EASTWARD, WESTWARD

EASTWARD, WESTWARD

A LIFE IN LAW

JEROME A. COHEN

Columbia University Press
New York

Columbia University Press
Publishers Since 1893
New York   Chichester, West Sussex
cup.columbia.edu

Copyright © 2025 Jerome A. Cohen
All rights reserved

Library of Congress Cataloging-in-Publication Data
Names: Cohen, Jerome Alan, author.
Title: Eastward, Westward : a life in law / Jerome A Cohen.
Description: New York : Columbia University Press, 2024. | Includes index.
Identifiers: LCCN 2024024403 | ISBN 9780231215923 (hardback) |
ISBN 9780231561044 (ebook)
Subjects: LCSH: Cohen, Jerome Alan. | Lawyers—United States—Biography. |
Human rights workers—United States—Biography. | Law teachers—
United States—Biography | Law teachers—China—Biography |
Criminal procedure—China. | Law Reform—China. | Human rights—China. |
Human rights—Taiwan. | Harvard Law School. East Asian Legal Studies Program.
Classification: LCC KF373.C545 A3 2024 | DDC 340.092 [B]—dc23/eng/20240602
LC record available at https://lccn.loc.gov/2024024403

Printed in the United States of America

Cover design: Noah Arlow
Cover image: Courtesy of Jerome A. Cohen

GPSR Authorized Representative: Easy Access System Europe,
Mustamäe tee 50, 10621 Tallinn, Estonia, gpsr.requests@easproject.com

CONTENTS

Preface: Better Late Than Never? ix
Acknowledgments xiii

1. CONFUCIUS SAID: "ESTABLISH YOURSELF AT THIRTY"—THE DECISION TO STUDY CHINA 1

2. GROWING UP AND GETTING EDUCATED 7

3. BEHIND THE HIGHEST BENCH: MY YEAR WITH CHIEF JUSTICE WARREN 22

4. AN UNPRECEDENTED SURPRISE: ANOTHER TERM, THIS TIME WITH JUSTICE FRANKFURTER 36

5. LAWYERING IN WASHINGTON: COVINGTON & BURLING, DEAN ACHESON, PROSECUTING CRIME, SENATOR FULBRIGHT 45

6. BERKELEY BECKONS: A BRAVE NEW ACADEMIC WORLD 67

7. STUDYING CHINA AT BERKELEY: SETTING THE STAGE FOR A LIFELONG EXPLORATION   77

8. HONG KONG BOUND: INTERVIEWING CHINESE REFUGEES   88

9. TRANSITION TO HARVARD   101

10. PASSIONATE PURSUITS: A NEW CHINA POLICY   109

11. BUILDING HARVARD'S EAST ASIAN LEGAL STUDIES: STIMULATING RESEARCH, TALENTED STUDENTS, AND TIMELESS TIES   133

12. KYOTO CHRONICLES: A YEAR AMID JAPANESE TEMPLES AND TURMOIL   145

13. MY FIRST TRIP TO CHINA: MEETING ZHOU ENLAI, ARGUING FOR JACK DOWNEY   154

14. PYONGYANG PERSPECTIVES: MAKING HISTORY IN NORTH KOREA   167

15. SAVING FUTURE PRESIDENT KIM DAE JUNG'S LIFE AND OTHER SOUTH KOREAN ADVENTURES   183

16. COOPERATING WITH TED KENNEDY ON AND IN CHINA   205

17. STIMULATING CHINA'S NEW LEGAL SYSTEM: THE COUDERT BROTHERS YEARS   217

18. LEAVING HARVARD TO ESTABLISH PAUL, WEISS LAW OFFICES IN BEIJING AND HONG KONG   230

19. LIFE, LAW, AND CHINA PRACTICE IN THE OPTIMISTIC 1980S   240

20. POLITICAL JUSTICE IN TAIWAN: FREEING ANNETTE LU AND PROSECUTING HENRY LIU'S ASSASSINS   255

21. THE DARK DAYS OF 1989: CHINA'S TRAGEDY AND VIETNAM'S PROMISE   265

22. ACADEMIC RENEWAL: CHARTING NYU'S EAST ASIAN LAW PATH   276

23. BEFRIENDING CHEN GUANGCHENG: THE VISION OF CHINA'S BLIND "BAREFOOT LAWYER"   282

24. WAS HELPING CHINA BUILD ITS POST-1978 LEGAL SYSTEM A MISTAKE?   298

25. "THE CURFEW TOLLS THE KNELL OF PARTING DAY": "TOMORROW WILL BE EVEN BETTER"?   307

Appendix   *319*
Index   *339*

PREFACE

Better Late Than Never?

This is not the first time I started this memoir. I began to write it in late January 1957, a few weeks after the arrival of our first-born child, Peter Lebold Cohen. It was a gloomy, rainy Sunday that seemed, at long last, an opportunity to come to grips with the past, especially some stimulating recent events. After all, I was already twenty-six and had encountered some memorable experiences.

Yet I was not really writing out of some feeling of duty to history or fear of forgetfulness. I was motivated by the hope of self-improvement, the acquisition of a skill essential to a successful professional life—the ability to express oneself accurately in writing in clear, interesting fashion. Until I began to work as a law clerk for Justice Felix Frankfurter at the United States Supreme Court in the fall of 1956, I had deluded myself into thinking that I had already acquired sufficient skill along those lines.

At law school, my literary talent had won me the coveted post of editor in chief of the *Yale Law Journal*, which enabled me to hone my editorial competence. Upon graduation, that experience led me to serve as a law clerk to Chief Justice Earl Warren of the United States Supreme Court, where I spent a profitable year drafting memoranda evaluating hundreds of petitions for certiorari seeking to command the Court's consideration, as well as bench memos summarizing the legal briefs submitted in advance of oral argument by those parties whose petitions had proved successful.

Working for Justice Frankfurter a year later, however, proved to be more challenging. Having spent a lifetime teaching about the Supreme Court at Harvard Law School before ascending to the nation's highest tribunal, Justice Frankfurter wanted no help with certiorari petitions or prehearing briefs. He asked his clerks to do serious, often original research on selected issues destined to come before the Court and to present their findings in well-composed memoranda. In addition, he sometimes gave his clerks the chance to do the first draft of one of his judicial opinions. Both these exercises—the research memos and the draft opinions—were where, at least in his eyes, I fell short of the optimum standard.

That is why Justice Frankfurter urged me to improve my writing and why he strongly suggested that the best way to do so would be to write something for at least fifteen minutes a day. "Write anything," he said. "It doesn't matter, so long as you keep practicing." I solemnly agreed to do so. Yet week after week, because of work, fatherhood, social life, or tennis, I never managed to follow through and felt increasingly guilty—until that fateful gray Sunday morning when I decided to make up for lost time by typing all day on my Smith Corona typewriter. And what better topic to engage my interest—and perhaps eventually that of others—than the work of the Supreme Court, including the vivid contrast and complex personal relations between Chief Justice Warren and Justice Frankfurter. This, I told myself, would not be mere selfish self-improvement but acting as a witness to and, indeed, a participant in history, helping to unveil the mysteries of the too little understood but critically important third branch of government.

So I attacked the task with excitement as well as vigor and dutifully ignored the distractions of my delightful wife, Joan Lebold Cohen, and our new heir, Peter. After I spent a couple of productive hours in isolation, however, Joan, cradling Peter in her arms, came over to show her appreciation for my belated determination. As they leaned over my labor, she said to Peter: "You see! Your Daddy is writing his memoirs!" At which point, Peter, an infantile but apparently severe critic, upchucked all over my emerging draft and the hapless Smith Corona! That put a premature end to my effort, and, after reflecting on the symbolism of the event, I decided to postpone renewal of the task.

The following day, when I reported the disaster to Justice Frankfurter, he said it reminded him of what one of his great mentors, Justice Oliver

Wendell Holmes Jr., had said about how to resolve the often difficult judicial dilemma of whether government misconduct amounted to a violation of the constitutional guarantee of "due process of law." Holmes, an earthy analyst of human frailty, had famously quipped: "How do you know a violation of due process when you see one? When it makes you want to puke!"

Well, Peter recently turned sixty-six, and I think it's time to try again, even though there is now much too much ground to cover for a memoir. Yet it's now or never! I only hope that, despite his subsequent Harvard Law School education and lifetime exposure to his parents' fascination with China, Peter's reaction to this humble effort will be kinder than his earlier one!

ACKNOWLEDGMENTS

Although it seems customary to thank one's family at the end of the acknowledgements section, I want to start by mentioning my family, especially my marvelous wife, Joan Lebold Cohen, a great companion for seventy-four years thus far and the person who has produced our happy brood. Three sons and their attractive consorts, seven grandchildren plus two husbands and six great-grandchildren to date make for a four-generation household. Given contemporary realities, we have not yet achieved the traditional Chinese goal of all actually living in the same dwelling, but, thanks to modern communications, we are very close and all those who can read have encouraged me to finish these memoirs. Indeed, it has been the desire not to leave them ignorant of their origins that has been my principal incentive for writing the book. I still deeply regret not having had the wit or interest as a teenager to probe the circumstances that led my father's father to emigrate in 1882 from central Europe to America at age twelve, alone with his fourteen-year-old brother.

I have also been encouraged to record these memoirs by my many former students and academic and law firm colleagues who have continued to share ideas, experiences, and values with me over the past seven decades. Literally, not a day goes by without their visits, emails, and phone calls. I mention many of them in the long appendix to this book and apologize to those I may have inadvertently overlooked.

In producing this book, I have benefited greatly from the editorial advice and cooperation of Richard Bernstein, a learned scholar, journalist, and critic whom I first met during his graduate study of China's history at Harvard almost half a century ago. Professor Yu-Jie Chen of Taiwan's illustrious Academia Sinica's Law Institute has also been of major assistance, more than amply compensating for whatever aid I could render during her able doctoral studies at New York University School of Law. Together they helped me through the painful and challenging task of reducing the first draft of the manuscript by about eighty thousand words to manageable proportions.

I am also grateful to Peter Bernstein, who, with his spouse and partner Amy, has done so much to shepherd important books on China and human rights to highly appreciated publication. Peter's advice, especially regarding the special problems of publishing memoirs, has been invaluable.

Finally, I want to thank Stephen Wesley and Columbia University Press (CUP) for undertaking this project. Stephen's support and the comments of the anonymous readers and CUP's review boards stimulated numerous improvements in the text. As the Scottish poet Robert Burns so wisely noted: "O wad some Pow'r the giftie gie us. To see oursels as ithers see us!"

EASTWARD, WESTWARD

1

CONFUCIUS SAID

"Establish Yourself at Thirty"—The Decision to Study China

anshi erli! I first heard this famous phrase before I could understand it. Every educated Chinese knows it as one of a series of maxims coined by China's greatest sage, Confucius, as advice appropriate to life's successive decades.

I was about to turn thirty and confronted my most daring career decision. As a young, untenured professor of American public and international law who had just finished his first year of teaching at the University of California at Berkeley, I asked myself, Should I take up an extraordinary opportunity to study China, one that I had failed to persuade others to pursue? Indeed, less than two years earlier, I had rejected the suggestion of UCLA's law dean, who said, "Somebody should study the law of Red China," as many Americans still called the People's Republic of China (PRC) in 1958. I had even turned down an offer from the University of Michigan Law School that I replace a retiring professor whose specialties included the legal systems of France and Germany.

In June 1960, I found myself teetering on the brink of deciding to learn a language more difficult than German or French and take on a great civilization I knew nothing about. At least I had spent a year studying in France and had traveled briefly to see Viennese cousins and German tourist sites. I had never been able to visit China or anywhere in Asia.

Although China had undergone one of the world's most profound revolutions during my undergraduate, Fulbright, and law school years,

I had paid little attention. Of course, I was aware of the PRC's entry into the Korean conflict and the issues raised by the 1953 armistice and the problem of repatriation of prisoners. I also noted China's 1954 sentencing of my college classmate, John T. (Jack) Downey, to life imprisonment for espionage, and Beijing's post–Korean War policy of "peaceful coexistence." When it came to East Asia, however, I was far more familiar with the American mistreatment of Japanese resident aliens and even American citizens of Japanese descent during World War II than I was with Mao Zedong and his comrades, even though the Maoists were lawlessly exterminating millions of "counterrevolutionaries," arbitrarily confiscating private property, and ruthlessly imposing "reform through labor" upon huge numbers of people who expressed dissatisfaction with "the people's democratic dictatorship."

So how did the opportunity to become a specialist in Chinese law arise, and why did I seize it when other law professors shunned it? The role of chance was important.

In April 1960, toward the end of my first year teaching at Boalt Hall, Berkeley's law school, my senior colleague Professor Frank Newman and I were driving to Sacramento, California's state capital, for a legislation seminar with our students. Newman, who was about to become the law school's new dean, told me of a conversation he had just had in New York with his former law school classmate, Dean Rusk, who was then head of the Rockefeller Foundation (and soon to become President John F. Kennedy's secretary of state).

Newman, a farsighted and innovative character, asked Rusk to have the foundation establish a chair in African law at Berkeley. Just before I left Washington, DC, for Berkeley in the summer of 1959, he had been inspired by the visit of a South African law professor named Dennis Cowan, who was on a barnstorming tour to heighten American interest in South Africa's human rights problems. This was also a time when the British and French colonies in Africa were coming to independence, and some observers were predicting that Africa might become the wave of the future, the way that many others—more correctly—saw the promise of East Asia.

Newman's request caused Rusk to ask a question that Newman thought distinctive enough to tell me about. Rusk wanted to know whether there was anyone in the United States specializing not in African law but in the legal system of China. Behind that question lay a story.

Before joining the Rockefeller Foundation in 1953, Rusk had served under President Harry Truman and Secretary of State Dean Acheson as assistant secretary of state for East Asia. That was his job when the Korean conflict broke out in June 1950. Several months later, a major decision had to be made about allowing the American-led United Nations forces, which had forced the North Korean invaders out of South Korea, to pursue them into North Korea and possibly bring down their regime. And that raised the critical question: Would China enter the war in order to prevent the collapse of its invaluable buffer state? As everybody knew in 1953, China, contrary to the opinions of many foreign policy experts, did enter the war, and one conclusion drawn by Rusk and others from the debacle that ensued was that both the U.S. government and American society needed a new generation of China specialists who might better understand the "New China" and more accurately predict its policies. By the time Rusk reached the Rockefeller Foundation in 1953, thanks to the depredations of Wisconsin senator Joseph McCarthy and other rabid anticommunist politicians, some of America's foremost diplomats and scholars specializing in China matters had lost public confidence as well as their jobs, or they had been relegated to obscure diplomatic or academic assignments in places remote from Asia.

That was why Rusk had turned Newman's request for a chair in African law into a question about whether any American law faculties already boasted expertise in the legal system of China. Newman assured him that they did not. About a month later, Kenneth Thompson, an able political scientist then advising the Rockefeller Foundation, called Robert Scalapino, one of America's best-known scholars of East Asian studies and the most prominent of Berkeley's impressive group of social scientists and historians working on China. Thompson told him that, while African law was a worthy and important subject, the Rockefeller Foundation had decided that it was more urgent to train someone in China's legal system. He asked whether Boalt Hall would be an appropriate institution to undertake the task and would it be willing to do so.

By then, Newman had begun to take the reins from retiring Dean William L. Prosser. When Scalapino called to tell him of this opportunity, Newman enthusiastically called me to ask for help in seizing what would be his first administrative initiative. In doing so, Newman was not thinking that I might grasp the opportunity to take over the new China law program. He recognized that it would require several years of almost monk-like seclusion while learning Chinese and acquiring the vast accumulation of knowledge associated with understanding the country and the place and future of its legal system. Rather, he wanted me to find someone else to take up the unique opportunity.

"Find me somebody for this offer," he said, "so the law school doesn't lose the chance. Find me an East German who has studied law in China. Find me a social science grad student who knows Chinese and is willing to study law. Find me a Chinese graduate of an American law school who can meet faculty standards. Find me somebody."

I dutifully tried all the above plus some of my young Boalt colleagues, but there were no takers. One of them said politely: "Don't you think that would be a rather narrow specialty?" Floored by his response, I said something like: "Compared to administrative law?" Administrative law was a topic he was pursuing.

Meanwhile, I had become increasingly interested in the importance of the challenge. I had failed to persuade anyone else, but I began to persuade myself. I had left Washington for academe after careful thought, and I remained convinced of the promise of independence of an academic life. I also admired those of my law professors who stood up to McCarthyism. As one of the greatest of them, Thomas Emerson, told me, permanent academic tenure's protection against external pressures was the best available guarantee of personal, professional, and political independence. Unless, of course, one had the good fortune to inherit a fortune, which I did not. I also wanted the chance to think, read, write, and publish in an unhurried way and to add to public knowledge and debate. Taking on the China challenge would offer me all of that.

As I began to consult academic colleagues in Berkeley and other friends about that possibility, many thought that the opportunity would be going too far afield and would even be outside the usual area of "comparative law," as that subject had been studied in the West. I was especially touched by the concern of Dean Prosser, who took the initiative, despite his impending retirement, to drop by my office in an effort to dissuade me from what he had heard I was contemplating. "If you don't want to teach torts [the subject that made him famous]," he said, "then at least teach constitutional law, although I don't think that really amounts to law. But don't throw away your career on China. No one will ever pay attention to your work except once a year when the Ford Foundation comes around and asks whether anything interesting is going on. Then the faculty will trot you out from the back room, but the rest of the year you will be forgotten."

Perhaps that kind of advice only strengthened my determination to challenge convention, something I had been tempted to do on lesser occasions. In addition, I liked the idea of becoming an academic pioneer. Why had I abandoned a stimulating and possibly lucrative career in law practice if it was only to join the already abundant ranks of able professors of American law? My Berkeley salary was only $10,800 per year, and Joan and I were expecting our third child. Yet we were comfortable with the decision to enter full-time scholarly life. Having made that decision, I asked myself, Why not take full advantage of it by doing something that no practicing lawyer or government official would have time to undertake, and no other law professor wanted to do—spend a lifetime studying the Chinese legal system, past and present?

Certainly, the challenge of China would be immense. The difficulty of acquiring the language was only the most obvious hurdle. How to learn about law and legal institutions as they developed through the millennia of one of the world's oldest legal systems would require knowledge of history, philosophy, society, economics, politics, and culture as well as analysis of usual and unusual legal materials.

Contemporary obstacles added to the task. In 1960, the United States and the PRC were still a long way from establishing diplomatic relations, and even unofficial government contacts were only occasional and extremely limited. Americans were not allowed to travel to China, nor were PRC nationals permitted to come to the United States. Communications between residents of the two countries were monitored, and access to current Chinese publications was restricted by the PRC.

Seven years after the Korean armistice, American public opinion remained very hostile to "Red China." In the 1960 federal elections, three of the four members of Congress who had supported a recent proposal merely to bring the PRC into the United Nations General Assembly, but not to replace Taiwan's rival government in the Security Council and General Assembly, were defeated. As President Dwight D. Eisenhower accompanied John F. Kennedy down Pennsylvania Avenue to his successor's inauguration, he reportedly warned Kennedy that the only thing that would bring him out of retirement would be an attempt by the new administration to negotiate diplomatic relations with the PRC.

Despite all the doubts, when a Chinese literature colleague I consulted shortly before my thirtieth birthday—July 1, 1960—quoted the Confucian maxim about establishing oneself at thirty, something in me immediately responded, and I decided to try to establish myself in this foreign and hostile terrain.

My wife Joan was very supportive. Smith College had given her a solid education in Western art history, but following her graduation in 1954, she had written Smith's president a letter noting the absence of similar offerings in Asian art. A subsequent year of work at Yale's art museum, while "putting hubby through law school," spiked her interest in China's legendary but mysterious artistic traditions. When she heard I wanted to accept the four-year Rockefeller Foundation fellowship, she said: "Fine. You study their law and I'll study their art, which I have always hoped to do."

Law school reactions to my decision were mostly polite but unenthusiastic. Fortunately, Dean Newman gave me his strong support.

U.S. Supreme Court Justice Felix Frankfurter's reaction, which he sent in a letter, was by far the most interesting and most important to me. His first response was understandable but disappointing; he emphasized that, by choosing China, I was declining to build upon the unprecedented experience of having served as law clerk to two Supreme Court justices. "You are throwing away a whole accumulation," he wrote.

I wrote back to him, saying, "Dear Mr. Justice, I quite understand the reasons why you are reluctant to support my decision." Then, knowing that, for obscure reasons, Frankfurter disliked Prosser, I continued, "Indeed, Dean Prosser said exactly the same thing only the other day." That drew a rapid second response. Written by hand on a sheet from a long, lined yellow pad favored by lawyers, Justice Frankfurter's note began: "Given the role that China is destined to play in your lifetime and that of your children, of course you are doing the right thing. Tell Prosser to go to Hell!!"

Both bolstered and amused by that reluctant assurance, I took my first Chinese lesson at 9 A.M. on August 15, 1960. It was the fifteenth anniversary of Japan's World War II surrender, which had marked the start of the Asian—especially the Chinese—century.

2

GROWING UP AND GETTING EDUCATED

Nothing in my background prepared me for a career devoted to China or Asia. I was certainly not a "missionary kid" like some of my future colleagues who were brought up in China. Nor was I introduced to the Chinese language and culture through military service as some others had been. Growing up in Linden, New Jersey, population 25,000, in the Great Depression of the 1930s and even in the World War II years that followed, I was unaware of Chinese civilization and the momentous events taking place in the Central Realm.

To be sure, every Sunday on maid's night out our family dined at the only Chinese restaurant in our county. But that was merely the occasion for my brother and me to make fun of the Cantonese waiter's inquiry whether we wanted "lice or bled" with our meal. It failed to inspire the slightest interest in the monumental developments then occurring in East Asia. Although for a time my mother kept an unread copy of Lin Yutang's 1936 *My Country and My People* on our living room coffee table, and she played mahjong every week instead of bridge with a few other Jewish housewives, we never discussed the Orient.

Yet we were inevitably internationalists of a sort by the time I was eleven and the Japanese bombed Pearl Harbor on December 7, 1941. But we were Europeans in origin and interests. My father's father had come to the United States in 1882 at age twelve from a Yiddish-speaking village near Krakow in what is now Poland. My father was born in 1896 in a lower East Side New York tenement. My mother's father had brought her, then three years old, and the rest of her German-speaking family to New York in 1903 from Chernowitz, the easternmost outpost of the Austro-Hungarian Empire. Both families settled in the poorer port section of Elizabeth, New Jersey. My father, Philip Cohen, couldn't afford college but managed to attend a few semesters of Cooper Union's free tuition in New York before spending his after-work evenings in a boring night law school in Newark in order to pass the bar exam. My mother, Beatrice Flora Kaufman, did two years at New Jersey State Teachers College, which qualified her to be a public grade-school instructor. Each was the only member of their respective families to study beyond high school.

When my parents married, they decided to live in the relatively new, nearby city of Linden. My father practiced law in both Elizabeth and Linden and made an unsuccessful attempt to get elected to the state legislature. That disappointment, however, undoubtedly helped him gain recognition in Republican Party circles, and in 1929, Linden's Republican mayor asked my father to serve as the city's attorney, a half-time job that guaranteed him $7,500 per year and allowed him to continue law practice. Thus, until Franklin Delano Roosevelt's (FDR)1932 Democratic presidential triumph swept even local Republican office holders from power, our family, despite the Depression that began in 1929, was comfortably off. From 1933, until his death in 1949, however, my father struggled to earn enough to cover the family's expanding expenses.

Nevertheless, my brother Burton, who was four and a half years my senior, and I had a very comfortable, secure upbringing. We never moved from the fairly large house that our parents built on Linden's main street shortly after Burton's birth. We received a surprisingly good education in the Linden public schools and had close friends. Burton was probably the most outstanding student the Linden schools had ever seen. Although not an athlete, he excelled in all other high school activities while scoring the highest grades possible, and in his junior year, he became extemporaneous speaking champion of New Jersey's public schools. I probably benefited from our high school teachers' memory of his accomplishments, but it was embarrassing to me on the occasions when teachers referred to him in my classes. Yet I loved most of my high school courses, even Latin and especially civics, history, and English literature and played prominent roles in school forums and other programs. After two years of trying to reconcile the demands of violin lessons and the school orchestra with the conflicting demands of playing on the school's basketball team, I finally decided to focus on basketball, even though I was never talented enough to be more than a varsity benchwarmer.

My biggest mistake in high school was my failure to study German. Linden High had a brilliant, dynamic German teacher named Hans Moldaschl who eagerly sought out good students. I had a slim exposure to German at home, occasionally overhearing my mother chat with her older sister Fanny in their native tongue and almost every night after dinner listening to my mother play the piano and sing sentimental German love songs, even during the darkest days of World War II. So I was disposed to take up formal study of the language. But the anti-German political atmosphere of the day proved overwhelming, and I chose Spanish instead. I had become hostile to Hitler as early as 1939 when World War II began with the German invasion of Poland. Although only nine years old, I began to follow the war in Europe eagerly, and soon other factors weighed in. Early in 1939, a distant German cousin, a woman of about twenty named Hella Ebner, turned up on our doorstep. Unlike the rest of her family, she was able to escape Nazi rule and obtain an American visa. She stayed with us a few days and this gave me some insight into the plight of the Jews in Germany before it became even worse.

By that time, my father's political activities had alerted me to the dangers of Nazi influence and anti-Semitism at home in the United States. Dad took time from his law practice to serve as New Jersey commander of the Jewish War Veterans of America and in the late 1930s spent a great deal of time traveling throughout the state to oppose the impact of the German American Bund. The Bund was a Nazi organization based in the nearby city of Union that marched its American trainees, dressed like Nazi stormtroopers, to many cities in efforts to drum up support for Hitler and intimidate opponents.

I accompanied my father on some of these motor trips, which gave us a long time for conversation. I also used to join him at home on Sunday afternoons to listen to the latest anti-Semitic national radio lecture by the influential Catholic priest Father Coughlin, whom dad frequently refuted in his many public speeches. In this environment, even if I had known the importance of the German legal system for the development of the nations of East Asia and had foreseen my interest in the subject, I don't think I would have been attracted to the study of German. And once the Allied invasion of France began on D-Day in June 1944, I was deeply saddened by periodic reports of the deaths in combat of several young men whom I knew.

Like many of my high school contemporaries, I wanted not only to see the Nazis and their fascist colleagues defeated but also to help organize the postwar world in ways that would prevent any similar conflicts from arising. In my senior year, after the war's end, I represented our school in New Jersey's first student model United Nations Conference. I also showed my interest in world affairs in my high school graduation speech that naively called for a richer, fuller, and more peaceful life, taking no account of the many postwar international problems that were already plainly in view. Fortunately, I was aware of how little I knew of the world and was looking forward to learning much more at college.

BULLDOG, BULLDOG, BOW, WOW, WOW—ELI YALE

Other than my brother, who did his undergraduate work at Columbia, only one other Lindenite had ever gone to an Ivy League college—Dartmouth. I considered both schools but was most attracted to Yale. Of course, I gave serious thought to Harvard and Princeton and visited both campuses, but I actually knew little about either. Harvard seemed like it might be too intellectual, while Princeton seemed too social. Yale, I hoped, would offer a balance. I was a bit put off by the warning of the white Anglo Saxon Protestant (WASP) lawyer who interviewed me for admission that "some doors at Yale are closed to Jewish boys" but remained optimistic.

My freshman year was not easy. I was well aware that many classmates had attended leading prep schools that offered more sophisticated educations than Linden High had. For example, although my professor of English literature was more boring than my high school teachers had been, some of my classmates knew about Spenser, Chaucer, and other early English literary giants and inspired my studious interest as well as my competitive insecurity. I also had other incentives to "burn the midnight oil." I needed good grades to obtain and retain Yale's scholarship assistance. Despite their financial plight, my parents had vetoed my plan to apply for financial aid when I filed my college application. They mistakenly believed that to do so might prejudice my chances of admission. Fortunately, soon after arrival, when I discussed the situation with my newly acquired counselor, he urged me to apply for financial aid, which I began to receive in the second semester. Unlike Harvard, however, Yale required all "bursary boys" to help earn their keep by working ten hours per week at an assigned job. For the remainder of my first year, I washed dishes in the kitchen of one of the residential dorms inhabited by students after freshman year. That, of course, made my schedule tighter and led me to give up thoughts of extracurricular activities.

Getting elected to the Freshman Prom Committee was the only exception I made. I did not want to become a complete "grind," and the prom committee seemed an opening to social life. Here I turned a vice into a virtue. Although the name of Cohen is obviously Jewish and undoubtedly diminished my chances for joining a college fraternity (no Jewish fraternities were on campus), I thought it might enhance my prospects for winning the votes of "the Jewish quota," which in those days was restricted to 10 percent of the class, enough to assure me the necessary support to join the committee. That analysis proved successful, and as a result I made several new friends and, together with a young woman I invited from home, enjoyed the dance.

Sophomore year was just as busy but seemed more relaxed. I found a better bursary job serving as assistant to the administrator of Saybrook College, my new dorm. I was able to select a few courses in European history and international politics that made a comfortable fit with my interests. I also liked the class in moral and political philosophy, although I found Aristotle more difficult to understand than Thomas Hobbes or John Locke. To meet the language requirement, I chose to study French, which was then considered the most diplomatically useful tongue after English. I should have chosen Russian, as a few classmates did. I don't recall anyone who took Chinese. I also made time for joining the campus radio station, WYBC, where I presided over a Saturday night program I called "The Ten Most Unpopular Songs of the Week." Two of my favorites were "Hitler Lives If We Hate Our Fellow Man" and "Dad Gave My Dog Away"!

Midway in the spring semester, however, tragedy struck. My brother called to tell me that my father had suffered a massive heart attack and that I should come home immediately. Burton, who was doing his post-MD resident's training at a Brooklyn hospital, and I sat with our dad, who was too weak to move from home, for several days while trying to comfort our mother. Dad was very depressed that he might become a cripple and a burden to the family and might not ever be able to return to his beloved work as a trial lawyer. As his condition worsened, I scribbled for my own comfort: "A strong man lies flat, Knows not where he's at, And, gasping for air, he mutters a prayer in utter despair." The next day he left us.

I felt guilty returning to school ten days later, but my mother was being helped by her three surviving siblings and a couple of their children as well as Burton and didn't want me to drop out. Happily for me, I soon met a lovely Vassar girl named Lee Florsheim, who lifted my spirits, and we continued to see each other occasionally the following academic year.

Junior year was very satisfying intellectually because I chose to major in international relations and began to focus on the increasingly bitter Soviet-American Cold War. Professor Cecil Driver's course in comparative politics gave me the chance to write my best undergraduate paper, a study of "White Australia" that allowed me to condemn the racist, anti-Asian policy that then prevailed "down under." I also enjoyed courses in American and Victorian literature. But I felt I had to start earning a living and accepted a summer job flogging Philip Morris cigarettes as part of an executive recruitment program that also employed me as the company's Yale campus representative during my senior year. This took little time from my fall semester so I was quite free to concentrate on my European and Soviet studies and the senior thesis that I had decided to write on the wartime Roosevelt-Churchill-Stalin agreement concluded at Yalta in February 1945. This also allowed time for the very significant improvement in my social life that occurred when I met Joan Florence Lebold on a blind date at Smith College October 13, 1950, at six P.M.

Joan's brother Don was a year behind me at Yale and a friend from Chicago of my roommate John Dreyfus, so we knew each other slightly. Don had encouraged his sister to accept my invitation for an informal pizza supper in a Northampton greasy spoon, and she and I hit it off immediately. By that Christmas, after Joan visited Yale several weekends, my mother and I headed to Chicago to meet her complex and charming family. As winter turned to spring, we were seriously committed to one another, and I finished writing my thesis in the Smith library during spring vacation. Yet the future was anything but clear.

The Korean War, which began June 25, 1950, was going badly for the United States, and my classmates and I, about to finish college, were struggling to decide about our options. Our dilemma actually began in 1948 toward the end of our freshman year when the Soviet Union took control over Czechoslovakia, and many of us worried that we would soon be drafted out of college by the military. I was attracted by a Marine Corps program that guaranteed that I could finish college before being commissioned as a second lieutenant and platoon leader upon graduation. But my father, whose approval was required since I was only seventeen, refused to sign even though he had volunteered to enlist in World War I. It was the only time I was ever annoyed with dad. But three years later, after a member of the Yale Class of 1950 who had joined the program had already been killed in combat in Korea, I recalled the remark of Mark Twain, who, at eighteen, had thought his parents ignorant and was amazed how much they had learned by the time he was twenty-one!

By senior year, several better options had occurred to me. I had always assumed that I would go to law school, but as the year wore on, doubts arose. Professor Samuel Flagg Bemis, a very senior specialist in American diplomatic history, liked my class performance and the research I was doing on the Yalta Conference. He offered to recommend me for a Fulbright Scholarship to spend the following year in France. A young political scientist named Barry Farrell who had only recently arrived from his Harvard training was so enthusiastic about my work in his international relations seminar that he insisted that I meet Professor Charles Cherington, head of Harvard's Government Department, to explore prospects for pursuing a PhD rather than a law degree. But in view of the war, there was also a strong possibility that, instead of selecting one of these opportunities, I might be drafted into the army. That led me to consider another alternative when I saw an announcement that a representative of the Central Intelligence Agency (CIA) would soon be on campus to interview graduating seniors.

As an international relations major, I wondered whether I might fulfill my military obligation by serving as a CIA analyst in Washington instead of risking my life in the mountains of Korea. So, with about thirty other classmates, I crammed into a seminar room to hear the CIA's pitch. It was hopelessly vague, however, and gave no clue about why they wanted to recruit us. So I asked the speaker to give us at least a hypothetical about the kind of assignment we might receive. Annoyed at my question, he nevertheless agreed to give us what he called "a pure hypothetical." He said: "We might want to train you and then drop you into Red China to stir up resistance to the newly established Communist regime." My jaw must have dropped as I replied: "That sounds awfully dangerous." Now plainly irritated, he told us that during World War II, the CIA's predecessor, the Office of Strategic Services, had fewer casualties than the infantry. When I responded: "You mean on a relative or absolute basis?," he said, "I don't think you're seriously interested." I said: "You're right!" and walked out, leaving my classmates to continue the conversation.

This, I much later discovered, was only one of many meetings conducted by the CIA at Yale that succeeded in quietly signing up a large number of classmates, including John T. (Jack) Downey, who was captain of the wrestling team and a star varsity football lineman, about whom I will have more to say later in this book.

In early spring, my choices began to clarify in positive fashion. Yale Law admitted me with a scholarship and loans, and Harvard came through with a spectacular four-year, all-expense fellowship to pursue a PhD in government. When I received the Fulbright grant, I was able to postpone for a year the difficult decision between Harvard and Yale and different careers. To my surprise, my draft board gave me the necessary deferment to study abroad, which I was eager to do because I had never been out of the country. I did, however, have to deal with the problems my absence would create for my widowed mother and my devoted girlfriend Joan. Fortunately, they both understood my situation and gracefully accepted my decision. Joan, who was only eighteen, and I, a mere twenty, each recognized that we still needed some time to grow up before deciding about marriage.

THE GRAND (FULBRIGHT) TOUR

Because I was not scheduled to embark for France until mid-September, Professor Cherington, in an effort to win my allegiance to Harvard, suggested that I spend the preceding summer enrolled in Harvard Summer School on a generous scholarship provided by the school. I had a wonderful time taking two courses with Professor Hans Kohn of Smith College, a well-known refugee from Hitler who was an authority on the history of European nationalism. I also sat in on some lectures by two other leading refugee scholars: Professor Hans Morgenthau, whose *Politics Among Nations* had been my undergraduate bible, and Professor Ernst Gombrich, a noted specialist on the history of art.

I thoroughly enjoyed the few weeks in Paris that all Fulbrighters were assigned for orientation before departing for our respective posts in the provinces so that we could become acquainted with "the real France." I knew that I would be located in Lyon because that was the home of the projected subject of my study, the Radical Socialist Party. The Fulbright Commission had arranged housing for me in the comfortable apartment of a sixtyish Jewish widow, Madame Levy-Hauser, who had lost both her husband and one of her two sons to the murderous concentration camps during the Nazi occupation. Although she and I had occasional interesting conversations, I learned more from her surviving son Jean Lardy, who had changed his family name to one not obviously Jewish in order to promote his prospects in business. Jean frequently drove to other places in the region to develop his work and sometimes invited me to join him, which enabled me to tap into his experience and thoughts as well as see different parts of France.

My stay in Lyon was indeed less glamorous than the weeks in Paris had been, but I did learn a lot about postwar French society and improved my ability to understand and speak the language. Although the French university students that I met were largely anti-American, and "Yankee Go Home" signs were plastered in many places, I did manage to make a few local friends. Most of my friends, however, were either fellow Fulbrighters or students from other European countries. I enjoyed a course in French conversation and, late in the spring, actually gave a student lecture in French about the situation of Jews in America. That was inspired by my reading of Jean-Paul Sartre's then recent *Réflexions sur la question juive*.

To save money from the modest monthly stipends so that I could travel during the holidays, I often ate in the government-subsidized student cafeterias. The food was not up to Lyonnais restaurant standards, and it made me sick about once a week, so I lost about ten pounds that year. But that did leave me money for travel, which funded three weeks in Italy at Christmas vacation and over a month in Spain and North Africa in springtime.

The latter trip, made with my fellow Fulbrighter and future *Washington Post* columnist Milton Viorst, was truly memorable. Even though it still under Generalissimo Francisco Franco's iron rule, Spain was a delight, and North Africa, especially Algeria on the verge of revolution against French colonial rule, was as explosively exciting as any budding political scientists might wish. Algiers on May 1, 1952, was saturated with trucks loaded with French submachine gun troops. After a day questioning future Lenins in the Casbah's caves, we took a small bus to the Sahara on a seven-hour ride that gave us a chance to ask some colonial businessmen to respond to the bitter complaints we had heard in the Casbah. Unfortunately, one of the "colons" reported us to the Sahara oasis police, claiming that we had said we were agents of the U.S. government authorized to represent its views. This led to a protest by the French government to the U.S. embassy in Paris that created a political challenge to the then still new Fulbright program.

On returning to Lyon from Algeria, I had to make some decisions about the graduate education I would pursue in the coming academic year. I reluctantly chose to study law at Yale instead of international relations at Harvard in the belief, as Hans Kohn had urged me, that law training would offer me more career flexibility than a PhD would. I was reluctant because I thought several years of political science study would be more interesting than three years of law study. In addition, I would have to work my way through law school and take out loans to supplement the tuition scholarship offered, while Harvard made the PhD cost-free. There was also the risk that my local draft board might not look as favorably on law school as the study of international politics. Nevertheless, law seemed the better choice for the long run.

Having made that difficult decision, I did not want to consider whether to choose Harvard Law rather than Yale. Harvard had four times as many students and was unfamiliar terrain to me. I felt comfortable at Yale and knew I could get a part-time job as counselor to freshmen in the college, which would provide room and board.

My Fulbright obligations ended in June and I arranged for my mother to come to France for two weeks of tourism that we both enjoyed. After that, I quickly visited Germany, which my mother had no interest in, and Vienna, where we had distant cousins who had survived the Holocaust. I then started the long trek home via a couple of weeks in Denmark and Norway and ending with a week in London, where I became better acquainted with Joan's dynamic Aunt Viola and her third husband, the British businessman Norman Laski.

LEARNING TO THINK LIKE A LAWYER

I loved Yale Law School from the first day. It was small—only 135 in my year—and informal. Most of my fellow students seemed very bright, and we shared many interests, particularly a desire to improve the world, whether by promoting social as well as legal justice at home or international peace and human rights abroad. They also seemed more diverse in their backgrounds than my classmates in the college. There was no quota restricting the number of Jews or other minorities, but I don't recall a single African American in my year. Another obvious limitation was the presence of only four women in the entire class. Competition there was but it was generally good-natured and relaxed, although some members of the class were feeling insecure.

Most of the first-year teachers were interesting and able characters, and a few were excellent classroom performers. By far the best was the lively German refugee scholar Friedrich Kessler, who had come to America because his wife was Jewish. I prepared for Kessler's contracts course more than I did for all the other courses combined. Each day was intellectual combat, consisting of stimulating Socratic exchanges rather than lectures. I was pleasantly surprised to see how much fun law study could be. I was a bit disappointed in my grades for two of the first semester exams but did well on the other two. I was also disappointed by my performance on a paper I had to prepare early in the second semester for a noncredit seminar on legal writing where I made my contract discussion so complicated that my instructor had no idea what I was trying to express.

Having thus learned the hard way that there is a technique for successfully dealing with law school exams and issues, I fared better on the second semester exams and was one of the charmed twenty-five class members invited on the basis of grades to join the staff of the *Yale Law Journal*. Because of that new responsibility, I decided to give up a second year as freshman counselor in the college. That meant I had the pleasure of residing in the pleasant and convenient law school dorm, although I had to take out a school loan to pay for the privilege.

Second-year classes brought more work than in the first year, but life seemed easier because there was less tension. I especially liked the course in public international law taught by Professor Myres McDougal. His innovative analytical system was stimulating but always seemed to favor the actions of the United States. When he supported the infamous Supreme Court decision validating the wartime detention of thousands of American citizens of Japanese descent, we had a robust but inconclusive class discussion that ended when I asked whether he would support the mass detention of American citizens of Scottish ancestry if the United States and Britain ever went to war again.

My journal obligations added to my burdens. In the autumn, each new staff member was required to prepare for publication a note, which was usually a relatively brief analysis of a recent judicial or administrative decision. I was assigned a rather humdrum case featuring a new ruling on a technical procedural issue of federal law. Before embarking on the task, I studied the format and mode of analysis commonly employed in journal notes and decided to try to emulate them to the extent possible. Apparently I succeeded because my third-year editor, Buck Finkelstein, whom I barely knew, couldn't have been more enthusiastic and said he wouldn't change a word.

Buoyed by that achievement, after Christmas vacation I set out on the more ambitious task of writing what was called a comment, which could be a substantial study of a major problem selected by me. Not surprisingly, I picked a public international law topic—the immunity of foreign governments from suit in American courts, a subject first made famous by the 1812 opinion of the legendary Chief Justice John Marshall of the U.S. Supreme Court and that assumed some importance in the years after World War II. I submitted my draft just before spring vacation in March, hoping to have some response from the editors within a week or two. For several weeks, there was silence, and I was beginning to feel neglected.

Then, in mid-April, it was suddenly announced that I had been selected to be editor in chief of the *Yale Law Journal* for the coming year. This was literally a stunning surprise because no one had breathed a word to me about the possibility, the assumption apparently being that no one would turn the job down. I had hoped to be among the journal's managing board, but it had never occurred to me that I would be chosen for the top spot. I subsequently received favorable evaluation of my draft comment, which was published in my third year.

I didn't allow the welcome news of my new responsibilities to alter my personal plans. Joan and I had become engaged the previous Christmas and planned to be married on June 30 and then take an extended honeymoon in Mexico so I could spend at least a month improving my Spanish. I had been thinking of becoming an international lawyer and scholar specializing in Western Europe and Latin America. My French was still usable, although I sometimes felt I had merely learned to speak English with a French accent. I had improved my high school Spanish by studying in Mexico's traditional city of Guanajuato after my first year in law school and wanted to make further progress by exposure during another summer. That seemed wiser than doing the customary second year summer in the bowels of a major law firm. Like my classmates, I had squandered many hours during the fall semester interviewing for a summer job but that interesting experience had not deterred me from making Mexican plans.

Indeed, it made me and my Jewish colleagues on the *Yale Law Journal* rather cynical about the "white shoe" firms where we interviewed. Ten of us on the journal had been interested in possible "big law" summer opportunities in New York. Seven of us were Jewish. Not one of the Jews received an offer from a "white shoe" firm, but the three non-Jews all received numerous offers. Tom Carruthers, a charming Princeton graduate, summed up the situation in his strong Alabama accent by saying with a straight face: "It's the first time anybody's offered me a job because I wasn't Jewish."

Joan and I had a marvelous summer in Mexico. We loved swimming in Acapulco, visiting Mexico City's museums, and touring as far south as Oaxaca. But we most enjoyed the weeks in Guanajuato staying at the home of former local law school dean Manuel Cortez and his ebullient wife with whom I had spent the previous summer. We made many friends and felt that we were accepted into their small community and improved our Spanish.

At summer's end, we started married life in New Haven, Connecticut. Joan, happily, had landed a job in the slide and photograph collection of the Yale Art Gallery and occasionally graded papers for the popular course given by the exciting art history professor Vincent Scully. I had my hands full managing the journal and planning for my professional future. I was hoping for a Supreme Court clerkship instead of immediately entering law practice, so I did not spend as much time as the previous fall interviewing law firms for a job. But I did have to take account of the possibility that my patient draft board might finally insist that I enter military service upon graduation, despite the fact that the Korean War had ended the previous year. To cope with that possibility, I arranged to take the Connecticut bar exam during Christmas vacation of my third year rather than wait, as customary, until I finished law school, which meant that if I passed the bar exam, upon graduation I could immediately enter service as a commissioned officer and legal expert rather than risk being drafted into the infantry during the months before the summer bar results became available in late autumn.

Two of my journal-related experiences are worth recalling. I got in a bitter dispute with Judge Charles Clark, then chief judge of the eminent federal court of appeals for the second circuit, over the content of a tribute I had asked him and several others on the faculty to write for the journal in memory of our current dean Harry Shulman, who had suddenly passed away early in the second semester. Clark, the author of a leading text on civil procedure, had been one of my first-year teachers, and I was not alone in thinking he had done a dreadful job. Yet I had invited his tribute at the strong suggestion of former dean Eugene Rostow, who told me this would heal some faculty wounds and assured me that Clark would only say nice things about Shulman. When a couple of Clark's sentences could only be regarded as belittling, I asked him to delete them. He refused, withdrew the essay, and wrote me an angry letter accusing me of doing the work of some unidentified but sinister faculty member. I wrote back to say that I made my own decisions and no faculty Rasputin hovered behind the throne.

The second incident was far more pleasant. One of my tasks as outgoing editor in chief was to arrange the speaker for the annual April banquet marking the ascension of the journal's new leadership. Justice Felix Frankfurter had been speaker at the previous year's banquet that had introduced my group. He was interesting but spoke far too long for the audience of inebriated alumni and students. I had always admired Frankfurter's famous protégé, former Secretary of State Dean Acheson, who was then the target of vicious McCarthy-ite Republican attacks as "the man who lost China" to the communists. Acheson, a member of our university's governing body, the Yale Corporation, accepted my invitation by return mail but we needed to pin down the topic. I suggested several of the hottest contemporary topics of the day, ranging from McCarthyism to our policy toward the Soviet Union. Acheson, however, to my disappointment, wrote back that he wanted to discuss Washington and the Supreme Court from 1919 to 1921, the years in which he clerked for Justice Louis Brandeis. I then sought the advice of Dean Shulman, known to be Acheson's close friend, and he advised me to "let Dean talk about anything he wants. He'll be superb." That may have been the best advice I have ever received because Acheson gave a brilliant, sparkling portrait of each of the nine justices of that remote era. The audience was enthralled and Acheson, quite pleased at this initial effort to recall the past, subsequently gave similar talks on many occasions in Washington and elsewhere.

By April, my immediate future was secured when I finally received a telegram from Chief Justice Earl Warren asking me to serve as one of his law clerks for the Court's 1955 term. Once again, my obliging draft board, proud of a Lindenite's achievement, granted a deferment. My only regret was that my father had not lived to share in the family's excitement.

Yale Law School was a happy choice. I benefited greatly from the intellectual stimulus and professional training and opportunity it offered, and I treasure the lifelong friendships made there with colleagues who became distinguished public servants, including Michael Heyman, Stephen Pollak, and Jon Newman.

3

BEHIND THE HIGHEST BENCH

My Year with Chief Justice Earl Warren

I can't promise that this chapter of my year with Chief Justice Earl Warren or the following one about my subsequent year with Justice Felix Frankfurter will be as interesting, brief, or focused as the wonderful Yale Law School talk by Dean Acheson about Washington and the Supreme Court from 1919 to 1921. Yet I do hope that they offer some insights as well as amusements that evoke the "spirit of the age."

The mid-1950s was a relatively quiet time politically compared to the immediately preceding years. Joseph McCarthy's star, while not yet extinguished, was descending. Dwight D. (Ike) Eisenhower's election as president had softened some of the partisan Republican sniping at the executive branch that had marred most of the first postwar decade. Soviet-American relations were moderating, Mao's China was beginning to end the initial period of domestic revolutionary convulsions that had accompanied the communist takeover and China's participation in the Korean War, and the most recent of America's periodic "Red scares" appeared to be winding to a close. Comforted by the Supreme Court's subsequent assurance that its 1954 landmark school desegregation decision need only be gradually implemented "with all deliberate speed," the country seemed, at least in principle, to be slowly assimilating this major social upheaval. It was a good time for me to hope to play a modest role in the Court's continuing sensitive political involvements.

Joan and I found a good, inexpensive garden apartment in Parkfairfax, a Metropolitan Life Insurance development in Alexandria, Virginia. It offered a tiny yard; nearby street parking; easy access to Washington, DC, and the Court in twenty minutes if there were no traffic jam; and four all-season outdoor tennis courts to which I was attracted. It wasn't as chic as living in some of Washington's districts might have been, but it seemed a practical suburban compromise. We bought basic furniture for the living room–dining area, and an eighteenth-century, four-poster, canopied bed that some friends of Joan's mother had abandoned in Chicago was shipped to us in pieces and put back together by a neighbor more talented in that sort of thing than we were. We still sleep in this bed almost seven decades later!

Having overcome the housing challenge, I embarked on my first day at the Court. I was greeted by Earl Pollock, a Northwestern Law School graduate who was just completing a two-year term as one of Chief Justice Warren's first law clerks. "The Chief," as Court personnel referred to Chief Justice Warren, had not yet returned from a vacation in his native California, Earl (Pollock, not Warren) took me into his office to introduce me to Warren's administrative staff.

The Chief's main assistant was a rather dour-appearing woman in her early fifties known as Mrs. McHugh. The second assistant, an attractive, unfailingly pleasant woman named Maggie, had come to the Court from Warren's staff when he was governor of California, his long-term previous job. She helped him with correspondence. The only other staff member was a genial and sometimes discreetly humorous African American limousine driver named Dodson, who also ran errands inside the Court.

Earl Pollock spent quite a lot of time briefing me on what would be my major obligations as a Warren law clerk. Roughly one-third of my time and that of my two co-clerks, he said, would be taken up by doing "cert memos" for the Chief. The Court each year received many hundreds of petitions for certiorari requesting it to exercise its discretion to grant jurisdiction to hear a broad variety of cases. Only a relatively small number would be granted, and the justices regularly voted to decide which those should be—with only four votes required for cert to be granted. Our job as Warren clerks was to do a relatively short memorandum for the Chief analyzing each petition and making a recommendation about how to dispose of the matter. We were to divide the work and have individual responsibility for the petitions we dealt with, although we were free to discuss any questions with each other.

Another third of the job would be to prepare in advance a much more substantial memorandum called a bench memo for each of the cases that the Court accepted and scheduled for a hearing. Bench memos analyzed the pros and cons of the arguments presented in the printed briefs submitted by opposing counsel. We were to end these memos with suggestions for an appropriate decision as well as supportive reasoning.

The rest of my time would be spent doing whatever needed to be done to complete the draft opinions the Chief usually liked to work on himself, at least in the first instance. There would also be ample opportunity to sit in Court and listen to oral argument of cases of interest, as well as to analyze the draft opinions circulated by other justices.

Earl Pollock also informed me about the Court's political flavor and personal relations. When I asked him to explain the evidently greater influence of Justice Hugo Black over the Chief than Justice Frankfurter exercised, Earl smiled and said: "Felix irritates. Hugo soothes."

I was pleased with my first day at the Court, but the second day was almost ruined when I woke up that morning with a recurrence of back pain that I had last suffered the previous winter at Yale. Oddly, my condition led to my first meeting at the Court with Justice Frankfurter, whom Mrs. McHugh sent me to see, saying he was a notorious back sufferer who claimed that not a doctor but a chiropractor had "cured" him on many occasions. The chiropractor didn't cure me, but my exchange with Justice Frankfurter on the topic of back pain laid the foundation for future acquaintance and eventual friendship.

By the time I was back in the office from a real back doctor, most of my fellow clerks had begun to arrive, and "fellow" was the right word because there were no females among them. They were, however, a very nice group, eager to make new friends. I shared an office with Samuel Stern, who had graduated from Harvard Law School three years earlier and, after two years in the air force, had spent the previous year as law clerk to one of America's foremost federal judges, Calvert Magruder, of the First Circuit Court of Appeals based in Boston.

Sam was very smart, professionally well-prepared for working at the Supreme Court, socially perceptive and fun to talk with. Joan liked him too, and, when our Chicago friend, the charming Elizabeth "Bibsy" Mayer, moved to Washington the next year, we introduced her to Sam, and they eventually married. Sam was not only helpful in my adjustment to the work we shared but also endlessly enlightening about Harvard Law School and its intriguing traditions and politics. This was a topic of considerable interest to me as I gradually began to firm up my interest in eventually teaching law. Sam was also a distinctive character. Not long after arriving in Washington, he became interested in horse racing and soon purchased a part interest in a horse named Cruiseville that raced once a week or so at the Baltimore racetrack about an hour away. One of my biggest challenges in the spring of 1956 was to invent excuses should anyone inquire on Wednesday afternoons why Sam could not be found in our office.

The third clerk in the Warren office was a Californian named Graham Moody. He was several years older than Sam, having worked in business before studying law at the University of California at Berkeley, where he had served as editor in chief of the law review. Berkeley's law school, called Boalt Hall, was the Chief's alma mater, and he had maintained contacts with some of the faculty while serving as chief prosecutor of Alameda County, including Berkeley and nearby Oakland, and then as California's attorney general and governor. Graham, appropriately enough, was designated chief clerk, which gave him some added administrative responsibilities. He came to Washington with a wife and two young children and so had family responsibilities in addition to professional ones.

I soon became very friendly with the Frankfurter clerks, Andrew Kaufman and Harry Wellington. Andy was from Newark, New Jersey, which I had some links to while growing up in nearby Linden and Elizabeth. We discovered through his father, a distinguished Newark lawyer, that we even have some family connection, although to this day Andy and I are still not clear what that is. Andy, after serving as president of the *Harvard Law Review* in his final year, worked with his father and older brother in the family law firm for a year before coming to Washington for the clerkship. We not only shared legal and New Jersey interests but, by the time spring came around, also an enthusiasm for taking part in the softball games that some young Washington lawyers organized on Sundays on baseball diamonds in the park near the Washington Monument.

Harry Wellington was a couple of years older than we were, having been a classmate and a sometime roommate of Sam Stern in the Harvard

Law class of 1952. Harry was already a dedicated law teacher. He came to the Court from a two-year teaching fellowship at the Stanford Law School. More important, he brought with him a brilliant, dynamic wife named Sheila who had a spontaneous personality and great sense of humor. Joan and I immediately liked both of them as well as Andy, who was still a bachelor. Sheila especially impressed us by her ability to dash home after a day's work at her job at the Library of Congress and produce an elegant meal featuring one of my favorite dishes—beef stroganoff.

At the same time, my friendship with Harvard graduates among the clerks expanded to include Robert Cole, who, like me, had just graduated from law school. He was clerking for Justice Sherman Minton. Through coincidence, Bob too had rented an apartment in Parkfairfax, only two doors down from ours. Bob quickly proved himself one of the world's most charming people and had just gone through a divorce, so Joan and I saw him fairly often outside work hours. Bob had a sports car and offered to drive me to and from the Court every day, which meant that Joan had full use of our car for her own work and household matters.

While I was learning the ropes at the Court and developing new friendships, Joan was landing a job at the Corcoran Gallery of Art, a smaller government museum that specialized in American art and was seeking a replacement for its retiring registrar. Joan and the museum director, the amiable and optimistic Bill Williams, thought Joan's Yale experience fit the bill, and he liked her energy and enthusiasm. Although the pay was not significantly greater than what Joan had earned at Yale, the job was an opportunity to enter the Washington art world of curators, artists, and scholars and to learn a great deal about the art history of this country. I was now being paid $5,000 per year, so we were not troubled by money considerations.

Of course, we three new Warren clerks were delighted when in midsummer the Chief returned from California to prepare for the opening of the 1955 term, which, as usual, was slated for the beginning of October. We met with him to review the schedule, the caseload, and his preferred work habits, which were essentially as Earl Pollock had described. The Chief was genial and friendly without being especially warm and made it clear that, on administrative matters, Mrs. McHugh ruled the roost. As the year wore on, each of us got to know him a bit more, although none of us developed the kind of close relationship that some justices, and some judges on other courts, develop with their law clerks.

One symbol of the continuing distance between us was that the Chief never invited us to his home for lunch, drinks, or dinner and, with the exception of an occasional Saturday afternoon office chat, made no other personal gesture to get better acquainted. His experience in California state government and politics had kept his relations with staff at the professional level. In Warren's case, this was particularly disappointing because not only did he come to the Court after an impressive, indeed historic, political-legal career that we hoped to learn about but he was also well-known for having an attractive family of five daughters who were roughly our ages. I used to console myself with the thought that, being already happily married, I had not been deprived of the opportunity to marry one of the boss's daughters and inherit the family business.

The Chief did not like to write elaborate opinions but rather straightforward ones. His drafts occasionally seemed more declaratory than analytical. I recall one draft where it was necessary to distinguish an annoying precedent, which he attempted to do merely by stating the equivalent of "This is not A v. B but C v. D." In our office discussions, he sometimes showed some sensitivity to the fact that he lacked an Ivy League legal education and had spent his professional life as a prosecutor and governor rather than as an academic specialist in constitutional law and the operation of the Supreme Court and wasn't accustomed to scholarly jousting with law clerks. As the term wore on, he showed particular sensitivity to the influence of Justice Frankfurter, who was always ready to get acquainted with the clerks of other justices and exchange ideas. Toward the end of winter, Warren actually instructed Sam and me no longer to socialize with Justice Frankfurter, whom he obviously suspected of trying to influence him indirectly through his clerks.

A couple of weeks later, when Justice Frankfurter dropped by our office, which didn't require passing through the Chief's other offices, and invited us to a lunch he was giving at home for a few of the clerks he found interesting, I had to tell him that we were prohibited from accepting. He laughed and expressed surprise. After a brief chat, just as he approached the door to leave, he advised us not to be depressed about the Chief's restriction. He then told us a story about one of the law clerks to Justice Clark McReynolds, a famously curmudgeonly conservative member of the same early-twentieth-century Supreme Court as justices Oliver Wendell

Holmes and Louis Brandeis. McReynolds was apparently unpleasant to work with, and, midway through his term, the law clerk decided that he could no longer tolerate the situation. One morning, he knocked on the door to the justice's office and, after being shouted in, approached the justice's desk and announced his intention to depart. The only reaction from Justice McReynolds, who reportedly never looked up from his work to acknowledge the clerk's presence, was, "Very well." At that point, according to Justice Frankfurter, the clerk, as he approached the door to leave, turned around and said: "Mr. Justice, there's just one more thing. I think you're a perfect son-of-a-bitch!" Justice Frankfurter, who obviously relished the anecdote, then said to Sam and me: "Can you imagine anyone having a greater feeling of satisfaction?"

Although the Chief, in his courtroom questioning of counsel and in his judicial decisions, demonstrated a clear policy preference for vindicating the procedural rights of many, but not all, state and federal criminal defendants, I never saw him act in public in an openly biased way toward any litigants. I do recall, however, one day when Philip Elman, an early Frankfurter clerk who long represented the U.S. Solicitor General's Office in cases before the Court, was seeking to uphold a federal conviction against the claim that the defendant's procedural rights had been violated. Warren obviously thought that the government should not have contested the claim in the nation's highest court. He kept asking Elman whether he personally thought that the prosecutors involved had behaved properly. Elman, increasingly uncomfortable, patiently responded each time: "Mr. Chief Justice, the issue is not my personal view but what the Constitution permits." The Chief, having made his point for the benefit of the other justices, finally moved on.

Warren was plainly biased in one matter, but perhaps it was only known to Sam and me. That was a civil case in which the Pacific Gas & Electric (PG&E) Company of California, a major public utility and a potent right-wing Republican political force that had long opposed Warren when he was California's liberal Republican governor, was involved. To Sam and me, the legal arguments on behalf of PG&E's side seemed to be clearly preferable to those of the other side. Warren, however, insisted on upholding the view of the other party. When Sam and I learned that, we asked for a meeting with him and spent an hour trying to persuade him to accept our position. The Chief listened patiently but would not budge. Finally, he amiably dismissed us by saying: "Well, fellahs, sometimes you just have to be wrong!"

As the winter of 1956 was drawing to a close, domestic political tensions in Washington began to rise. Eisenhower's health appeared to be declining, and the Republican Party was showing signs of anxiety as Ike, a hugely popular leader, developed ileitis and then had a mild heart attack. Republican propaganda attempts to relieve public concern were so ludicrous that they became the subject of media ridicule. I liked best the spoof that emanated from the congressional press box, which went something like this: "Last night at 2:21 AM, death, as it must come to all men, came to President Dwight D. Eisenhower. Presidential Surgeon Leonard Heaton told the press that the President remained organically sound. White House Press Secretary James Hagerty said this would make no difference in the conduct of the Eisenhower administration." When asked at a press conference what the party would do if Ike could not stand for reelection, even Leonard Hall, Republican national chair, frankly quipped: "When we get to that bridge, we'll jump off."

I don't recall the specific date, but it was an afternoon late in March, I believe, when my office phone rang. I was being called, the secretary on the line said, by William Timbers, general counsel of the Securities and Exchange Commission (SEC). I had met Bill Timbers only a couple of times at Yale Law School alumni association cocktail parties. He was perhaps twenty years my senior. Before he got on the phone, I thought that he must be calling to try to recruit me to join the SEC staff once my clerkship had ended. It turned out very differently. Timbers told me that he had been trying to reach the Chief Justice to invite him to join Attorney General Herbert Brownell and "a few other friends" for a drink at the Capitol Hill Club on the coming Friday afternoon. Brownell, before becoming attorney general, had been Republican Party chair and had played a key role in promoting Eisenhower's candidacy through the 1952 nominating process and the successful presidential election. Timbers complained that Mrs. McHugh had repeatedly turned away his telephone efforts to reach the Chief and asked me whether I would convey the invitation to the Chief in person.

With some hesitation, I did go in to see the Chief and gave him the message. He became angry—not at me but at this devious effort to elude the barrier to contact that he had instructed Mrs. McHugh to erect. He explained to me that the relatively more liberal politicians within the Republican Party were hoping to enlist him to throw his hat in the ring if indeed Ike could not run again. Warren, while still governor in the summer of 1952, had commanded considerable support among liberal Republicans from the West at the Republican national convention, where the conservative Senator Robert Taft had mustered much greater support for his own candidacy. When Warren moved his delegates to Ike's camp, that assured Eisenhower's nomination. Warren told me that when, one year later, after the unexpected death of Chief Justice Fred M. Vinson, Ike asked Warren to become the next Chief Justice, he decided to abandon politics permanently and embark on a judicial career. He did not want to be drawn back into the political realm now, and he asked me to make this clear to Timbers, which I did.

I admired the way Warren handled this matter, and I was favorably impressed overall by him, even though I believed he was better equipped to be president than to serve as the chief of the country's judiciary. In fact, I thought he would have been a better president than Eisenhower, and I would have been glad if he'd gotten the 1956 Republican nomination, though I was also aware that it would set an undesirable precedent for a justice, especially the Chief Justice, to leave the Court and enter politics. Warren lacked the legal sophistication on which major law schools placed a premium, but he was politically savvy and increasingly began to exude a moral force on behalf of the Court. Of course, one might say that his predecessor, Chief Justice Vinson was an easy act to follow. Vinson, a border state politician of the kind that senator and then president Harry Truman preferred to befriend for his poker-playing evenings, was neither an intellectual nor a moral force. Justice Frankfurter liked to deride him for making only two contributions to the Court's jurisprudence—the phrases "for my money" and "in my book."

Frankfurter more than once declared that, in a long life unmarked by religious belief, Vinson's death, on the eve of the argument of the school desegregation cases, was the only evidence Frankfurter had witnessed of the existence of a divine being! Had Vinson still presided over the Court when *Brown v. Board of Education* was heard, Frankfurter maintained, at best the Court might have reached the same decision but by merely a 5–4 vote. That would have strengthened the widespread popular opposition to the decision. Although Frankfurter often expressed disappointment over Warren's subsequent failures in some cases to follow his would-be mentorship, he gave the Chief full credit for marshaling his political prestige and government experience to produce a unanimous Court decision regarding desegregation that put the best public veneer on this momentous development.

I personally liked Warren's emphasis on protecting procedural justice. He showed considerable concern not only for curbing what he deemed unfair government restrictions on due process for accused criminals but also for condemning unfair administrative practices in the federal government's handling of controversial cases spawned by the turbulent political climate of the postwar era. It was his sympathy for the rights of the criminal accused that most surprised many of the ardent California supporters of his pre-Court "tough on crime" record as a vigorous prosecutor and a demanding California attorney general. I often wondered whether the Chief himself recognized the contrast and how he might explain it. I became particularly interested in this conundrum after the rare opportunity to spend an hour or so with him on Saturday afternoons when he and I happened to be the only ones in the office, and he dropped by for a chat. This gave me a chance to ask about his experiences as the district attorney of Alameda County.

The Chief evidently recalled those days with relish and didn't mention any inconsistency between some of his actions as prosecutor and his current efforts to improve standards for the administration of justice. I especially remember the zest with which he laughingly told me how he handled the case of a man the police had arrested for drunken driving one Friday night on San Pablo Avenue in Berkeley. The police called Warren to ask what to do because the suspect claimed he was a Latin American diplomat and had immunity from prosecution. The Chief told me that he simply asked the police two questions: had the suspect been driving and was he drunk? When both questions were answered in the affirmative, Warren told me he said: "Keep him locked up for the weekend and let him out on Monday morning." So much for international law!

Warren at several points recounted, with apparent pride, some of the informal, unauthorized tactics police and prosecutors under his supervision had sometimes used to interrogate suspected gangsters, such as detaining them in hotel rooms for a period of unrestricted interrogation before taking them for booking at the police station. His reputation for being "tough on crime" had been an important asset in his electoral rise in prewar California.

In this respect, little seemed to be mentioned in Washington about the Chief's prewar political record. There was greater interest, however, in his major role regarding the internment during the wartime period of over 120,000 people of Japanese descent, two-thirds of them American citizens, after the December 7, 1941, bombing of Pearl Harbor led the United States into war with Japan. I never raised this question in our occasional Saturday afternoon chats, and he certainly did not mention it. Yet many critics have condemned his leadership in advocating a shocking mass internment that appeared to be based on racist more than national security grounds. Some have also speculated that the zeal that Warren demonstrated in protecting procedural rights and civil liberties once at the Supreme Court, and freed from the need to win votes, may have been an effort to overcome that earlier black mark acquired while he was running for election in a different era.

Overall, the Court's 1955 term, although busy, was relatively quiet in terms of its impact on the public. Having created during its two previous terms what Professor Charles Fairman called "a storm of protest as severe as it has ever encountered," there seemed to be a tacit consensus among the justices to try to avoid further inflaming popular feeling. Via a variety of technicalities, it evaded, at least for some years, having to decide some potentially controversial cases, such as the constitutional validity of the Virginia statute prohibiting marriage between members of different races.

Yet the Court could not dodge all the bullets. The country was still churning with litigation that reflected its continuing concern with communism. In *Pennsylvania v. Nelson*, the Court decided that federal legislation, preeminently the Smith Act of 1940, "occupied the field" and precluded state legislation proscribing the crime of sedition against the United States. That decision did not sit well with the many anticommunist politicians who thought federal prosecutions insufficient to meet the perceived threat.

Also very sensitive were Court decisions grappling with the extent to which the Uniform Code of Military Justice could constitutionally be applied to certain civilians as well as military personnel. Most sensational were the two so-called murdering wives cases, *Kinsella v. Krueger* and *Reid v. Covert*. The Chief joined justices Black and William O. Douglas in dissenting from the majority's determination upholding the criminal convictions in both cases. The *Covert* decision, to the embarrassment of the Court and especially of Justice John Marshall Harlan, who changed his mind about the case, was subsequently granted a rehearing and reversed in the 1956 term.

Nevertheless, especially in the retrospect of almost seven decades, one might characterize 1955 term as the lull after the storm. That, of course, did not diminish my satisfaction at having been a minor participant-observer. The substance of the work was also importantly supplemented by the human experience of witnessing the personalities of each of the justices and their complex interactions. To be sure, I had only modest opportunities to observe justices other than Warren and Frankfurter, but there were occasional glimpses, particularly when cases were being argued in public hearings. I also learned a great deal from listening to the descriptions of their bosses offered by their clerks and listening to those justices who accepted my invitation to join the clerks for a luncheon discussion.

I much admired Justice Hugo Black for his evident legal skills as well as his adroit diplomacy in influencing the Chief. His years in Southern politics and the U.S. Senate before being appointed to the Court by Franklin D. Roosevelt (FDR) and his long experience as a strong proponent of civil liberties on the Court made him a formidable figure. He was also outwardly friendly and modest and sometimes displayed a sense of humor. Black, who did not have an Ivy League education and who was rumored to have had some politically advantageous contacts with the Ku Klux Klan in his younger days, liked to cite the wisdom of classical Roman scholars in some of his opinions. That annoyed Frankfurter, who sometimes seemed to resent the favorable attention in the media and in academe that some of the dissenting opinions by Black and Douglas attracted in civil liberties cases. Black was said to be an avid tennis player who had his own tennis court at home in Alexandria, Virginia. I was disappointed that, despite hints dropped to him by one of his clerks, he never invited me to play.

William O. Douglas was a puzzle, not only to me but to many who really knew him. A famous young Yale Law professor and New Dealer whom FDR had appointed to serve as chair of the SEC before placing him on the Court, he seemed a classic "loner." He asked fewer questions at oral arguments that I attended than Frankfurter, Warren, and Black and sometimes seemed to be reading unrelated texts during oral argument.

Reportedly he was not only unfriendly with his clerks but also, on some occasions, unpleasant and overly demanding. His widespread travels and his love of the outdoors and social life made the newspapers from time to time. Yet he could be surprising. I had hoped to get acquainted with him especially because of his Yale academic background. When Joan and I were planning a Christmas party at home, I asked Bill Norris, his clerk, whether it would be out of line to invite Douglas and his new young wife Kathy. Bill encouraged me to try, and, to my amazement, Douglas and his bride turned up and were sociable. Indeed, he seemed so relaxed in our overcrowded living room that he accidentally knocked over our artificial Xmas tree.

I respected Justice Harlan and found him an attractive figure. Still relatively new to the Court, he seemed the embodiment of the conscientious jurist earnestly seeking to follow wherever the Court precedents and sounder line of reasoning suggested. He freely consulted not only Justice Frankfurter but also his law clerks and seemed open to meeting other clerks.

I knew less about the other four justices and confess that I had less interest in them. Three of them—Tom Clark of Texas, Harold Burton of Ohio, and Sherman Minton of Kentucky, like the late Chief Justice Vinson, had all been Washington, DC, cronies of Harry Truman. To many of the clerks, they seemed to warrant no great professional respect, although they were all friendly and genial. Clark, a former U.S. attorney general, usually displayed a benign attitude while listening to oral argument but often seemed to be asleep and about to fall out of his judicial perch. He seemed to catch himself every time he was about to fall. Burton, a handsome and conscientious former Cleveland mayor and U.S. senator, was probably the quietest of the justices and almost naïve about finding the answers to the Court's issues through faithful study of the huge body of its precedents. Minton was a clever, humorous former senator who loved to chew tobacco while attending oral argument. When in midterm the Court introduced courtroom microphones for each of the justices, it took him a few days to remember to turn off his microphone before noisily expectorating in the receptacle at his feet.

The ninth justice, Stanley Reed, like Black and Douglas, had been appointed by FDR, and I expected him to be as outstanding in both ability and personality as they were. He proved to be very amiable and friendly but not, at least at that point just before his retirement, to be a stimulating figure. The only questions I recall his asking at oral argument always seemed to be along the lines of: "Counsel, at what page in your brief does that appear?" When I inquired why FDR had appointed him to the Court, I was told that the main reason was the president's confidence that this devoted New Dealer would never vote to invalidate a congressional statute, unlike the other members of the Court, who had repeatedly held early New Deal legislation unconstitutional.

4

AN UNPRECEDENTED SURPRISE

Another Term, This Time with Justice Felix Frankfurter

As the Court's 1955 term was coming to a close, I had an especially sensitive problem. My local draft board in Linden, New Jersey, had been extraordinarily flexible in allowing me not only to finish Yale College, take the Fulbright year in France, and complete Yale Law School but then also to spend a year with Chief Justice Earl Warren. Apparently, it had been motivated to allow me all these privileges because I was the only person from my hometown who had ever had the opportunity to do any of these things. In early June 1956, however, the board informed me that my time was running out and I should prepare to enter military service, either via the draft or by enlisting in a branch of my choice.

With this stimulus, I got in touch with the Office of the General Counsel of the Air Force. General Counsel John Johnson, a very nice person, invited me for a chat, and we hit it off. I left his office feeling so confident that I would join his group and become a commissioned officer rather than a drafted infantryman that I went to see the Chief to alert him that I would have to leave my duties at the Court a couple of weeks earlier than scheduled in order to meet the Air Force General Counsel's needs. Warren, ever the good patriot, was entirely understanding and wished me good luck, with perhaps a little less reluctance than I expected.

Then really good luck struck. Just a couple of days later, before I signed up with the Air Force for a tour that would have required three years of service, a sweeping overhaul of the draft regulations was announced. The new rules provided that men who had reached the age of twenty-six would be permanently exempted from service. I was about to turn twenty-six in a few days. In addition, men whose wives were pregnant were to be exempt from service just as those who had produced children already were, and Joan was already almost three months pregnant with our firstborn. This was a stunning turn of events.

At the same time, I became the beneficiary of an even more extraordinary development in Justice Felix Frankfurter's office, to wit: Justice Frankfurter was, at the recommendation of Professor Henry Hart at Harvard, to accept an able law school graduate named Jack Kevorkian as a new clerk, replacing Henry Wellington, who had accepted an appointment to teach at Yale. But when Kevorkian, who was serving in the military, was unable to get released from his army post in time for the next Supreme Court term, the post remained open, and Justice Frankfurter asked me to fill the vacancy. I accepted with alacrity. Until then, Frankfurter had never had anyone other than Harvard graduates as his clerks. I would also be the first clerk to spend successive full years with two different Justices.

Justice Frankfurter had only one condition. I would have to obtain the agreement of the Chief to this unique and surprising arrangement. I was worried that Warren, who had suspected me of being susceptible to Justice Frankfurter's influence during the preceding year, might suspiciously resent the proposition and veto it. Although almost as mystified as I was by my unlikely turn of events because I'd bidden him farewell not long before, he graciously acquiesced, and my immediate future was determined.

Suddenly, I was faced with the unanticipated prospect of having most of the summer free before returning to the Court, so I got in touch with Newt Minow, a dynamic Chicago lawyer, former Chief Justice Fred Vinson law clerk, and later Federal Communications Commission (FCC) commissioner who had visited me at the Court to explore the possibility of my joining his small law firm. His firm was openly political and largely a base for sponsoring the renewed candidacy of Governor Adlai Stevenson for president. Stevenson had lost to Dwight D. (Ike) Eisenhower in the 1952 presidential election but was poised to try again in the fall of 1956. I told Newt, one of the jolliest and most optimistic people I had met, that due to unusual unexpected circumstances, I could soon spend a month in Chicago helping with the Stevenson campaign.

Newt immediately took me up on the offer. After Joan and I made a swing to various western cities, I found myself working full-time, without pay, in his Chicago office assisting Stevenson's principal speechwriters. I did research memos on a host of topics, outlined some possible speeches, composed paragraphs for insertion in existing drafts, and edited various proposed texts. I worked for John Bartlow Martin, a veteran journalist who was the governor's main resident writer. Harvard professor Arthur Schlesinger Jr. made one or two cameo appearances during my stay but I did not get a chance to know him.

I never saw Stevenson, who was preparing for the imminent Democratic convention. Joan, who extended her summer vacation from the Corcoran Gallery of Art, also volunteered in Newt's law firm office. She was given a range of administrative assignments that included guiding the machine that appended Adlai's signature to large souvenir photographs of himself to be distributed to potential supporters. These duties barely left us time for family, tennis, and swimming, but they offered my first insights into national politics.

When late August 1955 arrived, we drove from Chicago to Washington in high spirits and in anticipation of more new experiences. I knew that working for Justice Frankfurter was to be very different from working for Chief Justice Warren. There were no cert memos to be done because Frankfurter liked to decide by himself which cases he thought deserved argument before the Court. Having spent a good part of his academic life studying the Court's operation, he had strong views on this question. He would look at the petitions for certiorari and quickly conclude, often by simply reading the issues presented, how he wanted to vote on whether the case should be heard. Occasionally, if he thought that a case might be worthy of the Court's consideration, he would ask Andy Kaufman or me to do some research that might cast light on the background of the case or its prospective outcome if accepted for Court review.

Similarly, I do not recall being assigned to prepare bench memos on cases that had been accepted by the Court. Justice Frankfurter would personally peruse the briefs submitted by respective counsel, carefully read those that dealt with sensitive or difficult cases, and sometimes ask us clerks to research specific questions that called for further analysis.

The justice took pride in writing his own opinions, both those he was assigned to draft on behalf of the Court majority and those in which he chose to express his views in a separate concurring or dissenting opinion. Of course, we would have the opportunity to offer a critique, make suggestions, and sometimes do supplementary research. We also might comment on drafts received from other members of the Court. I remember only one instance in which the justice asked me to do the first draft of an opinion. I was surprised and pleased, and the case, where Justice Frankfurter was to write for the majority, did not seem very complicated. The justice edited it intensely, however, and I could barely recognize the final product as something I had worked on. It plainly bore the mark of a Frankfurter opinion, written in his distinctive, crisp style with a bow to some historical references.

Not only was the clerk's work different from that in the Warren office, but the relationship with the judge was also very different. There was frequent and easy interaction with our mentor. He often came into our office, which was next to his, whenever he had an idea or bit of news to share or a question to ask, whether relating to the Court's work or the political events of the day. Although he had a full-time chauffeur, as did each of the justices, he liked one of his clerks to call for him at his home in the Georgetown section of Washington on weekday mornings and drive him to the office. This often provided a chance to chat with him about all sorts of subjects, including the life Joan and I were leading in Washington and his comments on the latest gossip about the affairs of state. I often sat with him as he concluded his breakfast, which invariably featured his appetite for grapefruit.

Yet driving Justice Frankfurter to the office proved to be no simple task because of his long friendship with Dean Acheson. That dated back to the former secretary of state's student days in the class of 1919 at Harvard Law School. Acheson lived only a few blocks away from the justice, and they had long developed the custom of going to work together. Walking was their preference if the weather permitted. That meant that on decent days I would drive the justice to Acheson's house at 28th and P streets, and then the two of them would walk to Acheson's office at Covington & Burling in the Union Trust Building at 15th and H streets in the center of the city. I was to wait there in front of the building and then take the justice to the Court.

The challenge arose from the city's parking rules. No cars were allowed to park in front of the building until 9:30 A.M. Yet there were always cars hovering in the area waiting to pounce on any free spot at precisely

9:30. The justice and Acheson usually aimed to arrive at the entrance just around that time, and I would try to get there about ten minutes in advance and wait for them. But an alert police officer would often wave me away. One morning, I said to him: "But officer, I'm waiting to pick up Justice Frankfurter." He responded: "Yes, and I'm Napoleon. Get moving."

Rainy days were often easier and more interesting because all I had to do was drive them both from Acheson's house to Covington and then deliver the justice to the Court. But certain days the conversation was too interesting, with the three of us bundled in the broad front seat of my Chevrolet. I was embarrassed one rainy morning when our discussion was so stimulating that I ignored the fact that 19th Street had recently become a one-way street and I started driving in the wrong direction. As the onrushing traffic approached us, Acheson, plainly worried, asked to be let off immediately at the next corner. The justice, who never learned to drive (Holmes also never learned), remained blissfully unaware of the situation.

In the evening, Frankfurter would occasionally ask Andy or me to drive him home. I always enjoyed that opportunity, which was more relaxed than the morning post-breakfast stint. As it happened, the justice was spending a great deal of time being interviewed by an oral historian named Harlan Phillips from Columbia University about his pre-Court experiences, and so on the drive home, he was often quite stimulated about the past and still reliving it. That gave me a great chance to soak up stories about the justice's exciting public involvements during his decades teaching at Harvard Law School, whether they concerned prominent civil liberties disputes such as the famous Sacco and Vanzetti murder trial or the staffing of Franklin D. Roosevelt's (FDR) New Deal with newly minted Harvard Law graduates. In those days, Republican critics sometimes joked: "How do you get to Washington? Go to Harvard Law School and turn left!" I also enjoyed the justice's accounts of his friendships with justices Oliver Wendell Holmes and Louis Brandeis. Much of this material soon appeared when Phillips published the oral history *Felix Frankfurter Reminisces*, the nearest thing to an autobiography the justice ever produced.

The justice was often personally thoughtful. Early in our year together, I noticed that, at least on days when Acheson was out of town, he was consistently late in preparing to leave home in the morning. That kept me waiting and increasingly irritable. One morning, as he luxuriated over his grapefruit, I gently asked, after ostentatiously looking at my watch: "Mr. Justice, were you ever late for Holmes or Brandeis?" I don't think he was ever late for me again.

On January 10, 1957, when Joan gave birth to our first son Peter, I felt comfortable enough to ask the justice not only to attend the bris, the traditional Jewish naming party given for boys shortly after their arrival, but also to serve as Peter's godfather. Never having had children of his own, he was, I felt, proud to play that role. He played the same role in early summer of 1959 after the appearance of our second son, Seth.

The justice even took Joan and me in to meet "Mrs. F" toward the end of the 1956 term. He had often talked about her, but she never appeared during visits to their home and certainly not at the office. By that time, Mrs. F was bedridden. I was never certain whether this was through physical necessity or her own choice. Perhaps the justice felt inclined to introduce us because he knew that Joan was an enthusiastic graduate of Smith College. The justice was proud of the fact that his wife "had led her class at Smith."

I often felt a touch of sympathy for the justice because he was denied her company on the many social occasions to which he was invited and at which he shone. Yet he sometimes joked about the situation. He liked to tell, and embodied, the story about the man who went to a party without his wife. When the man returned home, she asked: "Was it a good party?" To which he replied: "It was a wonderful, delightful, stimulating party. Of course, it wouldn't have been if I hadn't been there!"

Once, we discussed the problems raised by discrimination against women lawyers. No woman had yet been elevated to the Supreme Court at that point. The justice told me that occasionally he would report to his wife that the Court had heard a splendid oral argument by counsel that day. Mrs. F, knowing her husband's predilection for the fairer sex, would say: "Counsel didn't happen to be a woman, by chance?" At which point, he would compliment her on her perspicacity.

Once, Frankfurter was kind enough to suggest that Joan take the seat reserved for Mrs. F at the State of the Union speech, and Joan, although on the verge of giving birth to Peter, gamely seized the opportunity. She had a wonderful time sitting next to the ebullient Mrs. Burton, resplendent in a feathered purple hat and purple suit. When Mrs. Burton asked who she was, Joan said: "My husband is a law clerk." The status-conscious Mrs. Burton replied: "Well, my husband is a justice." Having thus established her position, Mrs. Burton gave Joan a detailed explanation of who all the various personages in the vicinity were. Neither of them paid much attention to the content of Eisenhower's speech, which soon became famous for launching what became known as the Eisenhower Doctrine about American foreign policy.

About a month later, we were invited to dinner at the elegant home of a middle-aged couple in Alexandria and our hostess told a story: Shortly after the Frankfurters arrived in Washington in 1939, she invited them to dinner in her Alexandria house, which had many African American neighbors. Justice Frankfurter, who had heard that Justice Hugo Black lived in Alexandria, focused on his young and excited hostess and asked: "My dear, where do the Blacks live?" The hostess said that she was so flustered by the question that she blurted out: "All around."

Like some of the other justices, Frankfurter often spoke at various law schools and universities, as he had done at our *Yale Law Journal* banquet in 1954. At the time of my clerkship, just after the Court's unanimous desegregation decision in *Brown v. Board of Education*, a counterattack against the decision was being launched. It included an effort to discredit the justices by claiming that their supposedly erroneous decision was a product of their lack of judicial experience before they came to the Court. They had been politicians, legislators, officials, lawyers, and academics but not state or lower federal court judges. Justice Frankfurter gave a powerful response to this attack in a long lecture delivered at the University of Pennsylvania Law School that emphasized the importance of the many great justices of the past who had come to the Court without previous judicial experience.

Nevertheless, this "prior judicial experience" attack became a Republican mantra, which led the Eisenhower administration to want to appoint new justices to the court with lots of prior judicial experience. The difficulty it confronted was that for twenty years, from 1933 to 1953, Democrats had run the federal government and, as a consequence, there were not many serving federal judges whom the Republicans considered attractive candidates for the nation's highest tribunal.

In early 1957, after two decades on the Court, Justice Stanley Reed decided to retire, and Ike swiftly appointed Charles Evans Whittaker to fill the vacancy. Whittaker had been a successful Kansas City, Missouri, business lawyer, but he'd only had a short tour as a federal district judge before being promoted to the federal appellate court in 1956, thereby entering the small circle of potential Republican nominees to the Supreme Court who could be said to have prior judicial experience, albeit precious little in his case.

I knew nothing more than the above about Whittaker on the day of his swearing in at the Court, but it soon became apparent to me and many others that he was out of his depth at the Court, and Whittaker knew it. One morning in May, Frankfurter asked me to deliver to Whittaker's office a note that Frankfurter had hastily scribbled. I gave it to Whittaker's secretary and asked her to pass it on to the justice. To my surprise, she urged me to take it to him myself. "He'll be glad to meet you," she said.

Whittaker greeted me cordially and asked me to sit down and chat. Before long he said: "Your boss is a genius, and I am totally inadequate. Unless I can do better, I will resign." To say I was startled by this revelation would be an understatement. After attempting to assure Whittaker that things would improve once the Court reached calmer days, I beat a hasty retreat to report this incident to Frankfurter, who was amazed at Whittaker's frankness to a law clerk whom he had just met. Whittaker managed to stay on in the Court for another five years before succumbing to a nervous breakdown and depression and stunning the political-legal world by announcing his retirement.

William J. Brennan, of course, proved to be a very different story. As in Whittaker's case, little was known about him in Washington when his appointment was announced. Because Brennan had been a Newark, New Jersey, lawyer and state judge, and because Andy Kaufman hailed from a Newark legal family, Frankfurter came into our office the morning the appointment was announced to ask Andy what he knew about Brennan. Andy said that, as far as he knew, Brennan was a competent, if not outstanding, candidate. The next day the *Harvard Crimson* reported that Professor Paul Freund, Harvard's revered authority on constitutional law, had told the student newspaper that Brennan "will make a great Justice." Frankfurter again came into our office and inquired about the discrepancy between Andy's cautious appraisal and Freund's enthusiasm. We were all puzzled until a handwritten note came from Freund the following day. "You may have seen the *Crimson*," he wrote. "A reporter woke me up by telephoning in the middle of the night to ask my opinion of the appointment. I told him that I did not know Judge Brennan or anything about him, but, since he was a classmate of three of us on the Harvard Law School faculty, I assume he will make a great Justice!"

Unlike Whittaker, Brennan did not lack confidence. In an early conversation with Frankfurter at the Court, he reportedly indicated his enthusiasm for "cleaning up" some long-festering constitutional questions, a remark that Frankfurter told me he found amusing. Nevertheless, the two became so friendly that in the spring of 1957, Frankfurter asked me to help the new justice with some research on an important issue of constitutional law that involved the extent to which each of the thirteen American colonies restricted freedom of speech before the Revolution. I found myself at work at the Court on a beautiful Easter Sunday instead of sharing the sunshine with Joan and our newborn son Peter. Fortunately, I was interested in the issue, and this also gave me a brief chance to become acquainted with the Court's newest member. Brennan proved to be a very nice and appreciative person. I came away believing that he would become a much more dynamic contributor to the Court's work than Justice Whittaker.

The year with Justice Frankfurter went by all too quickly. Looking back, I feel a bit guilty because I do not seem to have pulled my weight working in the office. This is probably because the justice relied more on Andy Kaufman, who had already won his confidence in the first year of his clerkship. Yet the justice never made me feel inadequate, apart from suggesting early on that I try to improve my writing. He proved a great, close family friend and adviser and became one of the reasons we finally decided to stay in Washington at the term's end. That, however, is the story of the following chapter.

5

LAWYERING IN WASHINGTON

Covington & Burling, Dean Acheson, Prosecuting Crime,
Senator J. William Fulbright

What to do after a unique two years clerking at the Supreme Court? Would it inevitably be a downhill career path after that? I thought of A. E. Housman's "To an Athlete Dying Young." Or might it be onward and upward? But in what direction? Private practice seemed the likeliest choice.

It was too early to consider teaching. Although academically inclined, I did not want to be a bookish legal philosopher or a learned legal historian whose scholarly work was unconnected to contemporary life. I have always been a "relevance monger." So I felt that I had to spend at least a couple more years acquiring some legal experiences beyond the refined and sheltered life of the Supreme Court to which I had been exposed. I had not yet spent a single day working in a law firm, not to mention all the other satisfying ways one can put legal training to work.

The previous summer, between clerkships, Joan and I had briefly toured several Western cities to make a preliminary survey of where we might want to live. We visited Seattle, Washington; Portland, Oregon; San Francisco and Los Angeles, California; and Denver, Colorado, and all of them had their attractions. But New York City seemed a much more conventional place to consider, and the "white shoe" firms were now more open to me than when I began looking for a job as a student. One firm was offering me $1,000 more than the $8,000 or so that all the others mentioned, and because Justice John Marshall Harlan had come to the judiciary via a long career as a partner in a major Wall Street firm, I asked his advice about how to evaluate the various opportunities. His wise advice was that a young person should not take a potential career job based on a salary differential. I said I agreed with the principle, but what, in the absence of other solid information, did an uninformed newcomer have to rely on?

Salary soon became a salient issue when a relatively small Hollywood firm named Gang, Kopp and Tyre offered me the then eye-popping starting salary of $25,000 per year to join them, but working in the entertainment business, including the representation of movie stars and aspirants, sounded too exotic and specialized for a starter. Joan was uneasy about my advising starlets, so we let that opportunity pass.

Private practice was not the only option I was considering. I also gave some thought to joining the federal government, particularly the U.S. Department of Justice (DOJ). Because of conflict-of-interest rules, Supreme Court law clerks were barred from appearing before the Court for the first two years after completing their clerkships, so joining the Solicitor General's Office was out of the question. I did think that there might be an opportunity to become a special assistant to a responsible DOJ official, which could be a satisfying start. Although I did not have any direct contacts in the DOJ, my years at the Court seemed a promising launch pad.

I had especially enjoyed the periodic lunch meetings that the clerks held in order to invite individual justices and other distinguished legal figures to share their views informally. Justice Tom Clark had been very frank with us about how to get ahead in Washington. In his broad Texas accent, he said: "Ah got where ah am because ma friends gave me a poosh. If any of you boys need a poosh, just let me know." Chief Justice Earl Warren was evidently well-connected with the Republican establishment, and I felt that he would give me a good recommendation. I thought I could also approach Attorney General Herbert Brownell, who in the late 1920s had been my predecessor as editor in chief of the *Yale Law Journal*. He had graciously accepted my invitation to lunch with the clerks, and I very much liked his honest and humorous presentation.

I will never forget how Brownell answered my question about the relationship within the DOJ between him and J. Edgar Hoover, the powerful and feared long-term director of the Federal Bureau of Investigation (FBI). Nominally, of course, Hoover was no more than the DOJ's number three official at best. Brownell was the obvious formal leader, but he gave a clever response to my question. "The other night," he said. "I had to return to work after dinner and, as I entered the Department garage, the policeman on duty asked to see my parking permit. When I told him that I couldn't find it, he refused to let me in." I said: "Look, officer, I'm Mr. Brownell, the attorney general. He replied: 'Listen, buddy, without a permit I wouldn't let you in even if you were J. Edgar Hoover himself!'"

I was also attracted by the Office of the Legal Adviser in the Department of State. My Yale Law adviser Jack Tate had been acting head of that office and spoke well of the opportunity. International law, after all, had been grist for my mill in student days. In addition, I was impressed by a long talk I'd recently had with Louis Henkin, an early Frankfurter clerk, when he visited the justice. Lou was very enthusiastic about the experience he was then enjoying in the Office of the Legal Adviser and had obviously found it an excellent base for the distinguished teaching career in public international law that he was about to begin at Columbia Law School.

I decided that, at my greenhorn stage, private practice, although a conventional choice, made the most sense. Because caution, as well as inertia, has often been a force in my life and because Joan and I liked Washington, we decided that the simplest thing would be not to move to New York, Chicago, Denver, or California but to stay put, at least for a while.

I did a few interviews, most memorably perhaps with a former Chicago lawyer named George Ball, who was close to Adlai Stevenson and the Democratic Party. After a tour practicing with the New York firm Cleary Gottlieb's office in Paris, Ball was leading Cleary's relatively small but growing Washington outpost. He took me to an elegant lunch at Washington's best French restaurant, where he and the headwaiter proved to be old friends going back to George's lunches at the Crillon in Paris. Working with Ball sounded like it would be fun. But, again, it seemed too narrow a slice of big-time law for a novice.

In the end, I decided on Covington & Burling, where I had so often dropped off Dean Acheson when I was a clerk the year before. I shared a small office with a pleasant University of Virginia graduate who had arrived a few months ahead of me, and he kindly showed me the ropes. I received a few administrative law research assignments and soon became the fourth person on a four-man totem pole for various mundane cases. This was less than thrilling becaue I was looking for responsibility on significant matters. Yet I liked the people I worked for. Stanley Temko, who had just made partner, was a congenial and wise supervisor. I also enjoyed Donald Hiss, a more senior but not powerful partner and younger brother of the brilliant Alger Hiss, who had not long before been convicted of perjury involving accusations of spying for the former USSR. Don, like Alger, had been a clerk for Justice Oliver Wendell Holmes and was a close friend of Justice Felix Frankfurter. Although I rarely worked with Don, we often chatted about international politics and foreign policy, and he took me to lunch a couple of times.

I liked the Covington environment and thought I would stay with the firm at least two years before deciding whether to remain in DC longer or take up a teaching job elsewhere. Joan and I wanted to have a second child, and even our larger second apartment at Parkfairfax was getting to feel cramped, so we decided to try to buy a small house in the nice residential neighborhood of Cleveland Park. It wasn't as chic as Georgetown but a lot more livable, especially for children as well as adults. The firm, through its close affiliation with its landlord, the Union Trust Bank, was able to offer its employees favorable real estate financing. So we found an attractive older house at 3415 Rodman Street and moved there in early November. We had some nice neighbors, including Henry Brandon, Washington correspondent for the *Sunday Times* of London, and my dear Yale College classmate Fred Pelzman and his darling wife Frankie. Alan Barth, editorial page chief for the *Washington Post*, lived across the street, and we played tennis with him a couple of times. To my disappointment, I never did meet another of our neighbors, the journalist Stuart Alsop.

At Covington, I finally got involved in an important case, with the chance to work with one of the most respected senior partners, W. Graham Claytor, a hard-driving and sober expert on government regulation of business. He was representing what was then called the Detroit Edison Company, a leading regional power corporation, in its recently begun project to build a nuclear power plant, the first to be constructed in the United States. It was already under way on the shores of Lake Erie, but it was proving increasingly controversial because of widespread concerns about its safety. As I read the extensive opposition briefs filed with the Atomic Energy Commission by labor unions, public interest groups, and other organizations, I became concerned that perhaps I was on the wrong side of the case.

After a couple of weeks of effort seeking to respond to the worries expressed by the media as well as others, things came to a climax on Christmas night of 1957, as Graham and I were working together in his office. I was not happy, not only about the case itself but also about the fact that I had had to abandon Joan and our son Peter at our new home on his first Christmas ever. That holiday had never held much positive significance for me, but Joan had grown up in a more assimilated Jewish family where it was a major occasion. About 11 P.M., I said to Graham: "My consolation for working late on Christmas night is that at least I know that you and I are working hard to blow up a better world." Stan Temko would have laughed out of similar concern, but Graham, with barely a half-smile, said: "You know. You may not be suited for private practice." I replied: "Perhaps you are right." This stimulated my thinking about how I should spend my time.

Like many associates, I wanted more meaningful experience and decided to take advantage of a pro bono arrangement that the firm had recently made with the local Legal Aid Society. Every month, it assigned a young lawyer to work in the Legal Aid Bureau to assist people who were in need of advice but could not afford to pay a lawyer. The perception in the firm was that those assigned this duty were usually the least valued associates in the firm, but I volunteered and in early winter got the opportunity. I enjoyed interviewing the variety of people who came in for advice, and I had to learn about different local law subjects and procedures ranging from property disputes to divorce. But this did not get me into court or involve criminal law, which was my principal interest, so it was not completely satisfying.

I think, to address my interest, Don Hiss may have suggested that I volunteer to take on a pro bono case in DC criminal court. I quickly drew an assignment that led to my first litigation experience and even a criminal jury trial. My client was a twenty-five-year-old Black man who had spent most of his previous seven years in prison because of three previous convictions for "unauthorized use of a motor vehicle." Not long after his last release, he'd found a job cleaning cars in an auto laundry. After keeping out of trouble for a few months, one cold January night, as he walked home, he could no longer resist temptation and again skillfully took over someone else's car. However, it stalled nearby, and an inquisitive police officer arrested him.

The case looked to be open and shut for the prosecution, which seemed determined to send this hapless fellow back for an even longer prison term than before. My client wanted to go to trial because previous plea bargains had disappointed him. He hoped that a jury might sympathize with his plight. So I decided on the only way out—to ask for a jury trial and to choose as our defense "not guilty by reason of insanity." It was a long shot, of course, but there had been recent stirrings of interest in the topic, and because I have always been offended by the criminal conviction and punishment of the seriously mentally ill, I thought it worthwhile to make the insanity effort in my assigned case.

How to do it? I decided on the following argument: here was a man who, for the fourth time, had been in effect charged with car theft. On his most recent release from prison, what kind of a job did he get? Stroking cars all day in an auto laundry. Some men like women, some like men, but my client had a clear, irresistible addiction to cars. He should not be condemned to another term in prison, where he would obtain no medical treatment for this relatively minor crime. Perhaps a sympathetic jury might be so persuaded, I hoped. I wanted to produce enough evidence at trial to create a reasonable doubt of guilt in the mind of at least one juror in order to prevent the unanimous verdict required for criminal conviction.

There was only one feasible possibility for accomplishing this—to produce the testimony of an expert witness, a psychiatrist, whose evaluation might foster the insanity defense. Of course, this was a pro bono case, and we had no funds to retain a psychiatrist. But a court clerk told me that I might be able to persuade a staff member from Washington's leading mental hospital, St. Elizabeth's, to assist us, because it was a municipal government institution. So I called on the hospital chief, and he graciously agreed to examine my client and then testify in court himself.

Unfortunately, in court, the psychiatrist seemed an unimpressive witness. Although he had frequently appeared in this capacity, he himself seemed a bit unstable as he walked into the room past the jury and unable to find the witness box. With some apprehension, after laying the groundwork, I put the key question of the day to him: "Doctor, on the basis of your examination, do you find the defendant to be psychotic or merely neurotic?" If the witness had said psychotic, the judge would have instructed the jury to find the defendant not guilty by reason of insanity if it believed the doctor. And my client would have been sent to St. Elizabeth's for treatment instead of to prison for punishment.

The expert concluded that the defendant was merely neurotic, and the jury promptly rejected our defense. After the trial, I briefly had a chance to interview my expert and asked him to elaborate on how he decided which conclusion seemed more appropriate. He said: "You know, I run a busy, crowded hospital. If we don't have any free beds, I generally testify that the defendant is neurotic!" Although this outcome caused disappointment in our justice system for me, I decided that I would like to learn more about the realities of the criminal process and try to improve the situation.

Despite my longing to get out of the confines of being a junior associate in a big commercial firm, I thought it too early to leave Covington and decided that it was time to try to do some work with Acheson, if possible. He was glad to hear from me and to keep me busy on both an assignment for the firm and a task for the Democratic Party. The firm's business involved helping him prepare a petition for certiorari to the Supreme Court on behalf of a Tulsa, Oklahoma, oil company that had come to him because of his well-known friendship with Justice Frankfurter and the respect that some others on the Court also had for him. The oil client, fortunately, didn't know that Acheson also irritated certain other members of the Court, including Warren, Hugo Black, and William O. Douglas by his Anglophile bearing and fastidious appellate arguments. In this case, however, the first challenge was to persuade the Court to grant the petition and set the matter for a hearing, usually an uphill struggle.

The Tulsa company's general counsel flew in one day to spend the morning with me reviewing the draft petition I had prepared. Acheson then invited us to lunch with him at the nearby elite Metropolitan Club. Acheson promptly ordered a round of martinis for us. This pleased our guest, who wryly noted: "Tulsa is dry." Acheson showed little interest in either the petition or the oil company but was in high form, full of stories about his meetings with Winston Churchill and Charles de Gaulle. Before long, a second round of martinis appeared, and the discussion went on. When a third round turned up and as we finally ordered lunch, the general counsel looked very worried and whispered to me: "Even in our club, we only have one before dinner. How does he expect us to finish our work?" I indicated that we need not indulge further.

It was plainly a memorable occasion, but the client and I had to steer a straight course back to the office to complete the petition by the end of the afternoon. Acheson told us to call him when we were ready for his review. Around 4 P.M., we were indeed ready, but when I called his office, his long-term secretary, the able Barbara Evans, told me that the boss had gone home for the rest of the day. I did my best to make amends to the client but assured him that Acheson would give our draft full attention in the morning, which he did.

Acheson was not as occupied as he would have liked to be on professional matters, but he was keeping busy advising the Democratic National Committee on foreign policy as it was gearing up for the 1960 presidential campaign. On a few occasions, Acheson asked me to draft strong rebuttals to a recent Republican Party attack on him and the Democrats' "Truman-Acheson" policies. He made it clear that he also wanted me to attack John Foster Dulles, his successor as secretary of state and long-term nemesis, on more recent controversies, which I felt was easy to do. Nevertheless, each time I came up with a draft, Acheson would say: "Can't you spice it up a bit more?" I was evidently still too cautious a young lawyer for political diatribes.

I enjoyed the opportunities I had to catch a few other personal glimpses of Acheson. As his biographer James Chace pointed out, he was devoted to vacationing on the island of Antigua, often with his Harvard Law classmate, the well-known poet Archibald MacLeish, and their wives. Early in the winter of 1958, I came down with a case of what became known as the Asian flu. After interrupting some of our work by having to stay home in an effort to recover, I twice returned to the office prematurely. Finally, Acheson said, in an avuncular way: "Why don't you go south for a week and get over it? I go to Antigua every winter and it makes me feel like a million dollars." I thanked him for the generous advice but pointed out that, while it made evident good sense for him to feel so well endowed, I was just starting out in law practice and had to live more modestly.

Acheson, like Justice Frankfurter, occasionally liked to mention his appreciation of female beauty. Alice, his wife, was still attractive in her sixties, and their talented, artist daughter Mary, who became our friend, was a very pretty young woman. In a story that illustrated the tolerance of his long-term secretary, Barbara Evans, Acheson once told me of the morning that his calendar revealed a forgotten afternoon appointment to grant an interview to a scholar of international politics from New Jersey. He asked Barbara to make sure, at 5 P.M., after the allotted one hour, to ring him up to remind him of the important board of directors meeting that was allegedly expecting him so he could gracefully exit the interview. The scholar, however, turned out to be a gorgeous, brilliant young woman who was remarkably prepared for the interrogation, and he loved every minute with her. Acheson laughed when recalling how annoyed Barbara was when he responded to her reminder by saying: "Oh, Barbara. You can tell the board to get along without me today! I'm unexpectedly busy."

Mr. and Mrs. Acheson were unusually kind and friendly to Joan and me. One pleasant Sunday, they invited us, together with infant Peter, to spend the day with them at Sandy Spring, their suburban vacation farm, which was a great treat. We sat around the large pool; had a delightful outdoor lunch; and listened to his tales of international intrigue, Washington politics, and law firm gossip. After lunch, our host showed us with pardonable pride his beloved workshop, where he usually labored from 5 to 7 A.M. producing attractive tables, lamps, desks, and chairs in order to take his mind off the many matters that had habitually awakened him so early beginning with his days in government. Mrs. Acheson, a serious and talented artist who showed us some of her paintings, occasionally interjected some apt political remarks or observations of relevant personalities. Visiting them was an entirely agreeable experience.

One of the attractions that kept us in Washington, of course, was the prospect of maintaining our close relations with Justice Frankfurter. He did not disappoint us. This led to our most memorable social event of the 1957–1958 year, my first after leaving the Court. Justice Frankfurter invited us to dinner at his house in mid-October. We had been dinner guests there before, of course, but it was clear that this was to be something as special as it was mysterious. He asked us this time to come "black tie," without explanation. To our surprise, he answered the door wearing a dark maroon dinner jacket instead of a conventional tuxedo. There were only about six other guests. Catherine and Don Hiss were there. We were all impressed when, instead of the usual cocktails, the justice served Bollinger champagne and particularly delicate hors d'oeuvres. Mrs. F did not join us but Mrs. Hiss and one of the other women seemed amused at the unusual elegance. When we sat down for dinner and the soup course was served, their suspicions seemed to be vindicated.

A delicious Alabama cream of almond soup gave away the secret to the socially attuned.

What the justice had done, on the very night that President Dwight Eisenhower, amid great local publicity, was entertaining Queen Elizabeth and Prince Phillip of the United Kingdom at the White House, was to reproduce for our benefit the precise menu that the British royalty were being served at the same time. The second course was filet of sole; the third, roast duckling; and the dessert, as also prescribed, was Nesselrode pudding. This was a huge and delectable joke, and we spent the evening in humorous comments and praise of our host. This was Frankfurter's innocent revenge for Eisenhower's failure to invite him to the White House dinner as Franklin D. Roosevelt (FDR) had done when the Queen's father visited just before World War II. Joan and I were still living in Parkfairfax at that time and about to move to Washington in a few weeks. Our next-door neighbors were then Dag and Bob Hamilton, who had recently become parents. Bob had clerked for Justice Clark during my first year at the Court, and Dag was a budding political scientist. Dag had been feeling a bit under the weather and was home in bed, so the day after the stimulating Frankfurter dinner, Joan dropped in to cheer her up, in part by giving her an account of the fun we had just had. The story did cheer her up, and we felt Joan had done a good deed.

A month later, however, in the *Washington Post*, the scandal-raking national political columnist Drew Pearson published a story that tried to make the innocent, fun-filled Frankfurter evening look like a secret meeting of the communist subversives Washington had spent years suppressing. According to Pearson, the supposedly left-wing radical of the prewar era, Frankfurter, greeted guests in a red dinner jacket, and one of the few guests was Donald Hiss, brother of convicted political perjurer Alger Hiss who had been attacked for allegedly betraying State Department secrets to the Soviet Union. The story went on to claim that the guests reportedly mocked the patriotic efforts of the Eisenhower administration to improve relations with our key ally, the United Kingdom. This story was embarrassing to the justice, but he took it in the stride of a Washington sophisticate.

We all wondered how the story, in its highly distorted form, had reached Pearson. The justice thought that Catherine Hiss had perhaps told the original version to a friend at the British embassy who had a connection to Pearson, but he soon confirmed that was not the case. After we told the Hamiltons about our puzzlement, they did a bit of investigation and came up with the explanation. Dag had liked our account so much that she told Bob about it at dinner. He thought it was delightful enough to mention it to his father, Walton Hamilton, the famous economist and former Yale Law School colleague of Thurman Arnold, who had joined Judge Arnold at Arnold, Fortas & Porter. Bob's father thought the story amusing enough to tell at the next week's firm lunch held for all its lawyers. One of the associates in the audience was Drew Pearson's son, who lost no time sending it to his father! We confessed error to the justice, and, since he loved Joan, he could not have been more gracious.

As I noted above, by late winter of 1958, I was beginning to get quite restless at Covington. I was starting to focus on teaching, either at one of several Washington law schools or elsewhere, especially because law deans were starting to contact me. Still, my view then was that it was too early to take up teaching. Of course, if Harvard or Yale had shown interest, I might have succumbed, but I preferred to get some more varied experiences first. I thought that, if a good law school asked me to join during my fourth year in Washington, I would do so. If no such offer came through, I decided that in my fifth year, I would take whatever I could scare up. I had noted at Yale that some of my best teachers had first tried their wings at relatively modest law schools. Myres McDougal, for example, had started at Mississippi, in his home state, and Fowler Harper had first taught at North Dakota.

That made me recall a favorite Frankfurter story about Justice Louis Brandeis. In 1932, following FDR's election, a young Republican lawyer who had been serving as an assistant attorney general in the DOJ during the just-defeated Herbert Hoover administration, came to consult Brandeis about whether to stay on as a Washington private lawyer or to return to the hometown practice that had spawned him. Without a moment's hesitation, the sage opined: "Young man, go back to your roots. Go back to where you came from." Brandeis, of course, had never done that. Louisville, Kentucky, had been his roots. Yet he had based his career in Boston until selected for the Court. On hearing this advice, the disappointed lawyer interjected a practical consideration: "But, Mr. Justice," he reportedly said, "I'm from Fargo, North Dakota." To which the sage responded: "Well, young man, that's your misfortune!"

Most immediately interesting to me was the prospect of perhaps joining the office of the U.S. Attorney for the District of Columbia. I had met the incumbent, a kind Virginian named Oliver Gasch, at a local bar association meeting, and he suggested that I contact him if he could ever be helpful. My brief, recent, and unsuccessful jury trial experience as an assigned defense lawyer had whetted my appetite for actual combat in litigation, and I knew it would take years to gain this opportunity at Covington. So I went to see Gasch about a possible job, and he could not have been more supportive. He seemed especially eager to tap into my two years clerking at the Supreme Court because he was occasionally confronted by constitutional issues that might eventually reach that elevated level, and he did not want to be embarrassed by mishandling. I was more interested in getting into the trenches of real-life, ordinary criminal cases that would introduce me to the many widely acknowledged defects of the administration of American criminal justice. The U.S. attorney's office in Washington was an attractive opportunity for this because Washington was not a state but a federal district; the DC federal office exercised both local and federal jurisdiction. Mundane offenses like car theft, as I had already seen, were prosecuted by the DC office, and lawyers there could work on local crimes as well as more sophisticated federal criminal, civil, and administrative matters. If I had gone to New York, for example, I would have had to choose between joining the federal U.S. attorney's office and, for example, the state's Manhattan District Attorney's Office, both famous and important training grounds but separate opportunities and not amenable to flexible assignments.

So I decided to join Gasch's office as soon as possible. I reported this to the Covington administrators and to Dean Acheson; Stan Temko, the junior partner who was primarily responsible for my work; and my closest friend among the middle-range partners, Don Hiss. The reactions were immediate but mixed. Acheson, himself restless from recent insufficient professional activity, understood perfectly and did not try to deter me. Don Hiss equivocated and said he would miss our lunch talks about the rights and wrongs of Eisenhower's foreign policy. But Stan Temko persisted in an effort to keep me at the firm, and we had an extended and lively chat.

Stan, who had taken an interest in me from the start and was eager to learn whatever I knew about the Supreme Court, told me that it was embarrassing for the firm to have me voluntarily leave after only eight months. He also thought I could benefit from gradually increasing responsibility in the administrative law matters that preoccupied us. I liked the lawyers I worked with and admired the firm's highly professional skills and widely recognized success. But I explained to Stan my deeper ambitions and possibly abbreviated Washington schedule due to my interest in teaching.

I told him that I had no serious complaints about the firm, but I did mention the frequently voiced belief that Covington practiced nepotism in deciding who would make partner. Stan conceded that the firm had long been dogged by nepotism, with various Covingtons and Burlings at the top, but then he said, "That was the past. We no longer have nepotism." I couldn't resist countering: "But, Stanley, on January 1, 1958, just a couple of months ago, the firm made David Acheson a partner." With a straight face, Stan replied: "That's not nepotism. He's Mr. Acheson's son!"

So I quietly left the firm, and a while later, when I turned up at the U.S. Attorney's Office for the District of Columbia, I'd got just what I was looking for. I was first assigned to "the Counter," which, I was told, was a kind of hazing process for would-be prosecutors. It was a bit like a bullpen. Every morning, about six to eight relative newcomers to law practice, now including me, would be seated in a row at a long counter in a large room filled with noisy, diverse people accompanied by police waiting in line in small groups for us prosecutors to make our determinations about how to dispose of their cases. Most of those present had just been detained for possible prosecution, and others were potential witnesses and family or friends. Occasionally there were complainants who had sought out the police. At 8:30 A.M., each prosecutor would begin the interviews, which might extend until midmorning, or later if the lines were long. I wanted to meet people involved with the administration of criminal justice, and here they were. No quiet law office pondering and writing about the interpretation of vague and complex statutes and regulations but throbbing life.

I liked my colleagues. This was the spring of 1958 so, of course, all of us literally manned the Counter. There were not only no females but also no minority representatives among us, unless two fellows of Irish descent and yours truly are so identified. A few had congressional connections. I remember Representative Charles Halleck's son, a very nice, snappy person, very favorably. Most notable, at least in the future, was a tall, impressive looking man named Jack Warner, who later became U.S. senator from Virginia and an important member of the Senate Armed Services Committee as well as the husband of Elizabeth Taylor. Most of my new colleagues had recently graduated from law school at Georgetown, George Washington, or American University, often after working their way through night classes while holding down daytime government jobs. They were all aware of my distinct background but treated me nicely and were helpful.

The key question in every Counter interview was whether to assign the case for criminal arraignment before a local superior court judge or to dispose of it via some noncriminal method. Judges didn't like to have their courtroom cluttered up with what one judge called "nothing cases." Sometimes I would mediate among the suspect, any present accuser, and the detaining police officer. There was a certain risk to this process. What would people think, for example, if I accepted the promise of a violent husband never to beat his wife again and then he went home and killed her?

The problem in most cases was that most of these people were too poor and ignorant to know what to do if they became entangled with the police. They did not know about public defenders and legal aid or how to locate and apply for such assistance. Many, but not all, were African Americans who had moved to the District of Columbia from the South and lacked standard education at the high school level. The people caught in the system were, for example, sometimes confused about our Counter discussions and thought that I was the arraigning judge rather than a prosecutor. Sometimes I would refer the suspect to a relevant nongovernmental organization for help. Every day I would inevitably recommend some formal arrests and send cases for hearing before a judge, who would decide whether to approve arrest, as usually occurred. Most judges, then all males, were former prosecutors and tended to follow our recommendation, at least at that early stage of each case.

There were often potential defense lawyers waiting inside or outside the courtroom. These were not prominent, prosperous counsel but hungry low-level lawyers hoping to snare a client among those being arraigned. Perhaps they might collar a quick fee and swiftly negotiate a plea bargain with the prosecutor. More reliable counsel was usually working in nearby offices. Some of them, often Black, were extremely able, dynamic former prosecutors with decent legal educations and lots of experience on both sides of the aisle. They, of course, were more expensive. The best of them hoped to become judges, and some eventually did.

Trials before a judge alone were often simple and sometimes not even seriously contested. I remember one accused who had broken a bottle of Jack Daniels over the head of an enemy who had passed him in the liquor store. I urged him to retain counsel for the hearing, but he insisted on defending himself. When the trial began, the police testified to the event in question. The judge then asked the accused whether he wanted to contest the account. No, he said. Then the judge found him guilty of the misdemeanor of assault and battery and asked whether the accused wanted to say anything before sentencing. Yes, he said regretfully: "I sure am sorry I broke that bottle." At that point, the judge and I couldn't repress a laugh, and the defendant was given a suspended sentence instead of a few months in jail. A lawyer could probably not have done as well for him!

After a few of these experiences, I felt overly ready to try my first jury trial as a prosecutor. The first case assigned seemed easy. I carefully interviewed in advance the arresting police officer, who confirmed how he had seen the defendant commit the theft alleged. So I confidently put the officer on the stand in front of the judge and jury and led him through this straightforward eyewitness story. The only problem was that the powerful Black defense lawyer knew the real story. Standing up in outrage for the cross-examination, he shouted at my witness: "Isn't it a fact, officer, that you had nothing to do with this case until your buddy told you he had a day off today and didn't want to testify? Aren't you just repeating what he told you?" I was stunned, as was the judge, when the witness admitted the truth. The judge promptly declared a mistrial, and I was left to contemplate the outcome of my first jury prosecution.

Things did not immediately get much better. It was May 1958, and I received a more substantial assignment. A young white male had been caught red-handed shoplifting in Washington's leading department store, Woodward & Lothrop. The store detective took him to a private room to discuss the matter and learned that this fellow, who was dressed like a civilian, was a member of the U.S. Marine Corps on active duty. The detective and his store superiors became reluctant to press charges and told the suspect that they would not turn the case over to the police if he would agree to sign a paper promising not to press charges for false arrest against them and the store. The marine stubbornly refused to do so, and the store referred him to the police, who brought him to see me at the Counter. I told the suspect that there was a clear case against him and asked him to reconsider signing the promise not to claim false arrest. That way I could, in conscience, drop the case. Yet he again refused and instead retained counsel and requested a jury trial. He was an attractive fellow who showed up for the trial wearing his full marine regalia and a few badges that made him look like a hero.

That might not have been enough to win the jury's sympathy except for the fact that international politics saved him from conviction that day. On the previous day, President Eisenhower sent a huge batch of U.S. Marines into Lebanon, and the Washington newspaper headlines made the most of it on the morning of our trial. During the hearing I easily proved our charges, and there really was no defense. But the defendant's lawyer rang the changes on patriotism and the importance of not harming a boy who might soon have to sacrifice his life on behalf of our freedom. The jury refused to convict the accused by a vote of eleven to one, resulting in a "hung jury." Because no unanimous verdict had been reached, the prosecution was allowed to try the case again, and I was instructed to schedule a new trial a month later. Again, the defendant and his lawyers refused to agree not to file false arrest charges, but this time they miscalculated. By the time the trial was held, the Lebanon crisis had subsided, the public had forgotten it, and a new jury convicted the accused unanimously after less than an hour of deliberation. This was my first experience with the relevance of foreign policy to the administration of justice in the United States. It was not to be my last.

Through the summer of 1958, I gradually acquired more conventional experience and confidence. I also grew closer to my big boss, Mr. Gasch, who began to ask my advice about a few concrete cases that, if pursued by our office, might eventually reach the Supreme Court. The most notable concerned what to do about the novel *Lady Chatterley's Lover* by the famous British author D. H. Lawrence. It had some frank passages about lovemaking that had aroused some segments of the population politically as well as perhaps erotically, and there was rising public pressure to prohibit publication and sale in DC and to prosecute those who violated the prohibition. I advised against pursuing prosecution on the ground that the increasingly liberal Warren Court would be likely to rule that suppression of the book was an unconstitutional violation of the freedom of speech guaranteed by the First Amendment to the U.S. Constitution. Mr. Gasch accepted my argument and indeed seemed relieved by it.

What neither of us realized, of course, was that our office was about to be confronted by a much bigger challenge in the area of alleged obscenity. The head of the Washington, DC, police vice squad, a man named Blick who had reportedly developed an impressive collection of obscene objects that had been seized in various criminal search and seizure operations, had long heard of the supposedly great collection of Oriental erotica in the home of a respectable Cleveland Park businessman named Lawrence Gichner. He had also heard that Gichner had been publishing a series of books based on his collection. These books were titled, respectively, *Erotic Aspects of Chinese Culture*; *Erotic Aspects of Japanese Culture*; and, reflecting the greater specialization of traditional Indian culture, *Erotic Aspects of Hindu Sculpture*. Gichner did not hold these books out for public sale. They were printed privately and either given or sold only to friends and acquaintances. The Gichners also liked to invite intellectuals, art historians, and officials for dinner at their substantial house and, after dinner, accompany them to the third floor of the house, which had been converted into a museum for discreetly showing their large accumulation of erotic Oriental paintings and sculptures. As the guests left, near the front door was a guest book that they would be asked to sign and record any impressions of the evening. Many, including a couple of federal judges, had noted with satisfaction what an interesting hobby the Gichners had developed.

As previously illustrated by the columnist Drew Pearson, Washington is a city built on gossip, and Mr. Blick, the vice squad chief, soon heard of the Gichners. Although reportedly eager to view their museum, he was never invited and became determined to use the law to pry the place open. He twice asked the U.S. attorney for approval of arrest and search warrants against the Gichners for allegedly violating the local and national laws against obscenity, but Mr. Gasch rejected his applications. But when Gasch went to Maine on holiday at the end of summer, Blick again applied for arrest and search warrants against the Gichners and their home museum, knowing that Ed Daly, a good practicing Catholic, had been left in charge of criminal justice in Gasch's absence and believing that he might approve the request. Without contacting his boss or anyone else, Daly did approve the request for a search warrant. On Labor Day at noon, two big police trucks carrying twelve cops descended on Gichner's peaceful home. The police served the warrants and then emptied the entire third-floor museum into the trucks, also carting away many copies of the allegedly offending books. The Gichners were summoned to appear in court the next morning, by which time Mr. Gasch had returned to work after almost losing his breakfast when he saw the front-page headlines in both the *Washington Post* and the *Washington Star*. Gasch was flabbergasted and called me in early to discuss the case before the Gichners were scheduled for their court appearance. This was exactly the type of situation he had been trying to prevent.

I then hustled to court and appeared as prosecutor for the arraignment. The Gichners, who didn't even have a lawyer yet, pleaded not guilty. When the judge asked about setting a trial schedule, I said that the prosecution had not yet had time to view all the seized material and that we needed a continuance of a week, which the judge granted. I then had to put all other work aside and not only evaluate the material seized, including the books, but also obtain the opinions of leading scholars of Asian history and art in Washington to try to address the key question: Was this a case of peddling prohibited smut or permissible scholarly activity?

By day, I did my best to master the hopelessly vague legal muddle over the identification of punishable obscenity. At night, I dashed through Gichner's three relevant art books, scrutinizing their text as well as the beautiful photographs of the offending material. The Chinese and Japanese photos were largely lifted from what in East Asia are known as pillow books, which were traditional, illustrated sex education volumes given at least to the affluent who were preparing for marriage. The photos in the India book depicted carvings on the walls of famous Hindu temples at Khajuraho, which featured oral as well as conventional sex. Needless to say, we had more visits than usual at home those evenings from friends and colleagues, some former Supreme Court clerks included, who had read in the press about the case and learned of my involvement.

I persuaded Mr. Gasch that this was not a proper case for prosecution. The Gichners were not selling high school kids pornography at local drug stores. And their books were not written in a salacious manner. Rather, Mr. G had polished a veneer of apparent scholarship. The family museum, of course, was private and only open to selected guests. But the problem was how to dispose of the case without suffering undue political embarrassment. Some religious groups and media opinions were panting for prosecution. The U.S. attorney's office did not want to be roasted in the press for admitting that it had erroneously initiated a sensitive prosecution.

I got an idea from loosely following a Philadelphia case involving Jimmy Hoffa and his notorious longshoremen's union, the International Longshoremen's Association. It had recently been settled by establishing a public trusteeship composed of representatives of different organizations. I thought we might adapt the idea to the Gichner situation. Why not have the Gichners establish a charitable foundation for the study of Oriental art and culture? They could contribute part of their collection and books to the foundation every year and thereby gain annual tax benefits granted to charitable donors. The foundation, in turn, would contract with the famous Kinsey Institute for Research in Sex, Gender, and Reproduction at Indiana University to give it the material annually over time. To ensure protection of the public interest, the foundation would be managed by a board of trustees in whom the people of Washington could have great confidence, including the local Roman Catholic archbishop. To my surprise and pleasure, this idea proved acceptable to all and was implemented rather swiftly. The media seemed satisfied at the unusual arrangement, the Gichner prosecution was quietly dropped, and the defendants seemed happy at the outcome, not only because of their tax benefits but also the accordant publicity it had generated for their pseudo-academic achievements and their charitable benefactions.

At that point, I felt that I had begun to learn about the realities of criminal justice and perhaps I should acquire some civil law experience. Again, luck came my way when Mr. Gasch asked me to assist the head of the Civil Division in a dispute involving fishing in Alaska. The major fishing companies were suing the federal government for trying to protect the embattled "little people of Alaska" by preventing the big companies from using expensive, high-tech fish traps to catch salmon off the coast of Alaska. Perhaps inevitably, those companies retained Covington & Burling to pursue their case in the federal courts of the District of Columbia. I was delighted when Mr. Gasch asked me to assist in handling the plaintiffs' appeal from an adverse Federal District Court decision because we had a strong case, and it would be fun to oppose my former law firm colleagues who had tried to dissuade me from leaving for the U.S. attorney's office just a year earlier.

The Covington team was very strong and led by one of the firm's leading lawyers, Howard Westwood, a fierce competitor who was reputed to work his younger colleagues to the bone. The legal question was whether the Alaska Statehood Act, passed by Congress in 1958, allowed the government to stop the major companies from using their high-tech fish traps. Westwood did a good job at the appellate hearing in presenting the case for an interpretation of the Alaska Statehood Act that favored his clients. Nathan Paulson, the head of our Civil Division, had thoughtfully asked me to respond to the appellants' case in court because I had done most of the preparation on our answering printed brief. I was thrilled, of course, and stood up to deliver what I expected to be an extended argument, when the judge told me to be brief, and then, when I went on too long, told me to be brief again. I then got the point and respectfully submitted our case. It was apparent that the court would affirm the judgment below.

It was now the spring of 1959, and I agreed to accept an offer to start teaching at the University of California at Berkeley in the fall. Berkeley's dynamic administrative law professor Frank Newman, soon to become the school's new dean, had come to Washington to interview both Michael Heyman, my dear friend from Yale Law School, and me. He so impressed us with the opportunities to teach public law at Boalt Hall that we easily succumbed. Mike was clerking for Chief Justice Warren at the time. We and our wives all felt the pull of California, unfamiliar but exciting to us all.

Of course, there were many Washington voices that advised me to stay on for a few more years before teaching. The 1960 presidential election was approaching. Eisenhower would not run for a third term. Jack Kennedy and other Democratic candidates were mustering their forces. William Bundy, then a high CIA official who had worked there to shelter from the McCarthy era, and his wife, Mary Acheson, had urged me to stay and sign up for the expected rejuvenating wave in American government, politics, and foreign policy.

Washington would again become more exciting and progressive than in the Eisenhower years. I had the connections to become some new leader's assistant, but I didn't want to become another Washington lawyer hanging onto some senior person's shirttails and going in and out of government in a revolving door, hoping eventually to land a major official position. My late father had always hoped to be appointed a judge. I had no such ambitions and had learned from his experience the disappointments that unexpected turns in politics could lead to. I liked to spend time reading books, learning, writing, and exchanging ideas with scholars and students.

Despite the attractions of remaining in Washington in our comfortable home and life with friends, it seemed better to start a new adventure.

But first, just before leaving the city, I wanted to complete my brief exposure to government. I had seen the Supreme Court up close and worked in the executive branch but had viewed the Congress only from afar. I felt the need to get better acquainted with the legislative process and the roles of lawyers and law in its operation. Once again, luck came to my aid. Somewhere I had met a very nice congressional staffer named George Denny, a lawyer a decade ahead of me who worked for the Senate Committee on Foreign Relations. When I told him of my interests and teaching intention, he suggested that I become a short-term consultant to the committee, which was then headed by the lively and independent Democratic Senator J. William Fulbright. Having benefited from an early Fulbright scholarship at the beginning of the 1950s, I was eager to meet my erstwhile benefactor, especially at a time when he was playing an ever more important foreign policy role. Carl Marcy, the committee's chief of staff, liked the idea of bringing me on to work on impending passport legislation, so he introduced me to the senator, who promptly approved the idea, albeit with little personal warmth.

I worked for the committee for several months before pulling up stakes for Berkeley. I did research; prepared memos suggesting possible amendments to existing laws; drafted some new legislative proposals; and, most interesting, developed questions for Fulbright to ask at the hearings he was holding on revising passport regulation. That gave me an opportunity to sit behind him at hearings and take in the scene. With George Denny's tutelage, I also learned a lot about where the committee fit into the congressional process. George also introduced me to some other senators and relevant players. I especially recall the meeting he set up for me to chat with Senator Alexander Wiley of Wisconsin, a liberal Republican. Wiley had generally earned good treatment in the media because of his contrast with Joe McCarthy, Wisconsin's other senator. I found the hour with Wiley disappointing, however. As we left his office, I said to George: "Well, I guess Wiley is becoming senile." "No," George replied in stout defense of the senator, "He always has been!" Little did I realize that, twelve years later, I would be testifying before Senator Fulbright and the Committee on Foreign Relations on national television as part of the effort to awaken the country to the need for a new China policy!

Joan and I had one last happy event before leaving for California. She gave birth to our second son, Seth, on June 25, 1959. Just before moving day, we had Seth's religious naming party at home, with Justice Frankfurter as principal godfather. This time he seemed more comfortable holding our new infant than at Peter's bris in 1957. Rabbi Balfour Brickner, who was married to one of Joan's cousins, presided and served as co-godfather. Brickner, son of one of America's rabbinical leaders, was both articulate and humorous, and a good time was had by all. That made for a splendid send-off to the Golden West.

6

BERKELEY BECKONS

A Brave New Academic World

En route West, we stopped in St. Louis, Missouri, to spend a short vacation with Joan's mother and stepfather, Milton Tucker, but after a few days, I flew to Berkeley to make sure things would be set for the family's arrival. We were going to spend our first year in the home of David Louisell, who was leaving for a tour as a visiting professor at Yale. I arrived in August. The weather was perfect. The house was in the Berkeley Hills overlooking San Francisco Bay. I bought a used and battered Chevy convertible that seemed to symbolize what I had previously thought of as an unallowable luxury. Beginning a new life in sunny California, however, made me feel liberated, but no one who saw this sad yellow vehicle could accuse me of extravagance. Students who saw me park in the law school lot soon labeled me "Cadillac Cohen"!

Of course, I immediately paid my respects to Dean William L. Prosser, one of the grand old men of American legal education and the famed author of the "hornbook" called *Prosser on Torts* that eased American law students through their first year. Justice Felix Frankfurter had not been thrilled to know that Prosser would be my dean. He remembered Prosser as emblematic of the anti-Semitic traditions of prewar American law school teaching. Yet I enjoyed my initial chat with the dean as well as his humorous presiding over faculty meetings. He was a clever curmudgeon, given to writing musical ditties and uttering satirical remarks. Not long afterward, Prosser moved from Berkeley to the University of California

Hastings Law School in San Francisco, which was famous for recruiting retired professors and for the occasion he crafted a song entitled "Over the Hill to Hastings."

I liked most of my new faculty colleagues. They were friendly, helpful, and diverse. My office lay between that of Richard Jennings, an earnest middle-aged expert in corporate and securities matters, and that of Sho Sato, a Japanese American specialist in land law who, as a child of American citizens, had nevertheless been interned for years in California with his family during World War II. Down the hall were offices occupied by three refugee scholars who had fled Adolf Hitler's persecution. Stefan Riesenfeld was the best known because of his prolific publications in various areas of commercial and international law. Despite occasional difficulties with English, he became a favorite of both faculty and students. One of his better-known malapropisms was uttered at a dinner party where he praised the dean as having "a lot on the balls."

Albert Ehrenzweig, author of a leading and readable treatise on the complex subject of conflict of laws, had been a lower-court judge in Austria. He offered an interesting course called "Comparative Jurisprudence," a merger of the traditional courses in foreign law and legal philosophy. Albert, much my senior, was thoughtful enough to escort me to my first faculty meeting. En route, he offered sage advice, which he rightly suspected I would ignore. He said: "You know, you are about to hear discussion of many important issues on which you will undoubtedly have ideas. You will want to speak about them at the meeting. My advice is to say nothing. It's all been said before!" The third native German speaker on the faculty was John Fleming, a tall, handsome man with a flourishing mustache and an Oxford accent who had escaped the Nazis as a child and grown up in England. He was always pleasant but rather formal and detached, and, because the law of torts was his specialty, I had little occasion to get well acquainted.

I was closer to Frank Newman, who was my faculty mainstay. As previously noted, when interviewing me in Washington, he had generated the excitement that led me to Berkeley. He mentored me through the course in equity that I had been assigned to teach, and he agreed to do some student seminar sessions with me in the spring regarding the sections we would be respectively teaching in administrative law, his major subject. Frank was rumored to be a likely successor to Dean Prosser, but some on the faculty thought him too progressive.

Joan and I were also attracted to Geoff and Bobbie Hazard, who had recently made the transition to Berkeley and whose Eastern education and backgrounds made us comfortable. In the late 1950s, west of the Mississippi and even in increasingly liberated California, "back East" still carried a distinctive connotation. I recall the party Joan gave for Berkeley area high school girls whom Smith College might have wanted to enroll. I urged one of our young guests to think seriously about Smith. She replied that she had already committed to go to college "back East." When I asked where that would be, she said, seriously: "Sacramento!"

We enjoyed the few faculty parties that were convened during our first semester. Eleanor and Bill Prosser held the opener at their well-furnished home, which was only a few blocks from the Louisell house. There was also a very nice wine tasting Sunday in the Napa Valley north of San Francisco. Yet there was surprisingly little "Western hospitality" of a more personal nature. Dinner parties that included us at colleagues' homes were rare. People were well set in comfortable patterns. They were busy with family, gardening, and work and felt that we were younger and somewhat different. I remember, toward the end of the first winter, as the Heymans and we were motoring toward an evening in San Francisco, I asked Mike Heyman, who was jollier and more open to people than I, how he thought we were doing. He said, with a smile: "They say they love us. But how would they treat us if they hated us?"

My major preoccupation, of course, was teaching, and I had to spend about eight hours per class preparing. In recent decades, top law schools have often eased beginning teachers into their new role, with modest initial assignments and lots of time to prepare for class. In my day, however, Berkeley believed in baptism by fire. I was asked to teach two three-hour courses in the fall semester, which was the usual faculty load for the law school. I had hoped to teach constitutional law, but that had been the lure for snaring Mike. I was content to have two public law–related courses each semester, however diverse and unrelated to each other they might be. As a newcomer, I was assigned to teach criminal law at 8 A.M. in the fall.

I loved teaching criminal law, although some of the theory and detailed differences among various offenses in California legislation and case law were not simple. Joan's uncle, Julian Weston, had equipped me with a couple of corny jokes to leaven classroom discussions. One that was quite apt, and I still use today when asked to analyze distinctions without significant differences, involved the law professor who asks the student: "Mr. Jones, what's the difference between adultery and fornication?" Jones, reportedly puzzled, replies: "Damned if I know, prof, and I've tried them both."

I tried to construct realistic and probing hypothetical cases to stimulate the Socratic conversations to which I was new at teaching. I had a wonderful group in that first class. Earl Warren Jr., a modest and attractive fellow, was earnest and friendly. Tom Prosser, the dean's son, was always pleasant and the subject of occasional good-natured ribbing because of his father's prominence.

Perhaps the brightest student to take part in the dialogue was John Niles, the son of New York University Law School's then Dean Russell Niles, whom I did not know. One morning John looked to be sound asleep as I was holding forth. "Mr. Niles," I said: "I'm sorry to wake you but . . ." He opened his eyes, smiled, and said, with a straight face: "Professor, I was not asleep but had merely closed my eyes the better to visualize the argument." I replied: "Mr. Niles, you will go far." He did, becoming a partner in one of New York's greatest law firms, Debevoise & Plimpton, before falling victim to the AIDS epidemic in the late 1980s.

One of the quietest among the ninety students in the large criminal law class became the one to go furthest politically. Pete Wilson was a handsome, somewhat shy, graduate of Yale College who was eager to get into government. I only learned this toward the end of the semester, when Joan and I entertained the class at home. Pete approached me to ask some personal questions, starting with why I had not chosen to enter politics instead of teaching. I sadly lost track of him after his first year, but was amazed some years later, while I was ensconced at Harvard, to learn that he had become mayor of San Diego, his hometown. Not long afterward, he became Republican governor of California. I was stunned and realized that this ambitious fellow might well become a candidate for the presidency of the nation. Unfortunately, he apparently lacked the stature, confidence, and judgment to handle state affairs competently and lasted only one term in office.

My equity class was also fun to teach and inspired me to take a more serious interest in the civil rights campaigns that were beginning to sweep the country. I was struck by the social composition of Berkeley's freshman law class, which was more than twice as large as my Yale law class had been and far more diverse. It was a state law school; tuition was relatively low; especially for California residents, and many students were on scholarship, some even discreetly holding down part-time jobs. There were more Black students and other minorities than I was accustomed to seeing in academic life, and more women, some of them very smart and even aggressive in class discussion. All this was enlightening and refreshing as I gradually got acquainted with my surroundings. Fairly often, students would come by my office for career advice as well as course analysis.

Students, of course, are shrewd observers. A one-semester exposure of forty-five hours gives them ample opportunity to scrutinize the foibles of their professors, and Berkeley students lacked neither sophistication nor humor. They were also extraordinarily talented in musical and theatrical expression. I was totally unaware of this until the students' annual pre-Christmas show given just before December exams. It was a very clever, well-rehearsed, partly musical extravaganza that smacked of Hollywood as well as radio and television. One of the early acts made fun of the four new young faculty members. We were represented by four slight fellows wearing shorts and sucking on large lollipops. When a big, grizzled student asked whether they were first-year students, they replied in unison: "Oh, no. We're the new faculty." Then followed brief individual portraits. When discussing my teaching method, one student asked another whether I used the "hidden ball" technique. "Oh, no" came the response. "Cohen doesn't even bring the ball to class!" I learned a lot from that remark and thereafter pitched my analyses to the middle talents of my classes rather than to the intellectual elite.

These portraits were plainly good fun and indeed helpful, as were some of those devoted to senior faculty. The sincere Dick Jennings, visibly upset one day by students' failure to prepare for his corporations course, had preached to them about taking legal education more seriously. "You people," he reportedly said, "have to treat this classroom as a cathedral of learning." The Christmas show played this theme beautifully, depicting Jennings as "Vicar Dick" leading the congregation in responsive reading of the state corporation code.

More devastating and perhaps harmful was the extended sketch making fun of my friend Geoff Hazard, whose Ivy League clothes and Eastern speech patterns seemed to have raised eyebrows, if not hackles. The satire, however, was brilliant. It purported to show a rather seedy, unemployed actor bemoaning to his clever agent the difficulties that he was having landing a job. The agent, fingering a copy of *Variety*, spots a University of California Berkeley School of Law announcement of a new faculty opening in civil procedure (Geoff's subject) and urging qualified specialists to apply for the position. "Here's your chance," says the agent. The actor, aghast, says: "How can I possibly do that?" "I'll show you," says the agent, who proceeds to come up with the classic wardrobe that identified Geoff: blue blazer; blue, button-down Oxford shirt; striped tie; gray flannel trousers; and, something of an exaggeration in Geoff's case, white buckskin shoes. After helping the actor meet the requisite sartorial standards, the agent then goes on to teach his protégé the legal patois of civil procedure. The audience, of course, roared as they watched this tony new person being created in front of them. Shortly thereafter, however, Geoff, a very able scholar and teacher, decided to accept an offer to join the University of Pennsylvania Carey Law School faculty, and I sadly lost a tennis partner and good friend.

Fortunately, Joan and I were not limited to friendships among the law faculty. A cousin of mine had somehow known of a Berkeley professor of Chinese history named Joseph R. Levenson. We looked up Joe and his British wife Rosemary, who didn't seem bothered by the fact that they couldn't recall my cousin. They took us out to a terrific, small Chinatown restaurant in San Francisco where I had my first taste of ginger ice cream as well as marvelous northern Chinese cooking. Some months later, this friendship proved to be a critical influence that helped determine my career.

Very interesting to me also was the political friendship I developed with William J. Coblentz, who had preceded me by about eight years at Yale Law but had come to know about me through the alumni grapevine. Bill was an active Democratic supporter of California's governor Pat Brown, who had put him on the university's board of regents. When we first met, the Berkeley campus chancellor was a man named Strong, who seemed, to this superficial new observer, to be too weak in dealing with the tensions within the university. Bill played a role in eventually replacing Strong, whom I usually described as a perfect host for a "no-host" cocktail party. His replacement, the able labor economist Clark Kerr, made more of a mark and became widely known for describing the functions of a university president as regulating football for the alumni, parking for the faculty, and sex for the students!

In the meantime, I began to get acquainted with campus political tensions. At the time, Berkeley was still seething quietly from the uproar created almost a decade earlier by the state government's insistence that all state employees, including Berkeley faculty members, sign an oath pledging to be loyal to the U.S. Constitution. This had torn the campus apart, led to some faculty departures, and ended good friendships. In 1959, people still occasionally referred to where they and various colleagues had stood regarding "the Oath." There was also more than lingering resentment among Japanese American faculty and spouses over the increasingly condemned wartime internment of not only West Coast Japanese nationals but also American citizens of Japanese descent. Joan even witnessed this bitterness in the weekly flower-arranging course that she managed to attend despite growing family responsibilities.

Our best faculty friends outside the law school, Carol and Eugene "Bud" Burdick, were neighbors living just one block up the street from us. Bud was already, although still only an associate professor, one of the university's best-known political scientists. This was not so much because of scholarly publications as because in 1958 he was principal author, together with the writer Paul Jacobs, of a leading popular book of fiction called *The Ugly American*. Although fiction, it offered many useful and timely insights into the problems of American foreign policy in Southeast Asia years before U.S. involvement in the Vietnam quagmire. Bud, a former Rhodes scholar intimately associated with Democratic politics in California, was recovering from a mild heart attack. Nevertheless, he and Carol, a warm and lively person (and both at least a decade older than we were), immediately welcomed us and our young kids. Theirs was Western hospitality that we had not received at the law school.

During our first summer in California, Joan and I decided to learn more about the area by attending the conference of the California Democratic Council in Fresno in the central part of the state. That was great fun. We heard Senator Hubert Humphrey of Minnesota give a terrific speech as he laid the groundwork for a 1960 presidential run. I had chatted with him briefly in Washington while I was working for the Senate Committee on Foreign Relations and was glad to get in a few more words with him in Fresno. He had been giving seven speeches a day, and I asked him where he got the energy to sustain such an effort. He said he drew his energy from the crowds and their support for his views.

By the time of the fall election campaign, with Jack Kennedy the Democratic nominee, Bud Burdick had enlisted me in the cause. That left me with two vivid memories. In early October 1960, Bud and Carol were giving a big fundraising party in their spacious house. Arthur Schlesinger Jr., the well-known Harvard professor of American history who was one of Kennedy's main collaborators, had agreed to fly out to be the major speaker. Bud asked me to pick Schlesinger up at San Francisco Airport and deliver him to the event. I was delighted because this gave me a chance to chat with our guest for roughly an hour in the car. What surprised me was how nervous Schlesinger was about this informal speaking engagement. Here was a famous scholar and public intellectual who had been successfully lecturing at Harvard for many years telling a first-year unpublished teacher that "public speaking is not really my métier. I'm much more comfortable writing."

My other political memory associated with the Burdicks that year relates to election night of 1960 when they gave a riotous blast of a party. Again, Bud assigned me a delicate task with another leading popular figure, this time the lionized British author C. P. Snow. His 1951 novel of English academic politics, *The Masters*, had been widely appreciated, even in America's academic circles, and that fall he was in residence at Berkeley as the holder of its most distinguished visiting chair.

My duty on election night was to sit next to Snow on a couch before one of the television sets, chat him up, and keep him supplied with his beloved martinis. I looked forward to the opportunity, eager to learn more about the Oxford atmosphere, which my failure to win a Rhodes Scholarship had denied me. The evening proved to be a dreadful disappointment. Snow was already rather soused when I got to him, and all during that long and tense election night he merely kept repeating two sentences. The first was: "I've said it before, and I'll say it again. Kennedy will win with 350 to 375 electoral votes," a prediction that looked increasingly dubious as the evening wore on. The second statement was always simpler. Nodding toward the nearby pitcher of martinis, without a touch of embarrassment, he would say: "May I have a bit more?"

One political incident in the Bay Area stole time from the end of my academic year's tedious work of reading many student exam bluebooks. The infamous Un-American Activities Committee of the U.S. House of Representatives had chosen to stage a hearing in the San Francisco

Federal Courthouse in May 1960. This caused a massive popular protest led by students from various universities who blocked access to the broad and impressive courthouse steps. City police finally dispersed them by spraying them with powerful hoses and arresting a large number. Several of my first-year Berkeley students were locked up. At the behest of their classmates, I retained a leading Oakland criminal lawyer who managed to get them released on bail. When I questioned him about the students' chances of avoiding conviction, he frankly answered: "It all depends on our government's relations with the Soviet Union on the day of trial!" I was surprised. He went on to say: "If there seems to be Soviet-American détente, the jury is likely to forgive them and let them go. If not, they will be convicted." Once again, as in my May 1958 experience prosecuting a U.S. Marine for theft in Washington at the time of the Lebanon crisis, I was exposed to the juxtaposition of American criminal justice, international politics, and public opinion. Fortunately, the prosecutors ultimately felt politically secure enough to drop the charges against my students.

All in all, the first year in academic life had proved busy and satisfying. I had gradually developed into a decent teacher, thanks in part to critical student reactions. I seemed to be accepted by the faculty, even if not warmly embraced. I loved the Bay Area and the environment and, in the autumn, came to enjoy the surprisingly hot Saturday afternoons at the Cal football stadium. We loved our rented house and its setting and ended up, through great fortune, being able to buy the house next door for a modest price! It needed a front deck to take advantage of the Bay view, and Joan wanted to have a spiral staircase leading up to it from the street. We asked our old friend from college days John Field, who was already acquiring architectural recognition, to help us, and he did a splendid job turning what had been a rather ordinary Spanish-style structure into an open, attractive residence.

I was pleased when newly inaugurated Dean Frank Newman asked me to run a summer workshop in international law for a month beginning in June 1960. This gave me the opportunity to invite any speakers I wanted from anywhere in the country to join me in training twenty or so young law teachers in a program I could devise. The workshop proved to be highly instructive and lively, and it was a chance to befriend many experts, including some from international organizations. It was also not difficult to persuade famous law professors from the East and Midwest to spend a few days in the summer sun of California after what had been for them especially grim winter weather. Yet the best of the speakers was a nonlawyer and a local—my new friend Professor Joseph R. Levenson from Berkeley's impressive history department. Joe, at my request, gave a three-hour morning lecture on Chinese history in relation to the world that was enthralling. Right afterward, a young British law teacher came up to me and said: "That was better than any lecture I have ever heard during my three terrific years at Oxford." Joe was delighted to learn this because he was married to a member of the distinguished Anglo-Jewish Montefiore family that had always treated their newly acquired American intellectual relative with uncertain skepticism. One of Rosemary's senior cousins, who had ultimately warmed to Joe's genial social modesty, had told her after their first meeting: "The nicest thing about him is that you'd never know he is clever!"

Life was plainly stimulating and fun, but I knew that a serious professional challenge lay immediately ahead. I had only a two-year, nontenured faculty appointment as an "acting associate professor." I had to win tenure before the close of the second year. I was confident that my improved teaching would pass faculty muster. Yet I had to write a significant research article for scholarly publication. That required me to pick a suitable topic, which meant I had to focus on a given field rather than continue squandering my energies among criminal justice, equitable remedies, administrative law, and the newly developing United Nations law.

What to do? I had come to enjoy teaching each of these subjects, including Frank Newman's beloved administrative law. The only subject I felt I knew something about in practice, other than my exposure to constitutional law at the Supreme Court, was the criminal process. But I was still attracted to public international law, despite the fact I had not identified any point of entry into relevant research. My acquaintance with the three German-language refugees on the faculty had enhanced my interest in learning about traditional European civil law, a vast area that, as I had told the dean at the University of Michigan Law School when I was job-hunting almost two years earlier, I was ill equipped to explore.

Then, out of nowhere, luck again intervened with an opportunity from the Rockefeller Foundation to study China.

7

STUDYING CHINA AT BERKELEY

Setting the Stage for a Lifelong Exploration

The University of California at Berkeley was a wonderful place to start learning about China in 1960. Of course, going to China—the real thing—would have been more exciting, but that option was not on the table. Soon after I began the long course of study required to understand the Chinese legal system, I actually wrote letters to both Chairman Mao Zedong and Prime Minister Zhou Enlai telling them of my quest to study the contemporary Chinese legal system and asking for the opportunity to visit the promised land. I never received a reply and supposed that they were too preoccupied with their angry correspondence with Nikita Khrushchev and the Soviet Union to take on any new pen pals.

I did, however, receive a surprise letter from Beijing soon after doing an interview with the Voice of America (VOA). VOA had focused on why an American law professor would devote himself to the study of communist China's legal system, of all things. I gave them the obvious message—"peaceful hands across the sea to a forbidden land"—not knowing whether this English-language broadcast would be heard in China. Yet this quickly produced a neatly typed letter from an American woman named Dorothy Fischer who was based in Beijing. She had heard the broadcast and was evidently interested in promoting my effort. Fischer identified herself as a former member of the American Communist Party, but she had quit the party because it "was insufficiently advanced" and chosen to live in China.

"Why don't you come to study in Beijing?" she asked. She told me that an African American named Robert White, one of the twenty-one American soldiers who had been taken prisoner during the Korean conflict and had rejected repatriation, was studying law at Peking University, and she offered to introduce me. I replied that I welcomed her idea but that I had two questions. The first was whether the U.S. government would allow me to travel to China, and the second was whether the Chinese government would allow me to enter. I said that I would work on the first question if she would work on the second. Unfortunately, I never heard from her again, perhaps because the political climate in China had again become very tense after the brief respite that followed the disastrous Great Leap Forward of 1958–1961.

BERKELEY CHINA COLLEAGUES

My first and closest colleague and mentor in my new field was Joseph R. Levenson, who, like many of America's outstanding China specialists in the post–World War II era, had trained with John K. Fairbank at Harvard. As mentioned previously. Joan and I had become friendly with Joe and his British wife, Rosemary, so naturally we consulted them while mulling over the Rockefeller Foundation opportunity, and Joe's encouragement and example buoyed my enthusiasm.

Once the decision to study China was made, Joan decided to take Joe's Chinese history class three times a week while managing our expanding family. I had to concentrate on my all-important Chinese-language lessons while introducing a seminar on Chinese law and government in the law school. Yet three nights a week, at dinner, I benefited from Joan's summary of the lecture Joe had delivered that morning. It quickly became clear that I too had to take the course, one of the most highly respected on the campus, the following year.

Joe was a marvelous lecturer—thoughtful, substantive, well-organized. articulate, clear, succinct, modest, and humorous. His mission, as Joe put it, was "to provide a little bit of instant China for busy people." He was also a great scholar. His three-volume *Confucian China and Its Modern Fate* had a major impact on a rapidly developing field that was groping to understand the extent to which Karl Marx, Vladimir Lenin, Joseph Stalin, and Mao Zedong had altered the course of contemporary China. Yet there was an enormous contrast between Joe's writing and his speaking. Listening to him was delightful. Reading him, although a pleasure of a different kind, was not easy. Every sentence was richly worked, virtually baroque or rococo in its jewel-like embellishments. I had to rest every ten pages or so.

Joe's life was tragically cut short in 1969, when, at age forty-eight, he drowned in a family canoeing accident in Northern California's Russian River. Joan and I will never forget his modest charm and delightful, self-deprecating stories. Because Joe's relatives were rooted in the Boston area, it was especially appropriate to hold a memorial service at Harvard, where he had spent many years as an outstanding undergraduate and graduate student and where I was by then teaching. Together with Benjamin Schwartz and others, I was asked to be a speaker and, overcome with emotion, managed to finish my remarks only with the greatest difficulty. For over half a century after that, I have generally declined all memorial talks and have even had a poor record in attending funerals of friends.

Joe Levenson was not an expert on contemporary China, but our Berkeley colleague Franz Schurmann was, and I was enormously lucky to become his friend. One of the handicaps I confronted at the outset of my study was that few scholarly analyses of Chinese government, politics, and society under the People's Republic of China (PRC) had yet appeared. The PRC was barely into its second decade and had witnessed extraordinary and profound upheavals since its establishment in 1949. Getting to know Franz Schurmann helped me to deal with this challenge because he was researching a magnum opus about the PRC and welcomed my interest. I read his informal academic papers, went to many of his public lectures, and talked with him extensively.

It was Franz who introduced me to the value of interviewing refugees from the PRC to put together, in a comprehensible way, the shards of relevant legal research materials that were slowly leaking out of a very non-transparent regime. Indeed, it was his influence that led me to spend the year 1963–1964 interviewing refugees in Hong Kong. That resulted in my first book *The Criminal Process in the People's Republic of China, 1949–63: An Introduction*. And it was Franz's own subsequent interviewing that enabled him to publish finally in 1968, the year that Harvard University Press published my book, the monumental work *Ideology and Organization in Communist China*, which turned out to be the best scholarly publication of his long career.

Franz's writing was neither as finely cultivated as that of Joe Levenson nor as pellucid as that of Harvard's Ben Schwartz, but it was clear, informative, and full of ideas imaginatively culled from the printed and human resources on which he was able to rely. His linguistic prowess permitted him personally to consult the broadest possible sources because he literally had a dozen languages at his fingertips, including German, Russian, and Serbo-Croatian as well as Chinese and the Japanese he acquired as a young American military specialist during World War II.

Although he was eighteen years older than I, Professor Choh-Ming Li, who was then chair of the university's already eminent Center for Chinese Studies and a distinguished expert on China's economy, proved to be another very nice colleague. C. M., as he was known, was always curious about my efforts. He had a rather formalistic view of what a legal system should be and how it should be analyzed, and his own work had made clear to him that, by 1960, the party's revolutionary twists and turns culminating in the Anti-rightist Campaign of 1957–1958 and the Great Leap Forward of 1958–1961 had decimated the Soviet-style legal system that Mao had imported in the early 1950s. He also knew how scarce conventional Chinese legal research materials had become. One day at a cocktail reception our center gave for graduate students, C. M. took me aside and said, with a hand sheltering his mouth: "Since China doesn't have a legal system and there are very few materials, confidentially, how do you spend your time?"

Neither Joe Levenson nor Franz Schurmann ever asked such a question, nor did Bob Scalapino, Berkeley's best-known political scientist in the East Asian area. Scalapino, another Harvard product whose Asia-related career had been launched by military service in World War II and who had found the West Coast congenial, was a remarkable scholar, policy wonk, public intellectual, and administrator. By 1960, he was eminent with respect to Japan as well as China, and, to me at least, seemed to simultaneously crank out thoughtful essays with both hands while on airplanes to Washington and Asia.

Bob was also a fine teacher who took pride in training and fostering the careers of his many outstanding graduate students in comparative politics and international relations of East Asia. Chalmers Johnson seemed to be his favorite and, when I began, Chal was a young teacher in the government department already noted for his analytical, acerbic, and prolific anticommunist scholarship and lectures. I was too new to the subject to want to adopt his firm views, but I admired his ability and presence while preferring Scalapino's more balanced and open attitude toward developments in mainland China, Taiwan, and Hong Kong.

Berkeley had so many other scholars specializing in various aspects of China that I could prattle on at even greater length, but I only want to say a word about Cyril Birch, S. H. Chen, and T. A. Hsia, three learned experts in Chinese language and literature whom I will always remember.

Cyril came to Berkeley from England in 1961 with a formidable scholarly reputation even though barely older than I, and he and his wife Dorothy became our friendly neighbors. Although I never got to know him as well as I did some other colleagues, I found him to be thoughtful, broadly informed, amusing, and interested beyond his professional brief.

S. H. Chen, Berkeley's senior specialist in Chinese literature, brought Cyril to our campus. S. H. Chen was the embodiment of the humane Chinese tradition. Warm, welcoming, and sympathetic to newcomers like Joan and me who were brash enough to belatedly take on the huge task of learning about the Central Realm's millennial civilization, he and his charming wife Grace did everything they could to assist us.

T. A. Hsia, who was not actually on the faculty but on the staff of the Center for Chinese Studies, was a delightful friend who often loved to call my attention to the many changes in the Chinese language that the Maoist revolution was bringing to his country. I rarely saw him without a copy of the latest issue of the *Renmin ribao* (*People's Daily*), the authoritative voice of the Communist Party, in which he had underlined or circled new terms and usages that illustrated often subtle, yet important changes in Chinese life. He shared them with an infectious enthusiasm that reinforced my determination to learn to read Chinese and to use these words and phrases in my efforts to speak. Long after I left Berkeley, I continued to benefit from the elegant essays that T. A., brother of the better-known C. T. Hsia, professor of Chinese literature at Columbia, published in English.

LEARNING CHINESE

Although I had recognized that my biggest gamble in choosing China was whether I could learn to use the language, I did not worry about it and actually looked forward to the process. I was a young man in a hurry, so I tried to accelerate my language study. Instead of enrolling in regular university classes, I joined a special new program for graduate student beginners that the Center for Chinese Studies was organizing four hours a week, and I decided to supplement that with private tutorials. That, including intensive preparation, was about all that my law teaching left me time for, approximately thirty hours a week.

I loved it. Our center program only enrolled three graduate students plus myself, and I enjoyed knowing them all, especially a very bright, humorous first-year student in history named Fred Wakeman. He was as committed as I was, and the two of us set the pace for the other two. One of them didn't have much talent for languages and dropped out before the end of the year. The other, Robert Scheer, was a very smart, would-be political scientist whom I liked, but he was much more enamored of Fidel Castro's then new and vibrant revolution in Cuba than Mao's and eventually threw in his Chinese towel. I later benefited from reading articles he published about Cuba in liberal journals. Fred went on to become a marvelous historian of modern China and a splendid successor to his beloved mentor Joe Levenson in Berkeley's history department. It is hard for me to believe that Fred too went to his heavenly reward prematurely.

Our principal tutor also deserves a word. Mr. Wenshun Chi was a middle-aged, displaced Chinese intellectual who had come to us after years of teaching Chinese at the Defense Language School in Monterey, California. I encouraged Mr. Chi to try writing in English and suggested, as a start, that he edit the mimeographed teaching materials that he prepared for us—mainland Chinese language essays and speeches—into a book that could be used by many aspiring Chinese language students. He later did publish *Readings in Chinese Communist Documents: A Manual for Students of the Chinese Language.*

My other tutor, Mr. Hsutu Chen, was very different and a delight. He too had been teaching in Monterey, but he was younger, age twenty-six, and came to Berkeley to be a graduate student in physics. His major interest, however, was the history and sociology of religion. I got to know

Hsutu better than Mr. Chi because he was a tennis player, as was I, and on a couple of occasions I tried to mix tennis and tutorials, thinking we might combine language learning and sport. Unfortunately, Hsutu was a much better player than I. He left me breathless and barely able to utter many new Chinese phrases such as *wo hen lei* ("I'm very tired") and *ni dade hen hao* ("you play very well") as we played.

I had to teach only one two-hour law seminar a week for the academic years 1960–1963, so I was able to spend a great deal of time learning Chinese and about China in our old Spanish-style stucco house at 647 San Luis Road in the Berkeley hills. I enjoyed the solitude required for the acquisition of new Chinese characters and found focusing on even the simplified characters adopted by the mainland to be an esthetic experience.

I made one major mistake, however. Having discovered that it was taking me at least 50 percent longer to learn to write a character than merely to recognize it and know its meaning, I decided to deemphasize writing to speed up my reading. I later regretted this decision when it became apparent that I would have remembered the characters better had I practiced writing them. Many years later, when our youngest son, Ethan, spent a year in Japan as part of his Harvard College concentration in Japanese studies, he developed considerable skill in one of the Japanese styles of calligraphy, and I witnessed the satisfaction that gave him as well as his parents. Finally, it has always been embarrassing to me, as a purported specialist on China, that I cannot write Chinese, particularly when some of my non-Chinese students became quite expert at it.

I tried to create opportunities to begin to speak Chinese at Berkeley beyond mixing tutoring and tennis. One was recruiting a Chinese student to live with us in order to talk with us in Mandarin while helping with the children and the evening dishes. The problem was to find the right one, someone who spoke in the four tones of standard Mandarin then practiced in Beijing and much of northern China. Many China experts and Chinese friends had stressed the importance of avoiding undue exposure to the accents of people from southern China, including the East coast natives of the Shanghai area, whose local dialects, at least at that time, often inhibited the proper pronunciations and intonations of the standard Mandarin that was my goal.

With the help of S. H. Chen, I found Shirley Wang, a first-year undergrad bent on medical school who had actually come from Beijing a few years earlier and seemed just the person I was seeking. She came to live with us and would have been perfect, except for one thing—she almost never spoke and, when she did, even in Chinese, it was invariably in one-syllable words or mere grunts. A typical exchange would go like this. Me: "*Jintian tianqi hen hao*" ("Today's weather is very good"); Shirley: "Ugh." Me: "*Ni qu tushuguan ma?*" ("Are you going to the library?") Shirley: "*Dui*" (Yes). Then silence! Shirley was a serious, deeply committed person who desperately wanted to do well in her courses, get to her homework as soon as possible after dinner, and move on to medical school. Because she was the first Chinese who lived with us, our children developed the misimpression that China was not populated by happy people.

We rode out the academic year with Shirley but, again with the aid of S. H. Chen, who by then better understood our needs, we found a very different student for the summer—a dynamic, talkative, humorous grad student from Taiwan. Her parents hailed from Jiangsu Province next to Shanghai, she had all the wrong tones and used some expressions peculiar to Taiwan at that time, but she was terrific, just what the doctor ordered. Irene Chang and I talked by the hour in Chinese. She responded to my questions about Chinese life and society with fascinating stories and examples that caused me to want to talk more with her and to lose my self-consciousness as she corrected my halting efforts in Chinese. By the end of the summer, I had made real progress, and, only years later, when Joan and I finally reached Beijing in 1972, did I regret that I hadn't paid more attention to my tones once I started speaking with Irene.

I supplemented all these efforts with one other technique—informal but systematic Chinese-language conversations with some of the few students who had recently managed to leave mainland China and find their way to Berkeley. I especially recall two attractive women introduced by S. H. Chen. One of them went by the English name of Stella and was very pleasant and moderately interesting; the other one, Sally, twenty-three years old and a bit livelier, had just left Shanghai in 1962. Although she was short, she wore her hair in an attention-getting high pompadour that brought her up to five feet six or thereabouts. When I asked her about it, she explained that, to her, America represented freedom from China's repressive social atmosphere, and she wanted to make the most of the new opportunity. She had hated the bowl-cut hairdo that was then being foisted on her and many young Chinese women and relished the newfound symbol of her personal liberation in America.

Sally helped me understand the pre–Cultural Revolution Maoist impact on Chinese daily life, from which Americans had been cut off for over a decade. One vivid example concerned changing the previous, bourgeois definition of what should be considered a "good" marriage in China. Sally's mother, ambitious for her daughter to make her way in radically restructured Shanghai society, repeatedly pressed her to marry a member of the People's Liberation Army, which would have relieved her of the miserable class status she had inherited as a child of the formerly elite but later condemned "national bourgeoisie." Sally, university-educated and extremely bright, persistently rejected the military *duixiang* ("target") selected by her mother. He was a pleasant but uneducated and uninteresting soldier whose companionship Sally could not abide. This proved to be the precipitating factor in her decision to leave the motherland!

BOALT HALL AND CHINA

Although a few of my law school colleagues looked askance at my weekly Chinese-language lunches with Stella or Sally at the Faculty Club, Boalt Hall, Berkeley's law school, proved to be a good and welcoming place to undertake study and teaching about China. Frank Newman, now the law school dean, was extremely supportive once he recovered from the shock of learning that, by asking me to find someone else to specialize in Chinese law, he had inadvertently set me on this unexpected course. Other faculty members were, by and large, accepting of the choice, even if surprised. A few were understandably skeptical.

Despite Berkeley's West Coast location, my colleagues had more to offer me in the field of German law, which had profoundly influenced the legal systems of East Asia beginning in the latter part of the nineteenth century. After considering whether to adopt French or English law as a model for its modernization efforts, Japan had chosen the German system instead. Because this decision was widely considered to have contributed to Japan's rapid rise to power, it exerted an important influence on Chinese reformers and revolutionaries who, throughout the vicissitudes of the first half of the twentieth century, continued to build on the German model, either directly or via its Japanese adaptation.

Following China's communist "liberation" in 1949, Chairman Mao, by importing the Soviet legal system during the first decade of his nationwide rule, had chosen a model that Lenin and Stalin had built on the edifice of pre-Bolshevik Russian law. Pre-1917 Russian law in turn had been modeled on late-nineteenth-century continental European, largely German and French, law.

So I had much to learn from my dynamic senior colleagues Albert Ehrenzweig, who had actually served as a young judge in Austria, and the great scholar of comparative law, Stefan Riesenfeld, who, before coming to study and later teach at Berkeley, had acquired law degrees in his native Germany and then Italy. Without their help, I might have made the mistake of thinking that some basic Chinese legal institutions and norms, in both the mainland and Taiwan, that seemed so different from their Anglo-American counterparts were rooted in China's history and culture rather than Europe's.

Ironically, the greatest help I received from a law professor during my initial preparation for China was not from a Berkeley colleague but from a Columbia University law professor, John N. Hazard, the nation's senior specialist in Soviet law. Not only had he arranged to spend the academic year 1962–1963 on leave at the Center for the Advanced Study of the Behavioral Sciences at Stanford University, but he was also planning to expand his research beyond the Soviet system in order to assess its impact on other countries in the "socialist," that is, communist world.

Hazard had blazed the trail for Western students of communists and their law by daringly arranging to study law in Moscow in the 1930s after his graduation from Harvard Law School. When this happy, charming scholar and generous mentor heard that I would be teaching about China in Berkeley while he was at Stanford, he suggested that we join forces in offering a seminar comparing the legal systems of the two major communist powers, and he volunteered to make the long trek from Palo Alto every week. This proved to be a golden opportunity for both my students and me, and the experience made me appreciate how valuable it would be to have a colleague in the Soviet field on the same faculty.

Teaching with John Hazard for a year was also fun. I liked his ability to make classroom learning stimulating and pleasant, and I noted how much I enjoyed coteaching, which I have often done ever since. One day, at the end of class, I said to John in genuine admiration: "John, you could sell soap!" Unfortunately, he at first misinterpreted my remark to mean I thought he *should* sell soap!! I immediately clarified my intent, but this incident did reveal his sensitivity to the charge of being superficial that I learned later had occasionally been leveled against him.

He may also have been reacting to criticism by some social scientists that his work was naively legalistic and too willing to accept Soviet norms and statements at their face value rather than analyze them in the context of political reality. Similar criticism was occasionally voiced regarding the work of Harold Berman, who also became my mentor and friend when I moved to Harvard soon after.

But I always believed that much of this criticism was inaccurate and more a reflection of some scholars' dismissiveness of the idea that law could play any significant role in a communist dictatorship, an idea that continues to generate controversy in Chinese studies even today. Yet I have always tried to ground my work on China's legal system in political reality and have more than occasionally worried that perhaps I leaned too far in that direction and failed to emphasize the extent to which some aspects of the system functioned with considerable nonpolitical autonomy.

By the summer of 1963, I felt that Berkeley had prepared me well for the final year of the four-year grant from the Rockefeller Foundation, which I decided to spend interviewing Chinese refugees in Hong Kong. That was as close as most Americans could get to mainland China at that time.

8

HONG KONG BOUND

Interviewing Chinese Refugees

In the spring of 1961, luck brought me an unexpected opportunity to make a brief, introductory visit to Hong Kong two years before our scheduled stay there. Out of nowhere came an invitation from the University of Hong Kong for me to be one of the speakers at the ceremony celebrating the fiftieth anniversary of its founding in 1911. I was dumbfounded, to say the least, and wondered how the organizers had possibly decided to invite me because I had, at that point, published nothing about China or Hong Kong and knew no one at the university. Nevertheless, I accepted gladly.

The mystery of why I had been invited to speak was solved almost immediately upon landing in the colony. At the opening night's dinner, several people congratulated me on the books I had supposedly written about China and Japan, and it became clear that the hosts had mistaken me for Jerome B. Cohen (I am "A"), an American scholar at the City University of New York and an economist twenty-five years my senior who focused on East Asia! The next day, when it was my turn to speak at the academic convocation, I, of course, had to make the full disclosure that I was not Jerome B.; had not authored the books he had written and; indeed, at that early point in my life, had not published any books. I made clear, to be sure, that I was nevertheless very happy to be there!

Almost half a century later, in 2009, by which time Joan and I had lived in Hong Kong at various times for a total of almost ten years and were well known there, I told this story to a large audience at the University of Hong Kong Faculty of Law assembled to listen to me lecture about the significance of the tragic slaughter that had occurred in Beijing two decades earlier on June 4, 1989. The amusement the story caused helped to lighten the burden imposed by June 4 commemorations.

I told the 2009 audience that, having published quite a lot on China during the previous five decades, I hoped to be invited to speak at the forthcoming one hundredth anniversary of the university, which might have made Joan and me the only people to have attended both the fiftieth and the one hundredth. That might have finally enabled me to assuage the sense of guilt I have always felt for having unwittingly freeloaded on the earlier celebration! Unfortunately, as I was later informed, my frequent public criticisms of the Chinese government's human rights abuses made me an unlikely choice to be a speaker on such a sensitive public occasion after Hong Kong had become a "special administrative region" of the communist motherland in 1997.

SETTLING INTO COLONIAL HONG KONG

It was one thing for Joan and me to make a quick visit to Hong Kong. It was quite another to set up shop long-term in 1963 for a family of five and to find a place to carry out my research on China's criminal justice system, even then a very politically sensitive topic. Housing was plainly the most urgent requirement. I learned that Ezra Vogel, a young Harvard sociologist specializing in Chinese and Japanese studies, was also preparing to spend the current year researching in Hong Kong with his wife and three children. Ezra was roughly my age and a friendly person, and, after I contacted him in Hong Kong, he told us that they had found an apartment in a rather newly developed area of Kowloon called Yao Yat Chun near the Boundary Street dividing line between Kowloon and the colony's New Territories. He believed that another apartment might be available there, and we were able to find one almost across the street from Ezra's. The area featured two- or three-story residential buildings rather than high rises, and the residents seemed to be mostly local middle-class Cantonese, some of whom spoke English, with a mix of a few foreigners.

The problem with the location, we discovered, was that it was remote from Hong Kong Island, where most of the diplomats, British and American officials, international journalists, and Chinese and Western businesspeople we hoped to meet made their homes. We did not have a car, public transport in our area was limited, and taxis were not easy to come by. Unlike today, no tunnels or bridges linked Kowloon and the island. We had to rely on public ferries to cross the harbor between them, which was colorful but inconvenient.

The next challenge, after finding some local people to help with cooking and cleaning, was to take care of the children's education. Our eldest, Peter, already six and a half, was able to enroll in a respected English-speaking government school in Kowloon. But Seth was only four and Ethan, two and a half, was just beginning to talk—English, to be sure. Joan heard that a British army wife, a Mrs. Foster, ran an informal school out of her apartment on a neighborhood street. Mrs. Foster ran a taut ship but the children loved it for the entire school year, despite the absence of a playground, and Ethan as well as Seth made great progress in learning to talk, albeit in their native tongue rather than Cantonese or Mandarin.

REFUGEE INTERVIEWING

With a roof over our heads and the children taken care of, Joan and I began to focus on our own interests. She found a stimulating, if somewhat bewildering, opportunity to teach English to young Chinese refugee children. They lived nearby in a bare seven-story walk-up housing development, one of many that had been newly constructed for the flood of mainland families that had descended upon Hong Kong in the wake of the massive starvation caused by Chairman Mao's utopian Great Leap Forward campaign of 1958–1961. Joan reported that their children gratefully relished the challenge of informally learning English as a second language in their makeshift rooftop school.

My own work also involved Chinese refugees, but very special ones. I had decided to do a book on criminal justice in China, in part because criminal justice materials were more ample than other legal materials relating to contemporary China. Yet the available materials were far from sufficient. Indeed, China in 1963, fourteen years after establishment of the People's Republic of China (PRC), still had very little published legislation of any kind. Nor did it publish court decisions, and, apart from the few books and law reviews that had appeared before the suppressive Anti-Rightist Campaign of 1957–1958, there was almost no Chinese scholarly commentary on contemporary law. Scattered, incomplete newspaper reports were often suggestive but incomplete. A couple of Russian-language studies of Chinese law as of the mid-1950s that had been translated into English were helpful but very much out of date.

As previously mentioned, my colleague at Berkeley, the brilliant sociologist Franz Schurmann, had convinced me that, in these circumstances, if one wanted to understand how the legal system worked as a system, it would be indispensable to resort to interviewing Chinese refugees, and that is what I determined to do during my year in Hong Kong. I decided that I needed to interview three categories of refugees.

The first, and easiest to locate, consisted of ordinary citizens who had had no specific contact with the criminal justice system. They could help me understand contemporary Chinese society, popular attitudes toward law and their own perception of the roles played by the legal system, and whatever seemed to substitute for a formal legal system under a government that was not emphasizing legal formalities.

The second category consisted of those who had actual experience as targets of the criminal process broadly construed—the accused. I interpreted my task to include all those who had been significantly punished by the regime, whether or not the sanction imposed was formally labeled "criminal." Plainly this included those who had been subjected to reeducation through labor (*laodong jiaoyang*) or other supposedly "noncriminal" sanctions that possessed a variety of names for what was all too obviously some form of incarceration.

The third category, the most important and hardest to find, was composed of those who took part in the administration of criminal justice, as I had defined it. I needed to meet police; prosecutors; judges; other relevant officials; and, to the extent they were allowed participation in the process, lawyers. This was a tall order, especially for an American academic with few Hong Kong connections who did not speak Cantonese—the local dialect—and whose command of Mandarin was a work in progress.

But my timing was good. We arrived in Hong Kong in early August 1963. In the spring of 1962, for a period of about six weeks, the PRC had suddenly let down the barriers that had made it difficult for Chinese to reach Hong Kong without official permission. This enabled roughly sixty thousand people who, in an effort to escape the starvation and other miseries of the Great Leap Forward's aftermath, had been massing near Hong Kong's border with Guangdong Province to enter the colony. Many more would have joined them had the colony not later closed the border to prevent utter inundation by the refugee wave that had overwhelmed its facilities.

Although most of these newcomers were rural people of lesser immediate interest to my project, many of the articulate, educated, urban members of the group had begun to assimilate and become known in Hong Kong. As I cast my net in the official, academic, and business communities, I gradually began to meet intelligent newcomers who could explain life in China and where law fit in. They in turn sometimes introduced me to others who were of greater interest, such as those who had been targets of the system.

Among the most interesting and pathetic in this second category of informants were those who had been condemned to long periods of the supposedly "noncriminal" punishment of reeducation through labor (RETL). That was usually enforced confinement, often in rural labor camps, that in practice was indistinguishable from the criminal punishment called reform through labor (*laodong gaizao*). In that era, members of the two groups were frequently confined together.

Many of the offenders who had received RETL had been declared "rightists" in 1957–1958 during the infamous Anti-Rightist Campaign. That had followed the campaign to "let a hundred flowers bloom, let a hundred schools of thought contend" that had seduced them into publicly expressing their criticisms of the communist government. Listening to their sad tales of the personal and professional lives that had been ruined when Communist Party and police officials imposed RETL, without regard for either freedom of speech or fair procedures for defending themselves against unjust charges, was a sobering exercise.

Those who administered the criminal justice system—my third category of refugee informants—were much harder to find, but, when I discovered one, it was a veritable treasure trove. The first of them was

Eddie Chen (Chen Zhongwen), introduced to me, if memory serves, by a British official who was interviewing refugees as part of an ongoing refugee-interviewing program in Hong Kong. Eddie proved to be a wonderful resource. He had been born and brought up in Hong Kong by a communist mother during the years Chiang Kai-shek ruled the mainland. His parents had separated, and his father served in Chiang's Nationalist government's military. When the communists succeeded in "liberating" the country in 1949, his father left the mainland, and Eddie, then seventeen, and his mother moved to Guangzhou in the mainland, where, despite his youth, he landed a job with the police. He eventually was assigned to a unit responsible for investigating and supervising religious organizations. By 1955, however, growing doubts about the nature of his work led him to act in ways that made him suspect to his superiors. The last straw for the security apparatus apparently was their discovery of the manuscript for a novel Eddie had written about a Chinese soldier who married a Korean woman during China's involvement in the 1950–1953 conflict with America in Korea. Eventually, Eddie was sent to a labor camp for a punishment that was the immediate predecessor to what, beginning in 1957, became known as RETL.

Eddie was highly intelligent, evidently fair-minded and balanced in his view of the issues, and he spoke well in Mandarin. He also had an excellent sense of humor. He did a great deal to help me understand the early days of the PRC's public security system and the thinking of those who staffed it. I was so impressed with Eddie that I introduced him to Ezra Vogel, who found him even more helpful than I did because Ezra was engaged in a much broader study of the city of Guangzhou that was ultimately published under the title *Canton Under Communism: Programs and Politics in Provincial Capital 1949–1968*.

Eddie was not the only public security officer I interviewed. A British official later introduced me to another, who hailed from Fuzhou, the capital of Fujian Province. Although a few years younger than Eddie, who was in his early thirties when I met him, this fellow, whom I will call Zhou, had much more recent experience in handling criminal cases than Eddie had and was extremely helpful to my research on the criminal process. He was able to speak of developments as recent as just a year earlier, 1962, because he left his job only when he decided to depart for Hong Kong. Interviewing him five mornings a week from 9 A.M. to 1 P.M., I totaled

120 hours with him, my all-time interview record. Zhou was detached, professional, and highly competent. He did not volunteer long answers or unsolicited stories but was crisp and responsive and occasionally came through with a remark that was memorable.

In 1963, because the PRC had not yet promulgated a criminal code, one of the topics of great interest to me was to determine what conduct was deemed criminal and sufficient to warrant prosecution rather than handling by administrative or informal means. Obviously, murder, rape, arson, and other major conventional offenses that plague every society were deemed criminal, and so too were the most serious political offenses that were then often included in the vague and broad term "counterrevolution." But how, in the absence of legislative guidance, was the borderline between criminal and noncriminal behavior delineated in those cases in which various societies draw the line in different places in both law and practice?

I wanted to know, for example, whether adultery was treated as a crime in the PRC and, if so, to what extent and in what circumstances it was prosecuted. In many countries and many American states, adultery was still recognized as a crime but was seldom prosecuted. Zhou seemed a bit fuzzy in his initial response to the first question but on reflection decided that, at least in Fuzhou at that time, adultery in principle was regarded as criminal. I pressed him about the extent to which it was actually pursued by police and prosecutors. He then said, in an utterly sober vein: "Look, if we prosecuted all the cases of adultery, we wouldn't have time for the counterrevolutionaries!"

Zhou was memorable for other reasons as well, especially because he focused my attention, as no other interviewee did, on the question of my obligation to my informants. They were indispensable to my work, helping me to see how Chinese criminal justice functioned as a system. Indeed, after my Hong Kong year ended, I published an article entitled "Interviewing Chinese Refugees: Indispensable Tool for Legal Research on China." But what duty did I have toward my interviewees? This was more than an ethical or academic question for Zhou and me.

My informants, whom I modestly compensated with "tea money" while we were interviewing, needed work once our collaboration concluded, and I felt a particular obligation to try to help those with whom I spent the longest time. They had become my friends, and I could not abandon them once they had met my needs. I didn't have to worry about Eddie, who found a good opportunity with Ezra Vogel, who ultimately helped him go to the United States for study and an eventual teaching job. But Zhou was different, and he wasn't easy to assist. He spoke neither Cantonese nor English, and I was his only substantial contact in Hong Kong. Fortunately, after a few failures, one of my few business friends agreed to take him on.

PETER WANG: A JUDGE TURNED LAWYER

It had been profoundly satisfying to have the opportunity to interview two public security officers at great length, but I also had to find at least one valuable former judge and one able lawyer to fill out my necessarily scarce category of legal professionals. I met several people who, having heard that I could provide "tea money" for those who could discuss judicial matters, tried to convince me that they had worked in Chinese courts before leaving for Hong Kong. But interviews quickly punctured their stories. One man had plainly worked in local government but his attempts to describe how local courts were organized and staffed and how they operated were pathetic. Another tried to persuade me that he had actually gone to law school, but he fell apart when asked to name the courses he had studied. But not Peter Wang!

I met Peter, whose name in Mandarin was Wang Youjin, through the editor of one of Hong Kong's many Chinese language newspapers, the *Tiantian ribao* (the *Daily Paper*). Peter exuded credibility. He was quiet, thoughtful, careful in his judgments and expression, and eager to help. He told me that, like many Southeast Asian Chinese, he had left his native Singapore in 1950 at age eighteen in order to get a free university education in the new China that had only been established the previous year. On arrival in Beijing, he was assigned to study law at the new Beijing College of Political Science and Law, which later became the prominent China University of Political Science and Law, the training ground for so many of the government's legal cadres, past and present. When I asked him about the courses he had studied at law school, he rattled off all the right names without a moment's hesitation, and I knew immediately I had a good catch.

Peter finished law school in mid-1954, just as the PRC was publishing its first constitution, one that was heavily influenced by Joseph Stalin's 1936 constitution. Upon graduation, he was assigned to work at the special Railroad Court based in Harbin, capital of Heilongjiang Province in China's industrialized northeast. He was the only court employee, including judges, who had the benefit of a formal legal education, and court officials, mostly former military men and police officers, came to rely on him for all technical legal issues.

Peter told many especially valuable stories about the effort made by the PRC after its years of revolutionary tumult to introduce law and lawyers rather than the cruel class struggle that was continuing but in a more minor key. The party decided to create legal advisory bureaus, which resembled the Soviet colleges of advocates, and to staff them with young, recently trained talent, Peter among them, so he moved from his court to the Beijing equivalent of a law firm in 1956.

That was an exciting period for law reformers. Many codes of law were drafted with Soviet assistance, including drafts of what were slated to be the PRC's first codes of criminal law and criminal procedure, and the legal advisory bureaus were expected to help experiment with and implement these drafts. But the effort came to a sudden end in June 1957, when the outpouring of criticisms elicited by the Hundred Flowers Campaign stunned party leaders and led Chairman Mao to unleash the Anti-Rightist Campaign. Peter's government-sponsored law firm in Beijing was closed and, like many other legal officials, he was soon declared a "rightist." Because of his Singapore origins, however, he escaped severe mistreatment and, by 1960, was permitted to leave for Hong Kong, where he was hired by the *Daily Paper* as a staff writer and commentator on mainland affairs.

I interviewed Peter for a total of eighty-five hours, and he helped me understand not only the era of Soviet influence in which he had taken part but also the period that followed it. Then, for the rest of the year that I spent in Hong Kong, he continued to assist me in research concerning China's criminal justice system, research that eventually helped me to publish my first book in 1968— *The Criminal Process in the People's Republic of China, 1949–63: An Introduction*. (Joan said Harvard University Press would have sold more copies had I titled it "Sex, Chinese Law and You!")

ESTABLISHING THE UNIVERSITIES SERVICE CENTRE

Peter also helped me to establish the Universities Service Centre in Hong Kong, which was not a task on my initial agenda. In the early 1960s, foreign scholars who chose to make Hong Kong their base for the study of a China that excluded them had few facilities available. In an effort to improve this situation, the Carnegie Corporation in New York decided to establish a research center that would welcome and assist foreign China scholars who had come to Hong Kong for visits of not more than a year or two.

Establishing a research center on the border of what was still called Red China or Communist China, however, was a delicate undertaking because the British colonial authorities, always concerned about offending the mainland government, were carefully scrutinizing the preparations for the center, which they seemed to suspect was going to be a Central Intelligence Agency (CIA) front or at least that a few American scholars there might be connected to "the agency." When the first person sent to set the center up was deemed rather inert and too intimidated by our suspicious hosts, Carnegie decided to replace him. Needing someone already on the scene in Hong Kong, it asked me, although still relatively junior, to take on the job temporarily until a permanent replacement could be found, which I did with some reluctance.

With the aid of the Union Research Institute (URI), a local Chinese organization that had amassed a large collection of mainland newspapers, we soon established permanent quarters on Argyle Street in Kowloon near the then Kai Tak airport. Before long, the center began to hum. I found the URI files to be informative when gathering materials concerning the operation of China's legal system, and the center proved to be a more suitable place for conducting interviews with refugees who were not accustomed to visiting an international hotel or a foreigner's apartment.

I served as the principal person responsible for the center for the winter and spring of 1963–1964, so the Hong Kong government showed a special, if informal, interest in my activities. I recall with some amusement, for example, a dinner party given in my honor by our new friend Solicitor General Denys Roberts. To my surprise and pleasure, I was seated across from the colonial secretary, who served as Hong Kong's de facto foreign minister. He seized the apparently prearranged opportunity to inquire systematically about the center, its sponsorship, and my role. His attitude, in a sophisticated way, seemed to be: if you fellows are professors, why aren't you professing instead of taking so much time off to study China? Through a bit of luck and the international legal "mafia," I had by then developed strong connections with not only Hong Kong's solicitor general but also its chief justice, Michael Hogan. These two high legal officials vouched for my good faith and good behavior.

A BROAD RANGE OF HONG KONG FRIENDS

Sir Michael loved tennis, as did I, and I soon found myself in a lively doubles match on the chief justice's court atop the Peak of Hong Kong Island, which was inevitably dubbed "the highest court in the land." Michael and his glamorous wife Patricia invited Joan and me to dinner several times at their residence, where they frequently entertained. Another regular guest was the solicitor general, Denys Roberts, the witty author of humorous books about the law, who became our best friend. Indeed, our friendship endured during all his subsequent years in Hong Kong as attorney general, chief secretary of the government, and then chief justice and during his visits to us at Harvard after our departure from the colony. Although he was discreet about revealing the interest of British intelligence in the establishment and operation of the Universities Service Centre, he managed to let me know about it and to confirm that he had reassured the authorities that my colleagues and I were genuine academics and not fronting for the CIA.

Friendships with colonial officials were not the only thing that made Hong Kong social life especially interesting. We saw quite a bit of Ezra and Sue Vogel, who had children close in age to our own. We also liked Lucian and Mary Pye, especially Lucian's humorous, if somewhat cynical, insights into Chinese politics that were shaped in part by his early days growing up in precommunist China. Several of the non-American scholars who came to our new Universities Service Centre also became good friends, such as Kenneth Walker, the English economist who focused on China's agriculture.

Our wealthiest and most distinguished local Hong Kong friends were Lawrence and Muriel Kadoorie, introduced to us by Joan's London-based aunt, Viola Laski. Lawrence and his brother Horace, scions of a leading family of Baghdad Jews who had emigrated to Shanghai in the late nineteenth century to make their fortune, were among the most prominent members of Hong Kong's business community, which at that time was still largely dominated by British moguls rather than the Chinese tycoons who later replaced them. The Kadoories, despite their fabled wealth, had been interned in Shanghai by the Japanese military during World War II and had moved to Hong Kong after Chairman Mao established the People's Republic in 1949. There they operated China Light & Power, the Peninsula Hotel, and many other businesses.

I will never forget our family's first Sunday lunch with the Kadoories. They were kind enough to send a car, a Rolls Royce with a telephone, to fetch us. The Rolls made an impression on our sons, especially because Joan and I had decided not to buy even a modest car for our Hong Kong stay but to rely on public transportation. What really fascinated the children, however, was the ability to use a telephone in a car, something they had not previously seen. We didn't even have a telephone in our apartment because, at that time, to get one without waiting eight months, it was necessary to pay a bribe to a phone company official, which I regarded as conduct unbecoming a law teacher!

I always enjoyed hearing Lawrence hold forth on China. Although the communists had confiscated the vast Kadoorie holdings in the mainland and turned their very large Shanghai residence into the city's Children's Palace, he appeared to harbor little resentment and indeed liked to show an understanding of why the revolution had succeeded and why closer Western cooperation with the People's Republic would be desirable.

Lawrence also liked to recall stories from the old days. Although he and Muriel were slower to reveal details of the hardships of wartime internment by the Japanese, he often told other tales of precommunist Shanghai. For example, when I asked him about the effectiveness of Chiang Kai-shek's legal system, he acknowledged its limited reach in Shanghai and the occasional need to resort to less formal methods to vindicate one's rights. A favorite anecdote concerned how he managed to recover a beloved rare chess set that he had left with a Chinese friend for safekeeping while the family was interned. After the war, when the friend refused to return the chess set even after Lawrence threatened legal action, Lawrence took advantage of the opportunity presented when the leader of Shanghai's infamous Green Gang called upon him for a favor.

Twenty-four hours after Lawrence related his problem, the chess set appeared on his doorstep!

The period 1963–1964 proved to be a good time for befriending American diplomats, and we met many young, dynamic, and able American Foreign Service officers and spouses who shared our interests in China, among them Heyward and Sheila Isham. "Hey" Isham was a specialist in Soviet affairs who had been assigned to the U.S. Consulate General in Hong Kong in order to analyze the Sino-Soviet split from that vantage point. Sheila was a very talented American artist who was working to incorporate elements of Chinese culture and calligraphy into her painting. Hey had preceded me by a couple of years at Yale College, where we both had studied international relations, and the "old school tie" reinforced our common interests. The Ishams not only had wonderful children who were kind to our slightly younger kids but they also had a boat, an invaluable escape from Hong Kong's circumscribed geography, and they were generous in sharing it. We continued to see the Ishams on and off over the years during our mutually peripatetic adventures.

Journalists were the other main components of our Hong Kong social life, and we especially enjoyed Stanley and Annette Karnow. Stan was a wonderful writer and shrewd political analyst who had worked for *Time* magazine in East Asia for many years before discovering the greater satisfactions of doing popular yet serious books. After long covering America's Vietnam War, he did a splendid, highly readable study of it and then followed, years later, with a superb account of China's Cultural Revolution that even many scholars continued to rely on long after publication. He also produced an excellent book on the Philippines.

9

TRANSITION TO HARVARD

Leaving Hong Kong was not easy emotionally for the family or me, but we knew we had another adventure ahead of us—a year in Cambridge, Massachusetts. I had been invited to be a visiting professor at Harvard Law School (HLS) and a guest of the university's East Asian Research Center for the academic year 1964–1965.

Joan and I decided that, although the boys were still young, they might well learn about the world along the way back to America in the summer of 1964. So instead of heading directly to the States from Hong Kong, we arranged an itinerary that called for heading home in the opposite, longer direction. We spent a few days in New Delhi with Indian friends and then five days divided between Moscow and Leningrad, as St. Petersburg was then known.

For our stay in Moscow, we had made advance arrangements and payment for Intourist, the official Soviet travel agency, to host us. On arrival however, Intourist claimed that it had no record of our reservation or payment, so, under our protest, which was much later vindicated, we had to pony up again in order to secure the hotel and guide that we needed. We always suspected, without any evidence, that, once Intourist saw how young our children were, it "lost" our reservation in an effort to separate itself from responsibility for a potentially unruly group. Our hotel, the venerable, pre-Bolshevik Metropole, proved worth the price of admission. We had reserved two rooms for five people but were assigned a five-room suite that included a living room and a dining room that gave the boys plenty of running space. The charming furniture was from the tsarist era.

We were happy in our Soviet digs until the evening of the second day, when Peter came down with a high fever and what seemed like pink eye. Within about fifteen minutes after we notified the hotel of our problem, the doorbell rang and a three-person medical delegation entered. It consisted of a doctor, a nurse, and an orderly/driver—a team who, we were told, roamed central Moscow in an ambulance ready to respond to any urgent calls. The speed of their response and the obvious competence of the doctor, who spoke basic English, left me with an impression that was almost as favorable as that made by the delicious blini we were served at their hospital while accompanying Peter, who received excellent care there for a couple of days.

Warsaw, which billed itself as "the Paris of the East" but was still recovering from its World War II devastation, seemed like a breath of fresh air to us because we had just come there from the two major, rather drab Soviet cities. London, of course, was even a sharper and more enjoyable contrast. Joan's Aunt Viola and her amiable third husband doted on our entire family. All we had to offer in return was the huge slab of Russian caviar we had bought in Moscow with the excess rubles we had not been allowed to exchange back into dollars as we exited the former Soviet Union. Joan and I had each visited the Laskis separately before we married, but this was our first time together to sample extraordinary theater, legendary museums, and other British treasures introduced by our own equivalent of the proverbial Auntie Mame, and the boys loved their first whiff of London's history, pomp, and circumstance.

GETTING "ORIENTED" AT HARVARD— GREAT EXPECTATIONS

Establishing ourselves in Cambridge was not simple but, in comparison with arriving in Hong Kong the previous autumn, everything seemed much easier. We had rented in advance a comfortable house near the Radcliffe campus, sight unseen. We knew our son Peter would be able to attend second grade in a public school a block away, and my omnicompetent Joan managed to enroll the younger boys in a nice preschool. Above all, we had many friends, both on Harvard's Asia faculty and in the law school.

I had already met Professor John King Fairbank twice before. The first time was in Berkeley, California, in 1962 when, at the home of his former protégé and our good friend Joseph R. Levenson, he broached the idea of my visiting Harvard. Fairbank, who was the dean of post–World War II China studies in the United States and always eager to add young scholars to the field, had twice before sought to train a specialist in Chinese law for Harvard but each time had been disappointed. So when he heard that I had already plunged into the field, he contacted Milton Katz, director of international studies at the law school, who in turn enlisted the support of Dean Erwin Griswold. Not long after Fairbank's visit to the Levensons, Professor Katz stopped in Berkeley to discuss the possibilities of my spending a year as a visiting professor in the law school.

The Harvard invitation was gratifying but upsetting. I had permission to spend up to two years away from the Berkeley campus, which was a generous concession from the Boalt Hall law school administration. At the time I was planning to go to Taiwan for one year and then to Hong Kong the year after that, so that a year at Harvard would have meant a third year away. Yet I wanted the benefit of a Harvard year because I knew I would find exposure to both the law school and the Asian colleagues in Cambridge very valuable to my slowly increasing sophistication in comparative law and China scholarship. I decided, regretfully, to give up the year on Taiwan in favor of a year in Cambridge.

On the law faculty, I especially wanted to learn from several well-known figures. Arthur Von Mehren had become America's best-known expert on continental European law. He was also then leading the impressive Harvard-Michigan-Stanford program that, with Ford Foundation sponsorship, had introduced serious Japanese legal studies to the United States in the late 1950s and early 1960s.

Harold J. Berman was another Harvard professor of obvious relevance to my work. Following the example of Columbia's John Hazard, Berman had decided, while still a student at Yale Law School immediately after World War II, that he would specialize in the Soviet legal system, which later profoundly influenced the People's Republic of China's (PRC) development in its first decade. I plainly had much to learn from Berman, who was spending the 1961–1962 academic year in groundbreaking research inside the Soviet Union. Shortly after his return from Moscow, he gave a lecture at Boalt Hall about this breakthrough in Soviet-American exchanges that was for me a genuinely exciting experience.

Two years before my interest in China, while I was interviewing for a teaching job at the University of Michigan in Ann Arbor, the faculty there received the disconcerting news that their beloved colleague Professor John P. Dawson ("Jack," as he was known), who had been visiting at Harvard, had decided to stay in Cambridge. I hadn't yet met this scholar of European legal history, but having witnessed the depressing effect the news of his defection had on my hosts, I decided that he surely must be worth knowing. He did indeed prove to be an encouraging and stimulating mentor who sat in on and discussed with me several sessions of my initial Harvard course on Chinese law as well as the relevance of French and German legal history.

Harvard faculty member Lon Fuller's publications on jurisprudence, of course, embraced many themes, and, by the early 1960s, had become very prominent. My initiation into comparative law relating to China and my conversations with my senior colleague at Berkeley, former Austrian judge Albert Ehrenzweig, made me fully aware of how deficient my preparation in jurisprudence, a field that I had previously undervalued, was. Fuller had shown some interest in China's unusual development and could, of course, help to remedy this deficiency. Harvard also had impressive expertise in Anglo-American legal history. Samuel Thorne, whom I had known slightly when he was Yale Law School's learned library director during my student days there, had become perhaps the world's most renowned authority on early English legal history. And Mark DeWolfe Howe Jr., scion of a famous scholar of American literature, was breathing new life into the field of American legal history, especially in public law.

I was also eager to expand my knowledge of public international law. One of the main reasons I later decided to enter Chinese studies was to promote the smooth entry of communist China, or Red, China, as it was then often called, into the world community. In the early 1960s, I already knew what the distinctive "Yale approach" to international law was but wanted to learn from Harvard's experts, two more conventional but eminent leaders in the field: Richard Baxter and Louis Sohn. In addition, their senior colleague Louis Jaffe's influential research in administrative law had often dealt with international matters.

Although I had been blessed with the expertise of my Berkeley China colleagues in the social sciences and history, I was also eager to become acquainted with Harvard's counterparts. I had already met Fairbank and Ezra Vogel, but I also wanted to know the historian and political scientist Benjamin Schwartz, whose analyses of both traditional Chinese legal philosophy and Chinese communist history and whose crystal-clear writing style I much admired. Because I still knew little about the Chinese economy, I also looked forward to learning from Dwight Perkins, the young Harvard economist who, although only my age, had already developed something of a reputation.

Harvard's experts on Soviet politics were also naturally of great interest to me. Merle Fainsod was then America's leading specialist in this field, having superseded Berkeley's Julian Towster, who never seemed to adjust to the reality of destalinization. I also hoped to see Adam Ulam, who had been nice to me when, in early 1951, I visited Harvard as a Yale College senior trying to decide between pursuing a law degree at Yale and a PhD in international relations at Harvard. By 1963 I especially wanted to understand why social scientists in the Soviet field, including Yale's brilliant law professor Leon Lipson, tended to downgrade the work of John Hazard and Harold Berman as unrealistically legalistic. I hoped that my publications on China would avoid a similar fate.

AUTUMN 1964 AT HARVARD

I loved settling in at Harvard. I had only previously spent two months as a beginning graduate student there, in the summer of 1951, when I'd taken two courses in European history before taking up a Fulbright Scholarship in France. Back in Cambridge in 1964 for a longer stay, I was plainly there in more comfortable circumstances and quickly felt at home. Colleagues in both the law school and the China field quickly vindicated the reasons why I had decided that a year in Cambridge would be worth giving up a year in Taiwan.

Joan and I were also happy socially. As previously noted, we had been disappointed by the "Western hospitality" shown us during our four years in Berkeley, and, except for our wonderful new law dean Frank Newman, who had welcomed my choosing to study China, few Berkeley law professors seemed enthusiastic about my choice. They understandably treated me like the junior newcomer to Asian studies that I obviously was. Boalt Hall, despite its location on the West coast, was heavily invested in European law and seemed content with that specialty.

By the time we arrived in Cambridge, however, especially after a year of interviewing and other research and experience in Hong Kong relating to China, I had begun to feel more confident about my knowledge of contemporary China and was eager to exchange ideas with new and stimulating people. We were often wined and dined by Harvard Law School faculty families who not only were curious to learn more about us and China but also seemed moved by an implicit sense of noblesse oblige about how to treat faculty visitors.

It was an era when most faculty spouses were women who had not undertaken full-time employment and had the leisure to squander on gracious entertainment. Indeed, the pace of Harvard social life seemed so swift that it began to infringe on my research and class preparation. Nevertheless, it felt good to both of us to be appreciated and even flattered.

I had a similar feeling at work, where, instead of being treated like a wet-behind-the-ears junior, I was regarded as a knowledgeable expert in a major, inscrutable area, not only by the many interested students but also by the law faculty and even my new colleagues in the Asian field. This gave me the confidence to undergo the scrutiny to which, it increasingly became apparent, I was being subjected in faculty-monitored classes and during faculty lunches, informal tea chats, as well as dinners. The law school, undoubtedly encouraged by Professor Fairbank, was seriously considering me for a permanent appointment.

My feelings were complicated when an offer to join the HLS faculty arrived in December. To be sure, I was pleased to have the validation of the impressive Harvard academic community. It would have been disappointing not to receive it. I also could foresee an agreeable and successful life if I accepted the offer because it was obvious that there was a felt need for the kind of research and writing I wanted to do. Because of Harvard's location and prestige, I saw that there might also be greater opportunity to take part in the national discussions that I felt were required to help forge a new and more enlightened policy toward China than the prevailing Cold War stalemate. As my Yale mentor Myres McDougal later said approvingly, but with some exaggeration, "Harvard is a much better power base than Berkeley."

Yet there were significant professional and personal reasons to decline the offer. I felt a debt of gratitude to Berkeley and especially to Frank Newman. He had recruited me to California; cotaught a course with me during my first year; and, when I surprised him by expressing interest in taking up the Rockefeller Foundation China fellowship, bent over backward to make sure I could use the four years to best advantage. He also undoubtedly persuaded the faculty to award me permanent tenure largely on the basis of future promise rather than demonstrated publications.

Yet Joan too was inclined to stay in Cambridge. Like me, she enjoyed the new friends and the Harvard community, and she also saw greater opportunities to pursue her interests in Asian art history. Not only was she excited about the possibilities for faculty spouses to audit the many courses Harvard offered in Japanese and Chinese art, literature, and history, but the staff of the great Museum of Fine Arts in Boston, Massachusetts, and its school for budding artists warmly welcomed her contributions to lectures and to weekly educational television programs on art.

What finally made my choice easier was the uproar that had been taking place on the Berkeley campus throughout the 1964 fall semester. Although when we arrived in Berkeley in 1959 there were still occasional echoes of the 1950 loyalty oath controversy that had bitterly divided the university faculty, our four years there provided a peaceful environment for serious academic work. I certainly had been outraged by the refusal of the university administration to allow philosophy professor John Searle and me to hold a campus program designed to protest the San Francisco visit of the notorious U.S. House of Representatives Un-American Activities Committee, but that had been the only substantial political upset I had encountered.

In the fall of 1964, however, while I was blissfully at Harvard, the Berkeley campus was consumed by the continuing political chaos that was presided over by the brilliant graduate student agitator Mario Savio, and that worried me. Berkeley's chancellor, the able labor economist and mediator Clark Kerr, was struggling to work out a compromise among the conflicting forces to achieve peace and restore sanity to the university. From afar, I supported as well as sympathized with him.

I received the Harvard offer just as the drama in Berkeley was reaching its peak. About one week later, as the time for my decision was drawing near, Bill Coblentz, a dynamic San Francisco lawyer about ten years my senior who had befriended me through our Yale Law School alumni association for the Bay Area, telephoned me in the hope of convincing me to reject the Harvard offer. I bluntly asked Bill, who was an ally of then governor of California Pat Brown and a university regent working to end the crisis: "Is Clark Kerr going to stay on as chancellor? That's important to me." Bill vehemently replied: "Jerry, I guarantee you that Clark Kerr will stay in office." Several days later, Kerr resigned, and I chose Harvard, with a diminished sense of guilt! And I was not alone. Several of my slightly older friends who had been my Berkeley colleagues also decided to move to Harvard, including Henry Rosovsky—an expert on the economy of Japan, and David Landes—a specialist in European economic history.

10

PASSIONATE PURSUITS

A New China Policy

My aim in moving to Cambridge, Massachusetts, was to build an East Asian legal studies program at Harvard. Yet few of us live in cocoons: I could not ignore the surrounding world, nor did I want to.

SETTLING IN CAMBRIDGE AND AT THE LAW SCHOOL

My first obligation was to my family. In 1960, when Joan and I decided to take on the challenges of entering the China field, it was a joint decision, one that she has never regretted despite the many difficulties, personal and professional, that it entailed. But our children, of course, did not have the option to consent, and I worried about the implications for their future of their parents' choice. But, as it turned out, I worried about the wrong thing. What had troubled me was the possibility that one or more of them might acquire some dreaded Asian disease of which I was ignorant. Fortunately, all three have generally been blessed with good health, whether in China, Japan, North and South Korea, Russia, or India, although there were a couple of potentially serious incidents.

What I should have been worrying about was the impact on their education and personal development of so much skipping around the globe.

Of course, they benefited enormously from the extraordinary experiences and stimuli to which this exposed them, but the price should not have been underestimated. Our eldest son, Peter, bore the brunt of our early travels. Instead of enjoying the sense of personal security that I had derived from a childhood unmovably anchored in a permanent community, Peter did kindergarten in Berkeley, California; first grade in Hong Kong; second grade in a Cambridge, Massachusetts, public school; and the following years in the Cambridge Friends School (CFS). What a series of adjustments for him, as basic as requirements that he learn different systems of English penmanship, and what feelings of guilt this inspired in his parents. Once we enrolled all three boys in the CFS, however, we could relax about their education for a time, despite growing doubts about whether it was technically as demanding as the more expensive and socially less inclusive alternatives of the other local private schools.

Eventually the boys matriculated at various prep schools just outside Cambridge that met their differing needs. Peter enrolled at the wonderful Concord Academy, which fortunately had just begun to admit boys. Seth went to the highly competitive Commonwealth School in Boston started by Charles Merrill, one of the heirs to the Merrill, Lynch investment firm's success. Ethan benefited hugely from the welcoming attentions of the Cambridge School of Weston. It would have been far easier for all of us if they had attended the public school near our house, Cambridge High and Latin, but in that era, it was widely reported to be a dangerous place. Peter responded when I suggested the possibility: "Do you want me to get killed?" Things ultimately improved by the time his own children were ready, and all three had satisfactory experiences there.

Finding permanent accommodation was another matter, but here some good luck intervened. Just as we were deliberating over whether to move to a nearby suburb, such as Belmont, Lexington, or even more distant Concord, we received a phone call from Dorothy Zinberg, the mother of a little girl who was in preschool with Ethan. She alerted us to the fact that the house across the street from hers had just been sold to Harvard and was about to be made available to a faculty member. Dorothy, a classic Cambridge insider, urged us to dash over to the Harvard University Housing office immediately, which I did the same morning. That proved to be one of the better instant responses of my life. The house at 21 Bryant Street was an attractive, large house with half an acre of lawn and a tennis court that was to serve the neighborhood—and it was a mere seven blocks from the law school.

For the next seventeen years, the Bryant Street house gave us splendid shelter, despite three burglaries, two occurring while we were away and the third while I slept. I particularly enjoyed the minimal responsibility of managing the adjacent neighborhood tennis court, which gave me the prerogative of posting the weekly schedule so that I could play with colleagues and family at convenient times. I'm sure that there were those on the faculty who thought we were living too high a life for a still relatively junior faculty family. When we invited Milton Katz, the director of international legal studies, to our first cocktail party, he looked around, as surprised as he was impressed, and snorted: "Pretty rich for your blood." This from the person who had conspired with John Fairbank to bring me to Harvard!

Joan quickly made the most of our move, professionally as well as personally. Not only did she become a docent in Asian art at the Museum of Fine Arts in Boston, but she also began to help produce programs for WGBH, the increasingly distinguished New England public television station. I was especially impressed by her one-hour program entitled *The Journey of the Buddha*, which depicted the impact of Buddhism on art as it made its way from India to China, Korea, and Japan. Not long afterward, Joan joined the faculty of the Museum's School of Fine Arts, which was part of Tufts University, where she lectured on Asian art history for roughly twenty years.

I soon settled into a comfortable professional routine. Joan generally drove our boys to school, so I was able to start my research and writing at eight A.M. and work uninterrupted at home in my basement study until noon. Then, often trailed by our lovable dog Simhala, I bicycled over to the law school to join a pickup lunch with whoever was available in the faculty dining room. I had chosen to make my office in our East Asian Legal Studies wing of the new Roscoe Pound Building, which was a couple of hundred yards away from Langdell Hall, the main faculty office center. After lunch, with the aid of my devoted secretary, Bertha Ezell, I saw visitors and students, made phone calls, and dealt with correspondence. Whenever possible, I also squeezed in preparation for class in order to free up time in the evening. Yet I enjoyed my meetings with students, especially those whom I was encouraging to enter the field of Asian law. I didn't realize at the time that many other faculty rationed their contacts with students more strictly, using "office hours" to limit their commitment, a technique that I never adopted. As word got around, however, that I welcomed students, their visits became more frequent, and I must have developed other techniques for limiting my availability. After a few years, I learned that I was known as "efficiently friendly." There were fairly frequent faculty activities that provided occasions for developing friendships with my new colleagues. Every autumn, the notoriously abstemious Dean Erwin Griswold and his voluble spouse, Harriet, gave an opening faculty dinner at home, which nevertheless proved to be a jolly party because most of the guests, well aware that the hosts would not serve alcoholic beverages, had taken the precaution of having predinner cocktails at the nearby home of Associate Dean James Casner.

Dean Griswold's legendary administration of the law school required a bit of an adjustment. He often stalked the halls, turning off the lights in any office that was unoccupied for the moment. My most amusing administrative experience in that pre-computer era involved typewriters. It turned out, to my surprise, that while Harvard Law School (HLS) provided secretaries and stationery to faculty, each professor was expected to provide the secretary's typewriter! Two years later, when Griswold gave up his long deanship in order to become solicitor general of the United States, and Jim Casner became acting dean for a year, I proposed, as one of Casner's first acts, that he authorize the distribution of the then new and highly touted IBM Selectric typewriter to each faculty member—free of charge. My argument: It was risky enough for the school to require the almost all-male faculty to share their offices with the often attractive female secretaries. By requiring a professor, in addition, to buy his secretary a typewriter, the school compounded the risk of social mischief. Casner, a humorous person who saw the possibility of quickly winning faculty favor, promptly endorsed my proposal.

ENCOURAGING THE TEACHING OF AMERICAN LEGAL HISTORY

Shortly after this bureaucratic triumph, my attention turned to more serious matters. My work on China led inadvertently to a chain of events that stimulated a reform in legal education that had no direct link to China. Early in 1967, I took part in a conference at the University of Chicago that discussed the Great Proletarian Cultural Revolution that had begun to sweep over China the previous year. By chance, at a reception for participants, I struck up a conversation with the University of Chicago's eminent expert on American history, Professor Daniel Boorstin, who, it turned out, was an HLS graduate. In the early 1940s, Boorstin had unsuccessfully tried to interest the law school in developing serious research in American legal history. I was fascinated to hear his account because of my own appreciation of the work of my senior colleagues Jack Dawson and Mark Howe in European and American legal history, respectively, and their struggles to interest our students in the compulsory, and widely disliked, first-year course, "The Development of Legal Institutions." My interest was further provoked when, Mark Howe, the first Charles Warren Professor in the History of American Law, died tragically of a heart attack. Dean Griswold at first tried to recruit Professor Willard Hurst of the University of Wisconsin, the country's best-known specialist in American legal history, to fill the vacant chair, and when Hurst chose to stay where he was, I saw an opportunity to help the career of a student who had impressed me as a great prospect for adding to scholarship in American legal history and for invigorating relevant teaching in a way that might increase Harvard student interest in the unpopular course everyone referred to as DLI.

Morton J. Horwitz had come to HLS with a PhD in political theory from Harvard's government department. In many conversations during his second year at HLS, I found him to be consistently dynamic, enthusiastic, and articulate, and a shrewd observer of human behavior. By the time of Howe's death in the spring of Mort's third year, in 0000, Mort had accepted a federal court of appeals clerkship for the year after graduation, but we had agreed that he should afterward embark on a law teaching career. The problem was to find an initial faculty opportunity and to do that would require some evidence of the promise he held for scholarship. What Mort needed was time to research and write the path-breaking law review article or book that we both felt he was capable of. That would require money to buy the necessary time.

Professor Hurst's decision to stay in Wisconsin meant that there was no immediate prospect for filling the Warren chair, which in turn meant that the income from that chair would be accumulating. What better use of it than to train what the Beijing leadership liked to term "revolutionary successors," in this case, a new generation of budding historians of American law? Morton Horwitz would be the first beneficiary, but there would soon be more once Harvard made attractive fellowships available and established a credible training program that boosted the prestige of a long-neglected field. Such a move would also tie in with the idea I had been helping to promote: creating an innovative, four-year dual degree program in cooperation with Harvard's history department that would allow our students to earn an MA in history while pursuing their law degree. That in turn reflected the younger faculty's awareness of the desirability of producing law graduates who were also trained in related disciplines ranging from business to psychology.

Could I persuade the faculty to adopt this idea? Fortunately, Dean Griswold, a slightly eccentric but farsighted leader who would leave the school six months later to become solicitor general of the United States, was still in command. He embraced the idea of applying the Warren funds to fellowships for a new generation and liked the concept of placing the fellowships within the context of a new program for offering, in conjunction with the history department, combined training in law and history. Griswold immediately established a small Committee on Combined Work in Law and Related Disciplines and appointed sympathetic faculty colleagues to join me and Professors Oscar Handlin and Bernard Bailyn, two famous Harvard historians, to work out the details. The other law faculty members were Abram Chayes, a former Justice Felix Frankfurter clerk who had returned to Cambridge from service as legal adviser to the State Department; Andrew Kaufman, my close friend with whom I had clerked at the Supreme Court for two years; Jack Dawson, the respected senior colleague who had mentored me in European history after my arrival at Harvard; and Detlev Vagts, a highly cultivated and helpful expert on international business law and grandson of the illustrious specialist on American history Charles Beard. We completed our labors by the spring of 1968 and, with the aid of Acting Dean James Casner, promptly obtained faculty approval. After another year, during which Horwitz completed his draft about the relationship of law and economics in nineteenth-century America and many major schools became eager to recruit him, the HLS faculty decided to offer him an assistant professorship to begin in the fall of 1970. The Charles Warren chair had begun to reap the benefits of its expenditures! The rest, if a pun is permitted, was history because Horwitz immediately began to vindicate his promise and sparked an extraordinary decade in which HLS became the center for developing more than a dozen young legal historians. By the end of that decade, Horwitz had won the American Historical Association's Bancroft Prize for his 1977 book *The Transformation of American Law, 1780–1860* and was appointed Mark Howe's successor to the Warren chair. Over two decades later, a Harvard conference of the new generation of American legal historians that our efforts had spawned gave me generous credit for originating the project.

Before leaving this topic, I should point out that my interest in American legal history was not entirely separate from my main work on China. Indeed, it was the relation of revolution to law in China that had inspired my curiosity about the impact of revolutionary developments on the legal systems of other countries. I had spent some time during my prelaw Fulbright year in France studying the French Revolution, and, of course, I had, as part of my study of communist China, absorbed a lot about the influence of Vladimir Lenin and Joseph Stalin on Russian and Soviet law. It occurred to me that we ought to experiment with a section of DLI that would be called "Law, Society and Revolution." I would rely on Bill Nelson, another of the fellows I'd selected, to coteach and take the lead in presenting the English and American material while I would take the lead on the French, Russo-Soviet, and Chinese coverage. We gave it a try in front of a large class in the fall of 1969, and it met with a good reception. Many years later, one student, who by then had become president of Amherst College, wrote to thank me for stimulating interests that led him beyond the law into the broader reaches of academe. Bill and I might well have repeated the course the following year had he not already been selected as a law clerk for Supreme Court Justice Byron White for the 1970 term. Twenty years later, when I joined the New York University (NYU) law faculty, Bill was ensconced there as the leader of the school's distinguished work in American legal history, and we renewed our friendship and exchanges.

REACTING TO THE VIETNAM WAR

It didn't take long at the HLS for me to get embroiled in what would turn out to be the major, devastating development of the next decade, the worsening American involvement in Vietnam. My attention to Vietnam began in October 1965, when I was asked to give a well-advertised talk at the law school concerning U.S. policy toward Asia. I focused on China and don't recall saying anything about the as yet relatively unnoticed topic of American relations with Vietnam. During the question period, however, my senior law school colleague, Harold Berman, an expert on the Soviet Union, asked whether I agreed with the policy of President Lyndon Johnson's administration toward Vietnam. Not having given much thought to Vietnam and knowing little about it, in answering Berman's question I acknowledged the problems but refused to reject Johnson's evolving policy. I said that I had confidence that the major architects of the policy— Secretary of Defense Robert McNamara, White House National Security Advisor McGeorge Bundy, and Secretary of State Dean Rusk—had access to every day's diplomatic cables and military intelligence, information that was unavailable to the rest of us, and I was not in a position to second-guess their decisions. Afterward, Hal Berman told me that he was disappointed in my view. That added to the incentive I felt to learn more about Vietnam, American policy, and the controversial involvements of China and the Soviet Union.

So I began to follow Vietnamese affairs over the next few months more closely, and the more I learned, the more concerned I became. By late January 1966, I was convinced that critics who charged the Johnson administration with misunderstanding the political-military situation in Vietnam and with misrepresenting it to the public were right. I admired and benefited from the extensive reporting of the independent American media, which cast a gloomy light on the embarrassing failures that our forces and those of the South Vietnamese regime were encountering. The *New York Times* published a letter from me criticizing the House of Delegates of the American Bar Association (ABA) for simplistically endorsing by resolution the U.S. government's actions in Vietnam as consonant with public international law. The ABA's reflexive and unreflecting statement, I pointed out, uncomfortably resembled the similar political statements that Chinese communist organizations of legal specialists had issued from Beijing in support of their government. That letter undoubtedly did not endear me to Dean Griswold, a prominent participant in the ABA House of Delegates.

After that, I became active on the Harvard campus in speaking out against the war, frequently accepting the invitations of various organizations as well as opportunities to join television and radio discussions outside Harvard's confines. I especially recall debating Averell Harriman on the nationally televised (on NBC) *Today Show* in 1967. Harriman was then assistant secretary of state for East Asia. I had long admired him as an exemplar of a person of inherited wealth who devoted his career to diplomacy and public service. But that morning, he had the unenviable task of defending alleged American bombing of Hanoi hospitals that were said to be plainly marked with red crosses symbolizing their right to humanitarian protection under international law. Harriman was not a skilled debater and became rather inarticulate when pressed by my arguments and questions from the NBC moderator.

The next day, back in Cambridge from New York, I received a phone call from my senior colleague Milton Katz, who had served with Harriman in Paris during the post–World War II Marshall Plan era. He told me that Harriman had just telephoned him to register a complaint about my performance in our debate. Katz asked me for my side of the story, which seemed to pacify him. Three days later, however, I experienced further reverberations. Dean Griswold's wonderful secretary, Janet Murphy, with whom Joan and I often played tennis, appeared in my office and showed me a letter that Griswold had just received from the widow of a wealthy HLS alumnus. She had seen the *Today Show* broadcast from the living room of her Louisiana plantation and protested my views as "pro-Communist." She said that I belonged in Moscow rather than Cambridge. Janet reported that the dean was particularly upset because the writer had been contributing the then princely sum of $10,000 per year to the school's alumni fund in her husband's memory. The dean expressed the hope that I would answer the letter. I politely declined on the ground that answering irate alumni missives was one of the burdens of deanship. The dean later sent me a copy of his soothing assurance to the protester that she had misunderstood me.

Students eager to attract faculty participation in antiwar rallies had their wiles. Once, because I was very busy finishing a law review essay under deadline, I tried to beg off appearing at a rally, but the organizers said that Professor John Kenneth Galbraith, the famous economist and John Kennedy–era ambassador to India, would be the other speaker there. Although Galbraith was a neighbor and our wives occasionally met at Smith College alumnae events, I did not really know this revered figure and thought that appearing on the same platform might launch a valued friendship. Yet when I turned up for our program before a large crowd in Sanders Theater that was undoubtedly attracted by Galbraith's name, there was no Galbraith to be found. When I asked the moderator what was going on, he told me that the esteemed professor had sent a voice recording of his speech from his Swiss ski chalet in Gstaad!

Although law school life seldom suffered interference from domestic political events, it could not avoid student tumult generated by the Vietnam conflict, especially because many male students were understandably concerned about being drafted into military service. This suddenly erupted at the time of a scheduled faculty meeting when a large group of angry students protested in the lobby outside our meeting room, where Derek Bok, our new dean, was presiding. With a nod from Derek, I went to the door and signaled the students to lower the volume and then locked the door in case there might be an attempt to break up our meeting. This did nothing to quell the noise, so our new associate dean, Albert Sacks, went into the lobby to give the students the opportunity to air their protests and hear a faculty response. I was one of the faculty then most identified with opposition to the war, so I accompanied him but stayed in the background. I admired the way Al Sacks dealt with the challenge. He heard the students with courtesy and gave reasoned responses, assuring them of the faculty's deep concern and willingness to take steps to make public its views. After about half an hour, this seemed to satisfy the group, who then disbanded.

After witnessing Al's successful dialogue with the protesters, I began to feel that he could play an important role in helping the university meet the growing challenges presented by student concerns. Although I liked Harvard president Nathan Pusey, who commendably attended most law school faculty meetings, he seemed inadequate to the current crisis. At that time, our senior law school colleague Archibald Cox was reportedly leading the university's responses from what was essentially a bunker in Harvard Yard at which, virtually every night, on behalf of President Pusey, he directed administration reactions to protean protests, some of which were massive and turned violent.

Indeed, the university was in crisis. There was talk of revolution, and the militant campus leaders of the radical Students for a Democratic Society (SDS) and other organizations were urging a series of coercive actions in all Harvard departments. Their main immediate focus was to use civil disobedience to end the university's cooperation with the government's Reserve Officers' Training Corps (ROTC) program, but their broader goal was to terminate all forms of university support for the Vietnam War and what they characterized as the imperialism of the American military-political-system.

I became involved in one of the last in a series of unprecedented protests in April 1970 when an angry mob of about two hundred campus activists who belonged to a group called the November Action Committee (NAC) invaded the university building at Number 2 Divinity Avenue. That building housed, among other organizations, the influential Center for International Affairs (CFIA), the target of the protest. The center's distinguished visiting committee was holding its annual evaluation of center activities and about to have lunch. A group of protesters swept up the stairs to the second-floor conference room, broke in, trashed the food, and harassed the committee members. At least one of the protesters reportedly poured a pitcher of ice water down the neck of committee chair John McCloy, an international lawyer and respected business figure who had served with distinction as U.S. ambassador to Germany and in other government positions. It later was revealed that the students' fury was in part unleashed because of their mistaken belief that Mr. McCloy was the director of the Central Intelligence Agency (CIA). They had confused him with the actual CIA director, John McCone, who was not present. Nor was the controversial secretary of defense, Robert McNamara, who had been rumored to attend.

Amusing as it may have been to some jaded observers of Wall Street and diplomacy icons, the violent student break-in was a major infringement of university rules and academic freedom. It appalled most of the scholarly community, including many students, some of whom supported the war and even a larger number who opposed the war but felt that violence went beyond the proper scope of protest. The Pusey administration, having issued ineffective warnings against these protests, felt forced to impose serious sanctions against the invaders of the center. The problem was how to do it fairly and without arousing further student outrage.

Harvard police, who had had some advance notice of the NAC's intended action, had not only identified those who broke into the conference room but also many of the larger number who had been milling around on the stairs and in the lobby below. The administration decided that the incident should be handled exclusively by the university and not involve the Cambridge police, who had been called in to quell a much larger demonstration a year earlier when radical students had occupied a major building, University Hall, and had only added fuel to the fire. Arrangements were made to press university charges against the most significant offenders for violating academic rules. Individual hearings were scheduled to take place before the university's Committee on Rights and Responsibilities (CRR), with the alleged wrongdoers given adequate opportunity to defend themselves. The widely respected political scientist James Q. Wilson was asked to chair the faculty group comprising the committee.

To my surprise, I was asked to take on the controversial task of presenting the charges. To the administration, I seemed an appropriate choice because I was a youngish, moderately well-known law professor who had long been active in campus programs and public platforms opposing the war. I had also had, a decade earlier, some experience as a federal prosecutor in Washington, DC. Technically I was identified as "legal adviser" to Robert R. Bowie, a former high State Department official who was the CFIA director and the complainant in the proceedings. To say that I was not happy to be asked would be an understatement. Yet I had a strong belief in the importance of preserving free and orderly discussion within the university and not allowing understandable anguish about the war to interfere arbitrarily with day-to-day academic activities. So I reluctantly agreed to take on the task.

My first challenge was to make sure that charges would only be pressed against the principal offenders. A careful investigation of the facts made clear that not all the students identified by the campus police had actually been protesters. The CFIA was not the only occupant of 2 Divinity Avenue, which also housed the famed Harvard-Yenching Institute and its library of Asian materials and a leading center for Jewish studies. Some of the students identified by the campus police had simply come to the building for academic purposes unrelated to the protests and were merely bystanders to the events in the lobby and the stairs. To the best of my recollection, formal proceedings were then brought only against those who had broken into the conference room.

The university decided to hold the hearing in a large room on the ground floor of the rather new administration building, Holyoke Center, in the heart of Harvard Square. That would allow attendance by some faculty, administrators, witnesses, *Harvard Crimson* reporters, and other students. But the announcement of the hearing had stimulated a huge student reaction, and, on the morning of the hearing, a large crowd of students had assembled in front of Holyoke Center and were planning to block entry into the building. According to the next day's story in the *Crimson*, they were chanting: "Get some feathers, get some tar, let's go get the CRR," meaning the Committee on Rights and Responsibilities which was responsible for the event. Fortunately, I usually moved around Harvard on a bicycle, so when I approached the building and saw the crowd, I decided to avoid the entrance and instead go around the corner, where I could ride my bike down the long driveway into the building's garage. It took the students, who had not expected participants to arrive by bike, a few moments to realize the situation and, although some chased after me, I easily reached the shelter of the garage. That proved to be the most exciting moment of the entire episode for me.

The only one of the accused whose name I can recall was Michael Kazin because I had known his father slightly in the early 1960s when I was teaching at Berkeley. Alfred Kazin, a famous writer, was a distinguished visiting lecturer on the Cal campus. According to an account of the hearings in the *Crimson*, Michael, a college senior who had been a leader of the previous year's occupation of University Hall, was the first of the protesters to have his conduct examined by the committee. He and the three student advisers he had allowed to accompany him reportedly pronounced the hearing process as illegitimate and tore up some of the photographs and witness statements that constituted evidence of their misbehavior. Because of that action, the CRR added another year to the one-year suspension from Harvard that it was preparing to give him as one of the protest leaders. Although many students were unhappy about the discipline imposed by the CRR, I never learned of any adverse reactions to my participation. Michael, who is now a well-known scholar of American history at Georgetown University, in response to my emailed request for information kindly confirmed the information about his hearing.

Although 1970 proved to be a tumultuous year for Harvard and other universities, it was the events of 1968 that had been the most shocking. The assassination of Martin Luther King in March was a stunning blow. News of it was transmitted while I was moderating one of a series of two-hour public affairs programs for the area's public television station, WGBH, and it was one of the few occasions during many television broadcasts that I have ever felt at a loss for words. Not long afterward, I began to hold some hope for an end to the Vietnam War as I listened, with excitement, to President Lyndon Johnson announce that he had decided not to run for reelection. That left the way open for a possible Democratic presidential candidate who favored withdrawal from Vietnam. Bobby Kennedy was the best-known possibility, although I was initially more enthusiastic about Wisconsin senator Eugene McCarthy. By the time of the California primary election in early June, however, I had come to agree with many others that, if Kennedy did well in the primary, the antiwar forces should join in his candidacy against Vice President Hubert Humphrey, who had disappointed many of us by publicly supporting President Johnson's pursuit of the war. Bobby's assassination at the primary's conclusion plunged much of the nation into crisis and had an immediate effect on Harvard, which canceled the year's final exams that were about to be held. Even the law school, which was relatively more insulated from political developments than the undergraduate school, canceled exams, and there was open demoralization on the campus. This tragedy also had a heavy impact on our children, ages eleven, nine, and seven, who struggled to understand what had taken place and why. The day after the assassination, as we sat on the steps at the side of our house, our youngest son, Ethan, broke my heart when he asked why things like that happen.

POLITICAL CONTACTS ABOUT A NEW CHINA POLICY

Preoccupation with the Vietnam War and its domestic reverberations did not diminish my interest in improving relations between the United States and China, of course. Many observers hoped that improvement in Sino-American relations might lead to an acceptable way of ending our mistaken Vietnam involvement. The challenge was how to bring about such an improvement after almost two decades of hostility and while China was in the throes of an unprecedented Cultural Revolution that was wreaking havoc on its foreign affairs as well as its domestic governance.

Because the status and future of Taiwan were crucial to any improvement in Sino-American relations, I visited the island on several occasions. Most memorable was the meeting that two academic colleagues and I had with President Chiang Kai-shek and Madame Chiang. When the president emphasized the importance of fostering the study of Chinese culture, I seized the opportunity to recommend the appointment to a position at the leading academic institution—Academia Sinica—of my student Chang Wejen, a legal historian who had just returned from Harvard. Wejen did receive the appointment and has had a distinguished career introducing China's legal traditions.

Liberal American political figures from a rising generation were increasingly interested in improving relations with China, and young HLS graduates who were recently recruited to the staffs of both Democratic and Republican politicians began to contact me for advice. I was first contacted by Jay Kriegel, who was newly advising John Lindsay, the young former U.S. Representative from the "silk stocking" Upper East Side of New York City who had recently been elected the city's mayor. I was delighted, given what seemed at the time Lindsay's bright future as a Republican, encouraging my hope that the Republican Party might evolve in a liberal direction. When Jay, who had taken one of my courses and was eager to promote reform, asked me to meet Lindsay in Cambridge, that was an easy sell.

I arranged a lunch and afternoon seminar at our home and invited a couple of more senior Harvard specialists to join us. Lindsay proved a genial and appreciative guest. At the end of the afternoon, after he had noticed the tennis court next to our house, he said he liked to play. I set up a doubles game that included Joan as my partner. Fortunately, John was approximately my size and I was able to provide him with a full tennis outfit and racket. He played well and enjoyed the break, and Joan still remembers him as the best-looking man she's ever played tennis with! Unfortunately, by the mid-1960s Republican politics had become increasingly conservative, and Lindsay ultimately felt forced to become a Democrat in a fruitless effort to advance his national ambitions.

Edward ("Ted") Kennedy, of course, had a brighter future in Democratic politics than John Lindsay. By 1966, Ted was preparing to run for reelection to his U.S. Senate seat and saw the need for a new American policy toward China as a useful issue to embrace. Again, an HLS graduate got me involved. Kennedy had hired Carey Parker as a legislative assistant a few years earlier. Carey, after a Rhodes Scholarship and a PhD in science from the Rockefeller Institute, had recently earned a law degree. Although he had not been my student, when the newly established National Committee on US-China Relations asked Ted to give a major address at a widely heralded conference, Parker got in touch with me and asked for a hand in preparing the speech. I was happy to help and get acquainted with Ted. His speech proved a hit, so Carey and Ted began to consult me regularly, leading to over a decade of cooperation. I will have much more to say about my work with Kennedy in later chapters.

As my cooperation with John Lindsay demonstrated, I was not so much interested in domestic politics as in China policy, and on a bipartisan basis. In the summer of 1967, James C. ("Jim"). Thompson Jr., a young Harvard historian just returned from service in the Johnson administration, and I chatted with Dick Neustadt on the deck of Dick's attractive Cape Cod vacation house overlooking Gull Pond in Wellfleet. We suggested forming a group of Harvard–Massachusetts Institute of Technology (MIT) Asia hands to discuss how Washington might begin to thaw the ice with Beijing. In the fall, Dick invited Harvard's John Fairbank, Edwin Reischauer, Benjamin Schwartz, Ezra Vogel, Dwight Perkins, Roy Hofheinz, and a few other colleagues, including Jim and me, to join MIT's Lucian Pye and Doak Barnett, who was visiting at MIT from Columbia. Although Fairbank was the senior specialist in the group, Jim, who was Fairbank's protégé, thought that John would be too busy to chair the group with the necessary dispatch and suggested that, because I already had tenure, Dick should ask me to be the chair, with Jim's able assistance. Dick agreed, and Jim and I proved to be an effective combination in convening regular meetings of the group throughout the 1967–1968 academic year and early in the following fall semester. Our goal was to prepare a confidential memorandum to submit to whoever might win the November 1968 presidential election, in the hope of persuading the new administration, whether Democratic or Republican, to take steps toward ending the long, unfriendly stalemate with Beijing.

By the time of the election, we had agreed on a thoughtful, balanced draft containing about a dozen recommendations. Our first recommendation called on the new president to dispatch the new secretary of state to Beijing to conduct secret, if need be deniable, conversations with the

Chinese leadership in order to explore possibilities of a thaw. Shortly after Richard M. Nixon's victory, however, when he appointed our Harvard colleague Henry Kissinger to be his national security adviser, we altered the draft's first recommendation so that Henry might qualify for the mission. The president, we urged, should select for the secret trip someone in whom he had the greatest confidence. Although we addressed our memorandum to Nixon, we asked Kissinger to transmit it, and our first recommendation provided some incentive for Henry to follow up on its delivery and implementation.

On several occasions during Nixon's first term, I met with Kissinger at the White House to discuss developments in Nixon's evolving China policy in the context of our Kennedy Institute memorandum. At each meeting Henry, who initially mentioned with Chinese modesty how little he knew about China, seemed more confident about his ability to meet the challenge. This was especially the case after he returned from the secret meeting with Zhou Enlai in Beijing in July 1971 that implemented our memorandum's first recommendation. After his return, our memorandum was leaked to the public by a republican opponent of the new development. Despite the fact that it turned up in the congressional record, it attracted little attention except from a few right-wing critics of Kissinger who claimed that Henry was the instrument of sinister left-wing forces at Harvard. I recall asking Henry what his impressions were of Chinese prime minister Zhou Enlai and enjoyed his response. "You know," he said, "that man is really serious."

As Nixon's 1972 reelection campaign heated up, I was supporting his opponent, Senator George McGovern, so I did not try to continue meeting Kissinger, who had indicated that the president was increasingly sensitive to Henry's contacts with his Democratic former colleagues at Harvard. I did continue, of course, with my pursuit of a new China policy during the remaining years of the 1970s in Cambridge.

NEW LAW SCHOOL RESPONSIBILITIES

My involvement in Harvard activities unrelated to both East Asian legal studies and the Kennedy Institute increased on my return from the

1971–1972 sabbatical year spent in Japan, which is the subject of a separate chapter. I was not enthusiastic about being asked, in the fall of 1972, to chair a controversial faculty-student committee to consider what to do about the law school's recent experiments with limited pass/fail grading. Of course, like most colleagues, I was eager to reduce student competition and tensions and improve conditions for studying law in various ways that would ameliorate the paper-chase atmosphere that had become Harvard's brand. Yet I had doubts about the wisdom of employing a pass/fail system beyond the first semester. I didn't realize at the time that, by asking me to shoulder this unwanted responsibility, Dean Albert Sacks was attempting to enlist me in general school activities instead of remaining more isolated in international and Asian-related matters.

I managed to survive the endless meetings of the committee on grades, but it did indeed take more patience and time than I felt was warranted. I was happy that our labors ultimately did not do away with grade rankings because, as my own career had demonstrated, in America success in legal education has traditionally been a path for the upward mobility of ambitious members of less-favored social classes. Pass/fail grading would deprive the socially disfavored of their principal vehicle for competing for the most desirable law jobs available. I was glad to hear my senior colleague Archibald Cox make an eloquent statement to our committee to that effect, warning us that a pass/fail system would result in a return to an earlier situation where law firms recruited on the basis of other factors than demonstrated legal talent. That made me recall a conversation I had had with an elderly Boston Brahmin HLS alumnus who told me, soon after my arrival in Cambridge in 1964, that, when a young man—and it was usually a man in those days—interviewed his firm for a job, he always asked the candidate what his father did and occasionally even asked what his grandfather did! The professional and social backgrounds of my father and grandfathers would not have met the expectations of a Boston Brahmin law firm, so I was not eager to extend the pass/fail system beyond the first semester.

The faculty was badly divided on the issue and ultimately rejected even our committee's proposal to permit pass/fail grading in the first semester. It did, however, endorse various other proposals we made for creating a more humane student environment. By the end of the academic year, the faculty members were so tired of wrestling with the problems that we decided to postpone further consideration for another few years. I was not unhappy with this outcome and glad to be free to return to Asia matters.

Almost immediately, however, Dean Sacks asked me to take on broader and more interesting responsibilities and become associate dean, director of international legal studies and chair of the school's graduate program. This was an opportunity that I did not want to decline. It offered the chance of not only invigorating Harvard's large and influential master of laws program, which seemed to be flagging, but also recognizing the increasing prominence of East Asia and the developing world generally in an environment that had been largely preoccupied with Europe, the British Commonwealth, and the Western hemisphere.

I had been impressed by the graduate program's potential from my earliest days at HLS in the year 1964–1965 and liked the fact that the overwhelming majority of the master of laws students came from other countries. Dean Griswold gave an opening dinner for graduate students each fall at which he asked each one to rise after dinner and give a short self-identification and statement of his or her purpose in coming to Harvard. I looked forward to attending, although I had been warned by senior colleagues bent on avoiding the evening to gird my loins for an endless, boring event at which there would be over ninety students to hear from. To my delight, the third speaker, a lively, red-haired young woman stood up and said: "I'm here from Ireland to study Soviet law and international law, and, when I return to Ireland, I'm going to become a spy!" That brought the house down and set the tone for the rest of the evening as the other students competed in entertaining us. The Irish lass was immediately followed by a fellow who said: "I'm here from Venezuela to study constitutional law. On returning to my country, I will teach constitutional law—*if* we have a constitution."

In the fall of 1973, increasingly impressed by Japan at a time when that country's economy had begun to make a world impact, the first thing I did in my new role as graduate program chair was to double the number of Japanese master of laws students we would accept. The second thing was to welcome a larger number of applicants from Taiwan, which I also felt was being underestimated. That facilitated the admission of students who were destined to become the island's future president, vice president, chief justice, and leading lawyers and scholars. I also spurred faculty support for establishing a program in Islamic law and Middle Eastern studies and began to raise funds for a chair that would be comparable to those already established for China and Japan. At one point, I wrote a letter to the government of Kuwait seeking the $1 million then sufficient for creating a professorship. Although Kuwait never responded, fortunately I had had the wit to send a carbon copy of my letter to Sheikh Yamani of Saudi Arabia, who had earned a Harvard master of laws, and he quickly responded with a check for $250,000! Nevertheless, it took more years, after my departure from HLS, for the teaching of Islamic law to be fully funded.

My concerns for improving the graduate student experience were not limited to the intellectual. I also thought of exposing the students to various cultural activities that were too often overlooked in their busy schedules. So, every year, Joan would give us a lecture tour of the magnificent Asian collection at the Boston Museum of Fine Arts, and we hosted the large group at our house afterward for a lively party that featured Joan's responses to questions about our own varied paintings and sculptures. Perhaps the most innovative activity I arranged was a violin concert given by Noriko Kozai, wife of our distinguished East Asian Legal Studies (EALS) visiting scholar of international law Shigeru Kozai of Kyoto University. Noriko, a talented and charming professional musician who is still performing in Japan almost half a century later, met with an enthusiastic reception from a packed house. All of this helped to build friendships that endure to this day, when we continue to be buoyed by the emails, letters, phone calls, and visits of former students who date back to those early days.

PRESIDENT JIMMY CARTER AND THE ALLURE OF WASHINGTON

In 1977, I almost succumbed to the allure of Washington after Jimmy Carter's presidential election. My contacts with Carter's advisers had begun in the spring of 1974 when, as frequently happened, another young HLS graduate, Stuart Eizenstat, asked me to draft a statement on China policy for Carter, who had just completed service as governor of Georgia and was taking steps to enter national politics. The statement, which ran to eleven typed pages, was prepared for issuance by a committee of U.S. Democratic senators. Apparently, the Carter people appreciated my effort. Early in March of the following year, Stuart called again to say that Carter had been invited to speak in Tokyo at the forthcoming meeting of the prestigious Trilateral Commission, and here was a chance for him to show some acquaintance with foreign policy problems. Stuart asked whether I would be willing to meet Carter, who would soon be making an exploratory trip to test the potential presidential waters in New Hampshire and could easily stop in Cambridge en route. I said I would be glad to see him and invited my senior colleague, former U.S. ambassador to Japan Edwin O. Reischauer, to join us for lunch at my house. I also invited my oldest son Peter, who was about to finish high school and was interested in politics. I thought he might want to volunteer in New Hampshire for the Carter campaign for a year after graduation.

We had a long and pleasant lunch with Carter that went on afterward for at least an hour in our living room. I liked Carter, who came alone and seemed earnest, intelligent, and analytical in his questions. He made no bones about his lack of knowledge of East Asia and of foreign policy generally. His international perspective, he said, was limited to that of an experienced naval officer who had been a submarine commander. We spent a lot of time discussing the wisdom of continuing to maintain American forces in South Korea, but his main preoccupation—and mine—was whether to advocate for U.S. withdrawal of diplomatic recognition from the Chiang Kai-shek regime on Taiwan as the legitimate government of China and establishment of diplomatic relations with the People's Republic of China (PRC) on the mainland. Carter repeatedly asked why we could not recognize both as governing the territories they each controlled. I had pointed out that some nations recognized both East and West Germany, North and South Vietnam, and even the two Koreas. Carter shook his head despairingly at our response that both of the competing governments that bordered the Taiwan Strait rejected that obvious compromise. His was a key question, of course, and one that he finally addressed in public only after the New York primary election that secured his nomination to the presidency in late June 1976.

By that time, I had joined the advisory committee on foreign policy that the Carter people had set up under the chairmanship of Cyrus Vance, a leading lawyer who had served in high positions in the Pentagon. I only recall attending one of its meetings but enjoyed the discussions with Columbia University political scientist Zbigniew Brzeziński, a brilliant international relations scholar; Mike Oksenberg, a leading China specialist; and others. Vance, whom I had not known, did not seem especially interested in my views, and I made no effort to contact him as the campaign wore on. However, I remember exulting with my friend John Kotch, a Vance committee member who was a Korea specialist, when Carter, in his press conference right after the New York primary, responded to a question about whether he favored recognition of the PRC by stating that he was prepared to withdraw recognition from the Chiang regime and establish diplomatic relations with Beijing. His answer jumbled the difference between the Republic of China on Taiwan and the People's Republic of China on the mainland but in the context, everyone knew what he meant.

Perhaps I didn't take part in the presidential campaign because I remained close to Ted Kennedy and his staff. Ted, who was still suffering politically from the adverse impact of his regrettable behavior in the 1969 Chappaquiddick tragedy, seemed to have a number of tensions with the Carter people. In any event, I was preoccupied with my Harvard duties as well as with trying to fathom events in China that were unleashed by Chairman Mao's death in early September 1976. I also continued to be concerned about the influence of corruption on Japan's domestic and foreign policy and published two essays in the *New York Times* in 1976 on that topic. My attention returned to Washington, however, when, in the winter of 1977, I received a phone call from Steve Orlins, my friend and former student who had joined the Office of the Legal Adviser to the State Department six months earlier. "They're going to appoint you legal adviser," he said with some excitement. I told Steve that this seemed unlikely because I had heard absolutely nothing about the possibility. Steve replied that he had heard the news from someone who had just left a relevant White House meeting.

I felt pleased but ambivalent as well as skeptical about this report. I was happily engaged in my work based in Cambridge and reluctant to either uproot my children or separate from them for most of the time by accepting a job in Washington. Yet the thought of serving as legal adviser attracted me, especially because the legal challenges of attempting to establish diplomatic relations with China loomed large, and I was a logical person for the job. Had I been clear about my ambition, I suppose I would have contacted Stuart Eizenstat, who by then had an important position on Carter's personal staff. I had a few chits to cash in. I also could have asked Ted Kennedy to go to bat for me. Although he and Carter weren't close, the new president plainly needed his cooperation in the Senate and the Democratic Party. I remembered the advice of Jim Thomson, who had managed the successful campaign to have his mentor Ed Reischauer chosen as Jack Kennedy's ambassador to Japan: if you want the job, you have to mobilize support. Instead, I did nothing and decided to leave the matter to fate. Eventually I learned that Carter, wary of having already appointed perhaps too many Harvard professors, left the question to Secretary of State Vance, who appointed a Yale Law School classmate of his then practicing law in Cleveland.

At that point I put thoughts of government service behind me until 1979, when my name circulated together with a few others about being appointed the first U.S. ambassador to the PRC. A well-connected *New York Times* columnist even published an op-ed identifying me; Leonard Woodcock, chief of the United Auto Workers union, which had strongly backed Carter's election; and another person as the three leading candidates for the Beijing embassy. I was even more skeptical about this prospect than I had been about the legal adviser opportunity. A couple of years earlier, I had criticized Dick Holbrooke, who had just become assistant secretary of state for East Asia, for what I believed was inappropriate handling of an essay that I published in *Foreign Policy* magazine while he was its editor. I also had had little contact with Mike Oksenberg, who had been assisting Brzeziński at the White House in negotiating with China and hadn't consulted me, despite the two widely appreciated essays I had published on the subject in *Foreign Affairs* in 1971 and 1976 and the massive 1974 book that I had published, together with Hungdah Chiu, on China and international law.

Again, although no one has ever accused me of being shy or perhaps even modest, I did nothing to promote my prospects. I seemed to lack the impetus that a good politician requires to overtly put himself forward, at least in public affairs. Instead of lobbying for the post in Washington, I spent the winter and spring of 1979 on sabbatical in Hong Kong, commuting regularly to Beijing in the hope of establishing a law office and a legal education base there. I even failed to keep in touch with Ted Kennedy and his staff while abroad, despite the fact that I had led Ted and eleven members of his family on a successful visit to China and Japan for three weeks in 1977–1978. Woodcock, a very nice and quietly savvy man, eventually got the ambassadorial job.

Yet I certainly was not passive with respect to academic, human rights, and professional opportunities to engage with East Asia, as the following chapters show.

11

BUILDING HARVARD'S EAST ASIAN LEGAL STUDIES

Stimulating Research, Talented Students, and Timeless Ties

Anyone who managed to wade through the previous chapter might get the impression that I made little time for the program I had come to develop at Harvard. Yet that was hardly the case.

PERSONAL MOTIVATIONS

During my early years at Harvard, I felt considerable guilt over the fact that I had come a long way in academic life in less than six years, but I hadn't produced any significant scholarly work. I had written two essays on American law published in the *Yale Law Journal* while I was still a law student and, subsequent to that, five brief book reviews and three insubstantial law journal articles.

Other than this slender compilation of written work, all I had to offer appointments committees at Berkeley and Harvard was my China preparation, preteaching professional jobs in Washington, student reactions to my classroom performance, and faculty evaluations based on personal interchanges as well as occasional class monitoring. My case was one of "promise or perish," not the customary academic "publish or perish." I did not want to be one of those professors who, having gained job security, loses their appetite for research and writing. My intrinsic interest in the daunting task of learning about China, its language, and its legal system continued to motivate me keenly. Yet I felt the additional need to take part in the broader Harvard Law School (HLS) community, justify my newly tenured existence among Harvard scholars, and gain their respect in a more general way.

CHINESE CRIMINAL JUSTICE AND LEGAL HISTORY

During my first Harvard semester in 1964, I focused on introducing the contemporary Chinese legal system, especially the processes of criminal justice that were among the most salient features of Chairman Mao's regime. This was a field I understood better than most others. At a time of China's maximum nontransparency, and because of the relative public prominence of criminal punishment and related sanctions in the Chinese communist order, the topic also presented me with the greatest possibility for accessing scarce relevant domestic materials for teaching and research.

Although the People's Republic of China (PRC) had not yet begun to promulgate and publish many formal laws, regulations, and judicial decisions, one could collect pieces of the criminal justice puzzle through Chinese newspaper reports and scattered material in occasional books, academic journals, and popular magazines. With the aid of my just-completed year of refugee interviewing in Hong Kong, and with the great help of, then a recent HLS graduate who had mastered the Chinese language and become my first research fellow, in 1968, I published, at Harvard University Press, *The Criminal Process in the People's Republic of China, 1949–63: An Introduction.*

I was proud of this book. It was grounded in the most varied and solid research possible at the time, presented an original interpretation of an important yet little understood aspect of China's new government, provided many useful translations and unusual refugee interviews, and raised many questions that needed to be addressed in order to promote further understanding of the subject. It appeared during the very worst days of the Great Proletarian Cultural Revolution, which had broken out in the spring of 1966 and by that summer had begun to smash the system I had labored to portray. As I said in the book's introduction, however, I was confident that the then current national madness would eventually subside, and Mao's successors would build on the foundations I had analyzed.

One of the reasons for this confidence was the link that I had noted between China's precommunist past and the PRC's post-1949 development of its criminal justice system. Three brief visits to Taiwan in the early 1960s had confirmed the similarities between the criminal justice system established by Chiang Kai-shek's noncommunist but nevertheless Leninist-type party-state before its forced departure from mainland China to Taiwan in 1949 and Mao Zedong's pre–Cultural Revolution system that had emerged from the new PRC's struggle to adapt Marxist-Leninist precepts and Soviet experience to China's needs.

Even more exciting was my discovery of the relevance of China's imperial legal traditions to the PRC's development. The year 1962 had proved key to my understanding of the connection between past and present because in that year, two books were published that influenced my thinking. I had already read with great benefit Professor Hsiao Kung-chuan's 1960 study, *Rural China: Imperial Control in the Nineteenth Century*.

That book was followed in 1962 by T. T. Ch'ü's monumental *Local Government in China under the Ch'ing* and Sybille Van der Sprenkel's compact *Legal Institutions in Manchu China: A Sociological Analysis*. These books together offered a detailed description, warts and all, of Manchu government and law and showed the extent to which traditional China's social and legal institutions often constituted a surprisingly efficient system for allocating responsibilities and administering justice in accordance with the then prevailing, largely Confucian ideology and norms. The books, especially Van der Sprenkel's thesis, led me to see an analogy between China's traditional, loosely integrated, sociolegal system and the new revolutionary one that the Chinese communists had gradually created for settling disputes and imposing punishments. Although Mao replaced traditional social agencies with different subgovernmental institutions, he sought to have these new institutions emulate their predecessors by handling many minor disputes and offenses in accordance with the new ideology and norms. This relieved the formal judicial system of a substantial workload and enlisted the broader population in revolutionary transformation.

While preparing the criminal process book, I summarized what I had been learning from secondary sources about China's traditional system for informally handling disputes and imposing punishments. In 1966, I published my first significant law review article entitled "Chinese Mediation on the Eve of Modernization." This essay stirred some interest among both lawyers and historians. The following year, Stanley Lubman, a Columbia Law School graduate who had succeeded me at Berkeley, followed with an excellent article entitled "Mao and Mediation," published, like my essay, in the *California Law Review*. It analyzed the early Chinese communist adaptation of traditional dispute resolution methods and emphasized the extent to which the contemporary version differed from the imperial practices I had described. On the basis of subsequent research, a UCLA historian of China, Philip Huang, later suggested that my essay had underestimated the role of the official county magistrates in settling disputes, and his response engendered further scholarly discussion, some of it critical of Huang's work. Even today, the debate over how to characterize the balance between society and the state in the Manchu legal system continues.

Not long after my arrival at Harvard in 1964, I learned that, coincidentally, the University of Pennsylvania Carey Law School in Philadelphia had introduced a seminar on Chinese legal history into its curriculum and had translated a large number of Manchu court decisions and used them for class discussion. Professor Derk Bodde, a distinguished sinologist, and Professor Clarence Morris, a leading legal scholar, twice invited me to Philadelphia to talk to their seminar, and I became so impressed by their labors that I urged them to publish a volume of their translations together with introductory chapters explaining the complex background necessary for proper understanding of the traditional court judgments. I suggested to Harvard University Press that it introduce a new book series called *Harvard Studies in Chinese Law* and that the Carey Law School manuscript become our first publication.

To inaugurate the series in 1967, the press asked me to give a public lecture at Harvard, and I happily complied. Because of my growing interest in Chinese legal history and desire to persuade others of its contemporary relevance, I decided to introduce the little-known but fascinating career of England's Sir George Staunton as a vehicle for attracting interest in the subject. I had come to regard Staunton as my scholarly and professional predecessor. He started learning Chinese at the age of thirteen when he wangled an invitation to join the historic, if ultimately frustrating, 1793 voyage to Peking of Lord George Macartney, who had been dispatched by King George III in an effort to persuade China's fabled Qianlong Emperor to authorize the Central Realm to open trade with England.

By 1810, Staunton had joined the East India Company's China trade group and found himself spending long periods of inactivity in the Portuguese colony of Macao. Having unsuccessfully tried to cope with boredom by resorting to wine and women, he found a better use of his time. With the help of Chinese assistants, he produced an English translation of the Great Qing Law Code to facilitate the East India Company's China negotiations, operations, and dispute resolution. Staunton's remarkable achievement vividly demonstrated the importance of China's domestic law to its commerce and international relations. Half a century later, his example helped to stimulate the imperial government in Peking to undertake its first systematic translation and application of any aspect of Western law—in this case, public international law.

PUBLIC INTERNATIONAL LAW

Given my interest in international relations, I naturally was eager to learn more not only about the domestic legal system of the PRC but also about its policies and practices relating to international law. With the aid of HLS's then doctoral candidate Hungdah Chiu of Taiwan, even before completing the manuscript for my criminal process book, I had begun to collect materials sufficient to introduce a second China-related course into the HLS curriculum, which over the years I tended to call "Chinese Attitudes Toward International Law." I first taught that course in the spring of 1966, just as the Cultural Revolution was breaking out. That weird and unprecedented upheaval temporarily restricted my acquisition of research materials for the domestic law course, but it suddenly inundated me with certain types of international law material. Much of it consisted of the PRC's blatant violations of a range of international norms relating to the protection of foreign nationals and diplomatic and consular privileges and immunities. Those violations were the result of the revolutionary struggles of the Red Guards and other domestic combatants, including Chinese government agencies.

Hungdah Chiu and I worked on those materials for the next seven years. We developed a smooth collaboration, first agreeing on a detailed outline of the book. He then did a superb job of collecting further materials for a documentary study illustrating the PRC's doctrines and practices in all available aspects of public international law.

I wrote an extended introduction, summarizing China's traditional international practices in East Asia, the entry of Western international law into China in the mid-nineteenth century, and the subsequent relevant actions of both the Chiang Kai-shek and Maoist regimes. I also wrote, with Hungdah's help, detailed comments about the many items we introduced on each topic. This massive two-volume work, titled *People's China and International Law: A Documentary Study*, seemed to take forever to finish, but it was finally published in 1974 and was awarded the American Society of International Law's (ASIL) biennial prize for the best documentary study in the field.

This was my second major scholarly contribution and, again, like the criminal process book, helped to open a new area of study concerning contemporary China. We were lucky in the timing of its appearance because the PRC had recently entered the UN and was seeking to complete the normalization of bilateral diplomatic relations with all major countries. American interest was especially high since the announcement of Henry Kissinger's secret July 1971 trip to Beijing and President Richard Nixon's spectacular visit to China the following February. Although the Watergate scandal and Nixon's resignation delayed Washington's formal establishment of diplomatic relations with Beijing until January 1, 1979, China's practice of international law was an attractive topic to many foreign observers throughout the 1970s.

Hungdah Chiu became a distinguished professor at the University of Maryland Francis King Carey School of Law in Baltimore and was recognized, especially in the Chinese-speaking world, as a great authority on international law because of his Chinese- as well as English-language publications. He is sadly no longer with us. The memorial talk I gave at his school reveals a great deal about our long and fruitful friendship.

FURTHER STUDIES OF CHINESE LAW

Although the criminal justice and international law books were my major works during this era, I had a lot to do with producing other volumes on a range of relevant topics. In an effort to induce young scholars to enter various aspects of the China law field, I thought it might be worthwhile to convene a conference of those of us who had already got our feet wet so that we could compare experiences and share our observations of the many sides of the elephant that is China. I solicited papers on a broad variety of practical as well as academic subjects.

Translation of Chinese and English legal terminology was inevitably one of our preoccupations. Hungdah Chiu contributed a stimulating and useful discussion of the challenges of accurately rendering into Chinese the standard English-language vocabulary of public international law, going back to the earliest Chinese attempts in the nineteenth century. He noted important differences between some of the formulations used by the Republic of China on Taiwan and the lexicon of Chairman Mao Zedong's communist system. In addition to writing the introduction to the conference papers, which I edited and published with Harvard University Press in 1970 as *Contemporary Chinese Law: Research Problems and Perspectives*, I produced an essay for the volume on the virtues of refugee interviewing for understanding how the nontransparent communist legal system then worked in practice.

In 1971, I published another edited volume designed to boost research in the field but focused on the experiences of various countries in resolving international legal disputes with China. In addition to writing this book's introduction, together with Professor Shao-chuan Leng of the University of Virginia, I contributed an essay on the Sino-Indian dispute over the internment and detention of Chinese nationals in India. This volume, again published by Harvard University Press, was titled *China's Practice of International Law: Some Case Studies*.

Law professors do not write books as often as they do essays, and I did not neglect law journal scholarship. I mentioned earlier my California article, "Chinese Mediation on the Eve of Modernization," which appeared in 1966. That year, I published in the *Harvard Law Review* a long essay that eventually became the introduction to my book on the criminal process. I followed it, three years later, with "The Chinese Communist Party and 'Judicial Independence': 1949–1959." I am happy to note that, since the Chinese Communist Party continues to oppose an independent judiciary, this 1969 essay continues to be occasionally cited in current studies of this critical problem.

The reader will be grateful that only one of the many other law review–type articles that I authored in the late 1960s is worth mentioning here.

It appeared in the 1967 *Proceedings of the ASIL Annual Meeting* and was based on the first speech I ever gave at the society's annual meeting, in April of that year. China was in the midst of the worst period of the Cultural Revolution, hardly an ideal time to urge international law experts to reconsider the fairness of almost two decades of harsh foreign criticisms of Beijing's many challenges to the world community. Yet I deeply felt the need for a new generation of American China specialists to start beating the drums for a less one-sided and hostile view of Sino-American relations than we had witnessed. I especially wanted to emphasize the need for a more balanced perception of the important role that some dubious American applications of international law had played in adversely affecting the relationship.

Finally, worried that the American public was not being adequately informed about the PRC's attitudes about public international law, I published a number of op-ed essays in the *New York Times* and elsewhere on various relevant topics. I particularly enjoyed trying to explain the complex legal issues involved in the UN's struggle to resolve the highly sensitive question of which government—that in Beijing or Taipei—should, under the UN Charter, represent China in the Security Council, where China had a permanent seat, and in the General Assembly. As will be discussed in a later chapter, in a 1971 op-ed in the *New York Times*, I also addressed questions of American espionage in China and Chinese criminal justice involved in the life sentence meted out by China's Supreme People's Court in 1954 to my Yale College classmate Jack Downey.

DEVELOPING EALS: HARVARD'S PROGRAM IN EAST ASIAN LEGAL STUDIES

At Berkeley, I had organized occasional lunch programs in the law school for interested students and faculty to hear a variety of academic experts relevant to Asia. I found that to be an informal and convenient way to get acquainted with the experts and the subject and stimulate cooperation and friendship. Once I decided to remain at Harvard, I developed a more systematic and energetic program and drew on specialists from many university departments. I would introduce the topic of the day and the guest speaker would usually talk for twenty minutes or so and then respond to comments and questions from yours truly and the group for about an hour. People brought bag lunches.

In addition to some of the obvious law school comparative and international law luminaries and the stars of Harvard's Chinese, Japanese, Korean, and Vietnamese disciplines, I invited some famous scholars on the Soviet Union, such as the political scientist Merle Fainsod and the sociologist Alex Inkeles, and some well-known social science generalists interested in law such as Talcott Parsons. Their talks not only broadened my horizons and those of our law school group, but they also spread the word around the university about what we were up to. In addition, I began to invite as speakers well-known experts from other universities, especially the Massachusetts Institute of Technology (MIT) and Tufts, and even leading foreign scholars and political-legal figures if I could lure them to Cambridge during their visits to Washington and New York.

Perhaps the outstanding speaker of the early years of our program was Singapore's legendary Prime Minister Lee Kuan Yew, who suddenly dropped into Harvard's lap right after Nixon's election to the presidency in November 1968. He had rightly foreseen that US-Asia policy was on the verge of change, and he believed that spending a month or so at Harvard, whose faculty he regarded as a generator of foreign policy ideas, might be a good way to take the pulse of developments. I met him for the first time at a session I organized for the China group of our Kennedy School Institute of Politics and invited him to speak at an East Asian Legal Studies (EALS) lunch program a week later. That session proved to be a longer than usual, extremely stimulating discussion, and we became friends.

The following week, he and Mrs. Lee, a successful business lawyer, came to dinner at our house. A few days beforehand, Joan and I received a letter in the mail from the prime minister's (PM) staff giving us the only formal instructions we have ever received from anticipated dinner guests. There was to be no smoking in the PM's presence, we were told, and the room temperature was not to exceed 70 degrees. It also helpfully indicated that the PM was not to be served certain foods.

The following July, while Joan and I were on a summer Asian research trip that included Singapore, the PM amply repaid our hospitality. In my honor, he convened a dozen of the city-state's main legal and foreign policy specialists for a lively and elegant dinner where conversation centered on what the PM deemed the latest outrage by the neighboring Malaysian government. Although he warmly entertained my questions about Singapore, I noted that none of the other participants dared to enter the discussion. As he drove us back to our hotel, Attorney General Tan Boon Teik said: "I liked the way you spoke up to the PM tonight," which only highlighted his and his wife's silence as well as that of the other guests.

My worst experience in this category occurred in the late 1970s after Chairman Mao's death had ended the Cultural Revolution and allowed a thaw to emerge in Sino-American relations. Because of the two-volume work that Hungdah Chiu and I had produced on China and international law, the then newly revived Chinese Society of International Law, through one of its recently rehabilitated leaders, Professor Chen Tiqiang, had invited me to lecture to its members in Beijing during one of my periodic visits to the nation's capital. Chen, a very nice man whom the Anti-Rightist Campaign and the Cultural Revolution had kept on the shelf for twenty years despite his published defenses of the regime's 1949–1957 international record, had looked me up in Beijing soon after his return to prominence. I warmly recall his greeting: "Although we have never met before today, because of your book [*People's China and International Law*] I feel we are already old friends."

I was eager to reciprocate his hospitality by inviting him to lecture at Harvard Law School, and he was delighted to accept. Thanks to my often-excessive enthusiasm, I asked him to give not one but three lectures on successive days. This was to be a major occasion for Sino-American relations and progress in international legal understanding. To be safe, although Chen had earned his PhD at Oxford before "Liberation" and still spoke English well thirty years later, I administered the usual two-rule admonition (speak loud and never read to the audience), and he guaranteed that he understood perfectly.

On his first day at Harvard, a very large crowd—larger than our lunch series had ever had before—awaited Professor Chen's talk in the ample meeting and library room of our EALS quarters. The atmosphere was electric. Sadly, Professor Chen, who had been left with a heart condition by the condemnation and isolation he had long suffered as a "rightist," was determined to avoid the risk of further personal attacks upon returning home after his potentially controversial Harvard lectures. So he decided that his personal security lay in reading from a prepared manuscript that could constitute the best evidence in case he had to defend himself once again back in Beijing. His somewhat quavering voice could only be plainly heard by those seated nearby and, despite his fluent English, the uninflected tone of his reading soon induced a feeling of soporific dissatisfaction among those who remained awake. The second day's attendance was down sharply, from about two hundred to fifty. By the third day I had to ask a few of the school's secretaries and other staff to take up places at the lunch table!

Distinguished South Korean guests proved to be among the most dynamic speakers. The great human rights politician Kim Dae-Jung, who, after enormous personal risk and suffering, eventually became his country's president, was inspiring. Everyone also marveled at the learned and stimulating talk given by Professor Hahm Pyong-choon, a Harvard Law School graduate who became national security adviser to the South Korean president before being assassinated in a failed North Korean attempt to kill President Chun Doo Hwan while visiting Burma.

One of the very best speakers among the American guests was Harvard's Edwin O. Reischauer, a famous authority on the history and politics of Japan, who returned in 1966 from five years as U.S. ambassador in Tokyo. I also did some television programs with Ed and marveled at his ability to give informed, crisp answers to whatever questions were raised and always within the allotted time. He might have been a great success in American politics or television as well as academe.

What made Harvard's EALS really special was the program's large number of able and devoted students—foreigners as well as Americans—and mostly from the law school but not entirely. Most of the Americans who took part in EALS (or "eels" as it was affectionately dubbed by those who enjoyed that East Asian delicacy) came for the regular LLB (later called the JD) law degree. Most of the foreign students came to pursue the LLM master of laws graduate degree. A small number of the latter, if qualified, stayed to obtain the prestigious SJD doctorate. Some of our participants never enrolled in the law school at all but earned MAs and PhDs in other university departments that allowed them to take my law courses and, of course, take part in our EALS activities.

For readers who are not themselves part of the field, any effort to mention the students who went on to make major contributions of their own in EALS might seem both a bit lengthy and too "inside baseball" to be of keen interest, and for that reason, I'm reserving my memories of those students to an appendix. Suffice it to say here that I've always believed in the hoary maxim, "Who acts through another acts himself." I was lucky to have been present at the creation of a newly developing field of study, which meant that many of the students I had, especially in the years at Harvard building the EALS program, went on to distinguished and influential careers of their own as teachers, builders of their own scholarly programs, and practitioners, and many of their students and protégés are now important members of a fully developed area of both legal studies and practice. This is a legacy of which I am enormously proud and grateful.

Perhaps the best way to sum up this account of my efforts to build our EALS program at Harvard is to call attention to a description of it that appeared in the HLS Yearbook for the class of 1978. "The East Wind is sweeping through the halls of the Harvard Law School," it began. "Today EALS has expanded to become an established Law School program that provides leadership for the study of Asian law in the Western World." The yearbook described our offices, "adorned with Chinese art treasures"; it spoke of our "Asian periodical browsing room" and our "small Asian legal library," and the variety of ways that EALS alumni "put their skills and enthusiasm to work on behalf of law firms, businesses, the government, international organizations and charitable foundations dealing with East Asia. Others have joined the faculties of law schools and university political science and history departments," not only in Western countries but also in Hong Kong, Singapore, Tokyo, and other Asian capitals.

I was more than pleased when, before ascending to Harvard's presidency, our law school dean, Derek Bok, made a surprise visit to our EALS quarters one afternoon. He concluded that the school's goal should be to create similar attractive and stimulating environments for every group of students with shared interests. Not long afterward, the student-run newspaper, the *Harvard Law Record*, published its April Fool's Day issue with the front-page headline: "Cohen Goes into Laotian Studies." It purportedly relied on an interview in which I allegedly claimed, "China is no longer interesting. Everybody has now been there. Even Alan Dershowitz!"

12

KYOTO CHRONICLES

A Year Amid Japanese Temples and Turmoil

By the spring of 1971, I was ready for a sabbatical. I wasn't bored with teaching after seven years at Harvard. My courses continued to be well received and well attended. The annual "Confidential Guide" to Harvard Law School (HLS) published by students, which, of course, was anything but confidential, generally gave favorable reviews to my classroom performance. A 1970 Harvard comment did perceptively note: "For Professor Cohen, teaching is just one aspect of a busy life." I took that as an implicit suggestion that perhaps the classroom was not the major focus of my day the way it was for some colleagues.

In truth, I did want some respite from daily obligations in the hope of completing a second book, this one about the preaching and practice of public international law by Chairman Mao's China. I also hoped to devote more time to learning about and taking part in an anticipated breakthrough in relations between the United States and the People's Republic of China (PRC). Bill Bundy had left government to become the editor of *Foreign Affairs* and had asked whether I wanted to contribute an essay about the need for a new China policy. TV programs were seeking interviews. Harrison Salisbury, who had just established the op-ed page in the *New York Times*, was eager for discussions of the complex problems involved in the PRC's impending replacement of the Chiang Kai-shek government as the representative of China in the United Nations. I was also being courted by the leading commercial sponsor of public affairs lectures to go on a handsomely paid tour to hawk China policies.

In those stimulating circumstances, the challenge was how best to take advantage of a sabbatical. I gave serious thought to staying home instead of spending the year in some distant residence in order to be free of law school obligations, as colleagues usually did. Staying home would not uproot the children's education and lives and would enable me to work with my talented assistant Hungdah Chiu to finish the book on international law that we had begun five years earlier. I had just received a Guggenheim Fellowship to support this effort and wanted to make the most of it. Staying put would also maximize my availability for participation in burgeoning China policy developments. But Joan was eager to free us and our sons from the intensity of life in Cambridge and have another exciting exploration of Asia, such as we all had experienced during the year we spent in Hong Kong in 1963–1964 before coming to Harvard. Although she would have to take leave from her academic responsibilities at the School of the Museum of Fine Arts, Boston, she was sure that renewed exposure to Asia would enhance her capacity for teaching and research on our return. Her arguments won me over, and we decided to prepare to go abroad.

But where to spend the year? We thought about several places, from Taiwan to India, where Joan was especially eager to spend some time. Yet Japan made most sense to me professionally. Sino-Japanese relations have always been extremely important. Japanese observers of China have often been well informed and displayed perceptions of the "Central Realm" that differed from those in North America or Europe. The Japanese government, keenly sensitive to the evident warming of Sino-American relations, appeared to be determined to improve its own ties to Beijing. Japan, the former colonizer of both Taiwan and Korea, also had a lot to teach about those two crucial areas as well as its evolving relations with them. I also wanted very much to study more about the Japanese legal system and its comparisons and interactions with China's and our own. Having long respected those relatively few East Asia specialists like Franz Schurman and Ezra Vogel who could use both the Chinese and Japanese languages, I wanted to take intensive Japanese lessons in the hope that, after a year in the country, I might be able to read Japanese sources and interview people in their own tongue.

Nevertheless, I felt an obligation to honor Joan's preference. We were in the seventeenth year of our marriage, and she had always loyally and enthusiastically adapted to my professional needs, accommodating her own to each new situation—in New Haven, Connecticut; Washington, DC; Berkeley, California; Hong Kong; and Cambridge, Massachusetts. Also, as it turned out, the Ford Foundation had recently decided to send an American law professor to Delhi University's law school each year, and it asked whether I might be interested in filling that post. I said yes, in deference to Joan's preference, and it all seemed to be too good to be true when we found out that the Delhi law faculty, after careful consideration, rejected my candidacy. They rightly calculated that, for what Ford was going to spend on luring the Cohens to India, the Delhi faculty could send three of its scholars to Harvard Law School for a year. Joan graciously agreed that the Ford fiasco had burst our South Asian bubble and was happy to accept the alternative because Japan had always been part of her own professional preoccupations.

But as we deliberated over whether Tokyo or Kyoto would be the best place for us to spend our year in Japan, fate again intervened to tilt the decision-making scales. When my dear friend Professor Fujikura Koichiro of Doshisha University Law School in Kyoto learned of our Japanese plan, he quickly arranged a visiting professorship that would only require minimal teaching responsibilities and that guaranteed us our own house within walking distance not only of the university campus but also of the old imperial palace. That was an offer I could not refuse.

So in the spring of 1971, I invited one of my favorite HLS students, Ko-yung Tung, who had grown up in Tokyo and was a native speaker of Japanese, to come live with us in Cambridge. Although Ko-yung was a diligent instructor, I actually had too little time for scanning more than a few chapters of the leading Japanese-language teaching manual. After landing in Tokyo, it didn't take long for me to regret that I hadn't devoted more time to language study. I thought we should start our new adventure with an authentic Japanese restaurant experience. I ordered a beer, or thought I did, telling the waiter "*O biru, onegaishimassu*" ("A beer, please"). When the waiter next appeared without the desired beer, I snapped, "*O biru, O biru*." Visibly upset, the waiter immediately returned, not with the requested beer but with the dinner check, even though we had not yet received our meal. In Japanese the words for "beer" and "bill" sound similar, at least as pronounced by the uninitiated. The whole family had a good laugh over this, and Peter, at fourteen our oldest son and open to new experience, gently criticized my exasperation by saying: "Remember, Dad, it's their country."

I gradually did better after settling into Kyoto, but not before one greater linguistic disaster. On our second night in Kyoto, while our boys were being looked after by our newly acquired housekeeper, Joan and I dropped in on a nearby little eating place, a sushi-ya. We sat at the oblong counter amid eight or ten local people enjoying our sashimi, sushi, and Asahi beer (I had already learned something from experience!) when, perhaps stimulated by the beer or the enhanced confidence I felt in being able to order it, I decided to let the chef know how delicious the food was. I smiled at him and said in a voice that those near us could hear, "*Damei dessu*," which I thought meant "It's good." To my surprise, the chef did not look pleased. Thinking that he may not have heard me, I repeated it in a louder voice that none of the patrons could miss: "Damei dessu." People looked surprised and the chef looked offended. Not understanding the unfortunate situation I had created, I quickly paid the bill, and we beat a hasty retreat. The next day, a look at my Japanese textbook revealed my mistake. "Damei" means "bad"! It took months before we dared to return to that delightful sushi-ya.

Given this incentive to learn the language, we managed to contact a senior woman who had taught some of my distinguished Harvard colleagues who had specialized in Japanese studies. Because of my Harvard connection, she was persuaded to admit us into her busy schedule. Joan signed up for three hours a week of private tutoring while I decided to do two hours every morning five days a week. Every hour required at least two hours of home preparation, so this was a major commitment, but I was determined to prove that, even at age forty-one, I was not too old to learn a new East Asian language.

As always whenever we moved the family to a new location, we had to act quickly to enroll the children in schools. We arrived in Kyoto well prepared, having made extensive inquiries before leaving Cambridge. Our two older boys, Peter at fourteen and Seth at twelve, had to board at Canadian Academy in Kobe—an hour train ride from Kyoto—during the week in order to receive the equivalent of an American high school and junior high school education, respectively. Ethan, at ten, was too young to enroll there. Having attended the Cambridge Friends School with his brothers for many years, he was devastated by their separation in Japan. It took him until the New Year to adjust to the Kyoto International School, where some of the local children made fun of him because he did not know Japanese and called him *baka* ("stupid").

Canadian Academy, by contrast, proved a welcoming environment for his brothers, although in principle it was a Christian school. I had little contact with the school apart from an initial visit with a few teachers and another at the academic year's end. But on one occasion I got an introductory whiff of what one Southern Baptist missionary parent was like. In the spring of 1972, Joan and I made a month-long trip to China, and the school's headmaster asked me to discuss what we'd seen at a specially convened parent-teacher meeting. After my fairly conventional overview, I got a question that I'll never forget from a fiftyish woman at the back of the room. She complimented me on a nice talk but expressed disappointment that I had said nothing about the Second Coming. Taken aback, I asked what she meant. She said: "I know that Jesus will return to Earth and that he will do so in China. Yet you have said nothing about finding any evidence of this." In reply, I merely said: "Madam, you apparently have access to sources denied to me."

Joan and I had little difficulty settling into our new Kyoto quarters, a wonderful house that had been built by Doshisha University for one of the early Christian missionaries who came from the West to teach English there at the start of the twentieth century. Our boys had a large bedroom upstairs, as did we, and we all slept on the floor on comfortable tatami mats. I also had a tiny study that benefited from the winter sun, not an inconsiderable feature in an old house that had a very cold front hall and needed heaters in each room. Downstairs we had adequate, simply furnished living and dining rooms and an adjacent kitchen that featured what must have been one of the earliest and most dangerous gas stoves in the country. We soon decided that eating dinner in one of the many inexpensive restaurants that dotted the area between our house and the university was the safest and easiest course of action.

My teaching obligations as a senior visiting professor had been arranged to be light, and I was assigned a typical faculty office. Because of unexpected political turmoil, however, I barely entered the law school during the entire fall semester. The university was suddenly captured by a branch of "the Red Army," the radical "Seki Gun," a national organization that was seeking political power in order to overturn Japan's evolving postwar democracy. The group assigned to Doshisha consisted of about eighty mostly young men armed with bamboo staves and wearing face masks. They boldly took over a campus of more than twenty thousand students, faculty, and administrators. They did not allow classes to be held, and the faculty was barred from going to their offices. Rather than call in the police to oust the invaders, an act that reportedly would have been broadly condemned by Japanese society, the university president retreated to the campus hospital, ostensibly for a mysterious illness that required many weeks of treatment. That left the academic community foundering and on its own.

For Joan and me, this sad educational and political travesty had a bright side. Kyoto was famous for a huge number of cultural and artistic attractions, and its autumn weather was perfect for touring. Joan, of course, was eager to see every legendary temple and garden, and I was happy to accompany her and benefit from her instruction. We had a good laugh when my mother, who was worried that there would be no way for us to mark observance of the start of the Jewish new year in September, urged us over the telephone to try to find a temple. We assured her that there were hundreds of temples in Kyoto, and we hoped to visit every one of them. We also had time for tennis. Remarkably, for the first month of my enforced exile from the law school, the Red Army allowed us to play on the university tennis courts. In October, however, they reconsidered and decided that allowing American imperialists to frolic amid revolution was not wise politics.

The Red Army's impact reached beyond the campus. In October, Joan was invited to give a lecture on American art at the America Center that the U.S. State Department had established in Kyoto. She had arranged to turn her talk into a discussion with a congenial Doshisha professor of English who was interested in Western art history. When the program began, however, he was nowhere to be found, forcing Joan to launch into her slide presentation without him. After about twenty minutes, the missing professor suddenly entered the hall, looking distraught and unshaven, and apologized for being late. He explained that he had been detained by the Red Army in recent days and had only belatedly persuaded his captors to allow him to honor his lecture commitment, but on condition that he return to captivity when the program ended!

I was stunned at these developments. In many autocracies, universities are islands of relative freedom. Yet in Japan's impressive democracy, Doshisha and many other universities had become islands of dictatorship because the government and society hesitated to take measures to subdue the Red Army and other radical organizations that competed with it. By winter, these rival organizations had begun to destroy each other, often through violence that included murder, and their grip on university life loosened. This allowed me the opportunity to begin to take part in law school life.

Doshisha was private and not as large and prestigious as the much better-known, national government–sponsored Kyoto University, but it had a relatively young and congenial law faculty, including a trio of criminal procedure teachers whom I soon got to know. They were receptive to my inquiries about law and practice in Japan but, to my surprise, their knowledge was strangely limited. They knew not only about their country's relevant legislation and court decisions but also the theory and content of the German legal system that was still a major influence in Japan. They also were somewhat aware of the increasing postwar legal impact, in Japan as well as other democracies, of American constitutional and legislative developments in criminal procedure. To their embarrassment, however, they knew nothing about actual practice of criminal procedure in their own country. None of them had ever been to the police stations and prosecutor's offices to which I had hoped they could introduce me. Instead, they asked whether they could accompany me to any such interviews that I could arrange so they too could learn the realities of the subject that was their professional focus. I could explain their presence, they suggested, by saying that they were serving as my expert guides. I did take them along on the few interviews I set up before time pressures led me to abandon the project.

My minimal teaching duties enabled me to spend time with Kyoto University experts in international law and relations, who were of immediate interest to me because of the impending normalization of relations between Japan and China. As the only relevant Harvard specialist then resident in Japan, I was frequently asked to speak in Tokyo on China matters, which made me feel that I had not entirely missed out on the growing American excitement about contacts with Beijing by leaving the United States for a year. I especially recall in April 1972 addressing the annual banquet of the Harvard Club of Japan. There, for the first time, I discussed the already sensitive Sino-Japanese dispute over islands in the East China Sea called *senkaku* in Japanese and *diaoyu* in Chinese.

Our best trip in Japan occurred during Christmas vacation when we went skiing with the boys on the beautiful northern island of Hokkaido. Everything about that trip proved noteworthy. Simply buying and renting ski equipment in Kyoto was a challenge, especially because I seemed to be larger than the usual male customers. Near the ski capital of Nisseko, we stayed in a traditional hot-spring (*on-sen*) inn, which we much enjoyed, but despite the season and the well-known ski location, there never seemed to be quite enough snow. One of the first Japanese phrases I acquired during that week was *yuki ga skunai-dessu* ("too little snow"). But we did have some good days, which exposed us to the hazards of out-of-control local skiers who roared down the mountain like kamikaze fliers on their final mission. Most bizarre was the time Joan and I rode the rather rickety ski lift in the midst of an icy blizzard. As we reached the mountaintop, through the blinding snowflakes, as though from Heaven came a recording of the voice of the late President John F. Kennedy admonishing us to "ask not what your country can do for you but what you can do for your country"! Joan eventually published essays about this memorable family excursion in *Skiing* magazine and the *Boston Globe*.

Immediately after returning to Kyoto from Hokkaido, Johns Hopkins University, which was seeking a new president, asked me to fly to Baltimore, Maryland, for an interview. I was a surprised and surprising candidate because I was then only forty-one and had never headed any institution more significant than HLS's East Asian Legal Studies (EALS) program. Also, the board seemed set on appointing the then provost to the post. But one of my protégés, Richard Pfeffer, and some of his colleagues on the Hopkins faculty pressed the board of trustees to consider me, too.

The board, as expected, appointed the able provost to the presidency but offered me the opportunity to become the next head of the university's influential School of Advanced International Studies (SAIS) in Washington, DC. That was a job that would have been appropriate to my career path and interests. Because I loved my China work at Harvard and didn't want to uproot our peripatetic family again, I surprised the board and perhaps myself by declining the opportunity. This despite my attraction to Washington, where Joan and I had spent four happy years, and to the national and international political scene. A few years after my return to Harvard, when Tufts' impressive president, Jean Mayer, pressed me to become dean of his university's Fletcher School of Law and Diplomacy, which would have allowed us to remain in Cambridge, I agonized longer over whether to abandon Chinese legal studies for broader administrative and academic pursuits. But with some reluctance, I decided to stick to my last. I later occasionally wondered about "the path not taken."

Not long after my return from Baltimore (and after Joan returned from a wonderful one-month trip to India on her own that I had agreed to as a consolation prize), came the international hullabaloo over President Richard Nixon's trip to China from February 21–28, 1972. I eagerly awaited the anticipated joint statement that would indicate the extent to which this long-awaited visit had proved successful. The Joint Communiqué of the United States of America and the People's Republic of China, referred to most often as the Shanghai Communiqué, was no disappointment, a hugely important, if necessarily ambiguous, document that still bears analysis five decades later. As I read the English text in the March 1 English-language issue of the Mainichi newspaper, especially the artful and controversial U.S. statement that it "does not challenge" the PRC position that all Chinese on both sides of the Taiwan strait regard Taiwan as part of China, I knew that a new chapter was actually going to open up not only in U.S.-China relations but also in my as yet unsuccessful efforts finally to enter the Promised Land.

Ironically perhaps, much of the time I still had left in Japan was taken up by negotiations with the North Korean mission in Tokyo for an unprecedented trip to Pyongyang for our entire family. Seeming to illustrate how fast things were changing, however, the opportunity to visit China suddenly opened up for Joan and me during the few weeks after the Nixon visit, and we readily took advantage of it.

13

MY FIRST TRIP TO CHINA

Meeting Zhou Enlai, Arguing for John T. Downey

As a new era of Sino-American relations dawned in the early 1970s, I had tried, like many other American specialists on China, many ways to be allowed to see the country for myself. The way in which I had invested the least effort was the one that ironically panned out first. A phone call that I got in Kyoto from the Federation of American Scientists (FAS), a group of liberal scientists seeking to initiate cooperation with China, suddenly brought an invitation to accompany its chair, the distinguished physicist and policy adviser Marvin Goldberger, and its executive secretary, the dynamic political activist Jeremy Stone, on a several-week trip to promote the first scientific exchanges between our countries. The three of us would be allowed to take our wives but not our children. So my wife, Joan, who had become a specialist in Chinese art on the faculty of the School of the Museum of Fine Arts at Tufts University, and I shared this first trip to China just three months after President Richard Nixon's famous China visit.

INITIATING CULTURAL EXCHANGE

We were guests of the Chinese Academy of Sciences (CAS). One of its able staff, Mr. Li Mingde, met us as we crossed the border from Hong Kong into

Guangdong Province and then escorted us by rail and then by plane to Beijing, where we were installed at the Minzu (Nationalities) Hotel. Excited to be in China finally, I awoke early the next morning and decided to explore the neighborhood before joining my wife and colleagues for breakfast. The area was bustling with people rushing to work, leaving no chance to strike up a casual conversation. I tried to talk with people in the nearby market, which would have been difficult at any time, but it was especially so at 6 A.M. I heard one vegetable seller say to another: "He's a Frenchman," perhaps because Americans were few at that point and I had a mustache.

I was hungry and getting nowhere in my marketplace effort at cultural exchange, so I decided after a while to try my luck at a nearby "little eating place." As I stood in line, the man behind the counter seemed friendly and asked what I wanted to eat. I asked him to give me what those ahead of me were having—hot soymilk soup called *doujiang* and a long cruller called *youtiao*. Armed with these props, I took the fourth seat at a table for four occupied by three middle-aged male workers. Everyone else in the room was watching but my new companions barely looked up. I was determined to get them to talk, but how to start? I remembered that foreign journalists who preceded me in China had told me that, every time they asked anyone about the mysterious fate of disappeared leader Lin Biao, the answer was always: "Have some more soup." So instead of explaining who I was and how I got there or reminding my companions about Chairman Mao's emphasis on being at one with the masses, I opened with what seemed a safe topic and said to the fellow on my left: "What's the name of this soup?" He didn't answer.

The room hushed, and tension began to mount, but I pushed on, saying hopefully to the man across from me: "Do you know the name of this soup?" He wouldn't answer either. At that point, the sympathetic man behind the counter looked unhappy at the cool reception I was receiving, and I noted a sign on the wall that said: "Heighten revolutionary vigilance. Defend the Motherland against spies." Standing in a corner staring at me with bulging eyes was a man who resembled a security officer about to make an arrest in a revolutionary opera. Meanwhile, the anxious man seated on my right was slurping his soup furiously in an effort to clear out and avoid the inevitable. He probably didn't want to be impolite like the others, but he may have feared that, if he told me the name of the soup, the next question would be "What happened to Lin Biao?" In some desperation I persisted and said to him: "You must know the name of this soup." He looked at me and then at the soup and said what Chinese often say when they don't want to answer: "I'm not too clear about that!" At that point, hoping that the official route to cultural exchange might be more successful, I decided it was time to return to the hotel!

On that first full day in Beijing, I underwent an unexpected name change. For twelve years, my Chinese name had been Kong Jierong. My first Chinese-language tutor in Berkeley, California, a learned former Beijing scholar, had given me this name. Kong, he had said, was the perfect family name for me because it sounded like Cohen and was the name of China's most famous sage, Confucius, who took a great interest in law. But in the China of mid-1972, Kong had become the enemy, the hated symbol of China's feudal past and anathema to every upstanding revolutionary. I had inadvertently arrived in the midst of a nationwide campaign to wipe out the remnants of Lin Biao and Confucius. So my hosts declared that I should have a new, more proletarian name. They decided that Ke En would do nicely since Ke was an ordinary name of the masses and, together with En (they knew I admired Zhou Enlai), would sound even more like Cohen than Kong did and have a favorable meaning.

I gave the matter little thought, but later, in 1977, when I escorted Ted Kennedy and ten members of his family to China to meet Deng Xiaoping and other luminaries, Taiwan's newspaper, the *Lianhe Bao*, used my new mainland name against me, claiming that I had abandoned the name of China's foremost figure. Of course, outside the mainland, I have continued to be known by my original name, and recently, since the resurrection of Confucius in China in the eyes of the communists, some mainland organizations and friends have also adopted it in referring to me.

We spent our first ten days in Beijing, preoccupied with the usual introductory tourist sites and meetings devoted to persuading our hosts to send their first science delegation to the United States, which they did six months later. A meeting I well recall was with a large group of "America watchers" convened by the Foreign Affairs Association (*waijiao xiehui*), an offshoot of the Ministry of Foreign Affairs. They were familiar with my July 1971 article in the American journal *Foreign Affairs* calling for U.S. recognition of the People's Republic of China (PRC) and disengagement from the Republic of China on Taiwan. At least a few knew that I had chaired the Harvard–Massachusetts Institute of Technology (MIT) committee that, in November 1968, had given president-elect Nixon a confidential memorandum recommending that he send a close aide for secret talks in Beijing with China's leaders. That was the origin of Henry Kissinger's famous 1971 visit.

Of course, my hosts, the "America watchers," wanted to discuss the problem of Taiwan and prospects for normalization of diplomatic relations between our countries, but they seemed most anxious about Senator George McGovern's chances of unseating Nixon in the fall presidential election. I was known to be an adviser on Asia to McGovern, although I did little for his campaign because I had spent most of the year abroad. At a time when China was looking to the United States to be a shield against the former Soviet Union, McGovern's pledge to cut the defense budget by one-third seemed very worrisome to my hosts. Also, it was obvious that the PRC had high hopes for cooperation with the Nixon administration, much of it based on the admiration that Kissinger and Zhou Enlai professed for each other.

I had agreed to talk with the group about these subjects if they would agree to discuss problems of cultural exchange, too. I wanted an opportunity to let them know how this initial effort looked to their guests. Because they hoped to establish diplomatic relations with the United States, I thought it useful for them to make their reception of Americans as smooth as possible. I especially wanted to ask about the most puzzling of our experiences in China, a visit to the subway. When our escort asked us if we'd like to ride on the Beijing subway that had been under construction, I said that the newspapers had reported that it was not yet in service. Our escort said that it was already in service and that we could ride on it.

At the appointed hour, while standing next to the track, we were given a long lecture about the history of the subway's development. During that time, only two trains came by, and neither had a single passenger. The next train, which we took through eight stations, also had no other passengers, nor did we see any people waiting in any of the stations. We were told they were all in waiting rooms, where conditions were more comfortable. When we got to the last stop, the Beijing railroad station, our escort still insisted that the system was in use. I embarrassed my wife by saying that we would like to wait a while for evidence that people really were using the subway. I had had doubts about some of the information we had been given on other matters and was disturbed that we could not successfully communicate about something as basic as whether the subway was in service. A bit exasperated with my determination to clarify an evident misunderstanding, my wife and a couple of others in our group went up the escalator to the main hall to wait. Down at the track, no trains came in for a time, but finally one did appear with about twenty assorted workers, peasants, and soldiers who seemed flustered when they encountered the escalator. With some satisfaction, our escort said: "You see, the system is in service." When I later asked the Foreign Affairs Association group about this mystery, our escort's leader, with the escort seated next to him, smiled and said: "It's very simple. Our subway is not yet in service."

Our escort had given me a more reliable insight into contemporary China earlier in the trip as we stood on a hilltop and viewed the beautiful valley of the Ming Dynasty tombs outside Beijing. By that time, I felt we had become friendly enough to talk politics and even international law. Just a few weeks earlier, at a lecture in Tokyo to the Harvard Club of Japan, I had discussed the increasingly tense dispute between China and Japan over the eight piles of rock in the East China Sea known as Diaoyutai in Chinese. On May 15, 1972, when the United States surrendered administrative jurisdiction over these islets to Japan, Sino-Japanese relations deteriorated further, and even today the dispute continues to fester. When I mentioned Diaoyutai, my escort became uncharacteristically emotional. "China," he said, "will never allow the Japanese aggressors to occupy one inch of its sacred soil. We will fight them to the death." But when I gently informed him that Japan had assumed jurisdiction over the islets only the previous week, he suddenly resumed his usual relaxed manner and said: "Oh, well. There is a right time and place for everything. We are in no hurry. We can settle this matter any time in the next five hundred years!" I had witnessed the two sides of contemporary China's politics—nationalism and pragmatism—in short compass.

MEETING PRIME MINISTER ZHOU ENLAI

One other question concerned us in Beijing—whether we would meet Prime Minister Zhou Enlai. We were told that we might, but there was no word by the time we left the capital.

We had ended our travels by returning to Beijing in order to fly to Guangzhou on our way out of China. Our hosts seemed slightly embarrassed that there had been no confirmation of a meeting with Prime Minister Zhou. Then, while en route, bad weather in Guangzhou required that our flight be diverted to the city of Nanchang, capital of Jiangxi Province. Because Nanchang was closed to foreigners, we were kept at its airport until dark and then taken to the People's Hotel, which we were forbidden to leave. At 4 A.M., we were to be awakened to return to the airport before daylight to resume our flight to Guangzhou. In the interim, however, big news came from Beijing. I received a telephone call at 1 A.M. from Professor Lin Daguang, a Canadian friend who had previously been an assistant to Prime Minister Zhou. Would Joan and I be willing to return to Beijing to meet Zhou? I said I would gladly return and would let him know about Joan. Joan understandably felt she had to return to Kyoto to look after our sons.

As Harrison Salisbury later commented in his book *To Peking and Beyond: A Report on the New Asia*, invitations to meet Prime Minister Zhou were often issued at the last minute, and it was not unusual to bring guests back from all over the country. There was also sometimes an air of mystery surrounding these meetings. For example, I was told to wait in my hotel room from 5 P.M., after which I would be picked up and taken to a preliminary meeting with an unidentified person, to be followed by dinner with an unidentified group, but with a strong hint that Prime Minister Zhou would be the host. The preliminary meeting turned out to be a private one-hour session with Deputy Foreign Minister Qiao Guanhua, a stimulating and self-confident interlocutor whom I enjoyed. I then went to dinner and met with Prime Minister Zhou, Qiao and some of their principal aides, at least two of whom eventually became ambassadors to the United States and heads of the North American section of the Foreign Ministry. Our interpreter was Tang Wensheng, known to many Americans as Nancy Tang, who had grown up in the United States while her father served at the UN. Although I had several short chats in Chinese with Prime Minister Zhou, Nancy did the heavy interpreting for the evening. The main guests were Professor John K. Fairbank, America's senior China scholar, and his charming wife Wilma. The Fairbanks had been friendly with Prime Minister Zhou in Chongqing during the mid-1940s before the

Communist Party's 1949 victory in the Chinese civil war. Foreign correspondents Harrison Salisbury of the *New York Times* and Richard Dudman of the *St. Louis Post-Dispatch*, and their wives also attended, as did Jeremy Stone and his wife.

Salisbury's book gives a long account of most of the conversation at our almost four-hour evening with Zhou and this group. I need not repeat it, although it was surely the high point of my first visit. Here I will mention only my most outstanding impressions, the deepest of which was left by Prime Minister Zhou himself. He gave us an hour of discussion sipping tea before dinner while seated in a circle. He was genial, informal, relaxed, humorous yet serious, and always guiding the conversation by asking questions. His first remark to me was: "Why didn't your wife come with you? We invited her." When I explained that Joan had wanted to join but was concerned about our sons, he quipped: "Oh, I forgot. In America, parents still have to look after children." Later, as we went into dinner, he said to me with a smile and a bemused twinkle in his eyes: "I understand that you have done many books on our legal system." This showed the respect he gave his guests by learning their backgrounds in advance. Yet he said it in a slightly quizzical way that gently implied that perhaps I had made more of China's legal system than China had. After all, the country was then still in its Cultural Revolution!

What I remember most vividly from the predinner conversation was the prime minister's preoccupation with cancer. Zhou knew, of course, that the purpose of Mr. Stone's and my visit was to initiate cultural exchanges in the sciences. He seemed especially interested in inviting to China America's leading cancer specialists, in theory and practice. The prime minister appeared so lively and healthy, so it didn't dawn on me that he might be inquiring on his own behalf. I did think that he might be asking on behalf of Chairman Mao Zedong, whose health had reportedly been deteriorating and was the subject of much speculation at home and abroad, and soon after our meeting, I wrote about this in an op-ed in the *Washington Post*. We later discovered that Prime Minister Zhou had learned in 1972, the year of our visit, that he himself was suffering from several kinds of cancer, which ultimately caused his death in January 1976, eight months before the demise of Chairman Mao.

Broader cultural exchange was one of our dinner talk's main themes. Professor Fairbank sat on Zhou's right and I on his left, so we were in a particularly good position to urge him to allow Chinese to visit and study at Harvard. Zhou deflected our efforts as well meaning but premature. He seemed to think that brief visits could soon be arranged but that study might better await the establishment of formal diplomatic relations between our countries. He appeared especially worried that Chinese students might have unpleasant encounters with students sent to America by Chiang Kai-shek's government in Taiwan. He even asked me, as an international lawyer: "If our students debated on the same Harvard platform with students from Taiwan, wouldn't that be implicit recognition of a 'two China' policy and signal Beijing's acceptance of the legitimacy of the Chiang Kai-shek regime?" I assured him that academic debate among students had no necessary international law implications. At that point, about an hour into dinner, perhaps to ease the pressure from Harvard, the prime minister suggested that we take a five-minute break. In the men's room, Professor Fairbank, indicating that perhaps we had put too much pressure on the prime minister, looked me in the eye somewhat sheepishly and said: "The missionary spirit dies hard!"

I had wanted to make one serious suggestion about international law to the prime minister and his colleagues and waited most of the evening until an opportunity presented itself. I said that, having already entered the United Nations the previous October, China should move quickly to take part in all UN institutions, including the International Court of Justice (ICJ). That gave the Chinese officials their biggest laugh of the evening. They thought I must have been joking. Why, after all, would a revolutionary communist government want to participate in a bourgeois legal institution where its views of international law would not be accepted and where it was sure to be outvoted? I explained that the world was entering a new era and China, having been acknowledged as a great power by being awarded a permanent seat on the UN Security Council, should obviously want to play a role in the application of international law by the ICJ. The PRC did not nominate its first judge to sit on the ICJ until 1984. Although Chinese judges have played a constructive role in the ICJ's work ever since, their government has only minimally expanded its confidence in the ICJ's deliberations.

CONCLUDING THE VISIT

After the memorable evening with Zhou Enlai, anything else that occurred during my first trip was inevitably anticlimactic. Yet the exchange of ideas at the dinner with Zhou encouraged me to offer one more suggestion on a very sensitive topic before leaving Beijing. We were meeting the next morning with Professor Zhou Peiyuan, then chairman of the Revolutionary Committee of Peking University, or, as he preferred to put it to us, president of that illustrious university. Zhou Peiyuan, a University of Chicago PhD in physics and a former Cal Tech professor, had already spent a great deal of time accompanying us as the senior person responsible for our visit. His mission was presumably to get acquainted with and hear the views of his fellow physicist and sometime U.S. government adviser, Professor Marvin Goldberger, the leader of our small delegation. But Goldberger had to return home earlier than the rest of us.

Professor Zhou had a sensitive topic to raise with us, even in Professor Goldberger's absence. He surprised Jeremy Stone, a knowledgeable Washington defense expert, and me by asking what we could tell him about the so-called smart bomb that the United States had reportedly begun to use in the Vietnam War. I, of course, knew nothing about this subject and didn't know whether Stone was informed. In any event, we told Zhou that if anyone in our group could answer the question it would be Professor Goldberger, who had already returned to the United States. I'll admit that I was a bit naive in feeling shocked at what seemed a blatant effort to turn cultural exchange into an intelligence operation.

Joan and I found our first trip to China enormously stimulating overall, despite the evident limitations on cultural exchanges in both law and art. I felt that my research, and especially the year 1963–1964 that I had spent in Hong Kong interviewing Chinese refugees, many of whom were former officials, had prepared me well for the visit. Every experience left me with vivid images. Joan, a professional photographer as well as art historian, was more struck by the drabness and austerity of contemporary life and the absence of amenities. After returning to Japan, we took our boys to see Charlton Heston and Ava Gardner in *55 Days at Peking*, a colorful film depicting the imperialist heyday of the Boxer Rebellion, which by coincidence was playing in Kyoto. As we left the theater, Joan said: "That's the China of my dreams."

JOHN T. ("JACK") DOWNEY JR.

In the meeting with Zhou Enlai and in a subsequent meeting with a PRC official, I expressed my concern for my friend and college classmate, Jack Downey, who had been detained in Chinese prison since November 1952 after his plane had been shot down over China on a Central Intelligence Agency (CIA) mission to foster armed resistance against the then still new communist government. I had been trying for many years to obtain his release and had previously suggested to both the Chinese ambassador to Canada (later foreign minister) Huang Hua and Henry Kissinger that this could be accomplished, to the satisfaction of both countries, if the United States would finally acknowledge the truth of China's accusations that this had been a CIA incursion. I had also revealed the truth of the Downey matter in nationally televised testimony before the Senate Foreign Relations Committee in June 1971 and in a *New York Times* op-ed.

Downey's story goes back to the winter of 1950–1951. American participation in the Korean War was going badly due to the hordes of "volunteers" sent by the PRC to support beleaguered North Korean troops. The U.S. CIA decided to intensify its covert efforts to destabilize Mao Zedong's recently established regime and embarked on a quiet campaign to recruit the able new talent required.

Because of some Yale University faculty contacts, the CIA focused on various ways of recruiting students from Yale, where both Jack Downey and I were members of the about-to-graduate class of 1951. Although many classmates were privately introduced to the CIA by informal means, the agency also attempted more open recruitment. I recounted in chapter 2 about my own experience at a meeting with a CIA recruiter. I didn't sign up, but I later learned that twelve in our group showed interest in joining the CIA, although ultimately half were rejected as being "insufficiently rugged." Jack Downey was sufficiently rugged. He had been a 195-pound varsity football player and captained Yale's wrestling team. Less than eighteen months after our graduation, his CIA plane was shot down in northeast China in a mission whose purpose was to exfiltrate a previously dropped anticommunist Chinese colleague.

Two years later, the PRC broke its silence about the case and announced that Downey and his American partner, Richard Fecteau, had been sentenced to life and twenty years in prison, respectively, for espionage.

Ignoring the persuasive evidence produced by the PRC's Supreme People's Court, the U.S. government denied any CIA involvement and issued a preposterous story that the defendants had been civilian employees of the army on a flight from South Korea to Japan and that a storm had blown them off course into China. The U.S. government maintained this false position for almost two decades, despite the fact that it frustrated the possibility that Sino-American negotiations might lead to the American prisoners' release. Under the influence of the Dulles brothers—Allen as CIA director and John Foster as secretary of state—in 1957, the U.S. government even rejected the Chinese government's offer to release all its American prisoners, if American journalists were allowed to visit China. Maintaining the pretense that the detained Americans were innocent hostages whom the Godless Chinese communists had subjected to arbitrary punishment, Secretary Dulles, a leading Protestant layman, claimed that succumbing to PRC blandishments would be "trafficking with evil" and "yielding to blackmail." So Downey and Fecteau were left to rot in prison for many more years.

In 1966, as the Yale Class of 1951 prepared to hold its fifteenth reunion, a group of classmates decided to mobilize an effort to press the U.S. government to obtain Downey's release. I was teaching Chinese law and government at Harvard Law School at the time, so they asked me to take on this responsibility. But there were no PRC diplomats to approach in North America, not even at the United Nations, and Americans could not enter China nor Chinese enter America, so there was essentially nobody for me to approach on the issue. Mao had just launched the chaos of the Great Proletarian Cultural Revolution, and it would be three years before the conclusion of its most violent phase and the beginning of the PRC's effort to seek friendly contact with the Western world.

Opportunity finally knocked when Canada and China established diplomatic relations in the autumn of 1970, and I was able to make several visits to Ottawa to call upon PRC Ambassador Huang Hua. I asked him whether it might improve Sino-American relations and promote the release of Downey and Fecteau if the U.S. government were to tell the truth finally about their case and publicly acknowledge that the two men had been CIA agents. Huang said he found the idea interesting and worth consulting with his ministry in Beijing about. I replied that I would do what I could to get the U.S. government to accept the idea.

I had occasionally been calling on Henry Kissinger, President Richard Nixon's national security adviser, to follow up on the Harvard-MIT policy memorandum that we'd sent to Nixon in 1968, so I knew that the plight of the American prisoners was a White House concern. Yet Kissinger was so tight-lipped about White House plans and communications with Beijing that I had no inkling of what the U.S. government might be doing about the matter.

So I decided to try to create public support for a change in the U.S. position, and an opportunity to do just that came when I was invited to testify on China policy before the U.S. Senate Committee on Foreign Relations on June 25, 1971. At breakfast with Kissinger on the morning of the hearing, he did not ask me to refrain from public discussion of the Downey/Fecteau case, so, toward the end of my testimony, I spilled the beans in a way that evidently caught the attention of committee chair J. William Fulbright. We then had a long colloquy that gave me time to confirm before a national television audience that Downey and Fecteau had indeed engaged in espionage and subversion, just as the PRC alleged. I will never forget the look of shock on Fulbright's face as he took off his glasses, leaned forward in his chair and said, "You mean our government has been lying to us about the case all these years?"

After the hearing, I called on Bill Brown, then the U.S. State Department's China desk officer, to try harder to secure the prisoners' release. Neither of us knew that Kissinger planned to visit Beijing secretly two weeks later or that the prisoners' release was one of the issues he intended to raise with his Chinese hosts. Brown patiently heard my pitch about the prisoners but was more interested in what I might have gleaned from my breakfast with Kissinger. As I began to leave his office, Brown said, with some embarrassment, "Henry didn't happen to say what our China policy is, did he?"

I was disappointed that news accounts of the Fulbright hearing failed to note my Downey-Fecteau revelation, so I decided to publicize it in an op-ed in the *New York Times*. Having recently reported about Downey to our college classmates at our twentieth reunion, I thought the reunion theme might attract interest. I was delighted when the *Times* editor Harrison Salisbury gave the piece the title: "Will Jack Make His 25th Reunion?"

The piece appeared just two days before Kissinger began his secret talks in Beijing, and those talks initiated a long effort by Nixon and Kissinger to persuade the PRC to release the prisoners. Their efforts did bring about

Fecteau's release in December 1971, and Beijing reduced Downey's sentence from life to time served plus five years, but the PRC was unwilling to release Downey earlier.

I suspected that Chairman Mao and Prime Minister Zhou Enlai might be waiting for a public admission of Downey's guilt from the Americans. I published another *Times* op-ed emphasizing that some U.S. State Department officials were privately acknowledging the veracity of the PRC claim, and I continued to advocate for Downey's freedom during my first visit to China, in the spring of 1972, which included a four-hour dinner meeting with Zhou.

But how could Washington deal with this problem in public, especially when Nixon was already campaigning for reelection in 1972? Although Nixon's repeated private requests to Beijing about Downey brought him close to dignified begging, one could not expect any similar public behavior, certainly not before the November election. But after his reelection victory, at a January 31, 1973, press conference—one designed to provide details about the recently announced U.S. withdrawal from the Vietnam conflict, along with the release of all American prisoners of war (POWs) in Vietnam—Nixon dealt with the Downey issue. After many questions from journalists regarding the exciting news about the POWs, one reporter asked whether this also meant the release of Downey.

Nixon, an able lawyer, might have dismissed the question as outside the scope of the press conference or simply not answered, but he replied, "Downey is a different case, as you know. Downey involves a CIA agent." He then went on for several sentences, emphasizing that Downey's release "would be a very salutary action." Kissinger soon made the most of Nixon's statement in negotiations with Zhou and, together with the sad news that Downey's mother was in seriously declining health, it proved sufficient to win his release, on March 12, 1973. Hong Kong reporters dashed to the Chinese border to meet John T. Downey, the confessed American CIA agent who had just been released after almost twenty-one years in a communist prison. "Are you going to write a book?" one asked. Jack replied: "What would it have? Four hundred blank pages?"

Downey could not have imagined that half a century later, China's rising prominence and a wider global concern about espionage, truth telling, and trust would spawn not one, not two, but at least three books based on his experience.

Jerome Cohen in front of the family garage, thinking about his first speech.

Jerry's and Joan's engagement party. Chicago, December 1953.

The Cohen family in Tiananmen Square. Beijing, 2002.

Harvard Law School's East Asian Legal Studies celebrates its fiftieth anniversary and the establishment of a professorship to honor Joan and Jerry.

John T. ("Jack") Downey, one of Jerry's Yale classmates, arrives in Hong Kong in 1973 after almost twenty-one years in Chinese prison for "espionage." Jerry played an important role in securing his release.

South Korean democratic leader Kim Dae-Jung visits the Cohens shortly before his kidnapping by the South Korean KCIA in 1973. Kim credited Jerry with saving his life. He was later elected as president of South Korea (1998–2003).

Famed Philippine democratic leader Benigno "Ninoy" Aquino. After gaining freedom from prison in Manila with Jerry's help, he spent the last year of his life at Harvard University at Jerry's invitation. He was assassinated upon his return to Manila in 1981.

Jerry and his former Harvard student Annette Lu. He engineered her release from prison while Taiwan was still under dictatorship. Annette later became vice president in the Chen Shui-bian administration (2000–2008).

Jerry presents the blind "barefoot lawyer" Chen Guangcheng to the New York University crowd that welcomed his release from Chinese Communist custody, assisted by Jerry. New York, May 19, 2012.

Source: Andy Jacobsohn / Stringer / Getty Images News via Getty Images.

The high point of Jerry's first visit to China in 1972 was a four-hour dinner given for him and Harvard University professor John Fairbank by Chinese prime minister Zhou Enlai.

14

PYONGYANG PERSPECTIVES

Making History in North Korea

One might have thought that trying to learn about communist China, to promote the normalization of diplomatic relations between the United States and China, and to urge American withdrawal from the Vietnam war would have been enough to keep me busy. Yet I was fascinated by the problems of Korea, its history and international relations, and the experiences of South Korea—the Republic of Korea (ROK)—in seeking to modernize its legal system after the termination of Japanese colonialism at the end of World War II. After all, before the Japanese occupation at the start of the twentieth century, the Hermit Kingdom had for centuries been under China's influence, often seeming more Confucianist in theory and practice than even the homeland of the Sage, and the arch example of how countries in the much-debated Sinocentric sphere often paid tribute to the Celestial Emperor in Beijing. The East Asian Legal Studies (EALS) center that I established at Harvard Law School (HLS) in 1965 aimed to focus not only on China but also on all of East Asia, the entire former Confucian culture area, including, of course, Korea.

Almost immediately after EALS was founded, relevant students began to turn up. Some, like Kim Young-Moo, were South Koreans who came to law school at Harvard on their own initiative after studying law in Seoul and were intent on becoming much-needed practitioners of international business law back home. Others, Americans and Chinese as well as Koreans, had done graduate work in history or political science at Harvard or elsewhere and wanted to begin law at Harvard for either practical or academic reasons or both. I encouraged them and often persuaded the cooperative HLS admissions office to let them in, even if their Law School Aptitude Test (LSAT) scores might not have quite measured up to those of the intense competition. Among the students whose credentials and knowledge most impressed me was a recent Johns Hopkins PhD recipient in international relations named Kim Joung-Won, or Alex, as he was known in the United States. Alex had already gained access to some of South Korea's leading politicians, and he gave me some interesting and useful background on the efforts of his country's rising democratic leaders to resist the serious repression of the nation's dictator, former general and then president, Park Chung-Hee.

In 1969, the Asia Foundation asked me to make a short visit to Seoul, the ROK capital, to deliver some lectures on comparative law. This was my first chance to set foot on Korean soil and expand my knowledge and acquaintances. It heightened my interest in learning more about Korea, including the mysterious rival government to the north, the Democratic People's Republic of Korea (DPRK), which no American had yet been legally permitted to visit. After my trip to Seoul, occasional visitors from South Korea to Harvard kept my Korean interests alive, as did international events and new students from both the United States and abroad. One such visitor in the academic year 1970–1971 was the rising South Korean democratic politician Kim Dae-Jung, who was in the midst of an unprecedented effort to challenge President Park's imminent bid for reelection. I liked DJ, as Kim Dae-Jung was known, who proved to be a dynamic and stimulating speaker, very good at amplifying the changes on why South Korea needed democracy instead of continuing dictatorial rule. When DJ asked me to introduce him to U.S. Senator Ted Kennedy of Massachusetts, whom I had been advising on China policy for some five years, I agreed and accompanied DJ to Washington to meet Ted in his Senate office.

This led to a memorable friendship between the two, even though the start was not smooth. Kim and I arrived at Ted's office at a bad time. It was a busy day for Ted; there was a surprise vote on the Senate floor, and Ted arrived late for our meeting, not even having had a chance to review the day's mail. To my annoyance, Ted seemed preoccupied with the mail as I introduced Kim, and I began to feel embarrassed at Ted's apparent rudeness toward an important foreign guest who had traveled from Cambridge to Washington for this meeting. DJ was a formidable figure, however. Sensing the need to get Ted's attention, in a firm voice he said: "Senator, there's one thing you ought to know about me and my election effort. At home I am known as 'the Kennedy of Korea' and I need your help." Hearing that with surprise, Ted looked up from the mail, smiled, relaxed, and said: "Well, we certainly can't let a Kennedy lose an election!" That was the opening DJ needed, and he won Ted's support for years to come.

In the fall of 1970, I began to benefit from the arrival at EALS of Ed Baker. We took advantage of a new program allowing Harvard and Yale law students to arrange a temporary transfer to the other school in order to spend a semester of intensive study in special subjects available only at one of them. Ed's timing was excellent because I was able to place him in an office with Judge Lee Hoi-Chang, who had been sent to America for advanced legal training and who later became not only a justice of the Korean Supreme Court but also prime minister and a three-time major candidate for election to South Korea's presidency. For the subsequent half century, Ed has been an invaluable adviser to me on Korean matters, starting with his participation in our EALS efforts. We cooperated closely with two other very able specialists, Professor Kim Suk-Jo, a human rights expert and visiting scholar at HLS from Seoul National University School of Law, and William Shaw, a Harvard PhD candidate in Asian history with an abiding interest in Korean legal history. We soon became a group focused on human rights, law, and politics in the ROK.

That was the situation when, in the summer of 1971 Joan, our three sons, and I headed off for my Guggenheim Fellowship year of research in Japan. Neither Korea nor Japan was to be my focus but once again luck intervened, as it often has in my life, and this time it involved me closely with North Korea. In this instance, it had to do with a Japanese journalist from the prominent liberal newspaper *Asahi shimbun* whom I'd helped during a visit he'd made to Cambridge some time before. When this journalist heard I had arrived in Kyoto, he asked what he could do to facilitate my visit. I didn't think there was much he could do, but when I found out that *Asahi* had assigned him to cover the activities of North Korea's unofficial political/diplomatic mission in Japan, my attention was aroused. When he asked whether I would like to meet the North Korean representatives in Tokyo, I quickly agreed. So the morning of America's Thanksgiving Day found me at the DPRK's de facto embassy in Tokyo, meeting Kim Byong-Shik who, although nominally second in command for the DPRK in Japan, was actually the mission's leader. Kim was a serious looking, bespectacled, solid character in his forties who greeted me with evident appreciation of what was for him the rare opportunity to meet an American. This was a time when North Korea was increasingly anxious about the impending visit by President Richard Nixon to Beijing slated for the coming February and the impact it might have on the DPRK's relations with China, Japan, the United States, and the Soviet Union. Pyongyang deeply mistrusted all the major powers, including Japan. Having heard that I had been helping to promote Sino-American rapprochement and also had access to some Americans who influenced our Japan policy, North Korea decided that there might be some benefit in our getting acquainted, at least at its remote but important outpost in Tokyo. Our first meeting was an innocuous start to what indeed seemed to develop into something of a courtship. Kim Byong-Shik's principal assistant kept in touch and occasionally invited me and the whole family to a meal in Kyoto with his boss.

Kim Byong-Shik's many publications in English as well as Japanese focused on promoting the *ju-che* concept, an intense Korean independence ideology made famous by the DPRK's maximum leader, Kim Il-Sung. Yet Byong-Shik's personal life appeared to be less proletarian than the leader might have approved. He seemed proud of the big black limousine in which he drove us around, and, like the Japanese industrialists whose lifestyle he mimicked, he liked to play golf on weekends. I believe his taste for what Chinese communists have long condemned as the "sugar-coated bullets of the bourgeoisie" may have eventually created political difficulties for him in his unsuccessful struggle to become unchallenged leader of the North's Tokyo mission. His invitation for my entire family to visit the DPRK may also have subsequently proved an embarrassment. After returning to Korea not long after that visit, however, Kim reportedly went on, many years later, to become a vice chair of the DPRK, a rank just under Kim Il-Sung.

The North Koreans had read my 1971 *Foreign Affairs* article calling for American diplomatic recognition of the People's Republic of China (PRC) and knew that, as the only Harvard specialist on contemporary China then residing in Japan, I occasionally spoke at various public programs in Tokyo. Joan and I had just been invited to make our long-awaited first visit to China scheduled for May 1972. The North had apparently also heard speculation that, if the Democrats were to win the 1972 election, I might follow the Harvard precedent and become the "Kissinger of the next American administration," as another Japanese journalist told me. These were no doubt among the chief reasons why my Korean friends embraced my idea of a visit to the DPRK in the summer of 1972. Before the DPRK invitation came up, we were planning to return home to Cambridge from Japan in July, after the end of the school year. Joan and I were reluctant to abandon our children (again because we had had to go on our month-long trip to China in May that year without them) if the two of us accepted the invitation to spend two weeks in the DPRK in July. But it would be ideal if the children could accompany us on this trip, especially because the only good way for us to get to Pyongyang would be via Beijing. In fact, in those days, Americans did not fly from Japan directly to Beijing. They had to fly first to Hong Kong and there wait a few days for the promised PRC visas. From Hong Kong, one entered China via the border village of Shenzhen, took the train to Guangzhou for several hours, and from Guangzhou flew to Beijing. To go on from the Chinese capital to North Korea meant another delay of several days while waiting for DPRK visas in Beijing and an appropriate flight to Pyongyang. All in all, that would mean a week in China en route to the DPRK, which would give our sons at least an introduction to the country, and we could take another week in China to return to Hong Kong after leaving the North for Beijing.

That clinched my determination to take up the DPRK invitation. Yet my interest in doing so was enhanced, of course, by the excitement of breaking new ground. A dozen years earlier I had been motivated by the desire to be a pioneer, to break new academic and legal ground by becoming America's first specialist in contemporary Chinese law and government. That offered the opportunity to promote a reconciliation between the American and Chinese people too long separated by China's civil war and revolution and the Korean conflict. Now suddenly this quest had created a new chance for adventure and a useful contribution, one that I had never considered: opening up relations with the mysterious and potentially dangerous Hermit Kingdom that was even more isolated from the world community than China.

By the time our DPRK invitation came, which included our entire family, Pyongyang had already taken the first step toward peaceful contact with Washington. It had permitted journalists from the *New York Times* and the *Washington Post* to visit. Our family would only be the third group of Americans ever permitted by both the DPRK and the United States to set foot in North Korea. No American diplomats, officials, congressional representatives, businesspeople, academics, athletic figures, entertainers, or others had ever legally preceded us. This opportunity was irresistible.

Still, there were a couple of unexpected problems, one from the North Korean side and another from right-wing Japanese activists. The North Korean mission in Tokyo surprised me one afternoon with a phone call saying that they hesitated to raise a sensitive issue and would I please be sure not to tell our oldest son Peter, then fifteen, that they had raised it. After some hemming and hawing, it turned out that they were worried about Peter's hair, which, as they had seen on several occasions, was shoulder length, like that of some seventeenth-century European monarch. "We can't have him go to Korea like that," the caller pleaded. "People will think all American youth are debauched," he said. "Please tell him to cut his hair."

I did agree to speak to Peter, whose first reaction to the short-hair request was, as he put it, to "give it to them cold turkey!" But then he got an incentive not to obstruct the trip. The Japanese journalist friend who had introduced me to the DPRK mission disclosed on the front page of the *Asahi shimbun* that I would be going to North Korea in July with my family. That afternoon CBS Television in Tokyo called me to ask whether I was a good photographer and would I be willing to take photos for them while in North Korea. I told them I didn't know the front of a camera from the back but that my fifteen-year-old son was quite expert, as indeed he was. "Send him up to Tokyo," the caller said, "and we'll try him out with Super 8 film in Ueno Park." When Peter returned from this test in the park with flying colors, they made him an offer he could not refuse—payment of $1,500 if they found usable any film he brought back from the trip. As for his hair, although he refused to cut it back to unnoticeable length, he did reduce it to less distinctive proportions.

The problem presented by the reaction of Japanese rightists to news of our departure was less amusing. Threats to our departure began to circulate. The Kyoto provincial police insisted on calling at our house; at first,

I refused to see them, suspecting that they were under rightist influence and might themselves be trying to intimidate us. Finally, one afternoon, while we were sitting in our garden—there were boxes and suitcases all over the living room—they simply showed up, and I asked them what they were worried about. The chief inspector said that there might be some incident that would make it useful for me to contact them urgently. When I asked what kind of incident he had in mind, he gave me a very strange answer. He said that there might be an explosion such as the one that had recently occurred on a Japanese plane at an Israeli airport, and he also mentioned a Japan Airlines plane crash in India. Perplexed more than intimidated, I said that it didn't sound to me that the Kyoto police could be of much use if we should be the victims of such an attack. Nevertheless, I did agree to cooperate with them in arranging the details of our scheduled departure for Hong Kong from nearby Osaka Airport. At their suggestion, we booked our flight under an assumed Japanese name, Nakamura, I believe, and kept secret our flight details.

The North Koreans in Tokyo were furious when they heard about the intervention of the Kyoto police. Kim Byong-Shik's assistant shouted over the phone: "There is absolutely nothing to be afraid of, *nothing*!" In the next breath, however, he said: "Just to be safe, please keep your children inside the house from now on. That will prevent the possibility of kidnapping!" That was surely the most intimidating thing that happened during the hectic days before we left.

We breathed easier when we landed in Hong Kong, from whence we crossed the border into the PRC. While waiting in Beijing for our DPRK visas, I had an opportunity to meet with some PRC diplomats whom I had got to know during the ten days in May that Joan and I had just spent in Beijing on our first trip to China. They took note, of course, of our unusual plan to visit Pyongyang, especially because the Intelligence column of the widely read Hong Kong weekly magazine, the *Far Eastern Economic Review*, had speculated that my former Harvard colleague, the newly famous Henry Kissinger, then President Nixon's national security adviser, might have quietly asked me to open contact with the North as he had secretly opened contact with the PRC the previous year. This was a shrewd but totally mistaken guess. The State Department had actually tried to discourage me from going to the DPRK. When I had to present our passports to the American embassy in Tokyo for removal of the prohibition against travel to the DPRK, the deputy chief of mission, Richard Sneider, dourly warned me that the North Koreans would seek to exploit me. I replied, perhaps too jauntily: "Dick, I'm going to exploit them!"

From the moment our DPRK commercial plane landed, we were in a new, different, and difficult world. It was the latter part of July, and the North was still marking its annual "anti-America" month, which began each June 25, the date the Korean conflict had begun in 1950. Although we were met at the plane by a group of young girls clad in traditional attractive Korean colors and offering us bouquets of flowers, that pleasant first impression soon faded. The guide assigned for our stay by our nominal host, the Korean association for friendly cooperation with foreigners, was actually an official of the Ministry of Foreign Affairs and an affable fellow who spoke English well. But he was under strict instructions to limit our activities.

We were whisked from the airport in three new black Mercedes Benz sedans that dashed through streets devoid of traffic to a remote wooded area 28 kilometers from the center of Pyongyang. There we were housed all by ourselves in a relatively plain but large and attractive villa that was surrounded by a few armed guards toting submachine guns, ostensibly to "keep away the snakes." The villa was isolated but near a lake, and the boys were invited to fish there with the aid of the staff, who were even assigned to put worms on the hooks of the fishing rods provided to the boys. Oddly, I don't recall that we ever went swimming. Our meals were provided at the villa, with an overemphasis on serving, at every meal, rather salty Korean caviar that did not compare with the Iranian or Russian versions. None of the other rather nondescript food had anything distinctively Korean about it, unlike delicious Korean dishes in South Korea and restaurants in Japan and the United States. The largely repetitive diet gradually began to feel oppressive and confining and ultimately became a family annoyance that turned into a political problem with our hosts.

Our immediate interest, however, was in our activities. Before leaving Japan, I had read the reports of Harrison Salisbury and Selig Harrison, the two American journalists who had preceded us to North Korea, as well as those of a journalist from the *Asahi shimbun* who had recently visited the country, so I had some preparation for what we were likely to be shown. Our hosts were surprised on our first day of sightseeing when, after they told us we would visit a public school, I said: "Oh, you mean school 26?" "How did you know?" our escort asked. I responded: "That's where you took the *Asahi* reporter in April." He laughed uneasily, but the same sort of thing occurred a few more times. When we asked to see a farm and were taken there, it was, as I predicted, the Mangyongdae State Egg Hatchery described in *Asahi shimbun*.

Wherever we went, we heard the same sort of "brief introduction" that invariably featured reference to how many dozens of times the Great Leader Kim Il-Sung had visited the place and "taken it to his bosom." The umpteenth time we heard this prompted our son Seth to say: "Mommy, he must have the biggest bosom in the world."

Perhaps the oddest day was our excursion to a park in Mangyongdae, which had been described to us as the traditional home of the Kim Il-Sung family. We were first taken to its museum and noted, as we entered, that a large number of people were exiting from another door. In fact, as we began our tour, we saw that the entire museum had been emptied out, apparently in order to prevent any social contact that we might have had. As we left the museum, we saw many people entering it from the other side of the building. This only became significant when, as we strolled down the path toward our next stop—the sacred place where, according to our hosts, in 1942 Kim Il-Sung's uncle had secretly buried a pistol for future use against the Japanese colonialists, Joan announced that she needed to use the bathroom. This created an unexpected crisis because we were told that we could not return to the museum and that no other building was nearby. Finally, after much discussion among our keepers, they relented and allowed her return to the museum under the vigilance of a woman official.

Almost immediately after surmounting that challenge, a greater one emerged, one that was not so amicably resolved. As we viewed the pistol's sacred burial place, the heavens opened up and a terrific rainstorm began. We had to run for shelter. The nearest was a traditional Chinese-style pagoda that had a roof but was open on the sides and appeared to offer insufficient protection against the sudden winds and rain. Underneath that open platform, however, I spied a cozy, dry room in which a couple of Korean tourists had already found relief, and I urged the family to follow me there. This upset our principal escort, Mr. Li, who shouted as he ran after us: "Professor and Mrs. Cohen, please go to the place above. It's much better." And he herded us away from the dry room below. Of course, the pagoda proved to be as wet and cold as it had appeared, and there was no place to sit. As we stood there battered by the elements, after days of trying to meet each absurd limit on our activities with relaxed bemusement, I lost my temper when Mr. Li came up with some preposterous rationalization of why we were better off than his compatriots below us. I recall snapping at him in a way my children had never before witnessed, shouting: "Why don't you tell the truth for once? It will make you feel good."

That put a temporary end to our groundbreaking Korean-American dialogue. The natural storm passed, and we returned to our isolated villa in a silence that lasted almost forty-eight hours before a truce and sightseeing resumed, with nary a mention of the preceding political storm. I knew that my "misbehavior" had probably ended any prospect of meeting Kim Il-Sung, which fortunately had not been an important reason for my desire to visit the Hermit Kingdom, nor did it alter our hosts' efforts to assure our isolation from their compatriots. We soon after were taken to the theater to see a martial music and dance performance. It was well attended in the orchestra seats below us but we remained on our own in a balcony devoid of other people. At intermission, we were treated to soda pop in a room assigned to ourselves.

Most nights we were left on our own in the guest house, but always with a film provided by our solicitous escort, Mr. Li, who remained available to answer questions. By the end of our two-week stay, we had seen films on eleven of the fourteen nights, so we must have been the world's leading foreign authorities on North Korean films. The DPRK documentaries were heavy-handed and not likely to impress a Western audience. When a propaganda film designed to show DPRK economic progress featured scenes of factories belching black smoke, our children asked our escort why the government would want to display such blatant fouling of the environment.

The feature films were also propagandistic but technically quite impressive, and one or two proved interesting. I especially remember *The Flower Girl*, the story of a famous concert conductor from Pyongyang who, while vacationing in his native village, heard a local high school girl singing in the park and recognized the voice of genius. He provided her a scholarship to the national conservatory in the capital and, after completing four years of study, she made her graduation debut singing before a huge audience. As she took her final bows, not only was she showered with bouquets of roses but also, emerging from the admiring crowd, came her father from whom she had been separated during the chaos of the Korean War many years before.

This heartrending film thus featured two major themes of North Korean life. The first was the possibility and desirability of upward mobility for talented, hardworking people. The movie reminded me of the original version of *A Star Is Born*, the American film that I saw as a child in New Jersey. The Korean film offered a vivid contrast to the themes allowed in Chinese movies of that era, which would never have emphasized the rise of individual talent during the Great Proletarian Cultural Revolution that still prevailed in 1972. The other major theme of *The Flower Girl* reflected the deep, continuing longing of the Korean people, on both sides of the 38th parallel that divides North and South Korea, for the reunification of the huge numbers of families that had been riven asunder by civil war and international conflict.

Although we were comfortable in our remote lodgings so far from urban Pyongyang, we became increasingly restive about our continuing isolation from real life. Joan was particularly irritated. Our hosts had especially alienated her at the outset of our visit when they insisted that she submit to a "health examination" more detailed and intimate than the rest of the family were subjected to. Things became worse when our repeated requests to see Korean artists and their work were rebuffed. We were told that would be possible when American military forces departed from South Korea! Joan, a specialist in Asian art history, finally successfully pressed our hosts to allow us to see some caves that revealed wall paintings by early Chinese occupiers of Korea. Our hosts, who were hypersensitive about Chinese influences and domination, at first had denied that the Chinese had ever occupied part of ancient Korea, a claim that we ridiculed.

Perhaps nothing I said annoyed our hosts more than any references made to China. They also showed distrust of "modern revisionism," which in their parlance meant the Soviet Union, as it was called at the time of our visit. But they clearly sought to imitate Russian behavior in their daily life. At our meetings, men's clothing often featured Moscow-style, dark, double-breasted suits as well as ties rather than Chinese-style cadre outfits. One day, after seeing long lines of people waiting at every bus stop along Pyongyang's broad but empty boulevards, I asked why I didn't see anyone on a bicycle. Pyongyang is flat and ideal for bikes. In China, I said, the transportation problem was alleviated by a massive resort to bicycles. That drew a rapid retort: "You are always talking about China this and China that. This is not China. Please don't forget that. We are a modern people and don't ride bicycles in the city. Bikes are for farmers. You will see them in rural areas."

One had to sympathize with our hosts having to cope with our three children as well as their difficult parents. Ethan at eleven and Seth at thirteen were rather polite, accepting guests. Peter, a more rambunctious fifteen, was more independent and demanding. They all enjoyed the sightseeing, especially our long early visit to the nation's major political museum. The first twenty-nine rooms were dedicated to the history of the sacred family of Kim Il-Sung, which allegedly traced back to his heroic great-grandfather who was said to have successfully fought off the Americans who attempted to sail up the Daedong River to Pyongyang in the 1860s. The boys seemed to catch on immediately and appreciate how political myths were created and nurtured by effective museum presentations.

After leaving the museum, where photography was not permitted, Peter turned his attention to his CBS assignment, hoping to capture images of ordinary Korean life and thereby meet the needs of the CBS film library and earn his handsome summer stipend. Despite his still unusually long hair, Peter at first hit it off rather well with the hosts. In the course of an early discussion about the cost of living in America, they learned that, in Cambridge, Massachusetts, a haircut cost US$2.50. To them that seemed an awesome amount to pay for a haircut, and one of them immediately remarked: "No wonder Peter doesn't cut his hair!" They at least briefly seemed to view him as a member of the proletariat!

Things quickly became more tense, however, as Peter began to snap photos like a normal tourist, and our hosts objected. Trying to reduce the tension, our main escort, Mr. Li, said: "There will be a time to take pictures next week." He flushed when he saw the guffaws this elicited from the family. Joan, herself an eager professional scholar-photographer on the verge of publishing, together with me, a Book of the Month Club volume on China with over four hundred of her photos, was, of course, irritated but restrained. But Peter was determined not to be penned in, despite the inevitable friction his actions would cause, and he would constantly take quick shots that annoyed our escorts. I would even conspire with Peter on occasion to distract our monitors, who were becoming increasingly frustrated. One afternoon, I went too far. Pointing upward, I asked our guide what was the design on top of a nearby tall building so that Peter could focus on some interesting street activity. As Peter began to snap his camera, two of the drivers of the three Mercedes that transported us leapt out of their cars, angrily shouting and gesticulating at Mr. Li, in apparent protest at his failure to curb Peter. We had always suspected that the drivers were minions of the secret police.

This flap led us to make a serious effort to ask Mr. Li to seek permission from his superiors to allow more reasonable scope for photography. They agreed but then insisted that at the end of the visit we had to hand over for their inspection all the film that Peter and Joan had taken. Joan steadfastly resisted, arguing that this would ruin the film, which was Kodachrome that, at that time in Asia, could only be developed in Australia. To our surprise they relented. Perhaps my threat to reveal their absurd restrictions in the speeches I was scheduled to make about the trip in Hong Kong, Tokyo, and New York played a role in the favorable outcome. This was a threat I was destined to repeat toward the end of our trip.

By the twelfth day, we were literally fed up. Eleven days in a row, three meals a day, we had eaten roughly the same food in the same small dining room of our guest house, all by ourselves. This was part of the host's program for "introducing us to the realities of Korean life." Finally, that morning, I protested that we were being subjected to a unique and bizarre regimen, and I warned, that unless we were allowed to eat in a real Korean restaurant together with real people and sample some authentic native dishes, I would have to emphasize this in my speeches and essays about the trip. That broke the barrier, it seemed, because they agreed to take us to Pyongyang that night for dinner.

To our amazement, however, they did not take us to a restaurant that featured Korean food but to the dining room of the International Hotel in the heart of the capital, where we feasted on that authentic Korean specialty Wiener schnitzel! At that point even the children made fun of our hosts. We asked whether there were any Korean restaurants in the capital and whether the hosts were ashamed of their country's poor food or whether they were reluctant to show us to their public. Greatly embarrassed, they vowed to do better on our last night, and they did.

Eager to end our visit with a good impression, they took us that night to a very attractive government restaurant on the banks of the Daedong River. There we dined outside—in isolation, to be sure—on a terrace that had a beautiful view, and we really did feast on delicious cold Korean buckwheat noodles, a perfect dish for a very hot night. This was followed by a dessert of marvelous lemon ice cream, clearly the best I have ever had. We then arrived a bit late for the famed Korean Circus that was to be the pièce de résistance of the trip and that, because of our presence, that night did without the usual political act where clowns mock the United States. I don't know whether our hosts were familiar with Shakespeare, but we certainly felt that "all's well that ends well." Still, we looked forward to our morning flight back to Beijing and, believe it or not, a freer life in communist China!

But bad weather intervened. The morning flight to Beijing was canceled, so our hosts took us to the railroad station in order to catch the daily train to Beijing. Instead of a three-hour flight, this would be a tiring, twenty-four-hour journey.

The train was quite nice, and we had a compartment for the exclusive use of the five of us. Yet it only had sleeping accommodations for four, so we were told that one of us would have to sleep in the next compartment, which was occupied by the departing first secretary of the Soviet embassy, an ethnic Kazakh who spoke Korean, and his Russian wife. They proved to be very agreeable, despite limited English-language skills, and even shared a bottle of Russian vodka with us as the afternoon progressed. We were amazed to learn, as they poured out their grievances about living five years in Pyongyang, that during that period they had traveled only slightly more than we had in our two weeks in the DPRK. Although North Korean urban society of that era was obviously deeply influenced by Soviet Russia, it was equally apparent that the DPRK government had little trust in its major ally, the Soviet Union, even though it evidently mistrusted China even more.

Our week in Beijing en route home seemed like a vacation except for one interruption. The Chinese foreign ministry made an unusual effort to locate us and to arrange a lunch meeting with Assistant Foreign Minister Zhang, who had attended the dinner John Fairbank and I had with Zhou Enlai two months earlier. Speaking in Chinese, he asked me how I estimated George McGovern's chances in his effort to defeat Nixon's reelection. I said that I had been in North Korea and had heard no news at all for the previous two weeks. Then I said that it wasn't clear how much McGovern's choice for vice president, Senator Tom Eagleton, whose selection had just been announced as we left Beijing for Pyongyang, would add to the ticket. At that point, my host looked me in the eye and said what I thought was the Chinese equivalent of "Eagleton has withdrawn." I must have appeared startled, so Zhang repeated the sentence in English.

The whole scene seemed so unreal that I at first thought perhaps this was a bad dream. I pulled myself together and responded that this incredible development, which demonstrated how poor McGovern's political judgment had been to pick Eagleton in the first place, would obviously damage his already weak candidacy even more. Sadly, this forecast proved all too true.

On returning to Cambridge, after giving talks in Hong Kong and Tokyo, I felt that I had to also publish some sort of account of our North Korean adventure. The journalistic reports of Harrison Salisbury and Selig Harrison about their trips had failed to emphasize how circumscribed their activities had been, even in comparison with the restrictions imposed on foreign reporters who visited China. The *Christian Science Monitor*, which unfortunately no longer publishes a print edition, was at that time still a respected print newspaper and was interested in my experiences in North Korea, and I agreed to prepare an essay that would reveal in detail how absurdly limited our Pyongyang exposure had been,

Before I got around to doing it, however, a very able Canadian journalist named Mark Gayn published a marvelous long article in the *New York Times Magazine* that gave an admirable portrayal of his own recent visit to the North, which featured exactly the same type of reception that the North had given the American journalists and my family and me. I didn't want to repeat Gayn's detailed observations in my own piece for the *Monitor*, so I settled for what I hoped would be a reflective overview of the experience. In fact, my family and I agreed that what was really called for was a musical comedy about our experiences, but I thought that might require one more visit. As things worked out, that next visit would not occur for another twenty-five years and will be the subject of a subsequent, slightly more optimistic account.

In the interim, I gave a great deal of thought about how to take the North Koreans seriously, not merely as props for Western ridicule and entertainment. On many occasions, I advocated establishment of diplomatic relations with the DPRK or at least an informal U.S. mission in Pyongyang, but American expert and popular opinion gave no support. I have always felt that the DPRK might prefer close relations with the United States because we were the great power furthest away and least likely to intrude on its often tread-upon sovereignty, unlike Japan, China, and Russia. President William Clinton and Madeleine Albright, his secretary of state, showed signs of receptivity toward this approach, but only at the very end of Clinton's tenure. The arrival of George W. Bush as America's president and his proclaimed "axis of evil" featuring the DPRK promptly put an end to this promising effort.

15

SAVING FUTURE PRESIDENT KIM DAE-JUNG'S LIFE AND OTHER SOUTH KOREAN ADVENTURES

Our groundbreaking family visit to North Korea in the summer of 1972 was highly publicized in South Korea and soon led to an invitation from one of Seoul's leading newspapers for both Joan and me to visit the South. I was committed to return to teaching at Harvard Law School (HLS) after my sabbatical year in Japan, so we waited until the January break following Christmas vacation. The South Korean visit proved to be a memorable ten days because our hosts, building on the accounts I had already made public about our Democratic People's Republic of Korea (DPRK) experiences, wanted to show how much freer and more progressive the South was.

They made an impressive start on day one. Knowing that Joan's efforts to learn about Korean art and history in Pyongyang had often been frustrated by our communist hosts, and although it was a Monday, the day of the week when the National Museum was officially closed, they opened it only for us and arranged a personal tour led by a leading scholar. The next day, they took us on an overnight tour to Gwangju, a revered cultural site several hours from the capital where we were introduced to interesting and beautiful artifacts illustrating ancient Korean culture. We were accompanied not only by the newspaper's publisher, a sometime Republic of Korea (ROK) high official, and his wife but also by several photographers and an especially attractive young woman who figured in most of the photos taken of our activities.

On our return to Seoul, there were meetings with officials, academics, and lawyers; a visit to Seoul National University (SNU) School of Law; a courtesy chat with the democratic leader Kim Young-Sam, whom I had met on my earlier visit to Seoul; an interview with journalists; and more sightseeing. I didn't ask for an audience with President Park Chung-Hee, and none was suggested. My position on the protection of human rights was already known to the repressive ROK government, and my trip to North Korea had complicated the situation even further, so a meeting at the president's office, called Blue House, never crossed my mind. It would have been nice to see the dissident political leader Kim Dae-Jung (who was often referred to as DJ) again, but at the time he was not in the ROK because he was based in Japan, a supposedly safer site for his continuing opposition to President Park, who had recently staved off Kim's notable campaign to defeat Park's reelection.

After our visit, on August 8, 1973, as I was in my law school office in Cambridge, Massachusetts, packing my papers for a long stay in Cape Cod, I received a frantic phone call from Kim Dae-Jung's Washington representative, a man named Lee. He told me that his boss had just been kidnapped from his Tokyo hotel suite and was undoubtedly about to be killed by the Korean Central Intelligence Agency (KCIA). Lee asked me to call Henry Kissinger, President Richard Nixon's national security adviser, who had just been selected to become Secretary of State for Nixon's second term, and ask him to do everything possible to save Kim. I immediately telephoned Kissinger's White House office. Kissinger was at a lunch meeting, and his assistant, Alexander Haig, later to serve as Secretary of State under President Ronald Reagan, took the call. He promised to have Henry return my call on his return to the office. I then picked up my family at home and we drove to Cape Cod. As we entered our Truro house, the phone was ringing. It was Kissinger, who was apologetic about the delay. I said: "Henry, they're going to kill Kim, and there's no time to delay." Kissinger said that my call had been the first to alert the White House of this development and that he would do all he could to save Kim.

I did not know it at the time, but apparently Lee, right after calling me, had also telephoned my senior Harvard colleague, the distinguished historian Professor Edwin O. Reischauer, who had served as U.S. ambassador to Japan during the John F. Kennedy and Lyndon B. Johnson administrations for five years. Ed was revered in Japan and presumably immediately got in touch with relevant Japanese officials to enlist their help because, like me, he was a friend of Kim's and a strong supporter of South Korea's democratic struggle.

I heard no further word about Kim's fate for another couple of days, until the newspapers reported that he managed to turn up in South Korea with a dramatic story of how he had been saved from a watery death by a mysterious last-minute intervention. Kim said that his kidnappers had chloroformed him in his Tokyo hotel and spirited him into a van that took him to the Japanese port of Kobe, where he was then transferred onto a boat that made its way through the ocean between Japan and Korea en route to Korea. In the midst of what the Koreans call the East Sea and what most of the world calls the Sea of Japan, Kim's captors, who kept him in blindfolds and had bound him in chains, forced him on deck and were preparing to throw him overboard. A devout Roman Catholic, Kim said he gave himself last rites and at that moment heard the whirring of what must have been a helicopter overhead. After some noisy, chaotic moments, the plane disappeared, and someone shouted: "Take the chains off him and put him back in the cabin."

I confirmed all this with Kim himself on my next visit to Seoul in late 1973, and he later published a long account in Korean in the monthly magazine of the leading Seoul newspaper *Dong-a Ilbo*. He gave me and Professor Reischauer full credit for actions that saved his life. Yet to this day, I do not know what actually transpired after my phone call to Kissinger nor do I know what Reischauer, who has long since gone to his reward, may actually have done. Kissinger himself has never acknowledged playing a role. His memoirs failed to mention the incident. When I later asked him about this omission, he simply said that discussing it probably had not fit into the book's structure, which I found unpersuasive.

Some cynical Harvard colleagues, who knew Kissinger far better than I and were among many critics who bemoaned the low priority he often seemed to give human rights matters, believed that he may not have done anything to save Kim. Philip Habib, at the time our very able and feisty American ambassador to Seoul, is rumored to have claimed credit for the swift humanitarian action required, reportedly reading the riot act to President Park and threatening a harsh U.S. response if Kim were killed. Whether he did so and was operating under White House instruction is unclear.

DJ's kidnapping drama had a happy ending, but my next exposure to KCIA lawlessness did not. Professor Tsche Chong Kil, a distinguished professor of comparative law from the faculty of the SNU School of Law, had spent the years 1970–1972 with our Harvard East Asian Legal Studies (EALS) program on a prestigious Harvard-Yenching fellowship. Shortly after his return to the ROK in the fall of 1972, President Park declared martial law and replaced the country's constitution with a new charter that guaranteed him permanent rule. This caused an ongoing series of largely student protests that created turmoil in Seoul.

Early in the fall of 1973, after another of many incidents of KCIA beatings, arrests, and torture of SNU and other students, Professor Tsche, a mild and usually nonpolitical person, was moved to protest the KCIA abuses at an SNU law school faculty meeting. Shortly afterward, on October 16, 1973, he was detained by the KCIA and never seen alive again. Four days later, after his body was found at the base of a tall KCIA building, the Park government announced that Tsche had been a North Korean spy and, after supposedly confessing to his captors, had committed suicide by jumping from a seventh-story window. His wife, a medical doctor, was not allowed to examine his body, and no one believed this story. He had obviously become another victim of KCIA torture; the ROK government finally acknowledged this with an ample payment of compensation to his family many years later after the country had come under democratic rule. In the interim, I did my best to publicize this horrendous incident by, among other things, publishing op-ed pieces about it in the *Washington Post* in 1974 and 1975.

Having become increasingly ensnared in Korean human rights issues, I made several trips to South Korea from 1974 to 1978. I recall visiting Kim Dae-Jung during the period when he was at home under heavily guarded house arrest. To avoid further adverse publicity in the American media, the Park dictatorship allowed me to spend a couple of hours with Kim. Kim, it turned out, had evidently used his time in compulsory isolation to work hard on improving his English. Because all conversations within his house were monitored, we sat together on his living room couch and used a Magic Slate, a child's toy writing pad, to exchange messages, lifting the translucent sheet each time we reached its end, which wiped out what we had written. I was amazed how well this gimmick worked.

On a subsequent trip (in June 1978, I believe), after the Park regime had imprisoned Kim, I called on his remarkable wife, Lee Hee-ho. The authorities had denied her permission to visit her husband in prison, and she asked me to help her wage an effective protest. We decided to go to the prison, together with a *New York Times* photographer, so that he could record our vain efforts to gain entry to the prison by knocking on the huge front door. We did manage to get a photo in the *Times* but Kim remained locked up.

Perhaps my most memorable visit to Seoul occurred in April 1974; it did not involve Kim Dae-Jung but his democratic rival Kim Young-Sam (or YS, as he was known), a very different but equally important figure in the ROK's struggle for political freedom. Kim Dae-Jung was not only a devout Catholic reared in relatively simple provincial surroundings but also a dedicated democratic ideologue who believed, with Thomas Jefferson, that sometimes the tree of liberty has to be nourished by the blood of patriots. DJ was a risk taker who did not shy away from active resistance to oppression. Young Sam, by contrast, was the product of a well-to-do, bourgeois urban upbringing who always sought to keep out of prison and remain safe in order to fight another day against the ROK's anti-democratic circumstances. DJ was a brilliant, incandescent public speaker. YS, as he was known, was a more measured yet attractive and sincere one.

I liked YS as well as DJ and, through my former Harvard Law School student Alex Kim, who was a remote cousin of his, came to know him fairly well. I recall having dinner at his impressive residence, and we sometimes met for drinks or a meal at a restaurant. Unfortunately, YS never worked hard enough to use English; this was usually not a problem because we normally had someone present who could interpret. Things occasionally got more complicated if the two of us were on our own because Japanese became our only medium of communication. He was fluent because his early education had been under Japanese colonialism. Mine was far less than perfect, having only recently been acquired during the year I spent in Kyoto in 1971–1972. My deficiency once led to an embarrassing fiasco where YS waited fruitlessly for me to show up for a 6 P.M. meeting, which I thought was meant for 9 P.M.—the difference between *rokuji ni* and *kuji ni*!

What I admired most about YS was his determination to try to use the nominally democratic, highly restricted institutions that the Park dictatorship continued to allow in its attempt to give the impression that South

Korea was a proper ideological ally for the United States, worthy of the controversial American commitment to defend the South against North Korea. President Park's pretense became increasingly difficult to sustain as he systematically tightened the domestic political noose as the 1970s unfolded. In April 1974, when Park promulgated a series of emergency decrees that banned his political opponents from publicly expressing any opposition to his repression, YS sought to use my visit to challenge the new mandate. He asked me to give a public lecture to his Democratic Party's assembled representatives serving in the national legislature.

I was happy to accept this challenging task, but we were all aware that foreigners as well as Koreans were subject to the new decrees and the criminal punishments that enforced them. The problem was how to say something meaningful without violating the prohibitions against any criticisms of the government. It occurred to me that the way to do that was to give a lecture devoted to the topic of why both Americans and South Koreans were all opposed to Kim Il-Sung's North Korean totalitarian system. In my talk, I carefully listed all the characteristics of the DPRK system that were intolerable to a free people.

North Korea, I solemnly noted, did not allow freedoms of speech, assembly, or publication. The DPRK was a police state that arbitrarily imprisoned, tortured, and even killed political opponents. It did not allow free elections, and its ruling party controlled all aspects of government. As I laboriously listed all the North's political sins, my audience, having caught on early to my act, began laughing uproariously. That afternoon was probably the high point of my human rights activism in the ROK.

Some other adventures proved to be no laughing matter. I recall, after a mass protest that was harshly suppressed, taking shelter in Seoul's Myeongdong Cathedral with a large number of dissenters who were relying on the reluctance of the police to be seen as infringing on the country's leading Catholic place of worship. Later, in the same visit, having been warned of a rumor that the secret police were about to arrest me, I hustled to the airport to board a flight to Tokyo at the last minute. I was later told that, had there not been a jurisdictional dispute between competing secret ROK police agencies over which had principal responsibility for controlling me, I would have been intercepted at the airport.

My June 1976 visit to Seoul received the most publicity because it was known that I was on the foreign policy advisory committee working for the presidential election of Jimmy Carter, who was about to clinch the Democratic nomination to oppose President Gerald Ford. I was not an influential member of the Carter team, having joined it late only after my preferred candidate, Representative Morris ("Mo") Udall, did poorly in the primaries, and I was not close to either Cyrus Vance or Zbigniew Brzeziński, who were Carter's main advisers on international matters. Because of my activities in South Korea, however, there were many anti-Park politicians and observers in both America and Korea who hoped that I might play a role in the federal government if the Democrats were to win the 1976 election.

The Park government itself was a bit nervous, especially because there were rumors that mistakenly tabbed me as an advocate of pulling American troops out of South Korea in response to the Park dictatorship. My admired friend, Professor Hahm Pyong-Choon, was then serving as national security adviser to President Park, a position that I wished he had not accepted. He proved eager to meet me in order to learn what he could about Carter's views as well as mine and be able to report back to anxious colleagues who were hoping for Ford's victory. Hahm, a brilliant scholar whom I mentioned in chapter 14, was known by 1976 as "the Kissinger of Korea" after disappointing many human rights supporters by joining the group of President Park's advisers. He hosted me for a remarkably delicious dinner of traditional Korean food at a leading Seoul restaurant.

To my surprise, early the next year, after Carter took office, Hahm came to see me at Harvard. I hoped that he had come to discuss some anticipated liberalization in the ROK dictatorship. It turned out, however, that he wanted me to try to serve as an intermediary between the People's Republic of China (PRC) and the ROK, which was being rebuffed in its efforts to improve relations with Beijing. I told him that I was surely not in a position to do so because the PRC was very unhappy with my 1976 *Foreign Affairs* piece, "A China Policy for the Next Administration," which had advocated far tougher conditions for U.S.-China diplomatic normalization than Beijing thought reasonable. By 1983, Hahm was chief of staff for Park's successor, President Chun Doo-Hwan, and he was one of the many Blue House staff who were killed in the unsuccessful North Korean attempt to assassinate President Chun in Burma in 1983.

My Korean-related activities tapered off during the first two years of the Carter administration. I continued to welcome occasional Korean visitors as speakers in our weekly Harvard EALS programs and to cooperate with Ed Baker, Bill Shaw, and Kim Suk-jo in our studies of Korean human rights problems. I also thoroughly enjoyed working with the increasingly distinguished South Korean specialist on the international law of the sea, Professor Choon-Ho Park, who spent most of the 1970s with our EALS program at Harvard. He and I coauthored an essay on China and the search for undersea oil resources in *Foreign Policy* magazine. I did manage the short June 1978 stopover in Seoul mentioned above in an attempt to press the Park regime for Kim Dae-Jung's release from prison. But my major preoccupation was with the slow process of normalizing diplomatic relations between the United States and China and the related legal hurdles.

Immediately following the January 1, 1979, normalization, I spent a sabbatical semester commuting between Hong Kong and the PRC, and then took what developed into a two-year leave of absence from Harvard in order to establish an informal law office in Beijing and to undertake the legal training of Beijing economic officials. That left even less time for Korean affairs. However, I did squeeze in a brief trip from Beijing to Seoul in late September 1979 that I made at the invitation of the Samsung Corporation, which had caught the then recent Western fever to invest in China and thought that I might help overcome Beijing's political ban on doing business with South Korea.

I spent the next decade immersed in China matters, principally the practice of law designed to improve Sino foreign relations and to enhance my understanding of China's progress and the development of PRC legal institutions. The ROK, to its frustration, continued to be barred by Beijing from participating in China's progress. Yet it became increasingly preoccupied with its own domestic problems. The dramatic late 1979 assassination of President Park by the head of the KCIA introduced a period of political instability and change during which the South nevertheless continued its remarkable economic transformation. The opportunity to cooperate with China finally came as a result of the tragic Chinese communist massacre of hundreds, if not thousands, of protesters near Beijing's Tiananmen Square on June 3–4, 1989. The PRC suddenly found itself bereft of eager foreign investors and decided to relent on its previous refusal to allow South Korean investment. Encouraged by their government, the major ROK businesses promptly seized the moment.

One of the leading ROK conglomerates, the Daewoo Corporation, headed by the dynamic and ambitious Kim Woo-Choong, sought my assistance in its hopes to expand into China. I was fortunate because one of my closest friends and research colleagues at Harvard Law School, former SNU law professor Kim Suk-jo, had by that time returned to Korea and become Daewoo's general counsel and adviser to Chairman Kim Woo-Choong. Thus, when visiting Seoul, I had the chance to become acquainted with the chairman, who was friendly and appreciative of my efforts.

The biggest Daewoo project that I worked on was its purchase of one of Beijing's finest hotels—the Kempinski—from the Deutsche Bank group of German investors that had built and managed it. I had stayed at the hotel several times during the 1980s and liked it, and I was delighted when Daewoo decided to take it on after Deutsche Bank opted to bail out following the June 3–4 tragedy. Little did I anticipate that Chairman Kim would ask me to stay in the hotel's presidential suite on my first trip to Beijing after the purchase. Of course, I accepted his offer, and staying there proved a memorable experience, but largely because I was then suffering from back trouble that made navigating the spaces of such a vast residence more painful than convenient!

For twenty-five years after our family's 1972 visit to North Korea, as my involvement with China and South Korea intensified, my contacts with the North evaporated. Then suddenly, in the summer of 1997, things changed. Tony Namkung, a good friend of my friend and former student Robin Radin, asked whether I would like to join him and Gordon Flake, a young economist specializing in Korean studies, in visiting Pyongyang for discussions that might open economic contacts as well as unofficial exchanges between the United States and the DPRK. Tony was a close observer of North Korea and well connected with the diplomats at its United Nations mission. The visit was scheduled to take place over the long American Labor Day weekend.

The first thing I did was to determine whether Joan or any of our sons might want to join me. My skepticism about their enthusiasm was promptly vindicated. Twenty-five years after the fact, Joan still harbored resentment about what she believed was the DPRK's misogynistic treatment of her, and she wouldn't dream of a second trip. All three of our sons were by then married and too committed to their own families and careers to consider the possibility. So I embarked on my own to join Tony and Gordon in Pyongyang for five days.

The North Korea I found in that brief 1997 visit was a different country from the one my family had discovered in 1972. It seemed a humbler place, much more open to learning from the West and more respectful of the PRC's accomplishments in drawing on foreign trade, capital, and technology to modernize its economic system. Our hosts plainly demonstrated their eagerness to learn what I could now tell them about how Deng Xiaoping's post-1978 Open Door Policy had in practice promoted China's recent success in international business. They soaked up every word of the three days of lectures I gave to a small group of specialists about the relevant roles of legal institutions, legislation, contract negotiations, and dispute resolution.

With the assistance of Gordon Flake, who proved to be a very effective interpreter and knew a great deal about China's progress, I worked hard on these lectures and felt considerable satisfaction with the results of our efforts. My exuberance showed up during the Labor Day phone call I made to my family in Cambridge, Massachusetts. When Joan asked how things were going, I said how pleased I was with the current visit, which seemed far more encouraging than the earlier one. After I said, "They really want to learn what I know about," Joan, somewhat incredulous at my optimism, said, "What have you been smoking?"

That brief 1997 visit led to two positive outcomes. One was commercial. My hosts made it clear that they would welcome it if I would bring to Pyongyang a few of the Western—not Japanese—companies that were my law clients in China in an attempt to initiate business discussions of mutual interest. The second outcome concerned education. With my academic hat on, the North wanted me to arrange training for their officials in relevant international business law and practice. Both propositions interested me, and I decided to pursue them simultaneously.

I knew that it would be relatively easy to find some companies among my China clients that were adventurous enough to want to explore opportunities in the DPRK. I found an immediate sympathetic ear in Jerry Wang, an intelligent American engineer of Chinese descent whom I had worked with during the early days of General Motors' (GM) entry into China. I felt that Jerry, who had left GM for a manufacturer of auto parts, had the patience, optimism, and intelligence required for this sensitive initiative. We soon had a successful couple of days in Pyongyang exploring the prospects for a DPRK company to manufacture and sell auto parts to meet the foreign company's prescribed needs. Although our discussions were preliminary, Jerry formed a favorable impression of the capacity of the Korean company in comparison with his similar early meetings with PRC counterparts. I was also pleased with the apparent ability of the host company's employees to understand the anticipated contract terms. In view of the DPRK's dubious reputation for honoring international trade contracts, both Jerry and I regarded this as an encouraging sign.

My new friends among Pyongyang's economic officials were pleased with this first business visit, but they were eager for more substantial cooperation, especially in the area of foreign direct investment, a far more complex legal undertaking than purchase and sale agreements. They were particularly interested in attracting foreign cooperation that would enhance their energy potential. Having recently represented an American power company that had already done a number of Chinese foreign equity joint ventures in China, I arranged for that client to spend a few days in the DPRK in order to test the potentially significant market there. That proved to be a fascinating experience as we observed our hosts' reaction to our presentation of the process involved in establishing a successful foreign investment in the field of electric power.

Our hosts' eyes almost popped in disbelief as we placed on the conference table the two large stacks of documents required for the conclusion of one of my client's recent China investment contracts. One pile was in Chinese and the other in English, all documents painstakingly crafted in the effort to achieve a common meaning. They had never seen such legal documentation, nor were they aware of the international financial and institutional arrangements reflected in them. It was as though we had come from another planet. The North Korean business officials had appeared knowledgeable and comfortable as I explained Western foreign trade contracts during my previous visit, but they were plainly dumfounded as I recited the intricacies of a joint venture investment. It was apparent to them that the DPRK lacked the institutions and trained personnel to undertake similar tasks.

That introductory experience quickly led the DPRK officials who had been facilitating my visits to the idea that the North needed to improve its international business education and to establish new legal institutions to meet its goal of benefiting from broader participation in the world's economic progress. The first thing that was needed, I said, was to organize a substantial training course in international business law in Pyongyang for hundreds of Korean officials. I offered to undertake the task without compensation and to recruit qualified foreign colleagues to join me in the presentations and the preparation of requisite Korean and English teaching materials. At the same time, I said, we could advise government officials and Korean academics about the development of the necessary new legal and economic institutions.

These ideas, while appreciated in the abstract, were much too much for my hosts to contemplate given the realities of North Korea's secretive and suspicious political environment. Yet they wanted to do something. Unlike the situation in China in 1979, an in-country foreign law training program on any scale was out of the question for Pyongyang. I was genuinely disappointed but not surprised at their reaction and asked what alternative they had in mind. They suggested a modest, short-term experimental seminar to be given abroad for a small group of Korean officials.

I immediately invited them to send a delegation to New York University (NYU) School of Law, where we had ample resources to launch such cooperation. The U.S. government had not shown much willingness to modify its embargo against the DPRK by approving U.S. trade contracts and surely not direct investment contracts of the kinds I had been discussing in Pyongyang, but I thought that there was a good chance that Washington might permit an U.S.-based academic training proposal. But the North Koreans immediately vetoed the idea. When I asked what place might be suitable in their view for our experimental training, we quickly realized that China would be the best place.

At that point they asked me to make detailed arrangements. I managed to persuade Peking University to allow us to use one of their seminar rooms because the Koreans said they would only send about fifteen participants. The university also agreed to accommodate the group in its main building for housing visiting scholars. I also had to arrange a program of instruction and to find the financial support required to pay the group's local expenses plus the costs of any instructors I felt it necessary to bring to China for teaching purposes. Fortunately, the Asia Foundation, based in San Francisco but with an office in Seoul, was thrilled to support this groundbreaking, politically significant development.

This first effort at cooperation was scheduled to last only two weeks, but we contemplated a series of similar periodic exchanges. The North did not ask me to take part in the selection of the participants, but we agreed that the group would consist of relevant business officials, including any specialists they might have on legal aspects of trade and investment. The group that did show up consisted mostly of legal officers of the Supreme People's Assembly and the Social Sciences Academy and economic and trade officials, plus a few other researchers and academics. One of the academics was a professor of international law at Kim Il Sung University Law School who knew more about public intergovernmental international law than the commercial side. A sometime court judge was also present, although he seemed more familiar with criminal law than civil and commercial matters. No practicing lawyer appeared, although two people officially belonged to the National Lawyers Association. I got the impression that perhaps Pyongyang didn't have any commercial law specialists. On the whole, the group proved to be appreciative, pleasant, and intelligent, eager to soak up what they could. There were occasions when they even appeared to share my humor.

Rather than start by bringing in some of my NYU School of Law colleagues or by drawing on some of my local Chinese friends who were experts in the field, I decided that it would be best for me to deal personally with the early days of this experiment. This made sense, especially because the Koreans agreed that their most immediate need was to deal with dispute resolution, an area of international business law and practice that I was familiar with through my work relating not only to China but also Taiwan and South Korea. The DPRK, as I previously mentioned, had a bad reputation when it came to honoring contracts and settling disputes with the relatively few foreign corporations with which it had done business, and any foreign company potentially interested in cooperation would place a lot of weight on making confidence-inspiring arrangements for preventing and settling the kinds of misunderstandings and disappointments likely to arise.

It was most important for the DPRK to become familiar with the standard institutions for formally resolving disputes that could not be settled successfully via negotiations. The two main types are courts and arbitration tribunals, both international and domestic. Arbitration, both outside and inside China, had become the predominant mode of formally settling business disputes with the PRC during the PRC's first three decades, when most of China's international business and disputes involved trade transactions with entities from other communist-bloc countries. When Deng Xiaoping opened the PRC to Western direct investment in 1979, foreign companies had little experience with Chinese courts and no faith in their independence, and Chinese business officials were skeptical of foreign courts, whether domestic or international.

Even less was known about the North Korean legal system. The DPRK's courts were a black box, and no foreign company could be expected to submit to judicial settlement in Pyongyang. Arbitration, however, offered some promise—more, to be sure, if conducted outside Korea, but possibly, in the right circumstances, even within the North. So arbitration became the topic of our first week. I had frequently negotiated the arbitration clauses in many types of contracts and served as an advocate before both Chinese and foreign arbitration tribunals. I had also served as an arbitrator in international arbitration institutions in both China and other foreign jurisdictions, and often gave speeches and published essays on the subject in various North American, European, and Asian forums, especially for business audiences. I was therefore confident that I could launch the proceedings effectively.

Yet language was a problem. I spoke only a few polite Korean phrases, and the Korean group had no one able to serve as an adequate interpreter on legal matters, although one or two spoke passable English. Fortunately, I was able to recruit one of my most talented former Harvard Law School students from South Korea to accompany me in this exciting enterprise. Myung-Soo Lee, after her basic legal education in Seoul, had earned her doctorate in public international law at Harvard; married a fellow Harvard law student from Korea; moved to New York with him; and, at my invitation, had undertaken research with me at my new NYU perch. She seemed an admirable partner for my DPRK venture and indeed proved to be that. Not only was she adept at the difficult legal translation tasks involved, but she was also remarkably skilled in getting to know the DPRK participants, who plainly liked and respected her. The all-male delegation was particularly impressed that a Korean woman could be so accomplished, and Myung-Soo's ability to win their confidence enabled me to develop a reliable insight into the group's aspirations and reactions to our program.

Our "students" were apparently under instruction to return to Pyongyang with plans for a DPRK arbitration law and establishment of a North Korean institution capable of arbitrating international commercial disputes. Myung-Soo and I discussed with them what would be required and offered to review the arrangements that they intended to draft on their return to Pyongyang, including a proposed arbitration law. They indicated that they would later send us their draft law for our suggestions, although this never occurred.

I thought that, in preparing their new system, the budding DPRK specialists should certainly become familiar with the PRC's already considerable experience in this area. I invited a man named Wang Shengchang, the head of staff of the PRC's leading international arbitration organization, the China International Economic and Trade Arbitration Commission (CIETAC), which had long been established by the China Council for the Promotion of International Trade (CCPIT), to join our seminar. To my delight, he proved to be an able, informed, and effective speaker, and the class listened intently and with appreciation. With Mr. Wang's help, we also spent an entire day at CIETAC. It was an eye-opening and exciting experience for me as well as my protégés. Although PRC and DPRK propaganda had very often told the world that relations between their countries were "as close as lips and teeth," political realities were often very different, as I had discovered in my 1972 visit to Pyongyang. By 1998, despite China's two decades of burgeoning international trade, economic ties between the two countries had not proved very successful, and many commercial disputes had remained unresolved. It quickly became clear to me that the two sides actually knew very little about each other's institutions for resolving business disputes and that they had experienced some unpleasant contract problems. I noted that no North Koreans were listed among the foreigners eligible for appointment as arbitrators in CIETAC's international dispute resolution roster. When I mentioned that, both sides admitted that they had had surprisingly few exchanges between their arbitration experts and welcomed more.

All this was a mind-boggling realization for me. It gave me a feeling of pride that I, an outsider to the communist world from the leading, often condemned imperialist country, had for the first time brought these "socialist" neighbors together in a meaningful way that might lead to their cooperation as well as enhance their cooperation with the bourgeois world.

I will spare the reader an endless recitation of the various topics covered in subsequent sessions but simply mention a few of the highlights. A detailed understanding of corporations and corporate law was crucial to dealing with foreign companies, so I decided that this should be the major topic of our next two-week session. How to provide such a comprehensive introduction in a short period would be a challenge. Unlike arbitration, corporate law was not a subject that I knew like the back of my hand but, fortunately, I found a solution to the challenge among my learned NYU School of Law colleagues. Professor Stanley Siegel, a veteran instructor not only in corporate law but also in the closely related topic of business accounting, proved a perfect choice, especially because, unlike many American counterparts, he was also expert in continental European corporate law theory and practice. I had not known Stanley well during my early years on the NYU faculty but loved the Korea week we spent together in Beijing. I learned a great deal from him and enjoyed my occasional injections of my own experiences into the mix.

To top off our corporate sessions, I invited the dean of Peking University Law School to join us for two hours because his specialty was Chinese corporate law. Dean Wu Zhipan proved to be a great favorite with both the group and me. He illustrated his legal points with clever drawings on the blackboard and, having been reared in a Korean minority area of Northern China near the DPRK, even regaled us with a few Korean-language folk songs that astonished us. No other speaker could match that performance.

Impressive in a much more low-key way was the seminar given by Myung-Soo Lee's husband Ji, who accompanied us for a week. Although still young and despite his foreign origins, Ji had already worked in a leading New York international law firm for a number of years after graduation from Harvard Law School and had already become a partner in the firm. He was able to communicate something of the tasks and atmospherics of foreign law practice. What I best recall about his appearance was his initial hesitation and uncertainty about the wisdom of meeting with the group, who were the first North Koreans he had ever met. Ji had been raised in a family who had fled to South Korea from Pyongyang to escape the communists during the Korean War and had been educated amid South Korea's intense hostility toward the North. Although Ji had already overcome the problems of dealing with Americans in the Western educational and business worlds, meeting North Koreans seemed to challenge him for the first few minutes of his presentation. Once launched, however, he quickly inspired the group's respect and illustrated the possibilities to which his auditors might aspire.

By the time of my third series of sessions with the group, whose membership changed little over time, they confided that Pyongyang did not have a law firm to welcome the foreign business community and facilitate international commercial cooperation. They were aware generally of the role that lawyers might play in protecting DPRK interests and, through fees earned from foreign companies, in adding to their country's depleted foreign exchange coffers. But they were baffled about how to proceed. It was apparent that they had come with instructions to learn as much as they could about this topic while in Beijing. So I suggested that they begin to acquaint themselves with both the foreign law offices in the Chinese capital and the local ones. It was easy for me to set up a meeting with the staff of our small Paul, Weiss office in Beijing, and a long afternoon of informal introductory exchanges interested and favorably impressed them.

What the group most wanted, however, was exposure to Chinese law firms. Here, in my enthusiasm, I made a mistake. Instead of continuing to ease them into the learning process by taking them to a small-scale, state-sponsored PRC firm for a first look, I arranged for us to visit one of China's most successful private offices. This major Chinese firm was delighted to have the chance to open contact with its mysterious but potentially important North Korean neighbors.

Our hosts had a large, splendid office decorated with contemporary Chinese paintings and modern, sparkling furniture. The Koreans were obviously taken aback by the surroundings, seemingly too stunned to follow the variety of sophisticated explanations of the firm's complex accomplishments that a succession of well-dressed local business lawyers offered us. My protégés found it difficult to believe that this was a communist institution and these were socialist personnel. Because I wanted the North to set up an international law firm, I regarded the afternoon as a setback.

I quickly decided that I had to do something to encourage the group and thought that it might be helpful to call upon a state-sponsored Chinese law firm the next day, even though that type of firm, initially the first allowed by the PRC regime as it sought to emulate the Soviet legal model, had soon been surpassed once private law firms were allowed to develop.

This visit was a great success. The North Koreans felt immediately at home in the run-down, shabby office. The rug in the entry hall was evidently worn out and stained. The conference room where we were received was small, dark, and cold. In this environment my protégés came to life and asked many questions. One exchange was memorable and demonstrated how far apart the two neighboring communist states were in their legal progress. The head of the firm, in giving an overview of its practice, mentioned that one area of importance was the relatively new subject of helping clients bring lawsuits against the local government. When the leader of our group inquired what this was about, our host explained this was the growing field of administrative law, which authorized citizens who felt that officials had illegally damaged their interests or rights to sue the government in court. The North Koreans shook their heads in disbelief, and their leader confirmed that such a concept was unknown in the DPRK!

One other incident that I clearly recall reflected the North Koreans' growing confidence in me. Toward the end of our second series of sessions, their leaders said that they hoped that I could make time outside the seminar room for the discussion of a sensitive matter. It turned out that they wanted my advice about a dispute that the DPRK had been having in Singapore. A ship that belonged to what we can call North Korean company B had been seized as a result of a lawsuit brought in Singapore's trial court by a local company that was seeking damages from North Korean company A for alleged commercial contract violations. The court had agreed and ordered the "arrest" of the ship on the theory, advanced by plaintiff's South Korean expert on DPRK law, that all North Korean companies had a single common owner—the DPRK government—and that the ostensible formal legal allocation of resources among different companies should be disregarded. Substance, it was claimed, should prevail over form.

My protégés said that their government was outraged at this result and that they had been instructed to seek my assistance. I, too, was surprised at the Singapore trial court's decision because I assumed that DPRK legal and economic arrangements were similar to those in China and other countries that had imported the Soviet legal model, which recognized the legal independence of individual state-owned enterprises. In those circumstances one could not legitimately take away the property of company B to satisfy the debts of legally unrelated company A. I was confident that the Singapore courts, reflecting their country's greater familiarity with PRC law than DPRK law, would never reach the same decision if a Chinese ship were involved in a similar case.

After verifying that DPRK legal and economic arrangements indeed followed the Soviet model, I agreed to lend a hand and overnight drafted a handwritten statement in support of the appeal of the trial court decision that the DPRK was making with the help of a Singapore law firm. I cited, in support of the DPRK position, not only its own formal legal and economic arrangements but also those of China that were similar and pointed out that the Singapore courts would obviously respect those arrangements if the PRC were the defendant. My unconventional expert witness statement made clear that I was submitting it in the public interest and that I was acting "pro bono publico" without compensation for my efforts. My grateful but skeptical students faxed my statement to the Singapore law firm that was preparing the appeal.

By the time of our next series in Beijing several months later, my students reported with some amazement that the appeal had been successful and that the appellate court had endorsed my view and released the ship. They seemed to regard me with enhanced respect, as though I were some kind of magician who could scribble mere words that were mumbo jumbo to them on a scrap of paper and achieve a momentous result. In reciprocation, they then offered me the highest tribute of all, an envelope containing ten crisp, new U.S. hundred-dollar bills. I was flattered and thanked them warmly but firmly declined their present because I had assured the Singapore court that I had submitted my expert statement on a pro bono basis. This seemed to puzzle my students but they finally accepted my suggestion that they spend the money on the purchase of a computer that would enable us to keep in close touch after my return to New York. Of course, I was never notified that the money was actually spent as I suggested, and we did not establish any means of direct communication. More than one knowledgeable observer to whom I have related this story has suspected that the proffered US$1,000 gift had been newly printed in Pyongyang by the DPRK's notorious counterfeit presses.

Myung-Soo Lee and I, both on the NYU payroll, were prepared to continue our DPRK training program into the year 2001 without additional compensation if the Asia Foundation continued its willingness to foot the bill for the program's expenses. But the advent of the George W.

Bush administration put an end to this distinctive cooperation once the new American president declared his great hostility toward the DPRK. I decided to await some future expression of interest from Pyongyang, perhaps from its UN mission. I had long maintained close contact with its deputy chief of mission, who was responsible for coordinating arrangements for our training seminars. Through frequent telephone exchanges, Ambassador Li had also become friendly with Vivian, my able and cheerful secretary at the law firm of Paul, Weiss, who had a charming telephone manner. He seemed eager to meet her as well as get together again with me and invited both Vivian and me to attend the annual April 15, New York celebration of DPRK leader Kim Il-Sung's birthday. The ambassador registered evident disappointment when he discovered that Vivian, although attractive and delightful, was an African American!

President Barack Obama disappointed me by being slow to recover the better relations with Pyongyang that President Bill Clinton had belatedly established. It was not until Obama's second term that the North Koreans signaled that they were interested in renewing our legal training programs. This time, it was suggested, they might accept Hong Kong if we preferred that to mainland China as a site for our meetings. I jumped at that opening because I believed that I could not only secure the cooperation of the University of Hong Kong (HKU) Faculty of Law, a school of distinction where I had much greater freedom to maneuver than in Beijing but could also draw on a more diverse roster of relevant local experts for our program. So we settled on the week of December 16, 2013, at HKU.

I remember our first session very well. It had been a dozen years since we had last met, and most of their participants were new to me. Our program started only a week after the stunning news of the execution in Pyongyang of Jang Sung Taek, uncle of Chairman Kim Jong Un, who had been suspected of overly close relations with the PRC. We worried that, in view of this momentous political bombshell, our delegation from the North might not show up on Chinese soil. Instead of the twelve people on the original list, only eight actually came. Most of them were very young, in their late twenties or early thirties, and belonged to the State Economic Development Commission (SEDC). Earlier in 2013, North Korea had announced its establishment of more than a dozen special economic zones (SEZs), and we anticipated that the participants were hoping to learn how to promote these SEZs quickly, as the PRC had done following the creation of its first four SEZs in 1979.

One of our most stimulating sessions was with the super-lively Shanghai-based American lawyer Gregory Miao Guanghua, who had been leading the successful Skadden, Arps law firm's entry into China practice for over two decades. Greg had become an important player in promoting Sino-American business cooperation, and I knew he would be an effective instructor for our Koreans because I had always thought that he was remarkably interesting and adept in expressing himself in English.

Although based in Shanghai, out of friendship for me and curiosity about North Koreans, Greg agreed to fly down for a long afternoon session with our group, and they loved it. North Koreans became more encouraged by the fact that Greg and his wife had recently visited North Korea as tourists. I also drew on my former Paul, Weiss partner Jack Lange to do an interesting corporate law session. Jack had been using his Paul, Weiss base in Hong Kong to pursue some major projects in China, including the projected Disneyland in Shanghai.

The most popular of that week's local lawyers was Y. J. Kim of the Hong Kong office of New York's prestigious Milbank Tweed law firm. Being of Korean descent, Y. J. had an intense interest in our effort to help North Korea make a successful entry into the bourgeois business and legal world. Speaking fluent Korean, he was able to make direct personal contact with our group and empathized with their situation. Not only was he an effective classroom teacher but he also proved to be a superb host for a lunch in the beautiful Milbank office and also for a grand final dinner at the city's glamorous China Club.

The North Koreans enjoyed their week in Hong Kong, and we easily agreed to meet there for another round during the first week of June 2014, again at HKU Law. Unlike the 2013 group, this one mostly consisted of high-ranking officials of the DPRK working group on foreign investment that had provided the participants in our original training programs of over a decade earlier. The most distinctive addition to that week's program was a long and impressive morning at the Hong Kong International Arbitration Centre (HKIAC), where we were hosted and lectured by its director Teresa Cheng, a leading lawyer-arbitrator. Teresa was thrilled to invite the North Koreans to the HKIAC because she was seeking to increase the prominence of her organization in a highly competitive international field, and she never before had contact with the DPRK. Some years later, as the PRC central government tightened its noose around Hong Kong on "national security" grounds, Teresa was elevated to become the city's secretary for justice, which placed her in the very controversial position of assuming responsibility for the prosecution of the huge number of criminal cases that political turmoil and repression spawned. I was happier with her performance as leader of the HKIAC, and our morning with her filled our guests with admiration for HKIAC's achievements.

This second Hong Kong program proved to be the last of my efforts to train North Koreans. Although the leaders of this group invited us to have our training program in September 2014 with a bigger audience in Pyongyang, Ebola broke out, and North Korea completely closed its borders until the epidemic was over. Unlike the final two years of the Clinton administration, the last two years of Obama's administration did not witness an improvement in U.S.-DPRK relations. Indeed, political tensions grew, and there was no signal of Pyongyang's willingness to resume our legal cooperation. Then, after the brief but failed spectacular political romance between President Donald Trump and Kim Jong Un, things soon became even worse. Since then, because of my ever more intense preoccupation with China matters, I have barely taken notice of the lack of progress on the Korean front. Yet I still feel nostalgia for my involvement with both North and South Korea.

16

COOPERATING WITH EDWARD M. KENNEDY ON AND IN CHINA

China looms so large in our consciousness today—and was so important to the United States even in the 1960s—that it is hard to believe that Senator Edward M. ("Ted") Kennedy's long and extraordinary life as a major American politician and statesman took him there only once. In the crucial period of 1966–1979, as the American people were developing a new image of China and considering a new policy toward it, Ted Kennedy played a significant role, albeit one that is now little understood or even remembered. Some of that role was played out in public, and some of it took place behind the scenes. I cannot give a comprehensive account of this story, but I know a good deal about it because I helped advise the senator on China during this period.

THE 1960S

I've recounted earlier how it all began, with a 1966 phone call from Carey Parker, the senator's legislative assistant, asking whether I would be willing to discuss China policy with Senator Kennedy, who was slightly younger than I and still in his first term in the Senate. That launched a series of occasional meetings designed to outline a new China policy for the U.S. government, which, during the Lyndon Johnson administration, was too timid to lead the electorate out of its hostility toward what was then called "Red China." The impact of the Chinese revolution that had culminated in communist victory in 1949 and of the brutal American combat with Chinese "volunteers" during the Korean War soon afterward was still very great, and any immediate change in China policy became even more difficult as the apparent madness of the Great Proletarian Cultural Revolution unfolded beginning in mid-1966. Secretary of State Dean Rusk became the symbol of the executive branch's frozen policy, intoning ad nauseam at congressional hearings and press conferences that "our China policy is under constant review," a proposition quietly denied by some of the restless China specialists in the State Department. I had a long talk with Rusk six months before he joined the new John F. ("Jack") Kennedy administration, and at that time he agreed that the United States needed to set a new China policy in motion. But because of domestic political considerations, he advocated more conservative views beginning with the time that he had to go before the U.S. Senate Committee on Foreign Relations to seek the Senate's advice and consent to his appointment.

For leadership toward a belated relaxation of tensions with Chairman Mao's regime, if it was to come at all, one had to look to either the U.S. Congress or the president to be elected in 1968. Indeed, Senator J. William Fulbright, the brilliant but idiosyncratic chair of the U.S. Senate Committee on Foreign Relations, had already shown the way forward. In spring 1966, Senator Fulbright had convened the first of several public hearings to urge reconsideration of our government's insistence that Chiang Kai-shek's remnant Nationalist Party of China (Kuomintang [KMT]) regime on Taiwan should still be deemed the legitimate government of China.

In this situation, the young Ted Kennedy saw a need and an opportunity to stake out a public position on a foreign policy issue where he could leave a mark. Despite the prevailing nationwide hostility toward what was becoming known as communist China, an improvement over the usual Red China, Kennedy's Democratic constituency in Massachusetts seemed ripe for change toward China, as did liberal opinion elsewhere in the country. This attitude was fueled in large part by growing opposition to our involvement in Vietnam's civil war. The Johnson administration was seeking to justify our Vietnam debacle as necessary to eliminate the specter of "a billion Chinese armed with nuclear weapons" carrying out alleged plans to gain control over all of Southeast Asia.

In a series of speeches, Ted gradually began to address the key problems that had long separated Washington and the communist regime based in Beijing, problems that, for the most part, continue to plague Sino-American relations today: How to maintain relations with the government on Taiwan while establishing relations with that on the mainland? How to provide representation in the United Nations and other public international organizations for both the government in Taipei and that in Beijing? What to do about the U.S. desire to protect Taiwan against attack from the mainland?

Kennedy initially had little political company in this quest. Only two independent-minded Senate colleagues, Democrat George McGovern and Republican Jacob K. Javits, prominently expressed similar interest following the first of the Fulbright hearings. Richard Nixon, maneuvering toward a second Republican nomination to run for the presidency in 1968, had briefly mentioned the importance of moving toward China in a famous 1967 article in *Foreign Affairs*, but he did not dwell on this subject, either during his 1968 campaign or even after his election.

By the time of Nixon's victory, a group of influential American scholars of East Asia and former government officials were in their third year of promoting an independent, nonpartisan educational organization called the National Committee on United States–China Relations. On March 20–21, 1969, just two months after Nixon took office, the National Committee held its first "national convocation" in New York, a huge event attended by 2,500 people, including as speakers and panelists thirty-five academics, business leaders, journalists, and government officials from various countries. Its purpose was "to elicit new perspectives, fresh insight and interactions of views on United States–China relations." The conference was widely reported in national and international media—press, radio, and television. Television networks NBC, CBS, and ABC covered the entire proceedings, as did some radio stations and networks.

Ted Kennedy was the banquet speaker and did exactly what the conference organizers had hoped for. He made many enlightened proposals for altering the country's China policy and gave them the publicity they had previously lacked. A front-page *New York Times* story by Peter Grose, for example, carried the headline "Kennedy Bids U.S. End Taiwan Bases." The subhead was: "In Speech Here, He Urges Withdrawal as a Part of New China Policy."

This is not the place to parse the details of Kennedy's recommendations but merely to stress his courage and far-sightedness in putting them forth. He urged the Nixon administration to offer Beijing "a clear and attractive alternative to the existing impasse in our relations." He continued, "Every new administration has a new opportunity to rectify the errors of the past. If the new Administration allows this time to pass without new initiatives . . ., it will have wasted this opportunity."

The National Committee convocation, and particularly Kennedy's speech, constituted a challenge to the Nixon administration, which was just beginning to prepare its own quiet approach to China. In the turmoil of the July 1968 Democratic convention following Robert Kennedy's assassination a month earlier, Ted had turned away efforts to persuade him to seek immediate nomination for the presidency, but by the spring of 1969, Nixon anticipated that Ted might be the Democratic nominee to oppose his reelection in 1972. And Ted, attempting to recover from the shock of Robert's death and the recent family and political responsibilities he inherited, did indeed appear to be taking on the new administration in many ways. I recall feeling that Ted was already forming an American equivalent of the British "shadow cabinet" that enables the party that is out of power to present a coherent opposition cohort to the incumbents. In any event, it was beginning to look like China policy might become a major issue in the 1972 presidential campaign.

THE 1970S

All this presidential excitement over a third Kennedy brother ended, of course, with Ted's tragic 1969 accident at Chappaquiddick Island, Massachusetts. By the time Ted was ready to take up foreign policy again in late 1970, the most violent days of the Cultural Revolution were ending, and China was showing signs of wanting to break out of its largely self-imposed isolation. In the spring of 1971, while the Nixon administration was quietly negotiating finishing touches on its plan to send Henry Kissinger, the president's special assistant for national security, to Beijing on a secret trip to break the ice with China's leaders, Ted decided that he wanted to visit China as soon as possible. He obviously hoped to get there before Nixon or any U.S. government official or any other American politician made the trip. I suggested this to China's ambassador to Canada, Huang Hua, whom I went to see in Ottawa from time to time, and he welcomed the senator to meet him to get acquainted and discuss possible arrangements.

Ted agreed to meet Huang, but before we pinned down the date it was announced in July 1971 that Kissinger had just made the sensational secret trip to Beijing that paved the way for the very public Nixon visit to China for February 1972. Although that news took some of the gloss off our project, we decided it was still worth the trip to Ottawa to see whether Ted might get to the Promised Land before Nixon. So in September, we made what we hoped would be our own, much more modest secret trip to the Canadian capital.

Once in Huang Hua's office, we began a several-hour discussion that focused on Taiwan. Ted had always been careful to keep Taiwan's security in mind, even while advocating U.S. recognition of the People's Republic of China (PRC) as the sole legitimate government of China and establishment of formal diplomatic relations with it. He did not believe that withdrawal of U.S. recognition and diplomatic relations from the Chiang regime on Taiwan should lead to reunification of the island with the mainland unless the majority of people on Taiwan made clear this was their wish. Nevertheless, we kept pressing Ambassador Huang to arrange for us to visit China before the end of 1971. He kept pressing the senator to issue a public statement that Taiwan was legally part of China and should be returned to the PRC. That would have strengthened Beijing's position in the behind-the-scenes bargaining that was taking place between the Nixon administration and the PRC government over what the U.S. position would be on this key question. It would also have put public pressure on the administration to recognize Beijing's claim to Taiwan.

Ted and I both had the impression that, if he yielded to Huang's request, it might have become possible for us to make a China trip that fall. Indeed, as Huang signaled an end to a long afternoon by asking Ted to "summarize his position on Taiwan," Huang put his hand inside his suit jacket as though he was preparing to take the necessary visas from his inside pocket. But, to my relief, Ted did not abandon his concern for the freedom of Taiwan's people. I then explained to the disappointed ambassador that Ted had to weigh his statements very cautiously, especially because he might someday become America's president.

Nixon's spectacular visit to China the following February was a master stroke for U.S. foreign policy and a magnificent presidential reelection maneuver that took the China issue away from his Democratic rival, George McGovern. But the Watergate scandal subsequently diverted Nixon from completing the task of normalizing relations with China in his second term, and the Gerald Ford administration, although it kept negotiations going, made little progress in persuading the PRC to show some flexibility on the many controversial questions involved.

In 1977, the new Democratic president, Jimmy Carter, renewed the normalization effort, but negotiations with Beijing proved to be even more difficult than before. Three issues were especially challenging. In normalizing relations, what position would the United States take about the legal status of Taiwan? After normalization, would Beijing allow the United States to maintain some form of official diplomatic representation in Taiwan, such as a consulate or a liaison office? And would China tolerate a continuing U.S. commitment to defend Taiwan and to sell weapons to its derecognized government?

Once again, Ted took the initiative to spur the normalization effort. On August 15, 1977, just days before Secretary of State Cyrus Vance was to set forth on a trip to resume the negotiations in Beijing, Ted gave another major China speech, this one before the World Affairs Council in Boston, Massachusetts, his home turf. The *New York Times* called it "the most forthright and detailed proposal made by a politician who is influential with the Carter Administration." Ted's speech was actually a blatant challenge to Carter and Vance, as well as to the PRC, to show more flexibility in their bargaining. The *Times* headline was: "Kennedy Calls for Diplomatic Split with Taiwan and Ties with China." Ted's theme was that we could continue to protect Taiwan by unofficial and informal means while formalizing relations with the real China. Ted not only "submitted a precise 'agenda' for Mr. Vance on his Peking visit," as the *Times-Dispatch* put it, but he also proposed a deadline for normalization, calling for the exchange of embassies "no later than 1978." He increased the heat on the administration by announcing a plan to submit a resolution to Congress containing his proposals the following month! By this time, Huang Hua had returned from his post as the PRC's first representative at the UN to become China's foreign minister and, not coincidentally, an invitation finally came for Ted to visit China—and not only Ted but whatever members of his family he wished to accompany him, as well as staff, journalists, and advisers. Until then, throughout the Nixon and Ford administrations, no Kennedy had been allowed to visit China because the PRC government felt that the need to cooperate with those in power in Washington had made a Kennedy visit "too sensitive" for China's leaders.

On Christmas Day, 1977, eleven Kennedy family members, two Senate staffers, two *Boston Globe* reporters, and yours truly left for two weeks in China, to be followed by a week in Japan meeting that country's leaders. I will mention later in this chapter some of the many interesting and humorous aspects of a major American politician's venture in early cultural exchange with the PRC bureaucracy. Most immediately, however, I want to focus on Ted's virtually unknown contribution to normalization—not his public stimulus of our own people and government but his private prodding that helped to convince China's leaders that, unless they too showed some willingness to compromise on their conditions for normalization, it simply would not happen.

In our hard-won ninety-minute meeting with Deng Xiaoping, who was suffering from flu, and in conversations with other Chinese leaders, Ted made it clear that, whatever the differences in details among the various American proposals for normalization, there was broad and firm unanimity among the public and its representatives that Taiwan had to be protected. He said the Chinese side, as well as the American side, had to be imaginative and practical in devising a formula that would enable us to establish formal and full diplomatic relations. My presence as his only outside adviser signaled what his position would continue to be. The Chinese government had loved my 1971 article in *Foreign Affairs* calling for recognition of Beijing as the sole legal government of China and establishment of formal diplomatic relations with it. But my 1976 sequel detailing the terms required for this "normalization" of relations had angered them, as Huang Hua had told me in no uncertain terms while he was still at the UN.

Although Ted's memoir modestly notes that "the trip produced no significant breakthroughs," this Kennedy initiative undoubtedly helped to restore momentum to Sino-American negotiations. On December 15, 1978, within the deadline proposed by Ted the previous year, the two governments announced their establishment of diplomatic relations as of January 1, 1979. Despite the fact that Confucius, now restored to heroic status in China, was at that time still being reviled by China's media as the embodiment of benighted feudalism, the normalization agreement was in the best Confucian tradition of settling disputes through mutual yielding by the disputants. Although the people and the government in Taiwan were understandably concerned that the Kennedy trip might support an impending sacrifice of Taiwan on the altar of America's broader strategic interests, history has demonstrated that normalization, including the U.S. Taiwan Relations Act, which Kennedy joined in sponsoring and was passed soon after his trip, has provided adequate protection for the island, at least until now.

To be sure, the problems of continuing American arms sales to Taiwan, of the scope of "unofficial" American contacts with the island, and of determining its relationship to the mainland have yet to be solved and may at any time upset the delicate balance among Washington, Beijing, and Taipei. Yet Ted was correct in his assurance to Taiwan that "the combination of improved Sino-American ties, continuing nongovernmental relations with Taiwan (including access to defensive arms) and Washington's statement of interest in a peaceful settlement of the island's future will give Taiwan increased security and prosperity." We, the Chinese, and the people on Taiwan should be grateful for his vision, statesmanship, and perseverance.

So many interesting things occurred during our 1977–1978 trip to China that a memoir seems the appropriate place to share at least some of them. One impression concerns our effort to visit a university in order to learn about the then recent resumption of education following Mao's death. Our handlers were evidently under strict leadership instruction not to allow Ted the opportunity to set foot on a university campus under any circumstances. The leaders were apparently convinced that Ted, if given the chance, would seek to harangue a large body of students by ringing the bells on themes of freedom, democracy, and the rule of law the way his older brother, the late Bobby Kennedy, had done in a well-publicized speech at Moscow State University over a decade earlier.

Our first stop was Shanghai, where we were told that there were too many other scheduled activities to permit a university visit. We were assured that such a visit would be possible in Beijing, our next stop. But, lo and behold, on arrival in Beijing we were told that the local universities were all closed because it was early January and everyone there was on

New Year's holiday, which we later learned was simply untrue. Our hosts said not to worry about the opportunity to visit a university because our third stop would be Changsha, the capital of Hunan Province, which had as many as eight universities.

When we arrived there and asked to visit Hunan University, we were told that a visit there was out of the question but that there were sixteen universities in Guangzhou, which was to be our next and last stop on the trip. At that point, my negotiations with our hosts—as the China specialist in our delegation I had the principal burden of these negotiations—began to become testy. I remember saying to my main interlocutor: "Mr. Qian, what difference does it make whether a city has eight universities or sixteen if we are not permitted to visit one of them?" I told him that by then we were convinced that they were giving us the runaround and that not only would the senator have to report this in various forums on leaving China but that the two Boston journalists who were accompanying us were beginning to catch on that the trip was not going smoothly. I emphasized that, in speeches I myself was scheduled to give about the trip in Hong Kong, Tokyo, and New York, I would ridicule their obstruction.

This pressure made an impact that led to an unforgettable scene. The next day we were taken to an attractive hilltop in a park that was near Hunan University. With some satisfaction, our escort, gesturing toward the university that was vaguely visible in the distance, said: "You wanted to see the university, and there it is!" He was unhappy when our group openly joked about this gambit, but that did not deter him from the next programmed maneuver. He led us on a stroll of about fifty yards to a nearby grassy knoll where, to his feigned surprise, we stumbled upon what we were told were several "worker, peasant and soldier university students." They happened to be dressed in colorful minority nationality costumes and were playing an assortment of traditional Chinese musical instruments while ostensibly taking a break from their studies. "If you want to meet university students," Mr. Qian said, "here is your opportunity."

At that point, I insisted even more vigorously that the senator be given an opportunity to meet with real university students. I said that, if he didn't, he would regard the trip as a failure. This was something of an exaggeration because, for Ted, the key to the trip was the already accomplished meeting with Deng Xiaoping. Yet my protest finally produced a serious response. We were told that, after returning from the next day's all-day visit to Chairman Mao's birthplace nestled several hours away in the fertile countryside, where tens of thousands of farmers were working largely by hand, the senator would be permitted to address a large group of university students, not at the university but in a suitable building. Indeed, that did happen, and it proved to be a serious and interesting occasion, although there was no Chinese publicity about it.

About seventy young Chinese, mostly men who appeared to be in their early twenties, were assembled in a simple lecture hall to listen to Ted's talk. They wore ordinary clothes—not colorful minority nationality garb—and may well have been students recruited from the newly reopened Hunan University. Ted's talk was conventional "hands across the sea" goodwill saluting the informal opening of PRC-U.S. relations and emphasizing the importance of moving forward to a broader and more formal engagement. There was no indication of an intent on his part to court publicity in China or abroad through bold statements about the importance of political freedom, human rights, and the rule of law.

There had been no significant question-and-answer period following Ted's Hunan University lecture. So the next day, as we traveled to Guangzhou, I pushed for an on-campus exchange of ideas with students at any of its sixteen universities. But our host resisted this effort. As a supposed compromise, they did arrange for a brief and uninteresting visit to the home of an elderly gentleman they claimed was a Guangzhou University professor.

At the time, Ted was the chair of the U.S. Senate Committee on the Judiciary and wanted, of course, to learn something about the PRC's legal system, which had been shattered by the decade-long Cultural Revolution and was being revived. This was of especial interest to me, as our hosts well knew, and they were aware of the book I had published on PRC criminal justice in 1968 and my other publications. But we were unsuccessful in our efforts to see a Chinese court in action. Our hosts did give us, however, the sop of seeing a traditional Chinese opera that concerned the operation of the imperial legal system. *Fifteen Strings of Cash* (*Shiwu guan*) had been forbidden during the Cultural Revolution when Chairman Mao's wife Jiang Qing presided over artistic life and only permitted the performance of six "revolutionary operas," all concerned with contemporary tales. I was fascinated by this imperial performance because it featured the struggle of an honest judge to resist the blandishments of a corrupt political environment. Ted also enjoyed it. I was a couple of seats away, and he said to me in a stage whisper that was audible to our hosts: "This is the closest we're going to get to a Chinese court!"

After some persistent badgering, we did manage to visit a Shanghai prison, and that produced one memorable incident. As we were being led through a workshop filled with perhaps fifty or more bemused prisoners who looked up from their labors at the foreign group striding past, Ted, hoping to have some unfiltered personal contact, suddenly stopped and asked the closest prisoner why he was being punished. Without the slightest hesitation, the prisoner said that he had negligently driven his truck off a bridge and killed nine people. In light of Ted's 1969 road tragedy on Chappaquiddick Island that had killed his female companion and his chances for the presidency, the prisoner's response had a stunning effect on our group, which included the two Boston journalists who accompanied us. We swiftly moved on, wondering whether our hosts on this occasion had outdone Potemkin in their anticipation and arrangements.

Before closing this chapter on Ted Kennedy and our China visit, I should recount some amusing details of our group's exciting visit with Deng Xiaoping. The meeting with Deng had been agreed in principle in advance of the trip, but on arrival in Beijing, his handlers told us it would be difficult to arrange because he was suffering from the flu. There were also hints that Deng was worried that, if he met with the first of America's 100 U.S. senators, he would soon have to meet all the others. Ted really wanted this meeting. At one point, he looked me in the eye more earnestly than usual and said that, if we didn't have this meeting, he would regard the whole trip as a failure. That put a lot of pressure on me. Although I had not negotiated the trip, in China I had become the principal instrument of communication with our hosts.

The challenge was how to persuade our hosts in the few days we had scheduled in Beijing. I decided to turn the vice of PRC monitoring of communications into a virtue, as I had done on earlier trips when our hosts had proved difficult. I convened a meeting of Ted and his staff in the living room of the large suite that he and his wife Joan shared. I made sure that our voices would be loud enough to assure we could be overheard, even via the still relatively primitive equipment the PRC had for bugging hotel rooms. For the benefit of our hosts, we had a long and frank discussion of all the disappointment, embarrassment, and other negative effects that failure to meet Deng would cause. In addition, two nights in a row I got on the phone to Joan back in Cambridge, Massachusetts, to tell her how unhappy I was with our hosts' reluctance to produce Deng, who had by then emerged as China's new leader. I recited all the reasons why not meeting Deng would adversely affect the mobilization of American public support for the normalization of U.S.-China relations. Having been with me on previous visits to China, my loyal spouse knew exactly what I was up to and went along with the game. Our hosts fortunately relented at the last minute and told us the meeting would indeed take place, and in the end Deng did greet the entire group, including the younger members of the family and then, after the usual group photo, held a serious discussion with the adults.

We spent a week in Japan after China, a visit that I had strongly recommended given Japan's growing prominence, the importance of China as well as the United States to Japan, and Tokyo's increasing sensitivity to America's budding romance with the PRC. We were cordially received by the mayor of Hiroshima, which was our first stop in Japan, because we wanted to demonstrate concern for the ever greater threat of nuclear war. The high point of the entire visit was a long-scheduled meeting with Prime Minister Eisaku Sato, who could not have been friendlier during the hour Ted, staffer Jan Kalicki, and I spent with him. We then returned to Washington, full of good stories and hopes for a peaceful future.

17

STIMULATING CHINA'S NEW LEGAL SYSTEM

The Coudert Years

In the summer of 1960, when Joan and I discussed whether I should seize the opportunity to study China rather than pursue a more conventional academic path, she pointed out that specializing in Chinese law meant that I would be selecting one area of law where few businesses or law firms would be likely to consult me. And, indeed, the only professional lawyer's fee that I earned during those early years was less than $1,000 for giving a 1962 opinion on a divorce dispute that involved the legal system of the Chiang Kai-shek government, which had preceded Chairman Mao's regime.

This situation began to change, however, because of the excitement generated by President Richard Nixon's spectacular 1972 visit to China. American business immediately saw the prospects created by the anticipated "opening" of the People's Republic of China (PRC). I had suddenly become professionally relevant, and Charles Stevens, one of my best Harvard students of the 1960s, recognized this. Charlie, who had majored in Japanese studies at Princeton before entering the Harvard Law School (HLS) class of 1966, had taken my courses and then joined Coudert Brothers, one of the traditional and most prestigious American international law firms. Charlie had already begun to mobilize a young group of colleagues to build a practice relating to Japan. Now he was quick to see the importance of the opening of China to a future East Asian practice, and he contacted me with the thought of enlisting me in this effort.

Charlie sensed that I might be interested in affiliating with his ambitions because Coudert's work would give me reliable insights into practical aspects of my law teaching and also provide my students specializing in Asian studies with a source of postgraduation employment that was then all too rare. I liked Charlie, admired his vigor and vision, and saw the desirability of cooperation. The problem was how to do it. Harvard, unlike a number of other law schools, did not permit faculty to form an exclusive affiliation with a law firm, which is the arrangement Coudert would have preferred. I was also then completing work, with my learned research associate Hungdah Chiu, on our massive two-volume documentary study *People's China and International Law*, and my extracurricular energies were largely absorbed by participating in the efforts to "normalize" relations with China. But I did agree to become a nonexclusive consultant to Coudert. I was to be compensated for time spent, which, although not remotely as beneficial as an exclusive counsel arrangement might have been, was nevertheless welcome.

Charlie lost no time in bringing me into action. During the January 1973 winter teaching break, he asked me to visit Tokyo, Hong Kong, and Singapore to explore prospects for establishing Coudert offices in those places. For a foreign law firm to open an office in an important Asian city in that era was no easy task. Local lawyers, many of whom had done graduate training at leading law schools in the West, did not welcome American lawyers. Japan, which had "grandfathered" a few small American firms that had been established during the U.S. occupation of the country, resisted any further intrusions into the market for legal services. The British colonial authorities in Hong Kong had just grudgingly admitted the first non-UK firm, a tiny outpost of an impressive Toronto firm. Singapore had allowed no foreign firms.

After making some preliminary courtesy calls on Japanese officials and law firms to assess the climate there, I flew to Hong Kong, where Coudert seemed to be making progress in its application to become the first American firm to set up an office. I was glad to renew my friendship with various officials, law firms, and corporate counsel that dated back to the happy year my family and I had spent in Hong Kong in 1963–1964 as I pursued research on the administration of criminal justice in China for my first book. I made it clear that I was lobbying for the entry of American firms generally, not only for Coudert. I believe my arguments proved helpful, and it soon became possible for not only Coudert but also others to set up shop, although they were authorized to deal only with foreign-related matters, not local ones.

Singapore was the most interesting stop on my route. I had become friendly with its brilliant prime minister (PM), Lee Kuan-Yew, during his month-long stay at Harvard following the 1968 U.S. presidential election, and he had warmly hosted Joan and me when we briefly visited Singapore the following summer. On this 1973 trip, I indicated that my mission was to persuade him to open Singapore as a base for foreign, especially U.S., law firms. Lee, who as a Cambridge student had earned a "double first" that had included law, proved to be an appreciative listener and questioner. He told me of the opposition of the local bar to foreign competition, but he seemed ready to countermand it in order to bring in the more high-powered and experienced international firms that would make Singapore a more attractive place for the growing number of foreign businesses that were seeking to establish regional headquarters in Asia. He also thought that foreign competition would educate and stimulate the rather sleepy and complacent local lawyers and offer them greater employment possibilities. I left our meeting with an optimistic feeling and shortly afterward was informed by my friend, Attorney General Tan Boon Teik, that the PM had decided to move ahead cautiously, admitting foreign firms one by one as needed, and that Coudert Brothers would be the first to be favored!

Although Coudert established offices in Hong Kong and Singapore and a few years later in Tokyo, I did little actual work for any of those offices until Washington and Beijing formally normalized relations on January 1, 1979. Once that occurred, my China practice and broader cooperation with the PRC began to soar. I was due for a sabbatical in the spring semester of 1979 and had long planned to spend it in Hong Kong, living a quiet life and occasionally dropping into the Coudert office to catch up on China matters with Owen Nee, an able, young Columbia Law School graduate, and his talented wife Amber, who was working as a paralegal in the Coudert office. I felt in need of a rest and a lot of reading and, having just been in Hong Kong and Singapore before Christmas to give some speeches, I didn't want to make more outside commitments, even though I knew normalization was stirring up widespread interest. Events, however, suddenly changed everything.

Not long after our early January arrival in Hong Kong, I was awakened one morning by a telephone call from Detroit, Michigan. It was from a fellow named Bob Rothman, who said he was assistant general counsel at General Motors (GM) and needed my help on GM's big plans for a joint venture investment in China. He said that he had met me over a decade earlier when I gave a lecture at the University of Michigan, where he was then a graduate student in Chinese politics before entering law school. During that first phone call with Bob, I cautioned him that it was far too early to think about substantial investments in China; GM nonetheless became my first significant client, a great way to launch a new stage in my career.

Other Western companies soon contacted me, but even more exciting was my first important opportunity to cooperate with the PRC on legal matters. In early December 1978, my distinguished Harvard colleague professor Oliver Oldman, who was director of the HLS International Tax Program (ITP), had dropped by my office. He was holding a letter just received from the PRC's national tax commissioner. It was a response to the annual invitation the ITP had sent out every autumn since 1954 to the ministries of finance of most countries inquiring whether they might want to send an able, English-speaking tax specialist to Harvard for a year of advanced training. For the previous twenty-three years, the ITP had never received a response from China. Now Tax Commissioner Liu Zhicheng, soon to be my friend, had written back, noting that the PRC had been considering the invitation for some time! How, he asked, could the PRC belatedly initiate cooperation with Harvard?

Oldman and I decided that it would be best to inform Liu that I would be taking up residence in Hong Kong within a few weeks and that I would be happy to hear from him at that time. Liu soon replied that he would welcome me to visit Beijing as a guest of the Ministry of Finance for a week in order to discuss cooperation, and we agreed to meet in early February.

The Ministry of Finance (MOF) and the National Tax Bureau were under great pressure from other central agencies to produce international tax legislation that would satisfy the needs of the foreign investors that were beginning to clamor for opportunities in China. The PRC was especially eager to entice U.S. oil companies to invest in oil exploration and development in the promising waters of offshore China. The companies were eager to do so, but only if they could obtain U.S. tax credits for every dollar they paid in PRC taxes. To obtain such credits, the U.S. Department of the Treasury had to certify that China's tax legislation met U.S. standards for creditability. So China's MOF and National Tax Bureau were scrambling for an adequate response to the demand for new legislation. In the absence of far greater knowledge than they possessed about international taxation, the PRC agencies felt stymied. That is why Commissioner Liu finally answered HLS's twenty-fifth invitation.

After conveying the urgency of the situation, Commissioner Liu asked for our advice. I expressed Harvard's willingness to cooperate. To meet the immediate needs, I proposed that the ITP offer an intensive course to a large number of the most relevant PRC tax officials. I said that I would assemble a group of leading U.S. tax experts to form the teaching staff. I also inquired whether any specialists from the rival Republic of China (ROC) government on Taiwan, which had a great amount of international tax experience, might be welcome to join us.

Commissioner Liu responded to these suggestions with enthusiasm. He offered to convene 125 officials for a one-month session of lectures. He also offered to make a sixtyish MOF official known as "Old Wang," who spoke excellent English, responsible for working with us to translate the necessary teaching materials, which would take several months. Based on this agreement, I went into action on returning to Hong Kong. As expected, the authorities in Taiwan unfortunately rejected the opportunity to assist "those Communist bandits in Beijing." But U.S. experts were eager to help and to make their first visits to China. In addition to ITP Director Oldman I quickly enlisted Professor Stanley Surrey, perhaps the most distinguished tax law expert in the United States, and other leading specialists from Yale, Columbia, New York University (NYU), and the University of Connecticut. With their aid, the process of selecting materials for translation got under way.

By all accounts, our July session, held at Liu's suggestion in the northeastern port city of Dalian, was an enormous success. Before it opened, the "students"—tax teachers as well as officials—had already met there for two weeks of orientation conducted by Old Wang in order to prepare them for what was to be a complex and unprecedented mass exercise in communist "thought reform" of a new type. Instead of drilling them in the usual ideological precepts of Marxism-Leninism and Chairman Mao's Thought, they were being introduced to the mysteries of "tax credits" and "tax sparing." We then proceeded to expose them to four solid weeks, six days a week, eight hours per day, of dense lectures designed to facilitate the drafting of the urgently needed legislation.

The Dalian experiment and the meetings that we held to organize it did a great deal to solidify relations with Chinese tax officials, to whom I remained close for the next four years as the PRC assembled the elements of a comprehensive international tax system. The U.S. government did certify both the PRC's corporate income tax and its personal income tax legislation as creditable. Indeed, I achieved a minor footnote in Sino-American tax history when, in 1981, the U.S. authorities made me the first individual taxpayer ever approved to credit payment of income tax to the PRC against his American income tax obligations.

My tax activities were far from my only unexpected involvements with the PRC in the spring of 1979. The Ministry of Foreign Affairs (MOFA), Beijing Municipality, and the China Council for the Promotion of International Trade (CCPIT) all asked me to fly from Hong Kong on various occasions to give lectures and arrange exchanges. Having waited almost twenty years for such substantial contacts, I found this a gratifying time.

Especially interesting was my cooperation with the CCPIT. It had been helping legislators to produce China's first foreign direct investment law and asked me to organize a full week of lectures in Beijing by American international lawyers. The goal was to introduce another very large group of economic officials and academics to the variety of investment vehicles that foreign companies might expect to establish in China. Like my tax efforts, this soon led to legislation that made possible the first Chinese foreign investment projects. On July 1, 1979, when the Chinese government promulgated the first seven laws enacted by the National People's Congress in many years, among them was the Sino-Foreign Equity Joint Venture Law, which attracted worldwide interest and made me feel happy on my birthday! The next day, however, a *New York Times* front-page story erroneously claimed that I had drafted the new investment law. The reporter had failed to distinguish between my merely arranging lectures on international experience with joint ventures and drafting national legislation.

All this exciting activity whetted my appetite. Many trips to the mainland from my base in Hong Kong had demonstrated how inconvenient and frustrating it was to come and go instead of residing in China.

I wanted to live and work in China at long last. Yet this proved difficult. All the national agencies that were eager to cooperate with me on an ad hoc, short-term basis became extremely cautious when I raised the prospect of inviting me to do more than make short-term visits. Deng Xiaoping's Open Door Policy was too recent. No one knew how long it might last. Having been badly affected in previous political campaigns, no responsible central government official seemed willing to run the risk of inviting a foreign law professor, especially one from the world's leading bourgeois country, to remain in residence.

Fortunately, my Chinese-language tutor at Harvard, Chuan Ruxiang, sympathized with my situation and offered to help. She was kind enough to introduce me to a friend named Xiao Yang, then head of the Beijing Economic Development Corporation (BEDC), which had just been created by the Beijing Municipal Government's Economic Commission as a vehicle for doing business with foreigners. Xiao, an extremely intelligent and nice Sichuan man who had studied engineering in Leipzig in East Germany, was unafraid to be an innovator and eager to make a mark as one of the new generation of reformers who were determined to transform the PRC economy. He saw the relevance of law to economic development and had already felt the need to train BEDC and other city officials for the foreign business negotiations that were daily being thrust upon them. We quickly made a win-win deal.

TEACHING BUSINESS OFFICIALS IN BEIJING, 1979–1981

I agreed to take a one-year leave from Harvard in order to offer a course, nine hours per week for an academic year, introducing international business law and dispute resolution to thirty local government officials. These cadres, aged twenty-five to fifty, had already been dealing with foreign businesspeople interested in concluding the customary range of commercial contracts—sales, purchases, licensing of technology, joint ventures, foreign wholly owned subsidiaries, and other arrangements. Very few of the Chinese officials selected knew English well, so the course had to be taught in Chinese. This presented a double challenge. I and my two able associates—Owen Nee and Stephen Orlins, from the then leading international law firm Coudert Brothers, for which I was a consultant—had never taught a law course in Chinese before.

Of course, Chiang Kai-shek's pre-1949 Republic of China government had a well-developed Chinese–English commercial law vocabulary. But not all its terms had endured on the mainland under the new regime, which had come heavily under the influence of Soviet law in the 1950s and which had only conducted limited business transactions with noncommunist countries before 1979. For example, even the pre-1949 Chinese term for contract—*qiyue*—had fallen into disuse on the mainland, which substituted in its stead the term *hetong*. We had to make do with the aid of a very nice general interpreter who had no legal training and little knowledge of English legal terms. During our lectures, he sat by our side, learning together with the other officials who were our "students," and occasionally helping as we sought to clarify the meaning of our poorly expressed attempts to convey complex legal concepts. Despite the difficulties, our 1979–1980 course was thought to be successful. We were asked to spend another year training a second group of city cadres, and I managed to persuade Harvard to extend my leave of absence in order to do so.

It is difficult to exaggerate the hunger for legal learning among Chinese economic officials who, in that era, suddenly had to deal with foreign companies and governments eager to do business. I vividly recall asking one dynamic and humorous Shanghai employee of the First Ministry of Machine Building who wanted to go to Harvard why he was so ambitious to study law. He said: "I work in my ministry's Law and Contract Division, and every day now we have to negotiate with the giants of the world's automobile industry, especially Volkswagen. We in the Law and Contract Division have only one problem," he said. "We don't know anything about law or contracts!"

Of course, many bright and eager Chinese officials were learning about law through actual negotiations. I witnessed that because, apart from teaching, I took part almost daily in negotiations between would-be foreign investors and Chinese state-owned enterprises from various industries. My arrangement with Xiao Yang and the BEDC facilitated this process. My two Coudert Brothers colleagues and I volunteered our teaching services in Beijing without charge, even for expenses. In return, however, the city government arranged for us to have three permanent two-room suites in the Peking Hotel at our expense. In those days, the

Peking Hotel was by far the best hotel in the capital, where every foreign delegation wanted to stay. Because Beijing then had no modern commercial office buildings, it was also where the large number of foreign corporations that were establishing representative offices wanted to set up shop, and even some UN officials and foreign diplomats wanted to live there. By assuring us three suites, the BEDC put us in the center of Beijing's growing international life, a comfortable place not only to live but also to work.

EDUCATION THROUGH NEGOTIATION

No Chinese lawyers appeared in any of the negotiations in which I took part during the 1979–1981 period. During those years, there were no licensed PRC lawyers because the legal profession, which had fallen afoul of the Anti-Rightist Campaign of 1957–1958, was not yet formally restored. Even after its reestablishment on January 1, 1982, it took several years before licensed lawyers began to take part regularly in commercial negotiations. Until then, Chinese companies, which were invariably newly minted, state-owned enterprises (there were virtually no private companies at the time), coped as well as possible by designating some staff members not formally trained in law to function as their legal advisers, as my BEDC "students" had been doing.

The absence of lawyers on the Chinese side added to the challenges I confronted in this work. I had to be sure to explain to the Chinese side what the relevant legal provisions of their own slowly emerging legislative environment were, how foreign and international law and practice dealt with the issues we faced, what were the legal implications of those issues for each side, and the pros and cons of the possible choices. As both a fair-minded lawyer representing foreign companies eager to gain China's trust and cooperation and an American law professor wanting to help China develop a satisfactory legal system, I felt acute responsibility for carrying out this difficult task. I also had to monitor the quality of the translation of legal terms and frequently supplemented the regular interpreters' translation, and sometimes even took over the job myself.

Chinese negotiators were quick learners. They carefully studied the English and Chinese language draft contracts that our side prepared for the negotiations and gradually began to piece together from various foreign draft contracts their own versions, in Chinese and soon in English, of negotiation drafts more favorable to them than were initial foreign drafts. Before long, the PRC officials began to provide Chinese companies with model contract drafts for initiating discussion of the various types of transactions. A model equity joint venture contract draft soon appeared, together with instructions and advice to Chinese negotiators about whether, when, and how to yield to foreign demands to alter its provisions. At one point, before Chinese law required all equity joint venture contracts to provide for arbitration of disputes in China, the PRC side was told to hold out as long as possible against foreign insistence that disputes be arbitrated outside China but not to regard the issue as a deal breaker that would preclude agreeing on the contract.

In those early days, there was an understandable sense of insecurity on both sides of the negotiating table. For the Chinese, establishing joint venture investment projects with Western firms was a new experience, and they were concerned about making mistakes of omission or commission as well as possibly even being tricked by the highly experienced foreign parties whom they had met only recently. This was well expressed by then vice premier Li Xiannian during an interview I had with him in April 1979. In response to my questions about the content of the equity joint venture law that was being drafted behind closed doors, he said: "You foreigners have nothing to worry about. You have been doing joint ventures all over the world for many years. We Chinese, on the other hand, have no experience in such matters."

Actually, we foreigners were also anxious because China's evolving legal and economic systems were a work in progress, and transparency was minimal. I recall trying to negotiate a joint venture contract to build Beijing's first modern hotel. My client needed to know about the financial situation and the governance of its potential Chinese partner, a recently organized Beijing city government company. Yet when I asked for copies of its balance sheet and its articles of association, I was told that these were "state secrets" and could not be made known to outsiders. I said that I hoped the Chinese government would reconsider this policy because no foreigner would want to invest blindly in a black box and that I would have to go back to Harvard because not much business cooperation could take place amid such secrecy. Fortunately, the policy of extreme secrecy did begin to change soon afterward, although in some cases the Chinese side still refused to make available "internal" regulations that they claimed supported their negotiating positions.

Not surprisingly, our discussions were also occasionally marked by misunderstandings linked to the difficulties of translating legal language. During our early hotel contract negotiations, for example, I said that our U.S. company client would have to ask its board of directors to "approve" (*pizhun*) the document we were negotiating. The chief PRC negotiator, showing some nationalist emotion, said that it was for the official PRC investment authority to "approve" contracts, not for the foreign side, which could only "agree" (*tongyi*) or not to the contract terms.

Some months later, an offshore oil project negotiation offered another illustration. Because of other commitments, I had to arrive a day after discussions had begun for what my U.S. client thought was to be an equity joint venture project. On arrival, I was told that the discussions had got off to a bad start for reasons no one could explain. When discussions resumed on the second day, I quickly saw the reason for the lack of progress. The China National Offshore Oil Corporation (CNOOC) believed that my client had wanted to establish not an equity joint venture but a cooperative joint venture, a different type of transaction for which no law had yet been enacted. The confusion had arisen because the Chinese names for the two different contract structures were very similar (*hezi jingying qiye* for equity joint ventures and *hezuo jingying qiye* for cooperative ones), and Chinese pronunciation and accents frequently varied. The entire first day had been wasted because of a mutual mistake!

Some misunderstandings were not because of language but because of the lack of detailed rules to guide the parties. Not only was there no cooperative joint venture law yet promulgated, but the 1979 Equity Joint Venture Law was short and simple. It stated only basic principles and obviously contemplated the subsequent announcement of administrative implementing regulations to give it concrete meaning. Those regulations did not appear, however, until September 1983, over four years later. They provided a good deal of necessary guidance, reduced the likelihood of disputes, and spurred foreign investors to enter into transactions about which they had previously been reluctant, thus making the equity joint venture their preferred investment choice for the initial period of Sino-Western cooperation.

OTHER EDUCATIONAL PURSUITS

Although teaching and negotiating were more than enough to keep me very busy, I also made time for other professional pursuits. The most prominent was the launching of cooperation with China's Foreign Languages Press in the publication of a series of volumes containing English-language translations by several of my law firm colleagues and me of much of the PRC's new legislation, which was inaccessible to most of the international community in the original Chinese-language versions. The first fruit of our collective efforts—volume one of three volumes on China's foreign economic legislation—appeared in 1982 and was followed shortly thereafter by our translations of the new criminal law and criminal procedure law. These tasks proved to be a valuable public service that also did a great deal to expand my contemporary Chinese legal vocabulary.

I also managed to give occasional lectures to a number of national and local agencies in Beijing, and I traveled to Shanghai and Tianjin to speak to large groups of local officials responsible for foreign direct investments in those major cities. Wherever and whenever possible, I met with law professors, who had begun to emerge from the shadows of the Cultural Revolution. I also met with a few relatively senior former lawyers who were waiting for the government to reestablish their profession after over twenty years of inactivity. The Beijing Foreign Economic Law Office was already functioning unofficially. I remember visiting its frigid premises on November 13, 1979, which was the coldest day I had ever experienced because, in accordance with local custom, the heat was not turned on until two days later. A German businessman residing near me in the Peking Hotel had been detained by the police for sleeping with his Chinese girlfriend. I had been asked to try to obtain his release and had been told that one of the legal experts at the Foreign Economic Law Office was familiar with criminal justice and had good connections with the Public Security Bureau. He proved to be receptive, knowledgeable, and helpful in securing the businessman's release.

In addition, I devoted some time to selecting the first PRC candidates, put forward by the State Taxation Administration, to study at Harvard Law School's International Tax Program. Other PRC departments soon indicated their hope to send young legal officials to Harvard, including the Academy of Social Sciences and the MOFA, which called me to inquire about sending someone to enter Harvard's full three-year JD program, so that person could become the ministry's expert on U.S. law. MOFA wanted me not only to arrange Harvard's acceptance of the very competent English-language interpreter it recommended—Zhao Jia—but also to procure the financial support for her entire American legal education. It may be hard for people today to understand that, in 1979, China's treasury had very little foreign exchange to spend. Fortunately, I was able to persuade Alexis Coudert, the very wise senior partner of the Coudert Brothers law firm and the trustee of a modest charitable foundation for the promotion of Polish-American law, to interpret the terms of the foundation's charter liberally in order to find the funds required!

Perhaps my most vivid memory of this exciting period was of something that I had witnessed only on television—the trial of the "Gang of Four." When that highly publicized trial began in November 1980, I hoped that it might be a useful instrument of public legal education. The criminal law and the criminal procedure law had both just gone into effect on January 1, 1980, and the trial, despite the enormous ballyhoo it had generated, seemed to be a possible vehicle for illustrating how the new laws should be applied. Unfortunately, the main defendant, Chairman Mao's widow, Jiang Qing, after listening to the chief judge's explanation of the role that defense counsel could play on her behalf, refused to exercise her right to counsel. Once she angrily insisted on defending herself, public attention shifted away from legal procedures and was quickly overcome by the extraordinarily intense political drama that unfolded.

Much more educational was a Chinese feature film that I was surprised to see on television some months later. Called *In and Out of Court* (*Fating neiwai*), it told the story of a woman appellate judge who resists heavy political pressure seeking to persuade her to reverse the criminal conviction of an important official's son. Instead, she courageously vindicates the principle of judicial independence of government authority. I was amazed to see the prominence accorded this critical principle in a popular movie made so early in the new law reform era. It reinforced my hopes for the future of the rule of law in China.

18

LEAVING HARVARD TO ESTABLISH PAUL, WEISS LAW OFFICES IN BEIJING AND HONG KONG

As Joan and I flew home from Beijing in early summer 1981, I knew I had to make some basic decisions. My Harvard leave of absence had just expired. Even former U.S. Secretary of State Henry Kissinger was not allowed more than two years away from the university. Because of my spring 1979 sabbatical, I had actually been away for two and one-half years except for two intense three-week winter-term teaching assignments. Was I prepared to walk away from the active and unique China practice and cooperation that had recently dominated my life? To put it the other way, was I prepared to forsake the marvelous academic life and position that I had enjoyed for seventeen years at one of the world's greatest universities?

Law practice was the obvious alternative to a return to full-time law teaching. Once Ronald Reagan was elected president in 1980, any aspirations I might still have had to take part in diplomacy or other government service relating to China were put on hold because I had neither Republican inclinations nor connections. Nor did I want to start a business career, although the blandishments of a major investment bank made me think of the prospect of earning a lot more money than I could with any law firm. I loved law practice relating to China and knew that it would be the most distinctive and satisfying thing I could do at the time. I have always had a practical bent and emphasized reality rather than theory and the printed page alone. Every day's practice on China issues constituted fresh and stimulating research. I worried that, if I returned to full time academic life, and although I could continue as a part-time legal consultant, my future opportunities for continuous learning about China might depend primarily on the fragmentary and occasional reports of former students and other lawyers who had filled my practical boots.

I valued the daily human interactions and friendships with the Chinese officials and scholars I had met and cooperated with in the country's attempt at modernization. Many of them thought I was useful, as did appreciative clients who urged me not to abandon what I had started. I enjoyed the challenge of negotiations—walking into a roomful of Chinese cadres I had never met before and winning their confidence and cooperation in a common cause. I also liked the sense of humor that Chinese negotiators sometimes showed. One day, after I had criticized their side's insistence that our side bear the entire risk of failure of our project, their chief negotiator said: "Capitalists take risks. We're socialists." Would I continue to be part of history in China or simply record it at home? Giving up on this adventure seemed inconsistent with the pioneering aspirations that had led me into Chinese studies two decades earlier.

To be sure, there was the other side of the coin. I had relished the life at Harvard. I had many diverse, stimulating, and interesting colleagues and friends, both on the Harvard Law School (HLS) faculty and in the university's Asia-related departments. My books, especially the 1968 analysis of the criminal process in the People's Republic of China (PRC) and the 1974 documentary study of the PRC's practice of public international law, done with Hungdah Chiu, had been regarded as groundbreaking. I was proud of the unique body of students I had recruited and assisted in the years since my arrival in Cambridge, Massachusetts, in 1964. I was also reluctant to leave the law school's East Asian Legal Studies (EALS) program. As previously noted, in fifteen years it had become, in Professor John Fairbank's words, a third center of academic China power at Harvard, like the East Asian Research Center later named for him and the Harvard-Yenching Institute.

I had enjoyed my status as a minor public intellectual as China and East Asia generally became a subject of national concern. My 1971 and 1976 *Foreign Affairs* essays; many op-eds in the *New York Times*, the *Washington Post*, and other newspapers; and television appearances on *Meet the Press*, *Face the Nation*, and the *Today Show* had brought me out of the academic shadows. It had also been satisfying to testify frequently before Congress; lobby the State Department and the White House; and join the various conferences and organizations that were dealing with normalization of diplomatic relations with China, solidifying our alliance with Japan, and protesting human rights violations in Mao's China, Chiang Kai-shek's Taiwan, and both North and South Korea.

Yet it didn't take me very long to gamble on the new, exciting, and uncertain adventure of attempting to establish a stable and significant China practice. Of course, I realized that becoming a partner responsible for a new and booming practice area in a major international law firm would inevitably change and restrict many aspects of the life to which I had become accustomed. Ironically, it would also diminish our living conditions. In Cambridge, after some years of renting the place, the university had sold us our attractive twelve-room house that stood on a tree-studded half-acre next to a nice neighborhood tennis court only six blocks from the law school. By contrast, when Joan and I were able to move from our single room into a two-room suite in the Peking Hotel, we thought we were living in the lap of luxury. Future China housing prospects were little better.

Although it may have been thought by some that the decision to relinquish my Harvard tenure was based on the promise of substantially enhanced compensation, that actually was not the case. By 1981, Joan and I were in comfortable shape financially and did not feel the need to earn a lot more money. Our two older sons, Peter and Seth, had both completed their undergraduate education, and our youngest son, Ethan, was halfway through college. Although they all contemplated some type of eventual graduate school, I knew that the consulting fees I could anticipate after returning to Harvard would meet anticipated financial needs, and Harvard also offered financial educational assistance to faculty children. The incentive to give up my permanent post at Harvard and become a mere part-time adjunct lecturer there was not in any way financial.

Perhaps some of my law school colleagues attributed my departure decision to Harvard president Derek Bok's appointment of our mutual good friend and colleague James Vorenberg, rather than me, to the school's deanship. But this speculation was also incorrect. The possibility of leading a major American law school had its attractions, but when I originally decided to study China, I had assumed that this unusual choice would preclude decanal prospects because it would put me out of the mainstream of U.S. legal education. Over the years, that continued to seem a minor price to pay for the privilege of a unique China career. In fact, there were rumors that my name was being bandied about for the HLS deanship, but when I got a handwritten note from my friend and Harvard president Derek Bok that, after deliberating long and hard, he had decided to ask Jim to be dean, I was surprised that I had even been carefully considered for the post.

Still, when I got Derek's note, I thought about how proud my late father, whose family financial situation had denied him a college education and limited his legal training to a third-rate night school, might have been. I didn't worry about what my mother, who was still alive and in her eighties, would think because she always wanted me to become secretary of state rather than a law school luminary.

As summer approached and I did decide to remain in practice rather than return to the university, the next question to resolve was which law firm to join. I saw no point in trying to stay with Coudert. Although I liked Alexis Coudert, Charlie Stevens, and a few other partners of what was a large, multi-office international institution, I knew that it was experiencing financial problems. That was probably the cause of some of the unattractive conduct that I had experienced in my contacts with a few of the firm's far-flung offices. I especially recall how the London office pressed me to spend a few days lecturing, meeting, and greeting there following a client trip to Switzerland so that the London partners could use the lure of possible China investment to attract potential clients to their office. I wanted to be cooperative, so I agreed and had an interesting time. I assumed, because this was principally for the London office's benefit, that it would pay my local expenses. When it failed to do so, I decided not to raise any question because reasonable people could differ over that situation, and I was new to the multi-office customs of international law firms.

But then I learned that the London office had charged our Hong Kong/Beijing practice with the very large expense that London, without consulting me, had incurred by renting an elegant hotel for my lecture and the elaborate dinner that followed it. I protested that maneuver to Alexis Coudert. Although I never did confirm how the issue was resolved, it left me with a bad taste. Alexis was a wonderful, able lawyer and a nice, mild person, but not a strict manager and too inclined to admit more lawyers to partnership than the firm could profitably absorb. I decided to seek my prospects elsewhere, and there were many places to consider. Charlie Stevens saw the handwriting on the Coudert wall and thought the time ripe for taking the whole Coudert Asia group of roughly a dozen lawyers, including yours truly, to a more profitable, less troubled "big law" firm. He had a connection to the large and growing Skadden, Arps firm that had made its fortune and reputation advising on major mergers, acquisitions, and takeovers and was eager to become more international. Charlie, Owen Nee, and I spent an interesting afternoon around the swimming pool at the Westchester home of Skadden's lead partner, Joseph Flom, who was keen to establish a position in China. But in the end, Skadden didn't move ahead, feeling that the risk of hiring a dozen lawyers was too great.

At that point, luck again intervened in my life. As I was leaving a breakfast meeting with Joe Flom of Skadden, I bumped into Arthur Liman, who had been two years behind me at Yale Law School and who subsequently had become a great and influential success at the law firm of Paul, Weiss, Rifkind, Wharton & Garrison. Arthur, a lanky, brilliant fellow whom I did not know well but who was always friendly, put his arm on my shoulder and said: "If you and Joe were talking about what I think you were, please call me this afternoon." I did call him, and he asked me to visit the Paul, Weiss offices before I made any decision about which firm to join.

I knew Paul, Weiss was a great American law firm and from afar had always admired it for several reasons, including that it was an important experimental example of a high-powered "mixed" law firm that was neither anti-Semitic and "white shoe" nor exclusively Jewish in composition. It had even begun to make modest progress in recruiting African Americans. What it still lacked, however, was a significant international practice. Apart from a tiny Paris bureau, it had none of the foreign offices and international legal experience of a Coudert Brothers or other traditional and even more prestigious and successful firms such as Sullivan & Cromwell or Cravath, Swaine & Moore or Davis Polk & Wardwell, none of which I found appealing.

There was one important obstacle, however—the seniority of the associates I could bring with me. Paul, Weiss was never prepared to absorb the full complement of a dozen Asian law specialists that Charlie Stevens had hoped to lead away from Coudert Brothers. But it was ready to allow me to bring two China associates plus Toby Myerson, a former student and close friend who, because of his expertise in Japanese matters, had actually been running the small Coudert office in San Francisco. Not long afterward, Paul, Weiss was willing to contemplate inviting Charlie Stevens to join us in an effort to consolidate our Japan practice. This was important to me not only because Charlie had become my close friend but also because, as I frankly told Matthew Nimetz and other Paul, Weiss partners who initially interviewed me, despite the new hoopla about China, I could not be confident that the China practice would actually develop as planned. I knew that our Japan practice would definitely prosper.

By that time, in what was early August 1981, I was at our Cape Cod house, and the time for decision had arrived. I'd also had offers from two other attractive firms: Cleary, Gottlieb, Friendly and Hamilton, which already had a thriving international practice and many foreign offices, and the major Los Angeles–based firm O'Melveny & Myers. Cleary, however, was reluctant to take on an associate as senior as Toby Myerson. Toby called me early on decision day and said: "If you join Cleary, we'll always be friends, and I wish you the best. But if you decide to join Paul, Weiss, I'll go with you." That proved decisive.

When I told Arthur Liman that I decided to join Paul, Weiss, he asked me to make detailed plans. The most important was which China associates I wanted to bring with me. My former student Steve Orlins was an obvious choice. We had just completed two years working cheek by jowl in the Coudert office in Beijing, and I greatly valued his ability and good judgment, as well as his broad interests in China affairs and three years of previous experience in the office of the Legal Adviser of the Department of State. And our wives had become close friends.

Jamie Horsley, another outstanding member of my former Harvard China group, had graduated from HLS two years after Steve. She had been practicing law in San Francisco rather than Asia for three years, but we had kept in touch. I knew that she had not lost interest in more direct involvement with China and would do a fine job in our Beijing office. In conversations with my prize client Amoco, which I very much wanted to follow me to Paul, Weiss, Bob Blanton, the oil company's China boss, was reluctant to accept Jamie as my Beijing replacement, not because of any doubt about her ability but because of her gender. "You know a woman won't be able to go out drinking with our Chinese hosts," he said. I assured him that Jamie was special in her capacity for holding maotai, China's strongest drink, as I had noted the night she and I first met at a group dinner in Taipei in 1974 before she had even applied to study law.

After I convinced Bob, Jamie agreed to join us, so I told Arthur we had our initial team. He then asked me to come to the firm one morning to attend a meeting with all the partners, many of whom I had not met during earlier interviews. Some of them, I knew, were understandably skeptical about launching a China practice or any expansion of the firm's modest international effort. Foreign law offices were notoriously expensive and often unprofitable. I was confident, given our continuing work for Amoco in Beijing, that a small office there would not break our proposed budget, and I believed that within a year or two a growing practice might sustain opening a Hong Kong office as well.

Steve Orlins, who had some friends at Paul, Weiss, was worried that more conservative partners might try to block Arthur's initiative. For a last-minute review of the situation, we decided to have breakfast together the morning of my meeting with all the partners. Steve became visibly upset at my appearance. "You're wearing a bow tie," he said. "This may be the most important day of my professional life, and you're wearing a bow tie!" He obviously thought that my tie would remind the partners that I was essentially an academic with limited experience in practice. I assured him that our new career would not require alteration of my sartorial preferences. After all, I pointed out, I was wearing a conservative gray suit! I had already heard a favorite joke about the firm's most senior partner, former judge Simon H. Rifkind, about whom it was whispered that his idea of a vacation was wearing a sports jacket to the office on Sunday.

Despite the bow tie, I passed muster at the large partners' meeting. One anxious tax lawyer, worried that I might mire the firm in an Asian financial debacle comparable to the recent U.S. political debacle in Vietnam, asked rather pointedly: "If we open a Hong Kong office in addition to a Beijing office, which company will walk through our door on opening day?" I pacified him by saying that we would only want to open a Hong Kong office when we had prospects and sufficient need for our services there.

So, on the morning of September 2, 1981, I turned up for work at the firm's headquarters, which was then located in New York City at 345 Park Avenue, conveniently near the Lexington Avenue Number 6 line's 51st Street station. My first office was not as glamorous as the one I would have had at Cleary's quarters at the tip of lower Manhattan. There was no inspiring view of the Statue of Liberty. But there was no long daily ride by subway or taxi from the small Upper East Side apartment that Joan and I had bought as a New York pied-à-terre. As soon as I arrived at Paul, Weiss, I received a warm welcome from Judge Rifkind and several other senior partners who assured me that a better office would soon become available. I had already met with the judge at an earlier lunch Matt Nimetz, then chair of the firm's international practice committee, had arranged. At that time, one of the judge's first questions was; "What should we call you?" I responded with a tired favorite of mine: "Call me anything but late to dinner," which showed that I shared the judge's taste for corny humor. I then said that everyone, including my student protégés and Coudert associates, called me Jerry. "Huh," the judge snorted to his colleagues, "very different from someone we once had here!" I wasn't sure to whom he was alluding. I was later told it was Arthur Goldberg, who had joined the firm briefly after serving on the U.S. Supreme Court and then as the U.S. ambassador to the United Nations. When Rifkind had asked him the same question, Goldberg had reportedly replied: "Let's keep it simple. Just call me 'Mr. Justice'!" This had not gone down well with Rifkind, who had himself been a distinguished federal judge for a decade before joining Paul, Weiss, but who liked to be called "Si" for Simon.

Never having been a partner in a law firm before, I had a lot to learn about organization, administration, finances, personnel, and other matters during the first weeks. I also had to spend time getting acquainted with the many partners who graciously accepted me. One of the most cordial was Lloyd Garrison, who fortunately did not recall my skeptical reaction to his recruiting pitch when he interviewed me as a second-year Yale Law School student twenty-eight years earlier. Lloyd not only insisted that I join the midtown luncheon and dinner club called the Century Association, but his lovely wife Ellen also recommended Joan for membership in an interesting women's counterpart, the Cosmopolitan Club. A couple of years later, when Woody Allen needed to cast someone as Mia Farrow's mother in his forthcoming film *Zelig*, a friend told him to visit the Cosmopolitan Club any weekday noon and he would have his pick of attractive gray-haired candidates for the role. So at eighty-three, Ellen Garrison, a delightful lady, became a movie star!

I was especially interested, of course, in getting to know partners who were developing the firm's modest international practice. The best-known was Ted Sorensen, who had become famous as John F. Kennedy's (JFK) speechwriter, first when JFK was U.S. senator and then president. Ted had assisted JFK in his award-winning book *Profiles in Courage*. I had known Matt Nimetz slightly during my first year teaching at Harvard, when he was the outstanding student in the graduating class of 1965. By the time we met again in 1981, he had recently completed service as undersecretary of state during the Carter administration.

I already had a passing acquaintance with the head of the illustrious Paul, Weiss tax department, Adrian ("Bill") DeWind, not through law practice or academe but as a result of my 1970s participation in efforts to improve the human rights situation in South Korea. Bill was an attractive, genial person whose interests and values gave me a favorable impression of Paul, Weiss long before I left Harvard.

Perhaps my friendship with Bill made me bold enough, early on, to speak at a partners' meeting held to discuss whether an able woman tax associate should be voted into the partnership. The partnership committee chair, summarizing the dilemma before the firm, said that the candidate was as brilliant as any tax lawyer in a firm that was known for its expertise in this field, but that she would never attract clients because she had the personality of a dead fish. Therefore, her mentors had concluded that she should become a law professor! Having just come from two decades in academic life, I said that among law professors, when a brilliant student had the personality of a dead fish, we always urged the student to become a tax lawyer! Bill enjoyed my comment, but I don't think it endeared me to everyone at the meeting.

One of the most interesting among my new partners was former Yale Law School professor and Stanford Law School dean Bayless Manning, who had served as a Japanese-language interpreter for U.S. forces during World War II and later as a diplomat. He was striving to build his own international practice and eager to foster my efforts. He was also curious about how well I, as a fellow refugee from scholarly life, would adjust to the realities of law firm existence.

For my day-to-day operations and decision making, I relied primarily on Arthur Liman and John ("Bud") Taylor, another dynamic, slightly older Yale Law School graduate who served as the firm's managing partner. Bud shared Arthur's enthusiasm and determination to make our

China practice successful. He and I also shared an interest in tennis, at which he excelled, and that strengthened our friendship.

A few partners did not seem equally enthusiastic about my arrival at the firm. I was apparently bringing in too many clients. Some of the multinationals I attracted created the potential for future conflicts with existing clients. One day a woman partner said to me, more in irritation than admiration: "You're going to bring in every Fortune 500 company there is." I reacted to this surprising implicit criticism by saying: "I thought that's why I was hired."

Not everything went smoothly in the early days. Arthur Liman, thinking that publicity might boost our new practice, suggested that I accept a *New York Times* request that he had arranged for an interview about why a senior HLS professor decided to abandon academe for law practice and China. I didn't know the reporter assigned and told Arthur that I felt a bit uncomfortable about the opportunity, but he assured me that the would-be interviewer bore goodwill toward the firm and would not distort my remarks. Nevertheless, that is precisely what happened.

Looking for an angle on which to hang his story, the reporter kept asking me to translate the three Chinese scrolls I had on the wall behind my desk. I was reluctant to do so because, like many similar scrolls that Chinese present as gifts, these flattered the recipient. When the reporter annoyingly continued to press for a translation, I finally complied. The reporter then said, rather sarcastically: "You're not modest, are you?" Really annoyed at that point, I said, even more sarcastically: "No, I'm not modest," a remark that the reporter then quoted without indicating the sarcasm with which it had been uttered.

Despite this bump in the road, we brought in so many new clients that it soon became time to plan on when and how to open a Hong Kong office. That introduced a new, more exciting stage in our progress, which will be the subject of the next chapter.

19

LIFE, LAW, AND CHINA PRACTICE IN THE OPTIMISTIC 1980S

The Hong Kong office for Paul, Weiss was going to start in 1983 as a very small outpost in order to keep expenses down. Four lawyers including me seemed the right way to begin. It was clear that I would need the cooperation of an experienced corporate partner to ensure proper handling of some of the business and financial transactions of the clients we were likely to attract, matters in which I had little practical experience. The Corporate Department, of which I was a member, suggested Allen Thomas, a dynamic, able, and experienced lawyer in his early forties. I didn't know him well, but I liked him, and, although he knew little about Asia, Allen was optimistic, outgoing, and eager to join me in this adventure. Our different talents and backgrounds seemed to be a good fit, one that inspired the firm's confidence.

We had to select two associates to bolster our operation. Steve Orlins was naturally my first choice, but what he really wanted to do was become an entrepreneur focused on China rather than a business lawyer, so I had to find another capable young lawyer with the training to assist me on China deals. Fortunately, Ellen Eliasoph, a very able and delightful 1982 Yale Law School graduate who had studied law for a year in Beijing before completing her Yale education, decided to seize the opportunity to help start our Hong Kong practice. I knew she would prove to be a splendid colleague.

Meanwhile, we were lucky to find Ruben Kraiem, a recent Harvard Law School (HLS) graduate to be Allen's associate and work with him on other international transactions. Ruben was known to be very smart, and he was friendly, interested in international practice generally, and laughed at my jokes. Although it was not apparent, he was Mexican and, having grown up in a foreign culture, seemed at ease with the prospect of practicing law in another one—China.

We were fortunate to find modest office space in the newly constructed Edinburgh Tower in Hong Kong's central business district. After all this careful preparation, we still had to answer the question that the skeptical tax partner had asked me on the day I was interviewed by the full Paul, Weiss partnership: "If we open a Hong Kong office in addition to a Beijing office, which company will walk through our door on opening day?" Here again, luck came to our aid.

During the year that Joan and I spent with our children in Hong Kong in 1963–1964 (chapter 12), we had come to enjoy the friendship of Sir Lawrence and Lady Muriel Kadoorie. Lord Kadoorie was Hong Kong's most prominent tycoon and presided over the electric power and hotel industries as well as other enterprises. In July 1972, when we spent a few days in Hong Kong with our children while en route from our year in Japan to China and ultimately North Korea, the Kadoories treated our whole family to a wonderful dinner with them in the premier restaurant of their leading hotel, the Peninsula. Later, during the time Joan and I divided between Hong Kong and Beijing in 1979–1981, we kept in touch with the senior Kadoories, their charming daughter Rita, and Rita's attractive husband Ron Macaulay.

In the autumn of 1983, as I returned to open a Hong Kong office and Joan and I established residence, the Kadoories were glad to welcome us back. This time, however, Lord Kadoorie, whom I called Lawrence, had more than friendship on his mind. He told me that the most important of his many companies, China Light & Power (CLP), which provided the electricity for all of the colony except Hong Kong Island, was contemplating a joint venture in China and that he would need my advice in bringing the project to fruition.

This was to be, by far, the largest foreign investment project China had yet seen. The total investment was to be roughly US$3.5 billion, an astounding figure, because the project called for the construction and operation of China's first nuclear power plant, a daring and potentially dangerous challenge. The plant was to be situated only thirty miles from

Hong Kong at Daya Bay in nearby Guangdong Province. This, Lawrence realized, would add to Hong Kong and foreign anxieties over the possible consequences of a nuclear mishap at the hands of inexperienced Chinese employees. Safety was obviously going to become a key issue in the anticipated negotiations.

I found myself in an ironic position. As I noted in chapter 7, I was a young Washington lawyer in 1958 and troubled by safety worries when I had chosen not to continue to assist the Detroit Consolidated Edison Corporation in its efforts to win approval to build America's first nuclear power plant. Yet in 1983, here I was, agreeing to take on the task of helping to establish China's first such plant. Of course, the two situations were different in some important respects. During the intervening generation, France, for example, had built and operated dozens of nuclear power plants without significant mishap, and China's vast southern region, lacking the coal resources of the country's north, had an urgent need for an alternative energy source to sustain its ambitious modernization plans. Knowing Lawrence Kadoorie and the track record of CLP in providing electricity to Hong Kong, and the project's intended reliance on the expertise of the experienced French nuclear company Framatome, I felt confident that the project was likely to be successful. The first problem was how to draft the necessary contract provisions, and the second was how to persuade our Chinese hosts to accept them.

This proved a complex task. China at that point offered very limited legislative guidance, even after detailed 1983 regulations provided some basic explanations of the very general 1979 Equity Joint Venture Law. We had no previous Chinese projects to rely on for appropriate clauses and language. Our joint venture contract and the related contracts and other documents had to anticipate and spell out everything for the first time. Fortunately, my Paul, Weiss colleagues and I were able to provide the required China joint venture legal inputs for a long first draft, and the CLP Legal Department, having carefully studied the legal documentation of French and other nuclear power projects elsewhere in the world, was able to supply us with the necessary knowledge and contract terms related to nuclear projects.

To be sure, we had to translate our English-language draft into contemporary People's Republic of China (PRC) Chinese because the PRC Equity Joint Venture Law required that all contractual investment documents be finalized in Chinese, as well as whatever language the foreign investors insisted on, and that the two versions of the contract be confirmed as substantially identical in meaning. By that time, I had managed to recruit a young Hong Kong lawyer named Kenneth Chan from the CLP Legal Department itself. Although a native Cantonese speaker, Kenneth was comfortable in Mandarin as well as English. Together we produced extensive Chinese-language contract documents that impressed our inexperienced but earnest PRC counterparts.

That did not mean, of course, that the Chinese side agreed with our draft. Negotiations dragged on for many weeks. They took place eight hours per day, five days a week, in the Shekou section of the new Shenzhen special economic zone (SEZ) just across the boundary between Hong Kong and Guangdong Province. Kenneth and I usually spent all week there, staying in a modest hotel. Conditions there were plain but adequate, although my mattress seemed lumpy and the toilet in my bathroom often broke down. I lay awake at night occasionally in Shekou wishing that my Harvard students could see me. Some believed that I had forsaken the mundane life of the Cambridge academic for the supposedly glamorous and more comfortable life of the international lawyer. My Shekou lodgings would have disabused them.

The most challenging issue in the negotiations concerned the safety standards that the venture would be required to observe in construction and operation. The Chinese side endorsed the standards promulgated by the International Atomic Energy Agency (IAEA), but CLP experts and their French technical advisers insisted on the significantly stricter standards that France had employed when establishing over forty nuclear power plants that were thus far successfully functioning without serious incident. The Chinese side, a newly created company organized under the PRC Ministry of Electric Power, persisted in rejecting our proposal.

The success of the negotiations seemed at stake. Kenneth and I were not the only members of our team who worried about the dangers of capitulating to the Chinese demand. Our client's engineers, all of them lifelong residents of Hong Kong together with their wives and children, were deeply concerned about the chances of a nuclear accident that could devastate their nearby community. China, after all, had no previous experience with such a sensitive project, and its industrial employees, only currently emerging from international isolation and still immersed in a socialist system that did not inspire foreign confidence, were an unknown quantity.

While our negotiations were going on, the political future of Hong Kong was being negotiated between the United Kingdom and the PRC, and the security of the colony was the subject of broad international discussion and concern. Anxiety over the colony's future reached its peak in late 1984, just when our negotiations were reaching their climax, as the United Kingdom and the PRC announced the conclusion of a Joint Declaration on the Future of Hong Kong. It called for the return of the colony to China in 1997 under a unique and untested arrangement characterized as "one country, two systems."

Fortunately, after some confidential talks between CLP leaders and then vice minister of electric power Li Peng, who later rose to become prime minister and preside over the tragic June 4, 1989, massacre of protesters in Beijing, the Chinese side returned to the negotiations and acquiesced to our demand. After that, the Daya Bay contract was relatively swiftly concluded, approved, and implemented. To my relief, and that of millions of Hong Kong residents, the venture has proved to be safe and efficient and, during the past four decades, a precedent for subsequent similar projects in China.

The CLP project was crucial to the successful opening of our Hong Kong office. We soon acquired other clients, large and small. As a result, we outgrew our original Hong Kong office and, after a few years, opened a large and glamorous office on the twentieth floor of Tower Two of the new Exchange Square development, the choicest location in the central district, right beside Hong Kong harbor. With Joan's help, we furnished the spacious quarters with tasteful Chinese art objects as well as some of her own very professional photos of Chinese life and scenery. The floor-to-ceiling windows in my office offered a mesmerizing view of the harbor, the adjacent mountains, and the ships and airplanes that dotted this gorgeous area. At our opening reception for clients and friends, Lord Kadoorie, whose respect for the Hong Kong dollar never allowed his companies to indulge in attractive offices, snorted in a friendly manner: "No wonder your fees are so high!"

We were very lucky to be able to recruit a talented, diverse, well-prepared, and energetic group of young lawyers to join Allen, Ellen, Kenneth, Ruben, and me in Hong Kong and Jamie Horsley in Beijing. Tim Gelatt, who worked closely with me at Harvard after a brilliant record as a University of Pennsylvania undergraduate sinologist, joined us after a brief tour working at our competitor Baker McKenzie. Tim Stratford, a member of what I liked to call my Harvard "Mormon Mafia," had come to law school after two years of mission service in Hong Kong and had worked as my student assistant. Hugh Scogin had been a learned graduate student in Chinese history at the University of Chicago until I persuaded him to study law with me at Harvard.

Larry Bates and Rory Macneil had written excellent third-year research papers on Chinese law under my supervision. Vivienne Bath, who had done her initial legal and China education in Australia, had proved to be an analytical scholar during her LLM year with me and came to Paul, Weiss after practical experience in Sydney. T. K. Chang, a Harvard College product who had studied with me as part of his four-year JD-MBA program in the law and business schools, joined us after a year in the trenches of the Wall Street firm Milbank, Tweed.

This group, of course, had its own contacts. That's how I first met David Pierce, who had studied at Harvard but was not known to me, in Singapore. Tim Gelatt urged the appointment of Alexa Lam, a Hong Kong resident who had studied law in the United States and worked at Baker McKenzie in Chicago. Steve Orlins introduced Laura Sherman to help with China issues that had to be dealt with in the firm's Washington office.

Stuart Valentine, a young Australian diplomat who decided to practice law, simply applied to our Hong Kong office. Mary Wong, originally from Hong Kong but who studied philosophy and then law in the United States, made it through the difficult Paul, Weiss recruiting process in New York as the first foreign ethnic Chinese woman ever hired as a regular associate. Michael March, who had studied law at Georgetown and done Chinese studies in Taiwan and the United States, came to us after a federal clerkship. Michael, after two years in the New York Corporate Department, like Mary, was happy to be posted to Hong Kong.

In 1984, I reluctantly decided that we had to ask Jamie Horsley, who had done a superb job running our Beijing office, to move to the New York office so that other firm partners could become more familiar with her work. Fortunately, Ellen Eliasoph agreed to move from Hong Kong to Beijing to fill the gap left by Jamie's departure. Ellen, while a Yale Law School student, had, like Tim Gelatt, spent a year as one of the first American law students to study in the PRC, so she felt comfortable returning to Beijing. There, she introduced two new Beijing acquaintances. Helena Kolenda was hired as a paralegal, but after two years returned to the United States to earn her law degree before rejoining us as a key lawyer in Beijing. Yvonne Chan, an outstanding young New Zealand lawyer who had been studying Chinese language and life in Beijing, became a valued contributor in Hong Kong as well as Beijing.

Our New York office always seemed to need new China hands as earlier hires were assigned to Hong Kong and Beijing. Tom Moore of New York University (NYU) School of Law joined us from the Simpson, Thacher firm. Jeanette Chan, originally from Hong Kong, had obtained college and law degrees in Canada but joined us after receiving an LLM from Harvard in 1986. I was also happy about recruiting Nicholas ("Nico") Howson and Matthew Bersani from Columbia Law School's elite China program run by my former Harvard collaborator, Professor Randle Edwards. Jeanette, Nico, and Yvonne all eventually became partners in the firm, a tribute to our expanding China practice.

I could not possibly take part in all the projects that descended on us and therefore had to pick my personal challenges carefully. I recall the satisfaction I felt from assisting one of the firm's traditional clients, H. J. Heinz of Pittsburgh, which I helped to find and develop a groundbreaking early consumer joint venture in south China. Not only did I and the Heinz representative have to struggle to obtain PRC project approval, but once the plant started, we also had to persuade Guangdong Province officials to suppress the many local trademark violators who soon began to market phony Heinz products with labels that almost looked like the real thing.

IBM then asked me to take on a much greater trademark challenge. Soon after it began to introduce thousands of new computers to eager Chinese consumers, it became plagued by local purveyors of rival models that purported to be IBM machines. To make matters worse, some of these even performed reasonably well. This was the first evidence I encountered of the commercial cooperation that had been secretly developing between mainland Chinese business entities and their counterparts in Kuomintang-controlled Taiwan The counterfeit IBM components were manufactured in Taiwan; the IBM-like logos, manuals, and packaging were produced in Hong Kong; and the finished products were assembled and sold by six enterprises operating in or near the Shenzhen SEZ in Guangdong Province, across from Hong Kong.

I thought that the central PRC government might welcome the opportunity to publicize favorably the efficacy of its new trademark law. The problem was how to enlist its support. I decided to call on Liu Gushu, the leading intellectual property official I had met a few times over the years. By the time IBM sought my aid in 1987, Liu had left government and opened a law office to make the most of his official experience and connections. With the help of Mary Wong, I put together a dossier on the case that enabled Liu to persuade the central government and the Guangdong authorities to crack down on the trademark offenders, which they did, showing both Chinese and foreigners that there were teeth in the new trademark law. IBM was happy with the outcome, and Mary and I published a detailed analysis of the case in the *China Business Review*, the magazine of the US-China Business Council.

I had already published many pieces on Chinese commercial law developments in this widely read magazine, and PRC officials often told me that they had carefully studied and benefited from government-produced translations of these essays. The one they most frequently mentioned had been entitled "Twenty Questions About China's New Joint Venture Law." A Ministry of Foreign Trade expert told me that I was sometimes referred to in internal discussions as "Twenty Question Cohen."

Whenever disputes arose, it was always better to try to settle them informally, as my Coudert experience had already demonstrated. Little was known about PRC courts in the 1980s, and what was known inspired more fear than confidence. Most foreign trade, investment, and technology transfer contracts with Chinese entities called for arbitration of disputes, either in China or abroad. Yet little was known about arbitration also. The best course, as I had quickly learned, was to seek to persuade relevant PRC authorities to come to our client's aid by ordering an offending Chinese company that came within its jurisdiction to cease its contract violations and provide other appropriate relief.

I demonstrated this to the amazement of the famous Honda corporation, which had been one of the first Japanese corporations bold enough to invest in the PRC. To obtain immediate access to the potentially great Chinese domestic market for motorcycles, Honda decided to take the risk of establishing a joint venture with a leading PRC motorcycle company based in Chongqing, one of China's largest cities and located deep in the country's interior. Honda was only interested in enhancing its sales in

China, not in producing Chinese motorcycles for export that might interfere with Honda's long-established and profitable operations in the United States and other countries. Its Chongqing joint venture contract therefore explicitly prohibited the export of the venture's products. Not long after production was successfully launched, however, Honda learned that the venture, managed by the Chinese, had been exporting its motorcycles to the U.S. market displaying the Honda brand and had even established a U.S. marketing operation that purported to have the exclusive right to sell Honda motorcycles.

This profoundly upset the Honda executives in Tokyo and understandably shook their confidence in China. In other countries, they would have immediately threatened to go to arbitration or court, as the contract permitted. But in China, they feared that any attempt to invoke formal legal remedies would render their company persona non grata and put an end to their business in the country, a belief that PRC officials did nothing to discourage. PRC officials often seemed to disdain or discriminate against Japanese businesspeople because of Japan's notorious wartime atrocities in China, so the Honda people were especially sensitive about what actions they might take, even in the face of outrageous bad faith on the part of their Chinese partner.

I assured them that there might well be a suitable response because they had both relevant legislation and explicit contract provisions on their side. I suggested that we approach the Foreign Investment Commission of Sichuan Province, which had jurisdiction over Chongqing investments. We did so, and the commission confirmed the facts and the law that we presented. The venture was ordered to cease its unauthorized exports, disband its marketing operation in the United States, and make appropriate amends to Honda. The Chongqing partner immediately complied, and I thereby earned the loyalty of my client, which in turn enhanced my reputation among Japanese companies seeking success in China. Before long, the Mitsubishi Corporation, which over a decade earlier had accepted my suggestion that it endow a professorship in Japanese law at Harvard, soon retained us for advice on several China matters.

In 1987, the United Nations was eager to cooperate with the PRC's State Economic Commission to review the progress that early foreign investment projects had made in China. It decided to convene a conference in Beijing of multinational companies from various countries to discuss their Chinese experiences to date and to recommend improvements in existing regulations and arrangements. I was asked to prepare a report analyzing relevant legal developments for submission to the conferees prior to the meeting. I invited my Paul, Weiss associate, Stuart Valentine, to join me in this research, and our report was soon made public and published. When I noticed that no Japanese companies had been invited to attend the conference, I pointed this out to the convenors, who made clear that the PRC hosts did not want Japanese to attend. I indicated that I thought this was a mistake for several reasons but had to acquiesce.

At the conference, PRC Vice Minister Zhu Rongji of the State Economic Commission, who was the host for the conference, made a passionate plea for the expansion of foreign investment in China. During his speech, without using the name of Japan, he made a bitter attack on "a country" that refuses to invest in China and promote the country's modernization but only wishes to sell its products. Having already been consulted by several Japanese companies and knowing their understandable concerns with China's legal system and the risks involved in PRC investments, I felt obligated, as consultant to the UN sponsors of the conference, to reply to Vice Minister Zhu's attack. I pointed out that no Japanese companies had been invited to the conference but that I was familiar with the thinking of some and could reflect their viewpoint. In particular, I cited the basic facts of the Honda experience as illustrative of the kind of problem that the Japanese feared might occur.

I had never met Vice Minister Zhu before and could not anticipate his response. In fact, he did not respond at all, but to my surprise remained silent. Yet my point evidently made an impact on the audience. I worried that there might be some adverse PRC reaction to my statement, but for two weeks there was no evidence of that. Then the *People's Daily*, the authorized newspaper of the Central Committee of the Chinese Communist Party, reported that Vice Minister Zhu had just delivered a lecture at a national business meeting where he emphasized the importance of all Chinese business units and officials respecting the provisions of contracts concluded with foreigners. If Chinese failed to honor their contracts, he said, China's hopes to attract foreign investment would never succeed.

I was naturally delighted to read this news, and after Zhu was promoted to the rank of minister, I had the opportunity to get acquainted with him. At one point, he invited me to join him and a Nobel Prize–winning economist from the University of Chicago named Miller for a delightful dinner, just the three of us. I later learned that Zhu's son was being advised by Professor Miller on his plans for study in the United States. Zhu, of course, went on to spur Shanghai's modernization as the city's dynamic mayor. That job then led to his designation as the country's prime minister and his persistent and successful effort to shepherd its monumental entry into the World Trade Organization.

Despite success in informally settling disputes for Heinz, IBM, and Honda, I was eager to test the reality of formal dispute resolution in China, and the opportunity soon came along. For several years, because both of us often lunched in the East Dining Room of the Peking Hotel, I occasionally bumped into the prominent British businessman Jack Perry, head of the London Export Corporation that had long been trading with China, even before Deng Xiaoping's Open Door Policy began in 1979. Jack was frequently identified as holding pro-Beijing political views and was a leader of the United Kingdom's 48 Group Club that had long taken the lead in conducting British trade with China, even during the dark days of Chairman Mao's most revolutionary years. In the summer of 1979, when Jack learned that I was helping the PRC to adopt its first foreign corporate and individual income tax legislation, he only half-jokingly criticized me for this effort, which was bound to have a financial impact on him and his company. In return, I only half-jokingly criticized him for surprisingly trying to deny revolutionary China the same right as other countries to impose taxation.

Nevertheless, several years later, Jack, without appointment, stopped by our Paul, Weiss office in the Peking Hotel one day, furious about what he deemed the most blatant PRC contract violation his company had ever suffered. He was determined to bring an arbitration against the offending PRC company, even though I cautioned him that, by doing so, he might risk a large amount of business because of the possibility of retaliation by a Ministry of Foreign Trade that had always denounced foreign efforts to invoke contract arbitration clauses. I recalled sitting in the bar of the Dongfang Hotel in Guangzhou night after night during my participation in the 1973 Canton Fair, listening to the grievances of foreign companies that had unsuccessfully sought to exercise their arbitration option against offending PRC companies.

Jack was well aware of the risk but insisted that arbitration was necessary to teach the Chinese side a lesson. Thus, against my better judgment,

I soon found myself as, I was told, the first Western lawyer ever to appear as advocate before the Chinese International Economic and Trade Arbitration Commission (CIETAC). This proved to be a memorable experience for all concerned.

The three-member arbitration panel was composed of Chinese foreign trade law experts, two of whom I had met briefly on other occasions. They ran the proceedings in a dignified, fair way and asked appropriate questions about the facts and law. As I faced them, I wondered why it might not be possible for three Chinese judges also to behave in similar fashion so that the courts could begin to inspire foreign confidence. My client Jack Perry, who attended the hearing, could see that I was having a good time, even when the Chinese contracts professor retained by the respondent sought to discredit my argument. At the conclusion of the hearing, and despite the fact that it left us with the impression that we might prevail, Jack had belatedly become increasingly worried that there might well be retaliation for his hubris. He told me: "You had a fine time at my expense."

The Chinese side, probably secretly in touch with the tribunal, must have been sobered by the experience and the prospect of loss, and settled the case before the tribunal rendered its decision. Although professionally disappointed not to have the anticipated arbitration award, I was delighted at the outcome, which pacified my client and apparently restored peace with his traditional trading partners. My able associate T. K. Chang, who assisted me in the arbitration, was later told by a Beijing lawyer who had served as a junior CIETAC staff member at the time of the arbitration that, if the case had gone to the award stage, we were expected to win.

The most curious assignment I undertook was to give modest tax advice to the mysterious Israeli businessman Shoul Eisenberg. Almost nothing except his presumed citizenship was known about him by his fellow denizens of the Peking Hotel. Day after day, for many weeks, we would see him sitting alone at lunch in the dining room of the East Wing, a kind of sixtyish sad sack. No one knew why he was there. In those years, the PRC, ostensibly devoted to the Arab countries of the Middle East, purported to be shunning Israel, with which it did not have diplomatic relations. Yet rumors occasionally suggested that Eisenberg was quietly providing Israeli weapons to China.

These reports were ultimately vindicated after Israel and China established diplomatic relations in 1992. It was later revealed that the Israeli

Parliament had accorded Eisenberg's international trading activity a special exemption from Israeli income taxation. At the time of his death in 1997, he was reported to be a hugely wealthy philanthropist who, in the 1980s controlled twenty companies doing business in thirty countries, most of them places where Western companies feared to tread. China continued to be prominent among them. During our brief acquaintance, however, his Beijing assistant only asked us to undertake the resolution of his company's tax status in China, a routine task that failed to reveal what they were actually up to.

Not all my China-related projects were strictly commercial, and among the noncommercial ones was my successful 1987 pro bono efforts to satisfy the demands of New York mayor Ed Koch to bring two giant pandas to the Bronx Zoo, if only for six months. After an innovative agreement with representatives of the Chinese Wildlife Foundation to lease the pandas—my idea—was finally reached in New York, T. K. Chang, then in charge of the Paul, Weiss office in Beijing, had to negotiate with the Chinese side to arrange for the air transportation of the pandas. The Chinese did not want the pandas to be shipped in the plane's baggage compartment, so a special compartment had to be built in the passenger section for them and their two keepers.

While all this was going on, Joan and I managed to keep our busy family life on track. We divided our time among China, Hong Kong, and New York. In Hong Kong, we rented an attractive flat in Century Tower at the foot of the island's Peak Tram in the midlevel district. When in New York, we continued in our small East 89th Street apartment, and every Friday took the 9 A.M. Eastern Airlines shuttle to Boston, where we spent the day. I saw students and colleagues at Harvard until I began teaching my 3 to 6 P.M. class, and Joan at the same time was at the School of the Museum of Fine Arts at Tufts University teaching Asian art history. After dinner with our oldest son Peter, who was practicing law in Boston following graduation from Harvard Law School, we would often drive to our house in Cape Cod for a relaxing weekend. During the week in New York, we kept in touch with our second son, Seth, while he completed medical school at Columbia and then advanced training in gastroenterology. Our youngest son, Ethan, after graduating from Harvard College in 1984, spent much of his time studying design at the Fashion Institute of Technology (FIT) in New York and then at the Haute Couture Center in Paris.

Despite her teaching, family obligations, op-eds, and frequent lecturing in many Chinese cities, Joan continued her art history scholarship. In 1987, she published her groundbreaking study of China's postliberation art, *The New Chinese Painting, 1949–1986*, replete with splendid photos of the rising generation of artists and their works. In addition, we published the third and final edition of our popular *China Today and Her Ancient Treasures* in 1986.

Joan also organized various art programs and exhibitions of her photos in New York, Boston, and other cities. As early as mid-1982, she curated "Painting the Chinese Dream: Chinese Art Thirty Years After the Revolution," which featured paintings and sculptures of the early post-Mao years. This exhibition, after four months at the Smith College Museum of Art, went on to Boston, where Mayor Kevin White presided at the opening ceremony and welcomed some of the Chinese artists whose works were on display.

Joan and I also sponsored the study in America of a few of the most outstanding younger artists we had met while living in China. Thanks to the generous hospitality of our dear friend Elizabeth Toupin, then dean of students at Tufts University, Yuan Yunsheng and then Qiu Deshu were able to spend successive years living in her house on the Tufts campus as distinguished artists in residence. I helped the dynamic and entrepreneurial painter Chen Yifei obtain his first visa from the American Consulate in Shanghai, and we assisted the Kong Boji family in adjusting to the New York area. Before he left China for Canada, Joan gave the promising and charming portrait painter Tang Muli requested advice about Western social life, and she made a trip or two to the murky bowels of New York's Lower East Side to help orient the recently arrived Ai Weiwei to Manhattan's harsh realities.

Our son Ethan, who always had his mother's talent for spotting artistic talent and had even organized an exhibition of contemporary Chinese art while a Harvard undergraduate, had befriended Ai Weiwei when both were new to the New York art scene. Indeed, as Weiwei recalls in his recent magnificent memoir, *1000 Years of Joys and Sorrows*, he put on his first solo exhibition, "Old Shoes, Safe Sex," in 1985 at the fledgling Art Waves/Ethan Cohen gallery in SoHo. Although no one except Ethan bought his work, Weiwei, Joan, and Ethan have remained friends ever since. At the time, I unfortunately paid no attention to the seemingly silent, shy fellow who occasionally turned up in our apartment. Only a generation later, after this now famous multi-achieving and courageous talent had begun to ridicule Chinese communist oppression openly, did we become friends, and, after his notorious detention, I published several op-eds that helped mobilize the public pressure that eventually led to his release.

Truly, until the tragedy of June 3–4, 1989, the 1980s were a stimulating, satisfying, and history-making time for the practice of law and cultural exchange relating to China and for me and my family personally. Things changed dramatically after that, as the next chapter will confirm.

20

POLITICAL JUSTICE IN TAIWAN

Freeing Annette Lu and Prosecuting Henry Liu's Assassins

I first heard of Annette Lu (Lu Hsiu-lien) from one of my prize students in the Harvard Law School Class of 1978, Jamie Horsley. Before entering law school, Jamie had done a year of graduate study and research in Taiwan during the academic year 1973–1974 and had learned of Annette's rising prominence as a newspaper columnist and activist for the cause of equal rights for women. Less well-known at the time was Annette's fervent belief in the cause of Taiwan's independence from Chinese governments on both the mainland and Taiwan, a belief that could not be publicly expressed under Chiang Kai-shek's dictatorship. Jamie suggested that Annette would be a fine candidate for a scholarship that would allow her to pursue an LLM degree at Harvard. Because I was then chair of the law school's graduate committee, that was easy for me to arrange, and Annette arrived in Cambridge in the fall of 1977.

One of Annette's LLM classmates from Taiwan was Ma Ying-jeou, who had already earned an LLM at New York University (NYU) but who was eager to pursue a doctorate at Harvard. My recent coauthor and respected junior colleague, Professor Chiu Hungdah, who had taught Ma in Taiwan, gave him the highest endorsement, and so I was happy to enlist a second outstanding academic prospect from Taiwan for our graduate program.

These two able scholars, both ambitious for an eventual political career back home, unfortunately did not get along well during their year together at Harvard. Ma, whose new bride had also earned an LLM at NYU and who served for a year as my research assistant on human rights issues relating to both the mainland and Taiwan, assiduously acquired further mastery of the field of public international law. Annette would periodically ask to see me to complain that she felt sure that he was reporting her support for Taiwan independence back to the Kuomintang (KMT) authorities in Taiwan. Although she never claimed that he was a KMT agent, she said that his attentiveness made her uncomfortable. Annette knew that I opposed Ma's support for the KMT dictatorship, but I could not take seriously her repeated wish "to throw him out of Harvard." I told her that the United States is a free country where she was free to make public her views and anyone else was free to listen and repeat them to others as long as they did not attempt to prevent her from expressing them.

At the end of the academic year, Ma, who compiled an excellent scholarly record, indicated his desire to stay on for admission to the doctoral program, which was granted. Annette, on the other hand, was more interested in immediately returning to Taiwan's political fray, which had become increasingly overheated. By June 1978, when Annette received her LLM, rumors were rife that negotiations between the United States and the People's Republic of China (PRC) on the mainland were close to establishing diplomatic relations, which would have resulted in termination of formal relations between the United States and the Republic of China on Taiwan. The implications of this anticipated move were momentous for Taiwan's political and legal status, bringing into even sharper focus the crucial issue of potential Taiwan independence. Annette wanted to play a role in this impending process, and the problem she confronted was how best to do this.

We had a long talk in my office at that time. Essentially she had two choices. One, which I preferred, was to work for Taiwan independence from outside the island, together with others who had long been active abroad in this quest. This could have been done in Japan, the United States, or Europe, and perhaps even Hong Kong. The other option was to return to Taiwan and gradually test the limits of freedom amid the accumulating tensions of the period.

Annette plainly preferred the latter. A strong speaker; energetic activist; and courageous, passionate person, she was itching to go home. I cautioned her with the words of the late President Harry Truman, who had famously warned would-be politicians: "If you can't stand the heat, don't go into the kitchen." To be sure, I was most worried that, after her return, she might soon be locked up and punished by the ubiquitous KMT secret police or even become the victim of foul play. When it became clear that she was determined to assume those risks, I said, half-jokingly: "Don't worry. If they lock you up, we [meaning the Democratic administration of human rights-minded Jimmy Carter and Senator Edward M. Kennedy, whom I had been advising for over a decade] will get you out." Those were words I later came to regret.

Annette did return to Taiwan in the summer of 1978, and on December 10, 1979 (International Human Rights Day), she and seven of her Taiwan independence colleagues were detained in Taiwan's second city of Kaohsiung after a KMT-sponsored gang provoked a riot during the activists' rally to promote their new flagship *FORMOSA Magazine*. This harsh KMT action came almost a year after Washington and Beijing had normalized diplomatic relations, isolating the Taiwan government then led by Chiang Ching-kuo, son of the late Chiang Kai-shek. Under strong pressure from the U.S. government and American public opinion, the KMT felt obligated to hold a public—albeit military—trial of the group that became known as the Kaohsiung Eight.

I was then working in Beijing and had hoped to be an observer at this trial on each of the dates for which it was initially scheduled. The trial, however, was held on a date that the Republic of China (ROC) government, which had been monitoring my phone calls from Beijing to Taipei, knew would make it impossible for me to attend because of an ironclad promise made to my most important China client, AMOCO, that I would take part in long-scheduled, crucial business negotiations in the capital. Fortunately, Timothy Gelatt, my protégé and friend, who became devoted to Annette during the year they overlapped at Harvard, was able to attend the trial. So too was my former Washington colleague John Kaplan, who later published a book about the trial.

To no one's surprise, a classic "show trial" took place, and the defendants all received severe punishments; Annette received a twelve-year criminal sentence. Recalling my ill-fated semi-humorous assurance that "we" would get her out of prison if worse came to worst, I was determined to try my best. Any influence I might have had with the KMT government had been reduced to nil, however, by my well-known, decade-long activities to facilitate what became known as "normalization of Sino-American relations." I did write a very long essay in the *Wall Street Journal Asia* condemning the trial and the continuing oppression by the KMT regime, even though the 1979 Taiwan Relations Act had ambiguously pledged the United States to protect Taiwan and thus the KMT.

For the next five years, I saw no political opening to help Annette, but domestic Taiwan and international developments gradually began to improve prospects for release of the persecuted. Then the KMT dropped the proverbial stone on its own foot. On October 15, 1984, three leading figures from Taiwan's most powerful criminal group, the United Bamboo Gang, sent to San Francisco at the behest of the Defense Intelligence Bureau of Taiwan's Ministry of National Defense, assassinated the Chinese American journalist Henry Liu, whose pen name was Jiang Nan (Yangtze River). That set off a political uproar in Taiwan-American relations once it was revealed that American intelligence agents had monitored post-assassination communications between the killers and the ROC government. The tragic assassination gave me the opportunity that I had lacked for freeing Annette.

I flew to Taipei from Hong Kong, where I was working, and arranged to see Ma Ying-jeou. After his 1982 return from acquiring his Harvard SJD degree, Ma had become a deputy secretary general of the KMT and President Chiang Ching-kuo's English-language interpreter. We had a frank but cordial chat. I emphasized that, because of the assassination, the KMT had never smelled worse in the United States and that it desperately needed to launch a new course designed to rehabilitate its dreadful reputation. I argued that the most immediate, effective step it could take, prior to the time necessarily required to deal with the killers and their government sponsors, would be the release of Annette Lu.

Of course, I remembered the animosity that had existed between Ma and Lu during their Harvard student days. Yet I believed that Ying-jeou would understand the need for "reform." I felt confident that he would see this occasion as an opportunity to begin to remedy the political damage done not only by the assassination but also by the earlier criminal convictions of the Kaohsiung Eight, and I believed he would urge President Chiang Ching-kuo to start with the release of his classmate.

Ma heard me out courteously and then suggested that I return to Taipei in two weeks to learn the response to my suggestion. When I did, he told me that the next day we had an appointment to meet Annette at the prison hospital, where she was receiving treatment for cancer. That meeting was probably the most emotionally moving one I have ever had. Ma looked healthy and handsome in a dark three-piece suit, and his mind was razor sharp. Annette appeared more forlorn than I had ever seen her, far from her former vibrant self and rather lethargic in a dull prison dress. We talked in English, and she spoke rather slowly and reflectively. I told her how embarrassed I was that I had not delivered on my semi-humorous assurance that "we" would get her out of any detention after returning to Taiwan. To my relief, she replied that she did not remember that assurance but did recall the admonition of President Truman that politicians should not enter the heat of the kitchen if not prepared to withstand it. Then she said: "I didn't realize how hot the kitchen could get!"

The three of us talked quietly for a bit over an hour before Ying-jeou and I returned to town. As I left him, he said that we might have an answer in about ten days, so I returned to my base in Hong Kong. As predicted, the good news that she was to be released arrived promptly—but with an unexpected condition. Annette had to agree to remain abroad for the next year. Of course, with delight I volunteered to arrange a fellowship for her to spend another year at Harvard, this time to take part in the university's Center for International Affairs, which I had twice before converted into an institution for the release and rehabilitation of persecuted Asian democratic leaders.

In collaboration with the family of Senator Benigno Aquino of the Philippines, I had helped to arrange for the senator's release from imprisonment imposed by President Ferdinand Marcos, who had a certain reverence for Harvard, if not for the lives of others. I had also organized a year's respite from dictatorial harassment for the courageous South Korean democratic leader Kim Dae-Jung, who had spoken at Harvard Law School's East Asian Legal Studies Program on two occasions and who was eager to enhance preparation for the term as the nation's president that he had long sought and ultimately obtained.

Annette returned to Taiwan from her second Harvard tour both intellectually and physically refreshed. In 2000, she was elected to the first of two successive terms as Taiwan's vice president under the banner of the Democratic Progressive Party. As this book goes to press, she continues to be politically active, although disappointed in her continuing failed quest to be elected the island's president. Ying-jeou, on the other hand, did manage to be elected president for two successive terms from 2008 to

2016 as the choice of a KMT that has had to adjust to Taiwan's impressive democratization.

The following will focus on the outcome of the Jiang Nan assassination cases, in which I also played a role.

A couple of weeks after the shocking 1984 assassination of the Chinese American author Henry Liu at his San Francisco home, and while I was supervising the Paul, Weiss office in Hong Kong, I received a phone call from one of my former Harvard Law School students who was practicing law on his own in the San Francisco Bay Area. He told me that he had just been retained by Liu's widow to pursue a wrongful death lawsuit for damages against the ROC government, which was widely believed to have orchestrated the killing. He asked whether the Paul, Weiss firm, well-known as one of America's most competent in civil litigation, might consider joining him in the case. He also specifically asked whether I would be willing to handle the Taiwan-related aspects.

Of course, I was thrilled to have an opportunity to be involved. I had not been in Taiwan since June 1978. In view of my prominent participation in the process of prodding the U.S. government to establish diplomatic relations with mainland China and withdraw formal relations from Taiwan's ROC government, many of my former students from Taiwan had urged me to postpone further visits until the island's domestic and international political situations had calmed down. I contemplated an eventual quiet return to Taipei on the occasion of some future uncontroversial business transaction.

The Henry Liu tragedy was not the opportunity for a quiet return that I had in mind, but it was too important to resist. I realized that, in addition to attempting to make progress on behalf of the case to be brought by Liu's widow, the visit would also give me the occasion for directly seeking the prison release of Annette Lu by renewing my friendship with her Harvard classmate Ma Ying-jeou, as discussed above. Yet I did not want to muddy the effort on behalf of Annette by also raising with Ma the claims of Henry Liu's widow. It seemed better, at least at that early stage, to pursue legal rather than political remedies regarding the Liu case.

I was proud of the Paul, Weiss firm for agreeing to represent Liu's widow and to do so pro bono, not even recovering all the expenses to be incurred on her behalf. The firm's senior partner, Arthur Liman, was excited at our chance to take part in the case, despite the fact this would put us in opposition to the still influential ROC government. With some obvious exaggeration, Arthur said: "I can't imagine taking on a more important case unless Gaddafi [then Libya's dictator] sends someone over to Israel to assassinate the chief rabbi of Jerusalem!"

Winning a wrongful death tort action against the ROC government in federal district court in San Francisco promised to be no simple matter. We expected the ROC to claim that, being a sovereign government, it was immune from such civil suits. The challenge was further complicated by the fact that, as of 1979, the ROC was no ordinary sovereign government but one that no longer maintained diplomatic relations with the United States. It required the skilled advocacy of Paul, Weiss appellate lawyers before the federal Ninth Circuit Court of Appeals to put to rest the issues involved in holding the ROC potentially liable. That left us, however, with the more difficult task of finding evidence sufficient to prove that the ROC was indeed responsible for orchestrating the assassination. That challenge was largely left to me.

Of course, if the killers from the United Bamboo Gang and the ROC officials who had allegedly commissioned them could have been brought to the United States to face prosecution for murder, our evidentiary challenge might have been a bit less complex. But by that time, the United States and the ROC no longer maintained diplomatic relations, and the two governments in any event had no extradition arrangement. The ROC refused to agree to ad hoc extradition of the suspects.

This subjected the ROC government, which, despite its loss of diplomatic relations, was still dependent on the United States for its defense, to enormous political and diplomatic pressure. Both the U.S. government and American opinion had reacted severely to the brazen assassination of a U.S. citizen on U.S. soil. The ROC also felt local pressure from a Taiwanese population increasingly resistant to the harsh dictatorial rule of the KMT. Thus, President Chiang Ching-kuo reluctantly agreed to prosecute those allegedly responsible in Taiwan.

PROSECUTION OF THE ASSASSINS

Announcement of the Taiwan prosecution of the United Bamboo Gang members seemed to offer a way to a successful civil suit against the ROC government in San Francisco. Yet that didn't solve our most difficult problem, which was to acquire enough evidence to establish the KMT government's responsibility for inspiring the assassination. To obtain the evidence we needed, and as the representative of Chiang Nan's widow, I decided to file a civil damage suit against the United Bamboo Gang killers in Taiwan court and to attempt to have that suit joined with the criminal prosecution to which the KMT government had committed itself, something that was allowed by Taiwan law.

My first priority was to find a competent Taiwan attorney who could serve as my counsel for this relatively innovative proceeding. My first attempts to do this failed. Even some of my best former students showed no interest in joining me in the case. It was too politically sensitive. Thanks to an introduction by another of my former students, the able legal historian Chang Fu-mei, I met Frank Hsieh Ch'ang-t'ing, a dynamic member of the Taipei city council known for his willingness to challenge the KMT. He obviously saw this case, despite its dangers, as an opportunity to enhance his political career. Frank seemed to be a very competent and energetic litigator, and we proved to be an effective team.

I was not permitted, however, to take part in the initial trial of the Taiwan prosecution against the United Bamboo Gang killers. After the district court judge's negative ruling on my participation as representative of the widow got plenty of press coverage, however, I was at least allowed to observe the initial trial, which was held under maximum security. At the end of each day's hearing, I continued, on television and in press reports, to criticize the trial judge's refusal to allow me to enter the case. After the defendants were convicted and while they appealed the judgment, Frank and I took the opportunity to appeal the court's decision to exclude me from the trial—and we won. The decision to exclude me was reversed and I could take part in the appeal, which, under ROC law, allowed an entire new trial. That in turn meant, following the examination of witnesses by prosecution, defense, and court in the criminal part of the trial, that in the civil part I and my lawyer Frank were allowed to question the witnesses and even the defendants. Of course, the proceedings were all in Chinese, which enhanced the challenge for me.

Even though most of the targets of my cross-examination testified, in Watergate style, that they could not remember the key events in question, and Admiral Wang Hsi-ling, the government mastermind of the plot, lied about the facts, I thoroughly relished the experience, which did enable us to get much of what we needed for the American case. Most important was that Frank was able to obtain the transcript of the pretrial interrogation of the accused by the police, which helped to verify the government's involvement in arranging the murder. It also brought out the intriguing detail that General Chiang Wei-kuo, younger brother of President Chiang Ching-kuo and then third-ranking official in the Ministry of National Defense, had been guest of honor at a housewarming luncheon given by a famous film director where the leader of the United Bamboo Gang and Admiral Wang, the orchestrator of the assassination, met for the first time!

General Chiang told the media that he had attended the lunch "for purely social reasons" and that there had been no discussion of the Chiang Nan problem at the lunch. Yet it appeared that, whatever his reason for attending, his presence demonstrated to the United Bamboo Gang chief, Chen Chih-li, that Admiral Wang was on very friendly terms with the president's brother. This demonstration proved useful when, the following week, Admiral Wang solicited the United Bamboo Gang chief to "teach a lesson" to Henry Liu, which would thus be seen as a patriotic act on behalf of the nation's highest officials.

Admiral Wang and his two closest aides in the Intelligence Bureau of the Ministry of National Defense were not prosecuted along with the United Bamboo Gang defendants in the regular criminal courts, but they were subjected to court martial instead. I was permitted to attend a public hearing of the case, the most notable aspect of which was the unusually bold defense made by Admiral Wang. He denied responsibility for Chiang Nan's murder. To back up his claim, he boasted that, if his Defense Intelligence Bureau had done the job, the killers would never have been identified. With some pride he told the tribunal: "You know, your honors, we are professionals. Ten or twenty years ago we used to do things like this all the time and were never discovered." When he said that, a hush overcame the courtroom audience of perhaps one hundred shocked people.

Admiral Wang's boast failed, and, like the principal defendant in the civilian trial, United Bamboo Gang chief Chen Chih-li, he was found guilty and received a life sentence. But he was treated like a distinguished prison guest while confined and, like Chen, managed to win release from prison some years later. For me and many others, this was a disappointing conclusion to what was said to have been Taiwan's most notorious criminal case up to that time.

Nevertheless, I believe that the "Chiang Nan ming-an," coming as it did on the eve of Taiwan's political reform era, played a helpful role in many aspects of Taiwan's progress. Both in Taiwan and abroad, the necessarily well-publicized trials plainly exposed the lawless violence underlying the KMT dictatorship, demonstrated that restrictions on the repressed media could be defied, promoted respect for human rights, and increased pressures for democratic reforms and a genuine rule of law. I have always been proud of my participation in this historic process.

It also made possible the successful outcome of our San Francisco litigation against the ROC government that we had brought on behalf of Liu's widow, Tsui. The KMT government, which needed to improve its image in the United States, offered to settle. Thus, after a couple of discussions between a Taipei law firm representing the ROC and me, we agreed on $1 million plus as payment to Tsui, which in the mid-1980s was a significant sum, especially because our firm claimed no fee for its services and did not even seek reimbursement for expenses. Nor did Paul, Weiss seek to publicize its accomplishment.

21

THE DARK DAYS OF 1989

China's Tragedy and Vietnam's Promise

When the student protests began in Beijing in mid-April 1989, I thought that this too shall pass, like the 1986–1987 student protests that Deng Xiaoping had condemned as "bourgeois liberalism" and managed to subdue without ending the country's favorable course of development. Those earlier protests had caused the unfortunate fall of the progressive Communist Party general secretary Hu Yaobang, whom the conservatives within the party held responsible for the political unrest. Fortunately, Hu was replaced by the dynamic Zhao Ziyang, who continued to promote political, economic, and legal reforms within the limits imposed by the party.

However, when the 1989 protests continued to grow and attracted workers as well as students from elsewhere in the country as well as Beijing, and when the protesters steadfastly refused to decamp from Tiananmen Square, I began to fear the worst. After martial law was declared on May 19, it became clear that this had become a much more serious situation than in 1987 and that the conservative Li Peng's replacement of Zhao Ziyang as the formal party chief would not end the matter. Several friends recalled what I had said so controversially on Ted Koppel's show *Nightline* in 1987: it's heartwarming when students go into the streets calling for democracy, but if that leads to less democracy rather than more, perhaps self-restraint might be preferable. On the night of June 3, when the People's Republic of China (PRC) military initiated the sustained massacre of many hundreds, if not several thousands, of protesters and bystanders, the China of the 1980s had plainly come to an end.

I had spent most of May in the Paul, Weiss Hong Kong office, from which we watched events in Beijing and other Chinese cities with increasing anxiety. Toward the end of the month, I returned to New York to deal with some administrative matters and spend the Memorial Day weekend at Cape Cod with the family. Although the situation appeared to be increasingly serious, I had not yet thought that events might soon develop in such a way that I might want to accelerate my eventual return to academic life.

In the fall of 1988 I was offered the attractive opportunity of being interviewed for New York University's (NYU) deanship, but I'd turned that down. I had also been regularly deflecting Harvard Law School's (HLS) dean James Vorenberg's annual offers for me to return to full-time teaching in Cambridge, Massachusetts, although I did continue my part-time Harvard lectures. Indeed, just before martial law was declared in China, I spent several hours in the Paul, Weiss Hong Kong office completing the very strong letter that I had promised HLS's new dean, Robert Clark, in support of a permanent faculty appointment for Professor William Alford as my Harvard successor in the Chinese law field. I was uncertain about when I might want to resume full-time teaching and whether I would want to return to Harvard, and thus it seemed unwise and unfair to all concerned, especially to students, to postpone any further a permanent appointment for a position that had remained vacant since my departure from full-time teaching a decade earlier.

The declaration of martial law did not prepare anyone for the brutal slaughter that was about to take place and that shook the world. Like most Chinese, most of us Hong Kong–based foreign observers were naïve enough to believe that the Chinese army would not kill masses of the Chinese people. June 4 changed everything. I remember lunching in our New York office with a few China associates on Friday, June 3, as word arrived about the beginning of the tragedy that was taking place in Beijing, where it was already early on the fourth. Someone came in with a portable radio that caused us a dyspeptic lunch. We knew something profoundly ugly was occurring that would alter the happy patterns of our existence. By the next day, the full horror of the occasion was upon us, and I had some preliminary thoughts about the implications.

My first thought had to be about personnel. We had to confirm the safety of our Beijing staff. There was no chance for them to leave Beijing, but we had to be sure that they continued to keep out of harm's way as young soldiers randomly continued to spray central residential areas with their bullets. We also had to worry about securing our tiny Shanghai office because that city was demonstrating unrest. Of course, we canceled plans for any of our people to travel to Beijing and indeed to anywhere in China. Oddly enough, the most immediately affected person was a Harvard undergraduate named Greg whom we had just hired for a year's internship in our Shanghai office. Greg had already shipped a suitcase of clothing and personal effects to Shanghai and was about to fly there himself, when we rerouted him to work in the Hong Kong office instead.

I also felt sorry for the two talented HLS women who, after completing their first-year studies, had already arrived in Hong Kong as summer associates planning to work on China transactions. There was no concern for their personal security, of course, because Hong Kong was not confronting protests, but there was some concern for their training and eventual future. Six months earlier, it had looked to be the start of an exciting career in the China practice for which Sarah Burgess and Ada Tse were admirably preparing, but it had suddenly been literally blown up in Beijing gun smoke shortly after they landed in Hong Kong.

I also began to speculate about the bearing of events on our practice generally. I estimated that it would take at least two to three years before we could return to the level of activity we had been enjoying. What would happen in the interim to my beloved Paul, Weiss colleagues in Beijing, Hong Kong, and Shanghai? Would we have to close our three China-related offices? Where would the lawyers go? Would the New York office absorb them? Would they want to return to New York to work on projects of less interest to many of them than China assignments? Might it be possible to expand the Vietnam practice that I had just begun and thus provide work for my colleagues? None of us had the same expertise regarding Vietnam that we did on China.

And what about me? Being a generation older than the colleagues I had recruited, I had witnessed previous sharp reversals in the PRC's pendulum-like progress and seemed better able than they, who had only known the largely optimistic post-1978 years, to withstand the emotional shock of June 4. Yet I was outraged by what had occurred and felt the need to express myself fully, regardless of the professional consequences.

I remember how angrily I rejected the invitation, just a few weeks after June 4, of PRC chief justice Ren Jianxin, who was also head of the powerful party political-legal committee that controlled the country's police and prosecutors as well as its courts, to be a featured speaker at an international rule of law conference that the PRC had the chutzpah to host that fall. Using a disdainful phrase often employed by party propagandists, I told patent expert Liu Gushu, who personally conveyed the invitation at the request of the chief justice, that I was not about to be "a running dog" of the party. Liu was visibly surprised at my vehemence, which implied that indeed he was one of the party's "running dogs." That is probably what ended our friendly contacts. I also published a very long essay attacking the party's massive violations of human rights not only during the June 4 massacre but also during its aftermath.

All our Western and Japanese clients that had been focusing on investments in China ceased their efforts, and revenues for the Hong Kong and Beijing offices dropped off sharply. I revved up our Vietnam prospects and canvassed all our major China clients to determine whether they might be interested in exploring Vietnam. Although a few, feeling the loss of China business as much as we did, promptly showed interest, again this was a long-run situation. To spur this effort, in 1990, together with a couple of associates, I published a modest book introducing Vietnam's preliminary efforts to attract foreign investment.

It didn't take many months before the Paul, Weiss headquarters in New York began to consider closing the larger and more expensive Hong Kong office as well as our one-lawyer office in Shanghai. Jamie Horsley and I naturally understood the pressure and began to discuss various options. When the firm even suggested the possibility of closing the Beijing office, however, that seemed an excessive and shortsighted reaction. I told the head of our international committee that, if that occurred, I would leave the firm.

Fortunately, patience prevailed. But our Hong Kong associates gradually began to scatter—enlisting in government service, academic life, business, and law practice elsewhere. A few continued with the firm either in Beijing or New York. Jamie herself decided to turn a vice into a virtue by resigning from the firm in mid-1990 as we closed the Hong Kong office in order to join her husband, an American diplomat who had been posted to the U.S. embassy in Manila. She had been commuting to Manila from Hong Kong on weekends for over a year, which had proved to be a strain and surely not the best way to foster their plans for raising children.

That last year of the Hong Kong office was a sad but diverse and challenging time. One had to be prepared for anything. One of the weirdest events occurred over Thanksgiving weekend of 1989. Joan and I were at our Cape Cod house for an annual family reunion. On Friday morning I received a rather frantic telephone call from the Canadian consul-general in Shanghai, whom I did not know. He told me that our valued law firm associate Jeanette Chan, a Canadian national, had been detained that afternoon at the Shanghai airport by the PRC customs authority on suspicion of seeking to exit China with illegal drugs.

Jeanette, who had been staffing our tiny Shanghai office, had been preparing to return to her home in Hong Kong for the weekend. Our Harvard intern Greg's suitcase had been shipped from Cambridge to Shanghai prior to June 4 and was still in Shanghai, although he had been rerouted to work in Hong Kong. He had asked Jeanette to bring the suitcase to Hong Kong with her, and she agreed. When a Shanghai customs inspector asked her to open the luggage, however, he spotted among Greg's clothing a jar of white powder labeled "Joe Wider's athletic supplement" that he suspected might be cocaine. The Shanghai airport lacked the technical capacity to test the material, and the customs officials said that they would have to send it to their Guangzhou facility and that the result would not be available until the next day. In the interim, Jeanette would not be allowed to leave for Hong Kong and would have to be detained under guard at the airport hotel. At that point, Jeanette called the Canadian consulate for help, and, at her suggestion, the consul-general called me for verification of her status.

Confident that the suspicion was baseless, I urged the consul-general to protest Jeanette's detention with the local government. When he seemed uncertain how to proceed, I said that he should act in accord with the provisions of the Canada-China consular agreement. With considerable embarrassment, he confessed that he could not find a copy of the agreement in his office! We agreed that he should immediately seek the guidance of the Canadian embassy in Beijing.

By noon the next day, Guangzhou customs officials confirmed that the white powder seized was not cocaine, and Jeanette prepared to fly belatedly to Hong Kong. By that time, however, word of the incident had spread throughout the Shanghai airport together with gossip that claimed this might be the biggest Shanghai airport drug bust in recent years. Understandably the local police decided to do their own investigation, and they decided that Jeanette could not leave the premises until their investigation had concluded. They detained her at the airport hotel for another day until they were satisfied that there was nothing to the suspicion.

At the same time, a local correspondent for Hong Kong's *South China Morning Post*, the leading English-language newspaper in Asia, reported that Jeanette, employed by a prominent U.S. international law firm with a Hong Kong office, had been detained on a drug charge, a story that unfairly inflicted harm to all concerned. I obviously had to take steps to correct the situation. Within a few days, despite my presence in the United States, I managed to obtain both an apology from the Chinese General Administration of Customs and publication by the *South China Morning Post* of a story that accurately confirmed the injustice suffered by Jeanette and the apology issued by the PRC officials.

Fortunately, no similar incidents marred my efforts to restore our law practice. Of course, I made several long visits to Vietnam in order to introduce some of the clients we had served in China to this new environment that was modeled on the PRC's experience during the 1980s. I even accepted an invitation to lecture in the Soviet Union about the success— until June 4—of foreign investment in China because, amid the turmoil of the late Mikhail Gorbachev period, there was increasing interest in Moscow and Leningrad in emulating the PRC's pre–June 4 accomplishments.

Despite the difficulties of the post-Tiananmen era in China, I did not want to abandon practice; Paul, Weiss; or my younger colleagues who chose to remain with the firm. Yet I did want to reestablish an academic base so I could securely devote more energy to attempting to defend the human rights of the Chinese people and help the PRC's legal system recover from the crushing blow of June 4. While debating about what to do, luck—both bad and good—intervened to delay my decision.

The bad luck came in Seattle, Washington, where I went after learning that I was being considered for the deanship of the University of Washington School of Law, a job I was offered but decided not to take. As I got out of bed the second morning in Seattle, I felt as though a sledgehammer had landed on the back of my head. I recovered in a few minutes;

managed to shave, shower, and dress; and arrived at my breakfast meeting on time. But in my second meeting that morning, with the university's vice president, I began to feel worse and wondered whether it might be wise to reveal my indisposition. I didn't want to be impolite and interrupt the meeting, but I thought it might be more impolite to try to stay the course and end up dying on the vice president's floor. Fortunately, my host was a man of action and, within what seemed like only fifteen minutes, I found myself in the nearby university hospital being attended by the head of neurosurgery, who turned out to be one of the leading specialists in the country.

I was soon diagnosed as having suffered a subarachnoid hemorrhage, an illness that, I was told, quickly killed about half of its victims. Indeed, a few years later, it claimed the life of my prized colleague and former student Tim Gelatt, who collapsed outside a Greenwich Village restaurant at age thirty-eight. I was luckier, especially because I did not even require the brain surgery that most survivors had to undergo. Nevertheless, the outcome in my case was not clear for several days. On day two in the hospital, as I began to feel a bit better, I asked my neurosurgeon what my chances were. His bedside manner was not as skilled as his medical talents, and he replied: "If you live to the end of the week, you'll be fine!" I already knew the situation was serious because, a few hours earlier, my son Seth, an orthodox Jew and a medical doctor, appeared in my hospital room, having flown overnight from New York, although it was Saturday, relying on the Talmud's exception to the rule against Sabbath travel in case of medical emergencies. After a full week in the intensive-care unit, I was released from the hospital on an outpatient basis on the understanding that I could not travel beyond Seattle for several weeks.

I did not regret my five weeks in Seattle. I recognized that the deanship opportunity may have saved my life and given me the more than three decades of active existence that have followed. Had I not stopped in Seattle, I might well have been stricken on the plane to Hanoi or in Vietnam itself, where the medical attention at the time would not have measured up to the treatment I received in the splendid University of Washington (UW) hospital. The period spent in recovery also gave me more than enough time to contemplate my future direction.

A return to Harvard was not feasible. HLS would not permit permanent faculty to practice law to the extent that I still intended. Indeed,

I realized that a law school in New York would be essential to suit my desire to follow the admonition of Chairman Mao to "walk on two legs." I knew that both Columbia and NYU would allow me to retain my law firm partnership while serving as a full-time professor.

At that time Columbia was the more prestigious of the two and would have seemed the better choice, but it already had a flourishing China program, thanks to Professor Randle Edwards. I wanted to renew teaching but continue in practice. Yet I felt that Columbia didn't need me and that it might be awkward for my dear friend Randy if his former Harvard boss were to "horn in on" his Columbia achievement.

By contrast, NYU was a blank slate with regard to China. So I got in touch with Professor Harry First on the faculty, who had called me two years earlier in an effort to enlist me in the deanship. I asked him whether the school might be interested in my joining merely as a regular faculty member while continuing to practice law roughly half-time. This produced an immediate, favorable response from NYU's new dean, the dynamic, imaginative, and ebullient John Sexton.

John had been an HLS student in the mid-1970s, but we had never met. However, he was a close friend and study group colleague of his HLS classmate Jamie Horsley, who had given him an enthusiastic endorsement of my teaching and research. John was also eager to raise NYU's profile by persuading as many Harvard, Yale, and Columbia faculty as possible to join his school. So the stars were aligned for my joining NYU as of July 1, 1990. Paul, Weiss graciously agreed to the new arrangement, with the understanding that my NYU salary would go to the firm as though it were income generated by my practice.

My hope was to keep the Paul, Weiss Beijing office going for the two- or three-year period that I estimated would be required before foreign business with China would begin to boom again. That meant expenses would have to be kept to a minimum. Staffing would have to remain thin and at junior levels of lawyer compensation. With the very competent help of a mix of our qualified young associates, we managed to do that until, following Deng Xiaoping's famed southern tour of South China near the start of 1992, business gradually began to pick up significantly.

I traveled back and forth as much as my new teaching duties would allow and managed to continue my public activities in China as well. One especially memorable event was the speech that I was asked to give in Beijing in early 1992 by the Foreign Correspondents' Club of China (FCCC), an important group that had been squelched in the aftermath of June 4 and that had not convened a public meeting since then. As the political climate began to relax in 1992, they invited me to give a talk at the Great Wall Hotel Beijing, the city's most visible Chinese-foreign joint venture project, in order to discuss the impact of June 4 on China's legal system.

Given the timing, the circumstances, and the sensitivity of the topic, it was not clear until the last minute that the event would actually take place. The Beijing police had previously forced the cancellation of one or two similar programs, and there were rumors that ours would suffer a similar fate. Despite the tension evident in the crowd that filled the large dining room, all went well, including the lively question period. Because of the prominence of the occasion, the Voice of America (VOA) recorded the entire session, which added to my sense of satisfaction. Little did I anticipate the consequences.

The next morning, I was confronted in the lobby of my hotel by the deans of Beijing's five major law schools. This was something of a shock, especially because I had just seen these colleagues two days earlier at a conference climaxed by a congenial cocktail party that the Ford Foundation's Beijing office had organized to promote our study of national legal education. At that time, the deans, all hoping that the Ford Foundation would renew its generous sponsorship of China's legal education, could not have been more convivial. But forty hours later, as they accosted me in the lobby of the Jianguo Hotel, there was nothing convivial about their demeanor. They were there to register "a solemn protest" against my FCCC speech, which had been rebroadcast all over the country by the VOA and which had even been heard by Prime Minister Li Peng. How could I, "a friend of China," the deans asked, have reported that after June 4, China's courts had become an instrument for repressing the Chinese people?

I claimed to be puzzled by their inquiry. After all, I noted, all I had done was to report what Chief Justice Ren Jianxin had repeatedly and publicly admonished the country's courts to do—to repress all counter-revolutionaries mercilessly. The deans replied that I had misunderstood the situation. Repression of counterrevolutionaries was surely not repression of the Chinese people because, by definition, counterrevolutionaries were not among "the people"! I laughed in scorn and told them that I had to hasten to check out of the hotel and make my way to the airport.

Ironically, I was in China with Nicholas ("Nico") Howson to visit provincial law schools and assess for the Ford Foundation the impact of June 4 on legal education. We fortunately did not meet any additional obstacles to compiling our report, which recommended further Ford Foundation support for China's legal education despite the huge setback inflicted by the June 4 tragedy. The Ford Foundation, virtually alone among major foreign charitable organizations, admirably understood the importance of not abandoning support for the youth and intellectuals of China because of the abominations committed by the country's elderly leaders.

By 1993, in the months after Deng Xiaoping's southern tour, the PRC announced that some foreign law firms would finally be allowed to register formally under their own names rather than as representatives of a client or as international trading organizations. It was made clear that not all firms would be immediately permitted to register. This set off a silent competition among the main U.S. international law firms to gain the favor of the local authorities and the Ministry of Justice.

Although I had been the first U.S. lawyer to set up shop in Beijing, initially for Coudert Brothers in 1979 and then for Paul, Weiss in 1981, I suspected that registration for Paul, Weiss could not be taken for granted, especially in view of my well-known opposition to June 4 and the subsequent repression. Politics is always a factor in PRC government decision making. Indeed, we were not the first U.S. firm to be granted permission and, as I began to become uneasy about our prospects, I asked my dear friend Xiao Yang at the Beijing Economic Development Corporation (BEDC) to inquire about the situation. He soon informed me that there was in fact political opposition that had been drummed up by another leading U.S. firm that was eager for registration. One of the young Chinese lawyers in its employ, whose father was a prominent PRC legal official in the commercial field, had argued against approving Paul, Weiss because of my human rights activities. Xiao was able to exert his considerable behind-the-scenes influence on our behalf, and we were ultimately registered along with several other firms.

By that time, Beijing had constructed its first office building, the Science and Technology Center, to accommodate international trade and investment firms, and we moved from our Beijing Hotel rooms into somewhat more satisfactory quarters in the building that came to be known as Sci-Tech. We were asked to handle many transactions involving knowledge of American securities regulations as well as project financing for power projects and other investments. Nico Howson and Helena Kolenda actually ran the Beijing office successfully for several years until Nico had to return to New York to undergo final pre-partnership scrutiny.

By 1994, it had become apparent, even to doubters in the firm, that we had to reestablish the Hong Kong office, which we did by asking Jack Lange, an able younger partner formerly at the State Department, to take the lead in accomplishing that task. Soon, both the Beijing and Hong Kong offices began to flourish and forged efficient cooperation not only with New York and Washington but also with the firm's Tokyo office. This was good timing because, by 1997, it was time for me, at age sixty-seven, to begin what the firm referred to as "the eldering process," which led to retirement at age seventy. I had mixed feelings about retirement. I had thoroughly enjoyed my two decades of China practice and was proud to have secured it by getting Nico, Jeanette Chan, and Yvonne Chan all elevated to partnership. Had I decided to continue in practice after my Paul, Weiss retirement, I had a few obvious options to join competing firms. But those offers actually helped me to realize that I wanted to be free of the restrictions and impositions on my time that practice imposed. I was eager to build on my decade of part-time experience at NYU and create an Asia-related academic institution similar to the one I had developed at Harvard.

22

ACADEMIC RENEWAL

Charting New York University's East Asian Law Path

Beginning in 1990, I had a wonderful three decades teaching at New York University (NYU) School of Law, especially after retirement from my Paul, Weiss partnership in 2000. That enabled me to devote myself full-time to academic and public pursuits. At NYU, I focused on three courses. In the fall semester, I usually offered a general introduction to the contemporary Chinese legal system that tended to emphasize criminal justice, legal institutions, and civil liberties. In the spring semester, I gave two courses relating to international law, one dealing with foreign business transactions with China and the other with intergovernmental relations, that is, public international law.

These courses were all quite popular, and I was particularly proud of the widespread interest in the legal aspects of doing business with the People's Republic of China (PRC). By the time I turned over that course to my former Coudert Brothers colleague Owen Nee, who gave a similar course as an adjunct professor at Columbia Law School, I had attracted an enrollment of 118 students, a very large number for a specialized course that had nothing to do with preparing students for the post-graduation bar exam.

In all courses, I was pleased not only with the numbers of interested students but also with their quality. Their classroom performance wasn't inferior to what I had been accustomed to at Harvard, and those who chose to do a research paper in lieu of a final exam occasionally produced studies worthy of law review publication. A few students were readily identifiable as excellent candidates for a career in academic life. And I found faculty-student contacts to be frequent, informal, and generally agreeable.

Because of my continuing responsibilities in law practice during my first decade at NYU, I played a less prominent role in the faculty than I did during my full-time years at Harvard. All I had time for from 1990 to 2000 was the development of Asian-related programs. I paid little attention to the many other issues that came before the faculty and didn't even attend the regular faculty meetings. I disappointed Dean John Sexton by my failure to integrate with the faculty, and on several occasions, he urged me to try harder.

I should have tried to pin John to a commitment to allocate several million dollars to the creation of an Asian law center to rival the one I had launched at Harvard Law School (HLS). I assumed, given his prodigious fundraising talent and the importance of China and Japan, that money for our activities would not be a problem. I didn't even insist on a faculty appointment with formal security of tenure. When John offered to start the process of assuring tenure, I said that the only tenure that interested me was one that he and NYU could not grant—continued long life.

When I learned that John had never been to Asia, however, I insisted that he promise to spend two weeks every summer with me for the next five years visiting the major countries of East Asia. This he readily agreed to do, and we had many remarkable and fruitful experiences. John was especially impressed by the experts from Japan, China, South Korea, and Taiwan whom in earlier years I had invited to be visiting professors at Harvard Law School. He wanted to invite them for teaching stints at NYU too. This was the origin of NYU's global program. John realized that we could not limit our global teaching opportunities to Asians but had to expand the number of visiting appointments to include outstanding scholars from Europe and other areas as well.

For several years, I ran the school's regular international program, which enabled me to invite a few promising academics, officials, and lawyers from China and Taiwan as visiting scholars. But until 2006, we had no NYU School of Law institution identifiably linked to China or Asia. I became increasingly aware of the need for such an institution, especially when chatting with applicants for law school admission who would ask why NYU didn't feature a specialized Asia-related center such as those that existed at Harvard, Yale, Columbia, Penn, and some other law schools.

I found the question to be slightly irritating and would assure the applicants that, in terms of courses offered, research produced, and relevant extracurricular activities, NYU compared favorably to any other law school in its Asia focus. Nevertheless, with the enthusiastic cooperation of Professor Frank Upham as codirector and the support of the law school's new dean, Richard Revesz, we finally established the U.S.-Asia Law Institute, which quickly became known as USALI. One of the law school's most outstanding recent graduates, Margaret K. Lewis, played a crucial role in assisting us at the outset, as did a very able young research scholar from Shanghai, Daniel Ping Yu.

I loved the institute's activities. Once or twice a week throughout the academic year, I invited some interesting guest relevant to East Asian studies to join me in a public lunch conversation. We also ran a separate set of late afternoon research seminars so that our visiting scholars could present their findings and benefit from comments from our USALI research group. Every year, we had about a dozen visiting scholars from China, Japan, Taiwan, South Korea, and occasionally Vietnam. Thus, we gradually developed a network of Asian colleagues that enhanced the possibilities and significance of our work in various ways.

A highlight of each year's agenda was—and still is—the one-day program on some aspect of Chinese law that we held in honor of the memory of the late Timothy Gelatt. Tim was an outstanding lawyer, teacher, and scholar who had taught Chinese law at NYU on a part-time basis and had made great contributions to our understanding of contemporary China before his untimely death from a brain hemorrhage on the streets of Greenwich Village in 1994. These annual events, which began before the establishment of USALI, benefited from USALI's administration and brought to the law school many outstanding experts for stimulating exchanges.

Within a few years of its establishment, and with the support of the Ford Foundation; the U.S. State Department's Bureau of Democracy, Human Rights, and Labor (DRL); and private donors, USALI managed to locate the funding required to house several full-time researchers on the PRC's legal system, and we began to produce both practical and scholarly comparative research studies that focused largely on legal institutions, criminal justice, and human rights in China.

Crucial to USALI's development was the recruitment in 2012 of Ira Belkin to serve as executive director. Ira, a 1982 graduate of NYU School of Law, had already become expert in the Chinese language through his prelaw studies, and he maintained that competence throughout sixteen years as a federal prosecutor. Ira finally decided to combine his Chinese skill with his legal talent and became legal adviser to the U.S. embassy in Beijing for six years. He subsequently left government and transferred to the Ford Foundation's Beijing office, where he assumed responsibility for the foundation's many projects designed to foster the growth of the Chinese legal system.

We were also quite successful in attracting some leading Western specialists in relevant fields to join our brief excursions in China. For example, U.S. federal judge Jed Rakoff, who had been my student at Harvard Law School, was always a great success in lecturing about, and demonstrating in mock trials, salient aspects of American criminal procedure. And Andy Griffiths, a well-known British police expert on the proper interrogation of criminal suspects, was another highly appreciated guest.

We also made good use of our knowledge of justice in Taiwan. Although PRC political-legal specialists recognized the value of their learning about Taiwan's impressive legal progress, political sensitivities usually barred any direct contacts between the two jurisdictions. Nevertheless, we managed to include Professor J. P. Wang of National Taiwan University College of Law, the island's leading expert on criminal procedure, in one of our most impressive programs on the mainland, and he was enthusiastically received by our hosts.

USALI devoted considerable attention to Taiwan, drawing on the unusual access to various legal institutions that my years of teaching Taiwan students at Harvard and NYU gave us. Ma Ying-jeou was always helpful, first while mayor of Taipei and then while president for eight years. Annette Hsiu-lien Lu also provided assistance during her eight years as vice president. In 2013, Margaret Lewis and I published a book about how Taiwan, as part of its democratizing process, put an end to the island's equivalent of Beijing's notorious "re-education through labor" that had authorized the police to subject perceived offenders to criminal punishment without providing the protections of due process of law.

Because the Republic of China (ROC) has been denied representation in the United Nations since 1971, its efforts to deposit its ratification of various human rights treaties with the UN were rebuffed. Thus, it could not participate in the processes for implementation of these treaties, which denied the ROC the right to have its implementation of the treaties reviewed by the treaty bodies that ordinarily subject a state-party's compliance to their review and recommendations. To compensate for this deprivation, the ROC engaged in a bold and imaginative move—it established its own committee of international experts to review ROC compliance. I was the only American among the dozen specialists invited to undertake this experiment and was glad to be joined by my distinguished NYU School of Law colleague, Professor Philip Alston, an Australian. I very much enjoyed the week in Taipei that these reviews afforded me on two occasions. I liked the chance to interrogate Taiwan government officials publicly about the detailed operation of their legal system.

During those years of learning about Taiwan as well as the mainland, I was lucky to benefit from the cooperation of Yu-Jie Chen as well as Margaret Lewis. Yu-Jie came to NYU to earn her LLM degree during the academic year 2007–2008. Although she did not enroll in any of my courses, we met in the winter of 2008 thanks to an introduction by Sharon Hom, a distinguished NYU law graduate who long served as executive director of Human Rights in China, one of the most dynamic of the nongovernmental organizations that focus on the PRC's treatment of civil liberties. Sharon, who has also served as an adjunct professor at NYU School of Law, had just selected Yu-Jie as the recipient of the fellowship in honor of Robert Bernstein that is awarded each year to an outstanding NYU law graduate who wishes to spend a year working for Human Rights in China.

The timing of my meeting with Yu-Jie was fortuitous. After a stimulating visit to Taiwan in May 2008, I had decided that I had to start publishing op-eds more regularly in order to reach a broader public, and that gave me the idea of writing regularly for the leading English-language newspaper in East Asia—the *South China Morning Post* (SCMP). The SCMP welcomed this idea, and we initially agreed that I would write one op-ed per week. It made sense to have these op-eds also appear in Chinese, so I arranged for Taipei's *China Times* to translate and publish my SCMP pieces. One op-ed per week may not sound like a lot, but it soon proved too difficult a pace for a busy academic. So I decided to do one every two weeks, and before long found myself coauthoring a number of these essays with Yu-Jie, whose interests covered the PRC as well as Taiwan.

After about a decade of regular contributing to the SCMP, I started to taper off for a variety of reasons. It was more convenient to do an op-ed only when the spirit really moved me. And I had discovered the new world of tweeting and blogging. Yu-Jie designed a website for me and, for the next five years, with the daily help of Maylin Meisenheimer, I turned most of my email contributions to my favorite listserv called China-Pol into tweets and blogs. Maylin was my assistant for two years at the Council on Foreign Relations and continued to help me for the following three years while working her way through NYU School of Law. Fortunately, before graduation, she introduced me to a remarkable law student successor, Soumya Kandukuri.

I have found this arrangement to be very satisfactory. I can send off comments on a range of issues in a very short time, whereas writing an op-ed tended to consume about eight hours. This leaves me more time to devote to these memoirs and to writing various essays at the request of several organizations. Recently, for example, I contributed to *Special Issue: Hong Kong's Changing Rule of Law* published by Taiwan's *Academia Sinica Law Journal*. My topic was "Hong Kong's Transformed Criminal Justice System: Instrument of Fear."

I also continue to work part-time on behalf of the Council on Foreign Relations, where my main responsibility is to organize six to eight roundtables per year on subjects of importance under the rubric "The Winston Lord Roundtable Series on Asia, the Rule of Law, and U.S. Foreign Policy." For over three decades, this has given me the opportunity to interrogate one or two experts per program and moderate the subsequent discussion in which a lively and devoted group of specialists take part. Prior to the COVID-19 pandemic, those sessions usually took place in person in New York City, with occasional meetings at the council's Washington, DC, quarters. Since then, with the aid of my able council assistant Kathy Huang, we have resorted to virtual meetings, and Zoom has enabled us to reach a broader, more geographically dispersed audience, especially because each session is recorded and made available to those who could not attend. This has made the experience more satisfying than ever.

All these activities have minimized whatever challenges my 2020 retirement from NYU might have brought me. I have immensely enjoyed the new freedom that retirement has given me, and I still have many opportunities to lecture and take part in public programs. I especially appreciate my continuing cooperation with Adjunct Professor Peter Dutton of the U.S. Naval War College, with whom I cotaught the seminar on China and public international law for seven years. His expertise on the law of the sea is of great benefit to our students and our U.S.-Asia Law Institute.

23

BEFRIENDING CHEN GUANGCHENG

The Vision of China's Blind "Barefoot Lawyer"

When I began writing this chapter, I was preparing to mark the tenth anniversary of Chen Guangcheng's highly publicized May 19, 2012, arrival in New York following his spectacular escape from detention in China. I first met Chen in the spring of 2003 at the request of the U.S. Department of State, which was hosting him and his wife, Yuan Weijing, as guests of the U.S. International Visitor Leadership Program (IVLP) that was designed to give promising midcareer figures from other countries a month's introduction to the United States. Chen had been blind since infancy but had acquired some stature because of his accomplishments as a "barefoot lawyer" in rural China; he was considered a possible future leader of his country. Chen had never studied law but had been favorably featured in the international media for his layperson's efforts to protect the rights of underprivileged farmers by resort to the court system in a countryside where professional legal representation was hard to come by.

When hosting Chinese visitors associated with the law, the State Department would often ask me to meet them and discuss the U.S. legal system. When I was informed that Chen had no legal training, however, I was not thrilled at the prospect of taking at least an hour from my busy schedule to help the State Department fill up the visitor's dance card. Nevertheless, I succumbed to the department's request, more out of a sense of obligation than curiosity. Soon after our session started, however, I became grateful for this opportunity.

Chen quickly proved to be fascinating: he was a handsome, articulate, and friendly man in his late thirties whose speech belied his lack of significant higher education and his impoverished village upbringing in Shandong Province. He did indeed seem like a possible future leader of his country. His responses to my questions about Chinese rural life and law—a topic little understood by foreign legal scholars and even many Chinese scholars—whetted my appetite to learn much more. Here was a frank, informative participant-observer, a rare bird even for seasoned specialists like me. I was reluctant to see our scheduled one-hour interview end, even after more than two hours.

In addition, I liked his wife, a pleasant, intelligent, humorous university graduate who had sought out and married Chen because of her idealistic endorsement of the social importance of his work as well as admiration for his talent and achievements. Reared in the more comfortable urban environment of coastal Shandong by a devoted middle-class mother who urged her to make a conventional marriage with a "more appropriate" partner, Yuan Weijing instead opted for a difficult life with a blind, less formally educated farmer who seemed determined to challenge and improve communist society and politics. Joan and I were preparing to return to Beijing for me to teach in a special training program established by Temple University at Tsinghua University School of Law, so I exchanged addresses with the Chens and invited them to see us in Beijing soon after our arrival.

Their visit in September produced some stimulating discussions with Tsinghua law professors and a couple of professionally trained lawyers, none of whom was well acquainted with the details of rural realities. Chen still knew relatively little about the burgeoning legal developments in China's cities, although he had applied his legal talents successfully to challenge the Beijing subway system's illegal discrimination against himself and other disabled riders.

I especially recall taking Chen to Beijing's large New China Bookstore. He was eager to acquire legal education materials that would be useful to his judicial outings to promote the interests of his varied and humble rural clients in the remote counties of Shandong's Linyi, his home turf.

I had no idea how many practical do-it-yourself pamphlets about different aspects of the Chinese legal system there were in print and how helpful and inexpensive they were. Civil procedure, contracts, administrative law, family law, criminal law and procedure, and almost every basic subject was covered in plain, simple language with typical examples of the kinds of problems and challenges that confront would-be litigants unfamiliar with professional realities. These short books were filled with homely illustrations and advice such as "If your opponent or the judge says X, then you can counter by arguing Y." I filled Chen's briefcase with the equivalent of over $100 worth of legal texts that he promised to devour during the coming months with the patient reading assistance of his schoolteacher brother and able spouse.

Before leaving Beijing to return to his village, Chen persuaded Joan and me to reciprocate with a visit to him. "You will never understand my situation," he said, "unless you spend some time in our village." And so we went, staying in a hotel half an hour away by car but spending all day every day with Chen and his family. We spent three days in the village, which was named Dongshigu, the first day walking around the community of about five hundred people. It quickly became apparent not only that Chen was regarded as a friend but also that he was treated with respect and often gratitude for the help that he had given many of the residents. I especially recall stopping to meet with a couple working on a tiny private plot of vegetables located on the small farm from which they scratched out a living. Chen explained that he had saved the family a considerable amount of money by persuading the government that they should not be taxed on the basis of having three able farmhands in the family because their mature son was mentally disqualified from working in the fields. To demonstrate their son's disability, they asked us to peer into a barred window of their farmhouse, where we saw a wretched-looking fellow in his mid-thirties aimlessly wandering around a room. He hadn't been allowed outside the room for two years, we were told, because he had previously used his freedom to try to strangle his mother. Rather than attempt to place him in the custody of an institution, his parents, like many in China, preferred to care for him under restraint at home.

We spent our second day indoors so Chen could introduce me to a broad range of his "clients," eight people in all, each of whom was eager to continue to benefit from Chen's help in dealing with the township and county governments and the local courts. Official tax demands were prominent among their concerns, as were their alleged violations of police regulations and occasional contract and debt disputes. Some needed help in seeking government benefits to which they were legally entitled but did not know how to pursue. Getting acquainted with the problems of these poor, uneducated, frequently disabled individuals was a moving experience for me as well as Joan, who sat in on most of the meetings.

We spent the third day reviewing Chen's progress and discussing his ambitious plans. It was plain that, buoyed by experience and his careful study of the pamphlets I had purchased for him in Beijing, he had become relatively comfortable in his contacts with the county court and local officials. Yet he felt increasingly overwhelmed by the growing demand for his services. Chen saw a tremendous need for many more "barefoot lawyers" in Shandong Province's rural areas and wanted me to help organize a training program in his district for as many as two hundred potential colleagues. He wanted to rent a hotel meeting room in the district for several weeks of introductory lectures to educate the large group he hoped to recruit for the project. He thought, quite rightly, that with my assistance we could invite several idealistic Beijing lawyers to join us in presenting the lectures. But he underestimated the strength of local government opposition. Chen's individual efforts, despite favorable international publicity, had already alienated city and county officials. It seemed unlikely that they would tolerate a plan designed to multiply the number of Chens they would have to contend with.

Nevertheless, I decided to work with Chen to take the plan as far as it might go. To promote support in Beijing, I invited him to return to the capital in a few weeks so that we could discuss it with various law professors, lawyers, and civic organizations that might be sympathetic. To my surprise, most of the lawyers and even law professors with whom I broached the idea were unenthusiastic, and some were actually hostile. They understood that, in counties like Chen's, there might be only five professional lawyers for a population of over 200,000 people and that those lawyers, whose livelihoods depended in large part on the patronage of the local government, were not eager or often even available to represent clients whose interests frequently opposed those of the government. This was indeed the situation in Chen's county that had stimulated his legal adventures.

Most urban professionals took a dim view of uneducated "barefoot lawyers," whom they believed were doing more harm than good and were damaging their efforts to develop respect for China's still new and uncertainly established legal profession. I recall how shocked I was at the meeting I arranged for Chen with the dean and deputy dean of Tsinghua University's distinguished law school and a leading Beijing lawyer who headed the school's clinical program in public law. The deputy dean and the lawyer were actually rude to my guest and openly read the newspapers while Chen was giving his initial remarks. It was the only time I was ever grateful that Chen is blind.

Dean Wang Chenguang, an expert in public law and society, fortunately had a broader view of the value of "barefoot lawyers." Indeed, not long before, he had himself made a rural excursion in another province to learn more about the accomplishments of such lawyers, hoping to enlist the support of the Ford Foundation for a project rather similar to Chen's. His interest in our idea was gratifying.

Ultimately, however, nothing came of Chen's project because of the Chinese government's intense campaign to enforce new and harsher birth control on an unwilling population. Thousands of women in Chen's district fled the prospect of compulsory abortion and sterilization and, in order to round them up, the police and other authorities arbitrarily detained and tortured many members of their families as hostages. Chen's attempts to protect the women and their captive relatives brought down the wrath of officialdom upon him, and he was subjected to ever greater restrictions and harassment. He compiled reports about his investigations into the horrendous situation and circulated them with the help of activist Beijing law professor Teng Biao and others from outside the area. Chen's frequent interviews with foreign journalists also infuriated the embarrassed Shandong authorities. A long interview with Philip Pan, Beijing correspondent for the *Washington Post*, hit them especially hard.

I became increasingly concerned about Chen's personal welfare, and our contacts were subject to ever greater surveillance. To facilitate our communications, I had bought Chen an IBM computer designed for the use of the blind, but the police confiscated it. Our telephone calls were closely monitored, and efforts, even by Beijing lawyers as well as other Chinese human rights activists, to visit his village were increasingly barred by local police and their hired thugs. Yet Chen did manage to leave his home on occasion.

Hoping to relieve the pressure on him, I came up with the idea of helping him attend law school. He had sometimes expressed interest in formal legal study, and I thought that if he could enroll in law school in one of the major cities it would remove him from the dangers of remaining at work in Linyi. So we went to Shanghai to see my good friend, Professor Tong Zhiwei, the courageous constitutional law scholar who was then acting dean of the KoGuan Law School of Shanghai Jiao Tong University.

Tong had grown up in the countryside and understood Chen's circumstances, and he could not have been nicer or more helpful. He immediately offered Chen a place in the school dormitory free of charge for the nights we were there. Although he said that, so far as he knew, no blind person had ever studied law in China, he welcomed Chen to join the university's night school program. I agreed to take care of the tuition fee and Chen's living expenses. However, Tong said, we had to get the approval of the Linyi authorities. I hoped that they would be delighted with the prospect of not having Chen in their hair for most of the next three years, but they refused to approve this novel proposal, perhaps fearing that, armed with formal legal education and a law degree, he would prove an even more formidable opponent. They were apparently confident that they could deal with Chen by other means.

I was more worried about Chen's security than he was. On his next visit to Beijing, he wanted me to meet the two human rights lawyers he regarded as his personal counsel, Li Heping and Jiang Tianyong. During a long and informative lunch in a quiet Japanese restaurant, they both made a deep impression on me. Yet I knew that neither could protect Chen from arbitrary arrest, and I felt that he was imminently threatened. After lunch, as we walked toward the taxi that was to take him to another interview with Philip Pan of the *Washington Post*, I urged Chen to prepare his family for the possibility of his detention.

That is what immediately happened, as Pan reported. When the taxi arrived at the appointed meeting place, a group of Shandong provincial police were there to bundle Chen brutally into the back of their van and transport him back to a series of torture-filled detentions on their home turf, followed by house arrest in Dongshigu. After Chen's frequent exposure of their harsh birth control measures, his captors decided to stifle him.

That lunch was the last time I saw Chen before his spectacular 2012 return to New York six years later. After being kidnapped from Beijing, he was kept under strict house arrest in his village until, in March 2006, he was criminally detained; formally arrested; and then unfairly prosecuted, tried, convicted, and sentenced to prison for four years and four months. We had no contact during his entire prison term. On his release from prison, he was subjected to further extraordinary house arrest involving almost two hundred local police and their hired thugs that effectively isolated him from all contacts with the outside world.

That was the discouraging situation until late April 2012, when word suddenly came that, amazingly, Chen had by himself managed an escape from his apparently airtight captivity and then, with the help of friends, made his way to the U.S. embassy in Beijing. His subsequently published memoir gives a hair-raising account of those events and the diplomatic crisis that they spawned. Secretary of State Hillary Clinton was scheduled to arrive in Beijing on May 2 for a meeting of the important U.S.-China Strategic and Economic Dialogue (S&ED) that the United States and the People's Republic of China (PRC) held periodically. Beijing's outrage and embarrassment over Chen's escape, his refuge in the U.S. embassy, and the problem of what to do about him threatened to collapse the S&ED before it began.

Of course, I had been excited about the news of Chen's escape to the embassy, but until noon on Monday, April 30, I had no knowledge of the actual situation. Then the phone rang in my New York apartment. It was a call from the embassy to discuss the Chen case. The first person to speak was Kurt Campbell, then serving as assistant secretary of state, someone I did not know. He was evidently tired, overstimulated, and feeling pressed for time. I didn't like his tone. Campbell told me that Chen wanted me to counsel him. He needed hospital treatment for an injury to his foot that he'd suffered during his escape, and he'd gotten assurances both from the PRC and the Americans that he would be treated fairly at the hospital and subsequently allowed to study freely at a Chinese university. Chen faced the fateful decision whether to trust those assurances. After filling me in on the situation, Campbell barked at me: "This may be the most important decision you will ever make. Tomorrow the whole world will know about this, and you'd better make the right decision." I responded that I was capable of making my own decisions and did not need his pressure. That exchange got the call off to a bad start.

At that point, Harold Koh, former dean of the Yale Law School and then Legal Adviser of the Department of State, wisely took over from

Campbell. I had known Harold slightly over the years because I had met his parents on several occasions, his father being a former South Korean diplomat and international law professor and his mother a dynamic sociologist. They had once sent him, while he was still a Harvard College student, to consult me about a career in the law.

Harold succeeded in improving the atmosphere and calmly told me that if Chen decided to stay in the security of the embassy, he might not have another opportunity to leave for a very long time and would be effectively isolated from society, separated from his wife and children, and branded a traitor by the PRC. On the other hand, if he decided to leave the embassy, he would be able to heal his broken foot at a good hospital for whatever time was necessary, rejoin his family, and then freely study at a PRC university for a couple of years. At this point he would be able to enroll at New York University's (NYU) new Shanghai campus and ultimately perhaps at NYU School of Law in New York. I hadn't previously known that Harold's and my good friend, NYU president John Sexton, had just committed NYU to accept Chen at its Shanghai campus. Having acquainted me with the necessary background, Harold, evidently hoping that I would urge Chen to leave the embassy, then put him on the phone for our first chat in over six years.

Chen and I reviewed the situation for about ten minutes. It was obvious that he was under immense pressure to make his decision immediately. Despite strong assurances from the American side, which was eager to resolve the diplomatic crisis and hold the S&ED, that he would be allowed to live freely while studying in China, Chen remained wary and asked my advice. I shared his doubts and asked what guarantees the PRC had given. When he told me that the PRC promised that he would have the same degree of freedom as any Chinese citizen, I said that was not good enough because we both knew the many restrictions under which Chinese university students lived.

The call ended inconclusively, but the next day, May 1, 2012—again at noon New York time, midnight in Beijing—the embassy called a second time. This time Harold Koh had a specific question that, he said, required an immediate answer: Would I confirm that Chen would be welcomed at NYU School of Law in New York immediately, not at some vague date in the future? I was almost flabbergasted because Chen had not asked to leave China and the PRC government had not offered that option. There was no opportunity to consult NYU School of Law dean Richard Revesz or university president Sexton. All I knew was that Sexton had committed NYU Shanghai to accepting Chen and had reportedly held out the possibility of Chen's eventual study at our New York campus.

I told Koh that I certainly did not have the capacity to approve Chen's enrolment as a student in the law school or any other university department. Chen could not speak, read, write, or understand English. But as faculty director of the U.S.-Asia Law Institute (USALI), and in view of Chen's extensive experience with the Chinese legal system, I could confirm an invitation for him to be a visiting scholar at our institute.

Of course, that left open the question of funding the expenses of Chen and his family in New York. Our USALI did not have the money to take on that responsibility, and I had no idea whether resources could be found elsewhere in the university. I did think that President Sexton was likely to help and that we might be able to attract funding from outside the university. If all else failed, I was willing to use my own funds until other sources could be located.

The challenge would be to persuade the PRC to allow Chen and his family to leave the country. In the interim, what was to become of them between departure from the embassy, and eventually the hospital, and departure for New York? I believed that, if Chen had refused to leave the embassy for the hospital, his family, which had been abused in many ways over the years, would be subjected to further suffering for perhaps even more years while Chen, who had earned the intense enmity of his government, continued to be confined in an embassy that no longer welcomed him. Although Chen told me that he was frightened at the risk of leaving the embassy in such uncertain circumstances—and I shared his fear—I told him that, on balance, I would not object if he decided to do so.

Fortunately, Chen did decide to leave the embassy, and that night, at the hospital, feeling insecure and abandoned by the exhausted U.S. diplomats who had left the hospital to get some sleep, he took his fate into his own hands. Recalling the telephone number of his trusted friend law professor Teng Biao, he called Teng and, after several conversations into the wee hours, decided to reject the PRC offer to have him study in China and instead go abroad with his family if possible. To promote the chances of success, he decided to tell the world of his decision immediately by contacting international media, which were eagerly trying to reach him. By morning, when the U.S. diplomats awakened, they and their PRC counterparts were confronted by a new situation—with the aid of Professor Teng, Chen demanded to leave China.

That led to another round of negotiations over his fate while the S&ED convened and later concluded. There were some anxious days awaiting the PRC decision about Chen's demand. Finally, one morning, as I was about to do a live 7 A.M. interview about the situation with the television anchor Christiane Amanpour, the PRC issued a statement that Chen, like any other Chinese citizen, was, of course, free to apply to the government for permission to go abroad to study. That was electrifying news. Although the PRC announcement did not indicate whether Chen's application would be approved, in the context, I was confident that this assured his release. The only question was, When would approval be formally granted so that Chen's departure, together with his family, could take place?

Although the University of Washington and one or two other schools showed willingness to host Chen, it was evident that he wanted to come to NYU and rely on our friendship to get him and his family settled. This welcome news nevertheless created a personal problem for me and my family. Joan, our son Ethan, and I were scheduled to leave New York to attend the second inauguration of my former Harvard student Ma Ying-jeou as president of Taiwan. After that, we were planning to travel to Beijing, where the Central Academy of Fine Arts (CAFA) had arranged a program to honor Joan's contributions to the introduction of contemporary Western art to China. Given the tense political situation in China at the time, the CAFA program promised to be a very sensitive political exercise, and I wanted to witness it and perhaps be helpful in Joan's dealings with the art establishment.

My bags were actually packed for the trip when the U.S. State Department called and told me that Chen's departure from Beijing was about to be approved by the PRC and that I must not leave New York because the Chens and the U.S. government would be principally relying on me to serve as Chen's host. This put Joan and Ethan, who had already departed for Asia, in the awkward position of having to attend Ma's inauguration in my absence. It also meant that I would have to make initial arrangements for the Chens in New York without the benefit of Joan's cooperation.

Finally, early Saturday morning, May 19, 2012, word came that the Chens were leaving Beijing and would arrive at Newark airport in New

Jersey that evening. The State Department asked me to meet them at the airport and to escort them to the spacious apartment that NYU had arranged in a faculty apartment building in the heart of the campus. At that point, U.S. politics reared its head. I had heard that Republican Representative Chris Smith of New Jersey, a leading critic of the PRC's harsh dictatorship, had wanted to meet the Chens at the airport. With the aid of Bob Fu, an able Chinese refugee and Christian minister who had become an important political activist in Washington, Smith's subcommittee had managed the feat of holding a public hearing that had enabled Chen to testify by telephone from his Beijing hospital bed. Smith obviously saw Chen's arrival as an opportunity to further his anticommunist activities and create favorable personal publicity in an election year.

I felt ambivalent about cooperating with Representative Smith at this stage. Although I shared his criticisms of the PRC's human rights violations, I associated him generally with right-wing Republican political views that I did not share, and I did not want Chen to become a tool of U.S. partisan politics before he even got his feet on the ground. I especially wanted to insulate Chen from the political sensitivities of an important presidential election year and give him some time to adjust to his dramatically new life before being exposed to the efforts of both Republicans and Democrats to exploit his sudden fame. Thus, I arranged for the Chens to leave Newark airport via a private exit that avoided whatever greeting Representative Smith had arranged.

In the weeks that followed, a number of people from Washington joined in this effort to enlist Chen in politics. Because of Chen's well-known opposition in China to forced abortion and sterilization, some people with Catholic religious and charitable connections seemed to want him to become a symbol of opposition to all abortions. Others were hoping to use him to attack Barack Obama's handling of China policy generally and to criticize specifically the efforts of Obama's State Department, headed by Hillary Clinton, to get Chen released from China. Still others saw him as a powerful vehicle for calling American attention to the PRC's many human rights violations. Because Chen spoke no English and evidently was following my advice, most of these efforts had to move through me, but Bob Fu established increasingly direct personal and phone contacts with Chen.

I rebuffed all attempts to involve Chen in politics on the grounds that he needed at least some months to adjust himself to life in the United

States before going to Washington. I distinctly remember a congressional staffer's long-winded effort in September 2012 to win me over. When I agreed to let Chen testify in January of the coming year, the staffer said: "But that will be too late." When I responded: "Too late for what?," the staffer remained silent but plainly had the November election in mind.

In the meantime, we had to organize a training program for Chen at our USALI. This had to be conducted in Chinese and focus on introducing him to U.S. law. We also hoped to enlist his enthusiasm for the simple English-language study sessions we organized for him. My colleague Professor Frank Upham, an expert on China as well as Japan, cooperated with several of our USALI research fellows in developing and delivering an informal curriculum for Chen. We also gave him one of our scarce offices for his exclusive use.

As spring turned to summer, Chen began to benefit from the quiet routine we had established for him. This was occasionally punctured by the visits of some distinguished and sympathetic public figures. The one I best recall was Nancy Pelosi, who seemed to be motivated by a desire to pay her respects and become acquainted with a leading Chinese human rights activist. I was delighted to sit in on this long and sincere meeting because Pelosi had been an active supporter of civil liberties in China for decades. Harold Koh also came for a long and sympathetic chat that both Chen and I enjoyed. Kurt Campbell, who had alienated me during the first phone call made to me from the embassy about Chen, promised to pay a visit but never turned up. Pastor Bob Fu was a fairly frequent visitor for meetings that I didn't always know about.

George Soros, who had sent us an unsolicited significant financial contribution to help cover the initial expense of hosting Chen, invited the entire Chen family plus Joan, our son Ethan, and me for a delightful summer weekend at his Southampton estate. I will never forget Ethan's and Chen's efforts to enable the blind Chen to hit a tennis ball from the sound of its bounce on the tennis court.

The dynamic international businessperson Andrew Duncan, an enthusiastic supporter of human rights in China and an admirer of Chen's accomplishments, was determined to do everything possible to ease the adjustment of the Chen children to the United States. The children—a nine-year-old boy named Kerui and a seven-year-old girl named Kesi—were bright and attractive poster children for the future of China, but they nevertheless needed a great deal of attention in meeting multiple challenges in the United States.

The major responsibility for hosting the Chens, of course, fell to NYU, and President John Sexton went all out to protect and support them. I don't believe any foreign newcomer to a U.S. university—even Albert Einstein—has ever been better treated. Although I sometimes believed that NYU went overboard in its expenditures, which totaled over $400,000 for the first year, I agreed with John Sexton that it was better to err on the side of generosity. I soon began to worry, however, about Chen's inevitable transition to a more permanent and realistic arrangement.

I had always indicated to the Chens that NYU's extraordinary hospitality had to be temporary. In the spring of 2013, we had even delivered a letter to him from the university confirming the need to think about the future. I assured him that the university would never abruptly cease its assistance and that I would guarantee that he could remain at NYU until some satisfactory, long-run opportunity had been secured. Indeed, with Andrew Duncan's backing, I did arrange what might have been a wonderful next move for Chen, namely, an offer from Professor Martin Flaherty of Fordham University School of Law's Leitner Center for International Law and Justice, for Chen to take up a position there with a group we called the Committee to Support Chinese Lawyers. I believed that if we could associate Chen with this group, we could make it a more vigorous institution. Andrew Duncan liked the idea and agreed that if we could negotiate an appropriate position for Chen at the Leitner Center for the following three years, he would donate a total of $900,000 so that Chen would receive a salary of $250,000 per year for his full-time services plus $50,000 a year for a full-time research assistant.

Unfortunately, by that time the New York media was reporting Chen's alleged dissatisfaction with his treatment at NYU, which made Chen look like an ingrate who was biting the hand that fed him. This unattractive publicity injected a spanner into the Fordham negotiations. Fortunately, the Witherspoon Foundation, a Catholic charity based in Princeton, New Jersey, was eager to support Chen and, after fourteen months at NYU, he moved to the Washington, DC, area, where he became associated with the Center for Human Rights at the Catholic University of America, a position that he has maintained to this day.

Because I was prominently linked with Chen's spectacular arrival in the United States, many people asked me whether my efforts to assist him brought down on me the wrath of the Chinese government. The PRC never criticized my role in bringing him to NYU, probably because this put an end to the huge public embarrassment that Chen's escape to the U.S. embassy had caused Beijing. A year later, however, once it was announced that Chen would visit Taiwan for several weeks in the summer of 2013, my relations with the PRC sank to a new low.

I was not responsible for Chen's decision to visit Taiwan. With no prompting from me, his invitation came from elements of the Democratic Progressive Party (DPP), the island's political opposition to then president Ma Ying-jeou's Kuomintang (KMT) government, and it arrived soon after Chen was ensconced at NYU in the fall of 2012. Chen was going to accept the opportunity immediately, but I persuaded him to wait until the end of the academic year so that he could take the children on the trip as well as his wife. I remained concerned that the DPP hosts were going to exploit him politically, and their proposed itinerary increased my concern. I didn't want him to alienate either the KMT or the DPP and thought it best for his program to focus on legal aspects, giving it a serious professional rather than political emphasis. Thus, I took steps to add some academic activities to his program, such as a major public lecture at the law school of the National Taiwan University and meetings with law professors, lawyers, and government legal experts. I tried to arrange sessions with judges and prosecutors also and asked President Ma to foster these arrangements, but Ma's support was not forthcoming, apparently because of worries about the impact on Beijing of appearing to promote Chen's visit.

As it happened, I was in East Asia just before the Chen family trip and agreed to travel to Taiwan for the first few days of his visit so I could facilitate his adjustment to the new environment. Our early activities were widely reported in the Taiwan press, and this undoubtedly gave Beijing the impression that I had initiated Chen's trip and was its de facto manager. Not long afterward, the PRC found an occasion for retaliating against me.

The National Committee on U.S.-China Relations (NCUSCR) had invited the new PRC ambassador in Washington, Cui Tiankai, to come to New York for a welcome dinner with the NCUSCR's board, and Cui had accepted. I was looking forward to the occasion. But two days before the

NCUSCR dinner, Ambassador Cui telephoned my former student Steve Orlins, the NCUSCR's president and one of my closest friends, and said that Beijing wanted to see a copy of the guest list. Steve complied with his request, and the next day Cui called Steve again to report that Beijing insisted that the ambassador could not attend the dinner if I was to attend. Consistent with the NCUSCR's policy of not allowing China to dictate who on the American side might participate in Committee activities, Steve explained that he could not disinvite me. Thus, the next night our board had a delightful dinner in the absence of the guest of honor!

This was not the only time the PRC attempted retaliation. Not long after, the NCUSCR invited the Chinese consul general in New York to give a talk to a small group of specialists interested in the Sino-Vietnamese dispute over legal issues in the South China Sea. The written invitation indicated that I would moderate the session, whereupon the consulate said that it would have to decline the opportunity because of my presence. Once again, Steve held the line and, to our surprise, a few days later a phone call from the consulate informed us that the consul general would be available after all!

One of the most interesting things I had to do on Chen's behalf was help negotiate a book contract for the memoir many people were eager to read about his unique experiences. Chen and I agreed that this project was necessary for two reasons. The first was the desire to inform the public about the nature of Chinese society and government under the communist regime. The second was the need of this penniless activist to obtain funds to provide a nest egg for himself and his family. We hoped to emulate those famous dissidents who had escaped from the Soviet Union and received very substantial financial advances for their memoirs. In my own mind, I had set the goal of achieving at least $1 million in advance. The problem was how to attain it.

The first challenge everyone emphasized was to find the right literary agent, and the name Bob Barnett kept popping up because he had recently represented some of the most famous public figures who had published memoirs of great public interest. He soon arranged for the two of us to spend several days in my NYU office negotiating with a range of leading publishers. They proved less enthusiastic about the book than I expected, perhaps because they recalled having been burned by large advances that had been paid to exiled Soviet dissidents that had never been recouped because of disappointing sales following the demise of the former Soviet Union. We did finally reach agreement with Macmillan, a highly respected division of Henry Holt and Company that offered an advance of some $550,000. Then the hard work of preparing a manuscript had to begin.

Chen was to write the memoir in Chinese, and the translation and editing proved extremely difficult. Nevertheless, the final product was a highly readable, fascinating insight into contemporary Chinese life and politics as well as an important chapter in Sino-American relations. Unfortunately, the book did not prove to be a commercial success, despite the favorable appraisals that it did receive. I had hoped that it would be made into a feature film because its exciting stories seemed made for Hollywood. This possibility was ruled out at the time because of Hollywood's increasing reliance on the Chinese market and its fear of producing anything that might offend PRC authorities.

Over the years since the book's publication, my contacts with Chen have been limited. We have occasionally greeted each other at meetings in Washington and have had a few friendly phone calls. Although I was saddened by his close public support for the Donald Trump branch of the Republican Party, I was glad to learn more recently of his new effort to take part in American discussions of China policy and to publish various commentaries in support of human rights in China.

24

WAS HELPING CHINA BUILD ITS POST-1978 LEGAL SYSTEM A MISTAKE?

Some thoughtful observers argue that the U.S. policy of cooperation with post-Mao China in developing its legal system has proved a failure. They claim that our engagement set out to produce a democratic, "rule of law" China that would become, in the eyes of the United States and other democracies, a protector of human rights at home and a responsible member of the world community. Instead, they argue, engagement has enabled a communist dictatorship to become increasingly repressive at home and a threat to world peace and the values we cherish. Implicit in this view is the belief that those of us who sought to assist in the early efforts of Deng Xiaoping's Open Door Policy to improve the legal system of the People's Republic of China (PRC) and its practice of both domestic and international law were not merely wasting our efforts but, like Dr. Frankenstein, had created a monster. From this perspective, we failed in the effort to export liberal-democratic legal values to China.

How should we evaluate this claim?

WAS POST-1978 LEGAL ENGAGEMENT WITH CHINA A POLITICAL MISTAKE?

Would it have been politically wiser if we had not positively responded to the post-1978 opportunities and challenges of helping the PRC to create a legal system from the debris of the 1966–1976 Cultural Revolution?

There is no doubt that foreign efforts to help the PRC reconstruct and develop a legal system in those years contributed to its recovery and its capacity for satisfying the demands of its people. At the time, the Communist Party, the PRC's government, and its people felt the need for the benefits that a decent legal system could provide. The three previous decades of pendulum-like political, economic, and social upheaval and transformation had created a chaotic legal vacuum. The country's new leaders wanted an organized, coherent legal system to help them implement their Leninist rule and carry out the center's commands. They wished to resurrect the PRC's pre–Cultural Revolution, Soviet-style system for settling disputes and enforcing official norms, but they believed that a simple return to the Soviet system would fail to meet the country's modernization needs. The courts, the procuracy, the Ministry of Justice, the law departments of other ministries, the legal profession, and even grassroots mediation committees not only had to be revived but also substantially strengthened, and so too the norm-producing institutions of the National People's Congress and its provincial and local legislative subordinates.

The educated and bureaucratic elites, having suffered the horrors of the Cultural Revolution, were awaiting some formal assurance of greater personal security. The promulgation of the PRC's first codes of criminal law and procedure on July 1, 1979, almost thirty years after the regime's establishment, was the new Deng Xiaoping government's first major legislative response to the era of lawlessness that had preceded it. Many believed that the new legislation promised greater public protection against still rampant crime. Others saw it as greater protection against the arbitrary detentions and harsh punishments that had for so long destroyed or scarred so many Chinese lives.

Deng Xiaoping's goals for feeding an impoverished country and rehabilitating and developing its economy also required immediate legal attention. The transition from a socialist planned domestic economy increased the importance of contracts, new commercial rules and regulations, and the means to enforce them. Buyers, for example, had to be sure that sellers would deliver per the agreed specifications or be made to compensate for their noncompliance. The PRC's ambitious hopes that Deng's Open Door Policy would expand foreign trade; earn foreign exchange; and attract foreign technology, loans, and investment also meant that appropriate norms, institutions, procedures, and personnel had to be created. I'm reminded of the moment in 1979, referred to above, when I asked a member of the Law and Contracts Bureau of the First Ministry of Machine-Building in Shanghai why he was so eager to study law, and his answer was: "Our only problem is that we don't know anything about either law or contracts!"

Among the seven important laws promulgated on July 1, 1979, was the rather vague but symbolically significant Chinese-Foreign Equity Joint Venture Law, which stimulated interest in mastering the mysteries of corporate transactions. In these circumstances, it was widely recognized that legal education and training for various roles would be critical to the success of the Open Door Policy. This meant not only reopening and retooling long-shuttered law schools but also attending to the suddenly large and immediate demand for officials capable of negotiating and implementing contracts and settling business disputes with foreign corporations as well as newly evolving Chinese ones. It also meant sending officials, law teachers, and advanced students abroad to foreign law schools. Relevant, helpful law had to come from somewhere.

Should those of us who cooperated with the PRC in its sudden hunger for Western law have refused on political grounds? Forty years later, fueled by hindsight, critics now gaining favor in Washington say that we should have realized that our efforts would strengthen an ever more repressive communist dictatorship that is said now to threaten liberal-democratic countries and international security as well as its own people. At the time, however, a PRC government that had repudiated the Cultural Revolution's killing of several million people and persecution of perhaps 100 million more was seeking our help in using law in various ways to prevent a recurrence of that national tragedy.

Even before the July 1, 1979, package of promulgated laws ended a legislative drought of more than two decades, the new, albeit truncated, Chinese constitution of 1978 had reflected the widespread popular revulsion against the violations of human decency and fundamental fairness that had too often marked the PRC's short history, not only during the Cultural Revolution but also from its inception. And the Chinese people, who were still experiencing the aftereffects of the homicidal, horrendous mass starvation inflicted by the 1958–1961 Great Leap Forward that killed over 30 million people, hungered for the benefits that could be conferred by foreign businesses eager to enter the Chinese market. From the perspective of the late 1970s, it was imperative to help China mitigate the risks of further impoverishment and renewed political chaos. In terms of international relations, the basis for the Sino-American rapprochement of the 1970s that led to the establishment of bilateral diplomatic relations in 1979 was the value each side saw in jointly opposing the oppressive power of the former Soviet Union. Many analysts also foresaw broader political, diplomatic, economic, and other benefits to be derived from finally welcoming the PRC into the world community. U.S. cooperation with the PRC in the context of the time did not need to come at the cost of sacrificing to communism the people of Taiwan, who at the time were still suffering under the repression of another Leninist-type but noncommunist regime, the Republic of China, which was dominated by the then recently deceased Chiang Kai-shek's Kuomintang (KMT).

By the late 1970s, the U.S. government and private U.S. law specialists had long been engaged in supporting the upgrading of the legal systems of both Taiwan and South Korea while they were still under dictatorial rule. That engagement later proved a wise investment. In the late 1980s, when both those societies managed to move toward democratic political regimes, they were bolstered by the more technically proficient and value-enhancing legal systems that U.S. cooperation had already helped establish. Political change and the opportunity it may provide for improvement in a nation's legal system is unpredictable. Yet change of some sort, however slowly it might appear, is inevitable. "Stop the world, I want to get off" is not an option, even for dictators. During the worst days of the Cultural Revolution, some of us believed that, although China was an unlikely prospect for genuine political democracy in the foreseeable future, the Chinese people might at least foresee development of a legal system that promised them essential decencies and basic protections. In 1979, Deng's Open Door Policy was beginning to vindicate that belief.

One could not know how much progress the Chinese Communist Party might be willing to make along these lines given its unpromising history, ideology, and policies. The 1983 attack against "spiritual pollution" and the subsequent campaign against "bourgeois liberalism" that removed Hu Yaobang from party leadership in 1987 were signals that the legal reforms of the Open Door Policy might be reaching their limits, at least temporarily. The 1989 downfall of the new party leader Zhao Ziyang and the following horrendous massacre of June 4 proved a devastating setback. Yet those sad developments were not inevitable, and history might have taken a different turn that would have been more likely to sustain the appetite for legal reform. Despite the impact of June 4, some important legal reforms were achieved in the two decades between Deng Xiaoping's famous 1992 southern tour and the ascent to power of Xi Jinping in late 2012. Even today, some improvements in the formal judicial system continue to be made amid ever increasing party and police oppression.

Unfortunately, the system has also organized other sophisticated measures for coercing the Chinese people to comply with the will of the increasingly oppressive party-state. Party discipline and inspection commissions have subjected many of the more than 80 million party members to incommunicado detention, during which confessions are often extracted by means of torture, and the police preside over a series of government institutions for inflicting similar administrative punishments on the broader population. The most notorious of these tactics—reeducation through labor—was abolished in 2013, but it has been replaced by a variety of other supposedly noncriminal sanctions, including the confinement of dissidents in mental institutions. In most aspects, the dominant, overwhelmingly Han majority has benefited from law reforms but not, of course, from the regime's use of the legal system to deprive them as well as minorities, such as Tibetans and Uighurs, of their political freedoms, their personal security against arbitrary punishment, and their resort to independent criminal defense. Thus, our efforts were incomplete even in Chinese terms and surely not largely successful in conventional U.S. terms.

They did help to change China, however, and largely, but not entirely, for the better. There is little doubt that the post-1978 legal reforms with which we assisted helped to make the PRC a stronger government than it might have been otherwise. A less chaotic, more prosperous China was then generally seen to be in America's interest and in that of the world community, and I believe it still is. Nor should we overlook the fact that, to a certain but unquantifiable degree, the post-1978 legalization effort of the communist regime has come at a political cost to its dictators. Their potential absolute power has been reduced to the extent that the system's personnel—its legislators, judges, prosecutors. legal administrators, lawyers, scholars, and even some officials within the police ministries—constitute an enduring, tacit professional and political interest group that contains significant silent dissenters to the party's current repression and its insistence that law specialists serve as instruments of that repression. Although the lack of transparency within the PRC prevents us from confirming the extent of dissatisfaction among today's legal elite, many of us receive more than hints of the adverse impact of the past decade's repressive policies upon this elite. Indeed, my respect for and loyalty to China's legal specialists who continue to work quietly toward liberal improvement of the system in very difficult and discouraging circumstances is one of my reasons for believing that we should not end our attempts to cooperate with PRC legal reformers despite the increasingly unattractive political climate for doing so in both the United States and China.

No matter how tightly Xi Jinping now controls the country, his rule will not last forever, and one can then expect another swing of the political pendulum toward a more moderate polity, just as that occurring following Mao's demise. Spurred by the informed reaction of citizens determined to allow their suppressed resentment to overcome their fear, there will be another attempt to improve human rights protections, permit civil society to recover from Xi-era persecutions, and free the country to become less censored and manipulated. When that day dawns, the sustained U.S. and other foreign law reform cooperation that persists to some extent even now in China may be highly appreciated and useful to further progress, as it proved to be in newly democratic Taiwan and South Korea.

On political grounds, I feel no guilt or regret about the years spent cooperating with the PRC during the halcyon days of the largely optimistic 1980s prior to the massacre of June 4. Nor am I doubtful about the desirability of continuing that cooperation today, as our New York University (NYU) School of Law U.S.-Asia Law Institute (USALI) and other foreign institutions struggle to do. Helping to reduce the number of wrongful convictions in China, assisting in lessening the amount of time alleged offenders spend in notorious pretrial detention, striving to enhance protections for the country's embattled human rights lawyers, and promoting the achievement of equal rights for women are useful services, even though success in these efforts may contribute to the stability of the communist regime by alleviating important grievances. As Chinese friends have privately emphasized, the Western effort has reinforced the Chinese people's longing for "equal justice under law." I believe in cooperation with the PRC where possible and sensible while also endorsing competition in economics and even containment, as necessary, in political-military affairs.

We were seeking to meet the needs of those Chinese citizens who were permitted to take part in our legal cooperation programs. Because the United States had emerged as the most prominent political and economic power in the post–World War II era, it was natural that we drew on what we knew from law practice and what had proved successful in our cooperation with other countries. Many meetings with PRC officials had made clear that, although they were understandably suspicious of our motives and insecure about their lack of international business experience, they were determined to take from us only what they deemed useful for their purposes, not to swallow wholesale what we had to offer. The PRC was no banana republic!

It is true that we failed to achieve our sub silentio hopes that, by helping provide international economic law to meet immediate Chinese needs, we might also promote eventual respect in China for our understanding of the rule of law, the fair administration of justice, and the protection of human rights. Certainly, few outside the Chinese Communist Party are likely to claim that the PRC has attained those goals. Nevertheless, the situation today, despite Xi Jinping's repression, is considerably better for most people—though surely not for Tibetans, Xinjiang Muslims, and the nation's human rights advocates—than it was in the dismal post–Cultural Revolution circumstances that we first encountered in 1979.

History is so adventitious. What if Hu Yaobang and Zhao Ziyang had not been ousted from their party leadership positions in the late 1980s, or if the People's Liberation Army, like the East German forces in the same period, had refused to kill its fellow citizens near Tiananmen Square? If we take a long-range perspective, we might say that the jury is still out on the consequences of our legal experiments during the early Deng Xiaoping period. Even in relatively tiny Taiwan, it took decades before the export of U.S. and other foreign law took full effect. It's not out of the question that over the long run, and despite the current and ongoing repression, the seeds of something different have been planted in China, that an ever more educated and sophisticated public might demand a more open, less controlled society with greater protections for personal freedoms than China has ever experienced in its three thousand years of recorded history. If that happens, the work that we did in China in the late 1970s and the 1980s may have left a more indelible, more enduring legacy than it's natural to assume in the country's current condition.

FINAL THOUGHTS

From an historical perspective one might ask whether my post-1978 hosts, wittingly or otherwise, revealed some deeper truth about the legal tradition that their country is still coming to terms with. Were they a contemporary embodiment of the quest in China's nineteenth-century "response to the West" that John Fairbank and his Chinese colleagues detected many decades ago—the desire to import foreign technical learning solely in order not to dilute but to preserve the Chinese essence that they thought was so different from that of the West and more appropriate for them? Does this help explain why the PRC has thus far successfully imported and adapted much of Western law in the cause of economic development but failed in other respects to practice Western versions of the rule of law, the administration of justice, and the protection of political and civil rights?

What indeed is the Chinese "essence" regarding law, at least on mainland China, if not Taiwan? Is it subject to significant change in response to future internal developments, foreign stimuli, or both? To what extent should this familiar Sinocentric interpretation of events be leavened with recollection of the initial profound shaping of the PRC legal system by the long-departed Soviet Union? The leaders of today's China, while seeking to exhume Confucius and the Chinese "essence" on behalf of nationalism, continue to extol Marxism despite its Western roots. Yet they are often reluctant to acknowledge the abiding Soviet impact on their legal system from Joseph Stalin's grave, except to invoke the fate of the former Soviet Union as a feared negative example. Despite Chairman Mao's attempt to exclude the influence of the pre-1949 Republic of China on the PRC, should we also take into account its inevitable impact as well as that of the Japanese and German systems to which the PRC often looked? And what of the unacknowledged but significant influence of Taiwan, which still purports to be the contemporary, democratic manifestation of the Republic of China? Should we regard the contemporary PRC legal system as an uneasy, evolving, contentious amalgam of traditional, Soviet, and Western elements?

What is at stake in our collective quest to answer these questions and to understand China is more than the theoretical and practical benefits to be derived from the detached academic study of comparative law. I like to believe that my perhaps excessive passion for the subject of arbitrary detention involves not so much personal ego as recognition of the need I hope we all feel to extend to Chinese people the benefits of "equal justice under law." Core among those benefits is protection against the cruelty and injustice of arbitrary detention, wherever it occurs. That is why I have emphasized my sympathy for all the victims of the PRC's increasingly sophisticated repression.

25

"THE CURFEW TOLLS THE KNELL OF PARTING DAY"

"Tomorrow Will Be Even Better"?

As this "plowman homeward plods his weary way," it is a challenge to conclude my account of a long and full life. I feel more energetic and enthusiastic than my reference to Thomas Gray's "Elegy Written in a Country Churchyard" would suggest. I actually much prefer the optimism reflected in Robert Browning's "Rabbi ben Ezra": "Grow old along with me! / The best is yet to be. / The last of life, for which the first was made." To be sure, both Joan and I often cite the observation made famous by the mid-twentieth century movie actress Bette Davis that "old age ain't no place for sissies." Yet, now in our nineties, we are glad to have avoided the alternative.

What can I say to family and friends and to readers I have never met? I recall that at a handsome dinner given in honor of my eightieth birthday at Georgetown University Law Center, when asked what wisdom I might impart to succeeding generations, I invoked the precedent of Conrad Hilton. When that emperor of the world's hotel industry was requested to summarize what he had learned in his forty successful years in the business, after a thoughtful pause, he replied: "Always keep the shower curtain inside the bathtub." I hope that my remarks will also be practical but of greater interest.

It should surprise no one that I begin by emphasizing the importance of family. Joan and I recently marked the seventy-fourth anniversary of our first date. We are currently in the seventy-first year of our marriage.

Although we both have met attractive members of the opposite sex, we have no regrets about staying together. Indeed, despite or perhaps because of our annoying illnesses of the past few years, this final era has left us closer than ever, especially because we are buoyed by the delights of a growing, four-generation family. Of course, we always hoped we could have three fine children, and it was not beyond expectation that they would produce, as they have, four grandsons and three granddaughters, each charming and wonderful. But living to enjoy five great-grandchildren—and a sixth is due soon—was a prospect that never crossed even our most remote horizons. And, we trust, more will be on the way, even, perhaps, while we endure.

I also take enormous daily comfort from my many former students and law firm colleagues who have become active members of our extended family. Not a day goes by—literally—that I do not hear from or have visits from one or more of them. Many have risen to prominent academic and professional positions and are contributing to public life in the United States and other lands. Especially during the recent COVID-19 years, the publications, emails, phone calls, Zoom meetings, and visits of this distinguished six-decade harvest of talent have informed and sustained me. They have made the retirement from teaching that I chose at ninety barely noticeable.

I did not, however, retire from my one remaining job—that of Adjunct Senior Fellow for Asia at the Council on Foreign Relations (CFR). That part-time preoccupation has allowed me to continue to indulge in the public dialogues with invited experts that I first experimented with at Berkeley and then developed at Harvard and New York University (NYU). Roughly once a month during the academic year, presiding over the Winston Lord Round Table on US Foreign Policy and the Rule of Law in Asia has given me great satisfaction, even when the pandemic required us to abandon in-person appearances in favor of Zoom sessions. I am now the CFR's oldest staff member. Perhaps by the time this memoir appears, the CFR's new leadership will have put me out to pasture, a decision I will accept with understanding and equanimity. Our relationship, dating back to the early 1970s, has been a happy and stimulating one for me and for Joan, too, because she was twice invited to mount CFR exhibitions of her photography of Asia relating to topics of our research. I was especially pleased with her recent show of pictures taken during our three trips to China's Xinjiang region. I wanted to remind CFR members that the repressed Muslim people whose rights we seek to protect are attractive individuals, not abstract statistics.

In view of Xi Jinping's ever increasing totalitarian control over China and its adverse consequences for the legal system of the People's Republic of China (PRC), which I have consistently denounced, people often ask whether I regret my career choices. Although there is perhaps inevitably an element of defensive self-vindication in my usual response, I tell them that I have never been plagued by doubts about the wisdom of the decisions made. To be sure, events not only in China but also in the United States have often confronted me with occasions for possible regret. The opportunity costs of a career specializing in China and Asia have been significant.

In New York, I live only about thirty blocks from Harlem. As a consumer of local and national news, I am well acquainted with the continuing enormous challenge of American racism and might well have devoted my energies to justice in that field. The battle against anti-Semitism alone, which so preoccupied my father in the years before World War II, could have attracted me. I sometimes also wonder how satisfying it might have been had I not decided to enter full-time teaching but instead remained a Washington lawyer serving the U.S. Department of Justice or the Department of State.

Unlike my father, I had no interest in becoming a judge. Although I warmed to my mother's thought that I might become a good secretary of state, I was never motivated to take steps that might lead toward that goal, including, as she offered, changing my family name to something more Anglo-Saxon. Even in early 1977, as President Jimmy Carter began to staff his administration and was reportedly preparing to invite me to become Legal Adviser of the Department of State, I did not seek the support of Senator Ted Kennedy, whom I had advised for years, or of Stuart Eizenstat, the Carter adviser who had persuaded me to help Carter in 1974 and 1975. Either might well have secured the job for me.

Similarly, I turned down earlier opportunities to lead the Johns Hopkins University School of Advanced International Studies in Washington, DC, and the Fletcher School of Law and Diplomacy at Tufts University in Massachusetts. Those positions would have enhanced eventual chances for a high foreign affairs government position or a university presidency, another possibility that I found attractive and for which I felt Joan would have been a superb asset. On those occasions, I remembered Justice Felix

Frankfurter's admiration for Harvard Law School Professor Paul Freund's decision to reject an appointment to be U.S. Solicitor General, which would have put him in line for a possible Supreme Court nomination. As Justice Frankfurter put it, "You shouldn't take a job you don't want because it might put you in position to get a job you're not sure you want."

I had a similar attitude toward law school deanships. I loved and revered Harvard Law School and knew that I had strong support among some faculty and even my friend, Harvard's new president Derek Bok, for leading the law school. Yet I decided to stay on leave in China for a second year instead of returning as expected to the school's overheated internal politics and selection process. I had many ideas for further innovations in U.S. and international legal education that might have burnished the school's luster as well as my own had I become dean. If lightning had struck, as it nearly did, I would have been thrilled to accept the call. Yet I was not prepared to alter my course in order to become an obvious candidate, and I subsequently declined to respond to the decanal blandishments of other law schools, including NYU, Columbia, and Chicago.

Those experiences made me recall my father's occasional observation about me during my grammar school years. With a humorous glint in his eye, he would say: "Ambition should be made of sterner stuff." His jest was evidently also an insight. In the end, I have always chosen to continue on the unique, if limited, path of creating a new and important academic and practical field. I frequently cited Justice Frankfurter's invocation of the Justice Louis Brandeis maxim that "self-limitation is the master's mark."

So, after more than six decades, what should one say about the chosen course? How much of an impact did it make? In what respects? And what does it enable us to foretell, if anything? "Who acts through another acts himself" is a hoary legal maxim that I have long admired. I am confident of the continuing impact of many of my former students and happily bask in the credit they often give me for inspiring and facilitating their accomplishments. Periodic birthday celebrations beginning with a memorable sixtieth party in Hong Kong, a seventieth conference that produced an edited volume, and an exhausting series of eightieth gatherings in various countries led to a marvelous ninetieth Zoom program. It culminated in a "liber amicorum," to which over 150 former students, younger colleagues, and friends contributed. Reading their tributes leaves me warmly reassured that I haven't wasted most of my time.

I also take pride in both my scholarly publications and my policy essays and op-eds, most of which are listed in the bibliography of this memoir. My 1968 book *The Criminal Process in the People's Republic of China, 1949–66: An Introduction* revealed the pattern of the unruly and hard-to-obtain facts of a new field and is still cited today. The prizewinning, two-volume 1974 *People's China and International Law: A Documentary Study* that I coauthored with the formidable Hungdah Chiu was another groundbreaking work and still awaits the sequel required to bring the subject up to date. And, although little noted, the 2013 study of Taiwan's progress toward the rule of law *Challenge to China: How Taiwan Abolished Its Version of Re-Education Through Labor*, largely the product of my imaginative and dynamic coauthor Maggie Lewis, should have an abiding significance on both sides of the Taiwan Strait.

My direct impact on U.S. policy toward China has been modest except for publication in *Foreign Affairs* of 1971 and 1976 articles that summarized the reasons why it made sense for the United States to establish diplomatic relations with the PRC and elaborated on the terms on which that could be achieved—terms very close to those finally agreed upon. Behind the scenes, I was pleased with the impact of the still little-recognized, confidential 1968 China memorandum that our Harvard-MIT committee gave to Richard Nixon via Henry Kissinger, and I felt that my long association with Ted Kennedy proved to be an effective indirect instrument for promoting Sino-American "normalization." Terry Lautz's 2022 book *Americans in China: Encounters with the People's Republic* recognizes in a lengthy chapter the contributions that Joan and I made to the China of the 1980s in our respective fields.

I immensely enjoyed my active law practice, whether as a human rights lawyer or as a facilitator of international business transactions with China. In 1973, when I finally succeeded in prodding the U.S. and PRC governments to agree on the release of my college classmate, the CIA's Jack Downey, from Chinese prison, I did not realize this would be merely the first of many cases where I would be asked to try to extract either foreigners or Chinese citizens from criminal detention in China. It was also exhilarating to play a similar role in other Asian jurisdictions: to help save the life of South Korea's Kim Dae Jung, to liberate my former student Annette Lu in the midst of her twelve-year sentence imposed by Taiwan's Kuomintang (KMT) dictatorship, and to arrange for the removal of Philippine senator Ninoy Aquino from his Manila prison to Harvard. I had also tried to deter Singapore prime minister Lee Kuan-yew from detaining his former solicitor general, Francis Seow, a distinguished lawyer who was imprisoned for seventy-two days without trial under Singapore's all-purpose national security law, and though I'd failed, the effort did lead to Seow's eventually finding refuge at Harvard Law School. I also continue to serve as an expert witness in litigation in various countries regarding not only PRC attempts to extradite alleged criminal suspects but also the applications of Chinese citizens for political asylum abroad.

I found my work as a Sino-American business lawyer to be surprisingly satisfying. Joint venture investment contracts were creative and constructive, if difficult, efforts that often benefited both the Chinese and foreign parties. I even enjoyed the process of settling the disputes that inevitably arose over their meaning. Although plainly the representative of the foreign company, with approval of the Chinese side, I often assumed the position of mediator between the disputants in settlement negotiations. And when informal discussions failed, I relished being the first foreign lawyer to take part as an advocate in the PRC's international arbitration proceedings.

As the end of my career approaches, it is gratifying to receive occasional public recognition of my efforts. The Harvard chair established in Joan's name and mine and the NYU chair in my name assure me that Chinese law will continue to be taught in the leading law schools to which I have long been devoted. The honorary degree that Yale University—my undergraduate and graduate alma mater—awarded me in 2020 means a great deal to me, as do prestigious decorations from the governments of Japan and Taiwan and the lifetime achievement awards of several academic organizations.

But what about the future? One of the PRC's most popular songs has been "Tomorrow Will Be Even Better." Because I am an inveterate optimist, I have often referred to it in China when ending lectures that were critical of current practices. I am not as depressed as many of my fellow foreign China-watchers are. Perhaps that is because I began my studies before the decade of the Cultural Revolution, managed to weather those ten bad years, and then felt vindicated when Deng Xiaoping led the enlightened reaction that I had predicted would be inevitable and that enabled me briefly to play a role in the nation's legal progress. China under the PRC has developed in pendulum-like fashion. We are now witnessing another extreme in the pendulum's swing toward repression. Xi Jinping is very likely to outlive me but "no life lives forever," and there will eventually be another profound reaction to the current totalitarian era.

Although temporarily silenced, millions of the PRC's elite who detest the current situation and suffer from it can be expected to attempt to alter it once the all-powerful "great leader" passes from the scene. I have long suggested that everyone in and out of China see the movie *The Death of Stalin*. Ostensibly a comedy, it is full of serious political meaning for all who now live under Xi's regime, which has exceeded Stalinism in the art of repression thanks to its masterful and massive application of twenty-first-century surveillance and information-control technology.

Even today, the idea of the rule of law and its virtues that was imperfectly nourished by Chinese legal education and limited law reforms and practice for three decades, beginning with the Deng Xiaoping era in 1979, have not been totally extinguished. Xi Jinping's frequent ideological emphasis on government doing everything according to law is well understood to mean "rule *by* law," that is, the use of law as an instrument of government control rather than "rule *of* law," which views law as a restraint upon government and a protection of the rights of citizens against the state's arbitrary coercion. Nevertheless, some distinguished Chinese constitutional scholars, although generally silenced, have occasionally managed to keep alive the concept of government under law as opposed to law under government, and even supporters of the regime sometimes—inadvertently or mischievously—invoke the term for "rule of law," which in spoken Chinese sounds identical to the term for "rule by law."

Contrary to the views of earlier communist leaders and many other Chinese modernizers, Xi Jinping has supported a revival of national respect for the wisdom of Confucius. Yet Xi's theoretical emphasis on "rule by law" has led many observers to note that he seems more accurately to be the heir to the "Legalist" philosophy of China's first imperial ruler, Qin Shi Huangdi. Qin opposed Confucianism and, in the third century BC, used harsh laws as weapons to unify what became the nucleus of the country.

Like his imperial predecessors and previous Chinese communist leaders, Xi has sometimes found it desirable in practice to rule through lawlessness as well as legislation. For many in contemporary China, the frequent acts of lawlessness of the party-state—the arbitrary detention, torture, disappearances and secret trials of dissidents and political rivals and the suppression of human rights lawyers and their clients—serve as vivid reminders not only of the absence of "rule of law" but also of the failure of the regime to practice even "rule by law" consistently.

When in China, I have often heard it argued that, because of the nation's history, we should not expect the Chinese people ever to practice democracy, individual rights, and the "rule of law" as these concepts have been developed in the West. Yet the experience of Taiwan since the 1990s and the related examples of Japan and South Korea all indicate that, in the course of modernization, East Asian political traditions need not inhibit the development of legal systems that earn Western respect. I have sometimes encountered Chinese who, on the one hand, argue that the people on Taiwan are Chinese and, on the other, maintain that history has disabled Chinese from developing the kind of political-legal system that has impressively evolved in Taiwan over the past three decades.

Despite the current comprehensive repression in China and the many challenges that will confront future efforts to establish a genuine rule of law of some type in such a vast and complex country, I remain optimistic about its long-run development. As argued in the previous chapter, I do not believe that my efforts toward that goal and those of many colleagues have been in vain. But I have one major caveat. The United States, China, and other major powers must act in ways that assure us that there will be a peaceful future rather than a nuclear holocaust.

Russia's invasion of Ukraine has immediately preoccupied the world with the gravest threat of nuclear war since the Cuban missile crisis of 1962. At the moment at least, the PRC appears to be influencing Vladimir Putin and his regime to moderate its brandishing of the nuclear rhetoric that has increasingly worried the international community. Yet there is also rising concern that the PRC's often-expressed determination to gain control over Taiwan may in fact constitute an even graver threat of nuclear war—between the United States and China—than that arising from the defense of Ukraine.

How to preserve freedom for the 24 million people on Taiwan without becoming involved in military conflict with the PRC appears to be the foremost of the immediate foreign policy challenges confronting the United States. Under President Joseph Biden, the United States has been gradually abandoning its policy of "strategic ambiguity" regarding whether it will join in Taiwan's defense if war should break out in the Taiwan Strait.

In recent years, even though the Taiwan government has been in the hands of President Tsai Ing-wen's more independence-minded Democratic Progressive Party (DPP), her careful administration has given no cause to believe that it might trigger Beijing's frequently expressed determination to launch an attack if the Taiwan government were to declare its independence formally. If conflict were to break out, the assumption now is that it will only be started by the PRC, and it is therefore very important for the United States to deter that possibility by leaving no doubt that, despite the absence of a formal defense treaty or even formal U.S. diplomatic relations with Taiwan, in those circumstances it would rise to the island's defense. That is why in recent months I have endorsed the idea of abandoning strategic ambiguity and replacing it with clarity, indicating that, unless conflict is provoked by Taiwan, the United States will defend the island.

Of course, we cannot know the future. We cannot be sure that any successor DPP government to Tsai's will act as responsibly as her administration has done. But Taiwan is blessed with many talented politicians, and I hope that those selected as future presidents will be as wise, cautious, and capable as Tsai.

Even if no uncertainty exists regarding the informal U.S. commitment to defend Taiwan, several other major issues are related to the island's security. Not only must the Taiwan government avoid provoking Beijing by declaring formal independence from China, but the United States, in supporting Taiwan, must do so within the framework of the "one China policy" that was first established by the 1972 Shanghai Communiqué negotiated with Beijing by Nixon and Kissinger. Thus, the United States must not have formal official cooperation and contact with Taiwan's government. That is why no defense treaty is possible, why the United States should not station military personnel and equipment on the island, and why there should not be official exchanges between the U.S. executive branch and Taiwan counterparts. As the 2022 visit to Taiwan by then Speaker of the U.S. House of Representatives Nancy Pelosi demonstrated, it is easy for disputes with the PRC to arise over whether certain U.S. actions violate the ban on official contacts. Although Beijing has not publicly pressed the point, there have even been occasional media reports that a small number of U.S. military personnel are actually on the island quietly training Taiwanese troops.

The most worrisome issue is the credibility and power of the U.S. commitment to defend the island. Although U.S. public opinion is currently hostile to the PRC and under the Taiwan Relations Act, Congress seems in favor of supporting Taiwan, even to the extent of engagement in combat, it is far from certain how strong the political support of the American people might be for actual warfare. Many observers have raised serious questions about whether the U.S. air and naval forces, in their present state of preparedness, could successfully defend the island against a PRC invasion. The prospect of Sino-American combat would quickly raise to a greater extent the specter of nuclear war that haunts the present struggle over Ukraine. During the Korean War, General Douglas MacArthur was desperate to halt the opposing Chinese forces, and he suggested the possibility of U.S. resort to nuclear weapons. At the time, China did not have the ability to retaliate in kind, yet President Harry Truman wisely refrained. Today's situation is vastly different and infinitely more dangerous.

I favor immediate substantial efforts to strengthen U.S. military capacity in East Asia; to improve Taiwan's readiness for combat; and to enhance Taiwan and U.S. cooperation with relevant allies, including Japan, Australia, South Korea, and major European powers, in order to strengthen the deterrent to PRC military actions. I also favor much greater emphasis on public education regarding the history of Taiwan–mainland China relations and the relevance of contemporary international law to the problem. Acquaintance with the history will help the international community understand that, from Beijing's viewpoint, the Taiwan question is a matter of restoring China's territorial integrity that is a relic of the KMT–Chinese Communist Party (CCP) civil war. But acquaintance with contemporary international law will make clear that, in settling such a dispute, the wishes of the island's population must be consulted and respected. Under international law, governments are no longer allowed to resort to force to resolve disputes over territory, a principle that the strong reaction to Russia's invasion of Ukraine demonstrated has substantial international support. In the Taiwan context, the United States and other major powers should become much more active in emphasizing and explaining relevant international law.

Perhaps the greatest diplomatic question is, Can China and the United States cooperate on those issues of crucial importance to the entire world community despite their often bitter bilateral and regional disputes? Climate, public health, food security, cyber/telecommunications, the Arctic, outer space, and arms control are only some of the outstanding immediate challenges that cry out for Sino-American leadership and cooperation. Even during some of the worst days of the Cold War with the Soviet Union, Washington and Moscow nevertheless agreed on certain key issues and agreed to manage, if not resolve, certain others. Deng Xiaoping certainly did not fear making compromises with foreign countries, including the United States, the United Kingdom, and Japan. However, Xi Jinping thus far seems unwilling to adopt a similar attitude even when, as in so many cases, it would appear to be plainly in China's interest to do so. Unless Xi moderates his existing stance, I hope that his government will not last as long as Chairman Mao's did.

As I prepare to leave the scene, it is sad and unsettling to note that the gravest challenges for Americans are domestic. Having witnessed my country cope with various national crises before, during, and after World War II, I did not expect, so late in life, to see the prevailing political and social turmoil at home, especially while economic conditions have generally been good. Democratic political institutions are more seriously threatened than at any previous era in my lifetime. The electoral process itself is under attack, and legislatures, courts, and administrations—federal, state, and local—are ever fiercer battlegrounds for the preservation and implementation of the basic principles upon which the United States was founded.

Despite all the progress made during recent decades, racism—against not only Blacks and Latinos but all people of color, including Asians—is still a daily reality and a dangerous stain on our public order, safety, and the administration of justice. There has even been a violent resurgence of the anti-Semitism that my father fought almost a century ago. Individual and collective violence has become increasingly prominent as political partisanship has become more intense, and mental illness that manifests itself in public expression and frequent tragedies has not been addressed adequately. Truth itself is at stake in our media and debates, and even our educational systems are not spared the impacts of our deteriorating political circumstances.

Should we be consoled that these challenges are not exclusive to the United States or even to liberal democracies but plague many other countries as well? We benefit from the experiences and ideas of others and to a huge extent from the immigration into our country of their people who, despite our failings, are attracted to join us. Our continuing welcome to immigrants, despite the controversies surrounding the policy, is one of the reasons I am hopeful about the future. The United States is changing its political complexion. If my great-grandchildren choose to study domestic politics in college, they will not learn, as I did in the autumn of 1947, that to be elected president of the United States, one must be white, Anglo-Saxon, Protestant, and the governor of a large state!

APPENDIX

MY STUDENTS IN THE HARVARD LAW SCHOOL EAST ASIAN LEGAL STUDIES (EALS) PROGRAM

[[A brief narrative account of my students in the Harvard EALS program who went on to distinguished and influential careers in the field.]]

My fear, as I embark on this appendix, is that I will inadvertently leave out the names of former students who ought to be included, and, if I have done so, my sincere apologies. Over the years, many students from all over the world took my classes, some of whom later created programs in East Asian legal studies of their own, and some who became leading practitioners in the field, senior judicial officials, and high-ranking government officials. I have done my best here to name as many of them as I can and to provide at least a brief appreciation of their accomplishments.

My outstanding student during the very earliest years of the Harvard Law School (HLS) East Asian Legal Studies (EALS) program was Victor Hao Li, an American of Chinese descent whose parents ran a Chinese restaurant in New Jersey. He did his initial three-year training in American law not at Harvard but at Columbia, then came to Harvard in the fall of 1965 to enroll in the LLM program. This was just at the start of my tenured teaching at HLS, and Victor arrived specifically to work with me, a surprising decision, given my own relatively recent entry into the field. Victor did well not only in my courses but also in others, wrote an interesting research paper on China's legal system as it was shortly before the Cultural Revolution broke out late in the spring semester of 1966, and decided that he would apply for the highly competitive SJD degree. With my enthusiastic recommendation, he was admitted, and we agreed that, to expand and update his research, he would spend the following academic year, 1966–1967, in Hong Kong interviewing refugees from China, as I had done three years earlier.

Because of the Cultural Revolution, that academic year proved to be a chaotic, challenging one for everyone in the British colony, but Victor made the most of it. He matured greatly during that experience and returned to Harvard in the summer of 1967 loaded with information and ideas for his doctoral dissertation. Of course, I worked closely with him, and Joan and I became very friendly with him as well as David Finkelstein, who was finishing his efforts to help me complete my 1968 book on criminal justice in China. Victor liked to play tennis, as did I, so we often mixed a bit of exercise with scholarship, whether in Cambridge, Massachusetts, or on his occasional weekends with us in Truro on Cape Cod. I still have in my Truro closet, fifty-seven years later, the sturdy blue sweatshirt that Victor brought back as a souvenir for me from Hong Kong with the famous Chinese saying "Let a Hundred Flowers Bloom" emblazoned in Chinese on the front.

Unlike most SJD candidates, who take considerably longer to complete the dissertation, Victor managed to finish his by the end of the academic year. He then returned to Columbia for a postdoctoral fellowship that, before long, enabled him to obtain an assistant professorship at Stanford University Law School. This was an exciting development for me because I felt great satisfaction in helping my first protégé establish another Chinese law beachhead that would propel this new field forward.

My social ties to students were enhanced by Joan's desire to get to know them and to welcome them to our house, which was only a few blocks from the law school. Although we had three young children and Joan was pursuing her own career in Asian art history, every semester we gave what became a leading student social event. We would assemble a group of students at the great Asian collection of the Boston Museum of Fine Arts at 7 P.M. Joan would then guide us around its many treasures for an hour or more. Then we would all repair to our house for a party for at least forty to fifty students who enjoyed seeing and hearing about our own growing collection of Asian paintings and sculptures. All of this helped to build friendships that endure to this day, when we continue to be buoyed by the emails, letters, phone calls and visits of former students who date back to those early days.

THE INCREASING NUMBER OF AMERICAN STUDENTS

The American students were a remarkable lot, and those interested in China, oddly enough, increased in number as the Cultural Revolution reached its insane apogee in the late 1960s. I found myself teaching roughly ninety students in each year's course on China's domestic legal development, a considerable number for a subject not on any bar exam and that was hardly essential to the conventional U.S. legal curriculum. In addition, the Chinese legal system was in turmoil, to put it mildly. Perhaps some of the students who enrolled without a prior interest in East Asian studies were seeking relief from their intense regular law courses, while others, reflecting the upheavals also then occurring in U.S. domestic life, were eager to learn about radical revolutionary experiences in another major country.

A few U.S. students with no serious China background, like Jon Van Dyke and Peter Trooboff, took my first seminar on China and international law in 1966 because they had already decided to become international lawyers. Jon went on to a great career at the William S. Richardson School of Law at the University of Hawai'i, where he became the leading expert in the United States on Asia and the law of the sea. Peter, after becoming a partner at Washington's largest law firm, Covington & Burling, ultimately served a term as president of the American Society of International Law (ASIL).

Among the nonspecialists who enrolled in my domestic China course during the Cultural Revolution era, I especially remember Jed Rakoff, with whom I had several very thoughtful conversations. Jed became a well-known Manhattan business lawyer, with an expertise in criminal justice that led to his appointment as one of New York's finest federal district court judges. We and our spouses have been good friends for many years, and I recently had the pleasure of reading his new book *Why the Innocent Plead Guilty and the Guilty Go Free* based on a series of essays that he published in the *New York Review of Books*.

Another nonspecialist American student with whom Joan and I both became friendly was David Halperin. After undergraduate days at Harvard, David had served with distinction in the U.S. Navy and then as an aide to Henry Kissinger. David became a well-known lawyer in Hong Kong and an innovative entrepreneur in the arts and crafts business. More recently he was the major contributor to the establishment of an HLS chair in Chinese law that honors Joan as well as me.

Many of the most dedicated EALS students in those early years were focused on Japan rather than China. This was natural because U.S.-Japanese relations were flourishing while the new China was closed to Americans—and soon others—as the Cultural Revolution gathered force. Princeton University's fine East Asian undergraduate program sent HLS a number of excellent prospects, some of whom had already spent time in Japan or elsewhere in Asia under the valuable Princeton in Asia program.

Charles Stevens in the HLS Class of 1966 was among the first Princeton graduates to turn up and, several years after his HLS graduation, he took the lead at the international law firm Coudert Brothers in recruiting later EALS students for that firm's ambitions, inspired by him, to establish offices in Tokyo, Hong Kong, Singapore, and ultimately Beijing. Another outstanding Princeton graduate a few years later was Anthony Zaloom, who claimed to have achieved his mastery of the Japanese language while working as a Tokyo bartender. Donald Clarke, among the very brightest of the Princetonians and a dual national—American and Canadian—arrived in Cambridge after having learned both Japanese and Chinese and lived in both countries. Don has subsequently made enormous, continuing contributions to teaching, research, and policy discussions in the Chinese law field from a base at George Washington University.

Yale also sent us some fine students of Japan. Alice Young and Toby Myerson, who both became successful international business lawyers specializing in Japanese transactions, arrived in the early 1970s. I later had the pleasure of working with Toby as a lawyer, first at Coudert Brothers and then for many years as his Paul, Weiss partner. Then came Jim Feinerman, who, while preparing for a PhD in the East Asian field, had studied both Japanese and Chinese at Yale and wanted to add legal training.

But Harvard College also did its part. I had "discovered" Ko-Yung Tung, one of the most interesting undergraduates attracted by EALS, at an anti–Vietnam War student rally in his freshman year in the college. Although bearing a Chinese name, he had been reared in Japan before coming to the United States for high school and spoke flawless Japanese. Following his HLS graduation, after a successful career in practice, Ko-Yung became vice president and general counsel of the World Bank and also an able part-time law teacher at Yale, New York University (NYU), HLS, and some foreign law schools while continuing his practical involvements. Other Harvard undergrads interested in Japan soon followed him, including Jeremy Hovland, who later became one of the EALS graduates to serve as general counsel of the Asian Development Bank (ADB).

Splendid students of Japan came to us from many other universities, not only the Ivy League. Arthur Mitchell, another eventual ADB general counsel, came from UCLA. He had honed his language skills as a foreign student living with the family of a leading Japanese politician, Ohira Masayoshi, who, before becoming prime minister, established Japan's diplomatic relations with the People's Republic of China (PRC) as foreign minister. Walter Ames, who later entered international business consulting, came to us after completing PhD studies at the University of Michigan, where his dissertation analyzed the role of Japanese criminal gangs in the broader society and polity.

Walter was one of what I came to call "the Mormon Mafia" originally introduced by Russell Munk, as I will note below. This was a growing group of students who had benefited from prelaw voluntary service in various East Asian jurisdictions as part of their practice of the Mormon religion. Another dynamic Mormon, Conan Grames, not only mastered the Japanese language but also spent a great deal of time developing ingenious ways of improving how to teach others to attain his linguistic fluency. Conan later became an important lawyer for the expanding Baker McKenzie law firm's Japan practice.

One of the most outstanding academic members of this Mormon group was Michael Young. I recall how, while at HLS, he spent at least two afternoons a week at EALS learning how to read Japan's civil law from a helpful Japanese scholar. Mike went on to launch the Center for Japanese Legal Studies at Columbia Law School and then to become not only dean of George Washington University Law School but also the distinguished president of several major universities.

EALS also developed a few American JD candidates who became interested in other Asian countries. Robert Hornick became a specialist in Indonesian law and government. Barry Metzger was attracted to India. Both later developed these interests while in broader Asian law practice, spending many years at Coudert Brothers and in related pursuits. Barry, who became an outstanding banking law expert, was the first EALS product to fill the general counsel's job at the ADB. Bob has been closing his career by teaching at the Sandra Day O'Connor College of Law at Arizona State University.

All these wonderful students and lifelong friends and colleagues made me glad that, after arriving at Harvard, I had not succumbed to the temptation, endorsed by some supporters of an innovating enterprise, to limit our new center to Chinese studies. Yet China gradually became the major arena for EALS as the PRC, after the worst days of the Cultural Revolution ended in 1969, decided to try to enter the world community on a conventional basis. An encouraging number of students were not intellectual tourists merely looking for diversion but seriously committed China specialists. One early arrival I best recall was the tall, lean Mormon from Salt Lake City named Russell Munk, who had transferred to HLS after one year of law school in Utah to learn about China. Russ was a man of relatively few words, but he was clever and devoted to studying more about the Chinese law and society than Mormon service in Taiwan had brought to his attention. He liked the work that we did together, and this experience led him to suggest to other Mormons interested in law and Asia that they apply to HLS. This was the origin of my soon-expanding "Mormon Mafia."

When Russ graduated, I helped him land a job at the U.S. Department of the Treasury, which by then was starting to prepare for a complex relationship with the PRC. After many years of valuable service, Russ ultimately became deputy assistant secretary of the Treasury for international affairs, a position he long held. He periodically used to recommend, after consulting me, the next EALS alumnus to be appointed general counsel of the ADB, a prerogative enjoyed by the U.S. government while Japan appointed the ADB president.

By early 1970, the flood of my would-be China disciples began in earnest. One of the first and most scholarly, Alison Conner, wrote me from Cornell, where she was completing her coursework for a PhD in Chinese history. She inquired about the possibility of adding legal training so that she might become more adequately prepared as an historian of China's vast legal traditions. Alison entered the HLS Class of 1973 and then earned a post–law school fellowship that enabled her to stay on at EALS to complete her Cornell doctoral dissertation on the development of evidence law in the last of China's dynasties, the Manchu or Qing. After a brief time in practice, Alison launched a distinguished academic career by teaching in Nanjing, Singapore, and Hong Kong before leading the China program at the University of Hawai'i.

At the time, and as long as Chairman Mao was alive, few firms had the vision to be interested in China. The Cultural Revolution dragged on, but things changed with Mao's death in 1976. By 1979, law firms began to compete zealously for our EALS graduates. Some even welcomed ethnic Chinese law students who had grown up in the United States and didn't really have a grasp of Mandarin as long as they could give clients the impression that they were knowledgeable about the PRC. In those days, I used to joke that any Harvard student who had recently eaten in a Chinese restaurant had become a China expert overnight.

The fall of 1970 also brought Frank Upham, another student destined to become my lifelong friend and even a teaching colleague for the past three decades. Frank had become interested in China while a Princeton undergraduate, so much so that he accepted a fellowship to teach English in Taiwan for two years after college. That opportunity allowed him to develop his Chinese-language skills and learn about life in a Chinese-speaking community during the heyday of Chiang Kai-shek's dictatorship over the island. After that, being an adventurous sort, Frank worked as a foreign journalist in South Vietnam as the tragic U.S. military conflict there went from bad to worse. He then decided to come to HLS and focus on our China program.

During his first two years at HLS, and although a self-described China "stalwart" among our broad EALS group, Frank gradually became interested in seriously learning about Japan. He recently reminded me that, when I heard that he was going to enroll in an 8 A.M. Japanese-language class five days a week before attending his third-year law courses later in the day, I urged him instead to take the academic year off and go to Japan for a more authentic and effective learning experience. Frank reportedly agreed that this would be a better idea but pointed out that he could not afford such an expensive project. At that point, he says, I offered to donate $3,000 of EALS research funds to him if he could manage to find the rest of the money required for the trip, which he did.

My idea was not to divert a talented would-be China specialist into another field of study but rather to enhance this budding Sinologue's capacity for a greater career in Chinese studies by adding the dimensions that knowledge of and experience in Japan might bring him. My early years at Harvard had made clear the fascinating interactions of law and society between China and Japan going back to the seventh century AD and the important comparisons, past and present, that were yet to be made by scholars capable of research in both languages. Indeed, I had just spent my 1971–1972 sabbatical year in Japan to learn Japanese, which seemed a good use of my time while patiently waiting for Red China to permit Americans to set foot in the revolutionized Promised Land.

After Frank graduated, he landed a clerkship with the Massachusetts state courts that gave him an opportunity to learn about the realities of the administration of justice in the United States and allowed time for the challenging task of finding an academic perch that would enable him to pursue Asian law. I helped pave the way for him to teach at Ohio State University, which he did for a number of happy years before moving back to the Boston area to teach at Boston College Law School.

Later, after I joined the NYU School of Law faculty in 1990, I urged our dynamic dean, John Sexton, to try to lure Frank to our faculty. At that time, shortly after the Communist Party's tragic massacre of many hundreds of citizens in Beijing, no one knew what direction China's modernization might take. Japan, by contrast, had begun to convince some observers that it might indeed become one of the world's leaders—*Japan as Number One*, as Ezra Vogel's famous book put it. I was confident that, with Frank's addition, NYU could build a credible East Asian program that would offer instruction and research on Japan as well as China, as Harvard, Columbia, and Michigan were already doing. To our pleasure, Frank decided to join us and has been a valued and popular teacher as well as a leading scholar for the past thirty years.

Academic year 1972–1973 brought us an unusual student opportunity. It was made possible by HLS's marvelous dean of admissions, Russell Simpson, who, unlike some admissions directors, always gave me maximum sympathetic and efficient cooperation in helping to build our

East Asian program. Charles W. Freeman Jr.—"Chas," as he was already known—had actually started at HLS in the Class of 1966. He left after two years and an indifferent academic record, however, to join his true love, the Foreign Service under the U.S. Department of State. After some years of extraordinary training, he acquired the reputation of being the State Department's outstanding Chinese-language interpreter. That had landed him the position of interpreter for Secretary of State William P. Rogers when Rogers accompanied President Richard Nixon and national security adviser Henry Kissinger on the famous February 1972 trip to China that Nixon, as part of his 1972 reelection campaign, had modestly described as "the week that changed the world."

I had already come to know Chas through State Department contacts and saw his potential for becoming an expert on China's practice of international law. I urged Chas to consider taking leave from the State Department for the year necessary for him to finish his legal education, offered to facilitate his readmission to HLS, and said that I would try to persuade the State Department not only to allow him to take the year off but also to keep him on its payroll while he was in Cambridge. All this came about. Chas had a spectacular record as a committed third-year student, contributed greatly to our activities, and then returned to Washington to forge a distinguished and occasionally controversial career not only in U.S. diplomacy and foreign policy relating to China/Taiwan matters but also on Middle East issues. He at one point served as U.S. ambassador to Saudi Arabia.

There were many other outstanding students who went on to do great things, too numerous for all of them to be mentioned. Clark Randt Jr., a recent Yale alum known as Sandy, was studying at the University of Michigan Law School but came to HLS for a year to join our China courses and EALS activities. We also occasionally played tennis, usually doubles, because he was much better than I and doubles reduced the discrepancy between us. One morning in October 1973, he telephoned to ask whether he might bring one of his former Yale College suitemates, then at the Harvard Business School (HBS), to join our game that afternoon. I said of course, and contacted Steve Orlins, a China specialist in the HLS first-year class and a fine player, to make our fourth.

Sandy's ex-suitemate turned out to be George W. Bush, son of George H. W. Bush, who had already achieved notoriety as the U.S. ambassador to the UN who had unsuccessfully tried to delay the PRC's 1971 replacement of Chiang Kai-shek's Taiwan regime as the representative of China in the UN. By the time of our tennis game, Bush senior had been rewarded (ironically) for this effort by President Nixon, who had recently named him as the head of the new U.S. Liaison Office in Beijing that was serving as a proto-embassy before the eventual establishment of formal diplomatic relations between Washington and Beijing at the end of the 1970s.

I got a kick out of meeting young George, or "W" as he later came to be known, because, as I mentioned in my discussion about my own Yale College days, I had met and liked his grandfather, Prescott Bush, who, while preparing to run for the U.S. Senate in Connecticut, had managed to attend some of the Saybrook College faculty dinners that I staffed as a poor bursary boy. "W" turned out to play a good country club level of tennis, not quite up to Sandy and Steve but better than mine. After some lively sets we repaired to the backyard of my house for a beer, which gave me the opportunity to ask George a few questions about the "B School" and his post-MBA ambitions. He was amiable and responsive, but there was no hint of the political future that lay ahead for his father and himself as presidents of the United States.

Almost thirty years later, not long after "W" was elected president in November 2000, he appointed Sandy Randt, his erstwhile suitemate, to be the U.S. ambassador to Beijing. Sandy, who had not been a career diplomat or a foreign policy pundit but a China-focused business lawyer and sometime government trade official, set a record that still lasts today by occupying this most challenging diplomatic job for over seven years and serving with distinction.

Fortunately for my tennis and more important for our EALS program, after Sandy's departure, Steve Orlins still had two more years at HLS, and during that time we began what has often been an almost daily lifelong friendship. I first learned about Steve in the fall of 1971, when his Harvard undergraduate mentor, my brilliant younger colleague James C. Thomson Jr. of the history department, telephoned to introduce one of his best students, one who was determined to come to the HLS in order to enlist in our China activities. I invited Steve to join our weekly lunch programs and, after considering his immediate postcollege options, we decided that he should spend a year in Taiwan living in a Chinese society and honing his language skills before entering HLS.

Steve had a fabulous year in Taiwan, even learning to sing in a Chinese opera, where he was cast as a sinister foreigner. Steve understandably had his postgraduation sights set on joining the State Department's Office of the Legal Adviser, a goal that had typically been out of reach before young law graduates had acquired several years of training and practical experience with a high-powered private law firm. Yet the mid-1970s was a special time in the gradually improving but still not formalized Sino-American relationship. "L," as the legal office was known within the State Department, recognized an immediate need for a young legal scholar steeped in contemporary Chinese studies and able to analyze the complex political-legal challenges that "normalization" of diplomatic relations entailed regarding the rival Chinese governments on both sides of the Taiwan Strait. So they made an exception: Steve got the job and played a useful advisory role not only in President Jimmy Carter's negotiations with its PRC counterparts but also in the intense congressional-executive jousting that culminated in the all-important Taiwan Relations Act of 1979 that is still crucial to the island's security today.

Another former student who deserves mention is William Alford, who came to HLS after he had already done graduate work in Chinese history with the renowned scholar and immensely popular lecturer Jonathan Spence at Yale. Because of his additional graduate study of law in England, he was admitted to HLS as a second-year student, and during the two years I knew him as a student, I tagged him as an excellent prospect for an academic career in the China field. Little did either of us suspect that, a dozen years later, he would succeed me as professor of Chinese law at HLS and that three decades later he would be chosen as the first occupant of Harvard's newly established Joan Lebold Cohen and Jerome Alan Cohen chair in Chinese Law. One really can't expect more than that from even the best student.

Yet it was the class of 1978 that brought the China activities of EALS into full flower. One of the stars of that vibrant group was Jamie Horsley, a woman I first met in Taiwan in the spring of 1974 and who was then pursuing advanced Chinese-language and area studies on the island as a graduate student in political science at the University of Michigan. Jamie proved to be an excellent law student and became a wonderful friend to both Joan and me. A few years after her HLS graduation, I recruited her to succeed me in the Beijing office I had just established for the Paul, Weiss law firm, and she soon became a partner in the firm. Jamie is currently associate director of Yale Law School's impressive Paul Tsai China Center, where she does groundbreaking scholarship on PRC law and government.

Another outstanding member of the class of 1978 was Natalie Lichtenstein, who for some three decades was the World Bank's expert on China's legal system and eventually played a key role in the establishment of the Asian Infrastructure Investment Bank in Beijing.

James Feinerman was a third prominent China specialist in that class. Following a tour as a lawyer with the DavisPolk law firm in New York, Jim entered academic life by joining the faculty at Georgetown University Law Center in Washington, where he established its important center for Asian law, organized some influential special programs for training young Chinese lawyers, and introduced Chinese law courses to JD and graduate students. Jim has managed all this while maintaining his scholarly publications and serving as the law school's associate dean for many years.

Susan Finder graduated with the class of 1979 just as China, because of the ascension of Deng Xiaoping, had begun to produce evidence of legal reform. Over forty years later, her daily blogs continue to be a fount of reliable news and keen insight into contemporary developments in the PRC legal system. Susan has rendered monumental service by creating and editing the very useful *Supreme People's Court Monitor*, which tracks China's latest significant judicial developments and benefits from her own close cooperation with PRC efforts to develop international dispute resolution arrangements attractive to foreigners.

Although he did not graduate until 1980, Michael J. Moser was another star student in Susan's entering class. After graduation, he began an outstanding career in law practice relating to China, first with law firms and then as an independent arbitrator acting as either an advocate or an adjudicator.

Paul Theil overlapped with Mike and blazed a trail that others have followed by choosing to combine the law degree with a Harvard MBA in a then new four-year joint program that I had helped shepherd through HLS approval. After a period as one of the EALS alumni who, like Sandy Randt and Jamie Horsley, served at the U.S. embassy in Beijing as an adviser to U.S. business, Paul soon made a successful career, much of it with Morgan Stanley, investing in China as well as Taiwan.

THE CONTRIBUTIONS OF FOREIGN STUDENTS

Although the PRC did not begin to send us talented law students until the 1980s, students from Taiwan arrived much earlier and made the most of their opportunity. Especially memorable was the group who arrived in the late 1970s. Annette (Hsiu-lien) Lu got her Harvard LLM in 1978 and, after bravely deciding to return to the island to combat the Koumintang (KMT) dictatorship that still prevailed there. With other members of the so-called Kaohsiung Eight, she was sentenced to a twelve-year prison term for the political offense of advocating for Taiwan's freedom and independence. Later, after serving five years of her sentence, she was released from prison on my suggestion to her erstwhile Harvard LLM classmate Ma Ying-jeou, who had become an important KMT official after his return from Harvard. After her release, following a year of rehabilitation at HLS, Annette resumed her Taiwan political career in the gradually freer environment of the late 1980s. In 2000, she became Taiwan's first woman vice president and for eight years helped lead the first non-KMT administration since the island was subjected to Chinese occupation after World War II. After Annette's second term expired, Ma Ying-jeou, who had stayed on for the Harvard SJD, was elected president of Taiwan for two four-year terms as the KMT returned to power.

Joan, our son Ethan, and I attended Ma's first presidential inauguration ceremony in 2008. There I was delighted to see the oath of office administered by another Harvard SJD recipient, Lai In-jaw, who, after a distinguished career in government, had become the country's chief justice. What an extraordinary event that was for the two of them, who had overlapped at HLS; for EALS alumni; and for me!

Of course, many other HLS graduates from Taiwan during my era also went on to illustrious careers in law practice and academe. Jack J. T. Huang, C. Y. Huang (Huang Ch'ing-yuan) and Jennifer Lin have all proved to be among the outstanding business lawyers in Taiwan. C. V. Chen (Chen Chang-wen) became both head of Taiwan's biggest law firm, Lee & Li, and an influential public commentator. He was succeeded at the firm by Nigel Li (Li Nian-tzu), another HLS LLM who, by that time, had become Taiwan's leading constitutional lawyer. For some years both C. V. and Nigel also continued to teach law part-time in China as well as in Taiwan.

Chang Wejen spent years as an EALS researcher working in the field of Chinese legal history, later received Harvard's SJD degree, and established an important and productive center for the study of China's legal traditions at Academia Sinica in Taipei. He also frequently lectured at many mainland law schools as well as on the island. Chang Fu-mei earned a PhD in Chinese legal history from Harvard before deciding to give up her subsequent scholarly pursuits at Stanford's Hoover Institution in favor of a prominent career in Taiwan's government.

After earning his HLS doctorate and a brief excursion in democratic politics, Eric Wu (Wu Dong-sheng) played a major role in Taiwan's business world. Li Chun, a lawyer and Yale JSD who was the first to greet me on my initial visit to Taiwan in 1961, later came to HLS with my assistance and earned the regular U.S. JD degree, an unusual feat, to be sure. Not to be outdone, both his daughter Florence and his son Fred soon followed him in earning Harvard's SJD and JD degrees, respectively—an extraordinary family!

Here, I name only those HLS graduates from Taiwan with whom I have enjoyed the closest contacts. Many others populate the legal profession, government, the courts, and law faculties on the island.

Harvard had attracted outstanding legal specialists from East Asia long before we established EALS. Although on arrival at HLS, I overlapped with the LLM year of Singapore's future scholar-diplomat Tommy Koh in 1964–1965, I was so new and preoccupied that I missed the opportunity to have more than a nodding acquaintance with him, a defect we happily cured in later years. South Korea's impressive scholar-diplomat Hahm Pyong-Choon, as previously mentioned, acquired his Harvard JD degree before my arrival but returned for a memorable EALS talk in the early 1970s. Several very promising law professors from Japan had already become academic leaders at universities in Tokyo and Kyoto on the basis of their prestigious Harvard doctorates earned before my arrival, with mentoring given them by my senior colleague, the distinguished Arthur Von Mehren. And long before the communist victory in China's civil war, the famous Dean Roscoe Pound had attracted splendid Chinese scholars to study at HLS.

My contribution to our early EALS Japan work was to make creative use of the new opportunities provided by the opening of the HLS Pound Hall in 1970. That made a huge difference to our program. Half of the fourth and fifth floors of that sleek classroom structure became available to our program. I moved quickly to invite for one year, each as visiting scholars, a stream of able Japanese law professors to cooperate with our faculty and especially our students. Yasuhei Taniguchi, whom I had first brought to Berkeley for the LLM in 1962, came as a dynamic young teacher from Kyoto University. After I spent the academic year 1971–1972 as visiting professor at Doshisha University in Kyoto, I invited several other very capable young teachers from that beautiful city to Harvard. Shigeru Kozai of Kyoto University, one of Japan's experts in United Nations law, and torts specialist Fujikura Koichiro of Doshisha, both of whom and their wives had been very helpful to Joan and me while we were living in Kyoto, were among my favorites. Professor Akio Morishima of Nagoya University was another very able visiting scholar.

Not long afterward, professors Morishima and Fujikura joined me and Julian Gresser in teaching a course on Japan and environmental law. Julian was an enterprising and talented U.S. lawyer specializing in Japanese studies whom I had befriended in 1965 while he was still a Harvard undergraduate. The three Japan experts ultimately produced a very useful book on the subject. This project was supported by the income from the $1 million grant I secured for HLS from the Mitsubishi group of companies during my stay in Japan in 1971–1972.

The Mitsubishi grant not only sustained legal research on Japan by EALS-related scholars but was mainly designed to enable HLS to introduce a permanent course on Japanese law into the curriculum. It proved a challenge every year for me to propose to our faculty suitable visiting professors from Japan, and it was only my agreement to coteach the course with the visitors that smoothed faculty approval. This was a new burden for me but a pleasurable one. It not only added to my learning about Japan and enriched my comparative studies of China but also stimulated interest in the relevance of Asian law among a larger and more diverse body of law students and Harvard graduate students from the arts and sciences. It even reached some students from the Fletcher School of Law and Diplomacy at Tufts University in Massachusetts, who were allowed to enroll in select HLS courses.

My law school courses and our EALS activities were also enriched by the participation of some brilliant foreign graduate students from a variety of countries. Albert Chen of Hong Kong later became dean of the University of Hong Kong Faculty of Law and a leading expert on the PRC's legal system as well as Hong Kong law. Others, while not conversant in any of the Northeast Asian languages, proved to be excellent interlocutors because of their insights into comparative law and legal history. Roberto Unger from Brazil was the outstanding example. His ability to place Chinese legal development in the broadest world context and to generate significant hypotheses and generalizations captivated other students as well as their professors. Roberto was soon rewarded with a place on the HLS faculty, where, over four decades later, he still holds forth.

I enjoyed the contributions of other lively foreign comparativists as well. Neelan Tiruchelvam of Sri Lanka was always a pleasure to listen to. After successfully entering election politics in Colombo, however, he was the victim of a dastardly political assassination. One of the most delightful challengers of some of my criticisms of PRC repression of human rights was Olara Otunnu of Uganda, who became a good friend of our entire family and whose younger brother Omara we helped escape from dangerous Ugandan political violence. Olara, an articulate speaker with lilting, anticolonial rhetoric and a dynamic manner, later became an influential voice for African interests at the UN. I was disappointed that a push to make him UN Secretary General never succeeded.

Gabriele Crespi-Reghizzi of Italy was our earliest example of an invaluable foreign student. He was at Harvard during the academic year 1966–1967, shortly after the start of EALS. A young teacher of Soviet law in Milan who had an excellent command of Russian, Gabriele had already begun a comparative study of PRC law. During his LLM year, he did a valuable early analysis of the legal aspects of Beijing's international trade disputes. At my suggestion, it was published in the *Harvard Journal of International Law*. His conclusion, written with continental savoir faire, was a useful one at a time when the Cultural Revolution had turned world opinion against the PRC. He assured us that the situation regarding China's conduct of foreign trade prior to the Cultural Revolution, at least in European eyes, had been one of "normal difficulty."

Years later, Matthias Scheer, a young lawyer and law teacher from Hamburg University whose specialty was Japan, gave us many helpful German perspectives on approaching the legal systems of both Japan and China. And Frank Munzel of Hamburg's Max Planck Institute was one of several able Chinese law experts from Germany who spent a year at EALS as a visiting scholar.

Before closing this appendix on building the East Asian Legal Studies program at HLS, I should say a word about our efforts to promote the study of Southeast Asian law and legal history. Vietnam was of particular interest. Like Korea and Japan, it had long been part of the traditional Confucian culture area. Imperial China had exerted enormous influence over Vietnamese government, law, and society, and in the last centuries of China's Manchu dynasty, Vietnam's rulers, first the Le and then the Nguyen, formed an important part of the tribute system that the Son of Heaven in Beijing had established to regulate relations with the lands on China's periphery.

The successful communist revolutions in China and North Vietnam after World War II did not end China's influence on its neighbor, but much remained obscure in their relations, including interactions between their Leninist-type legal systems. In the spring of 1975, when the South Vietnamese regime fell to Hanoi's communist forces, it became clear that the legal system of the newly reunited country, whose population seemed destined to soon exceed 90 million, deserved careful study in its own right. Like study of the Soviet system that inspired both the Chinese and Vietnamese revolutions, knowledge of Vietnam's modern experience would cast comparative light on the role of law in Chairman Mao's China.

I knew very little about Vietnam but became increasingly interested, especially after the arrival in the fall of 1972 of the first Vietnamese legal specialist to appear during my tenure at HLS. His name was Nguyen Ngoc Bich, and he was a Saigon lawyer who had been cooperating with U.S. officials in improving police administration in noncommunist South Vietnam. The Americans liked him so much that they urged him to undertake graduate legal education at Harvard and wrote to ask me to accept Bich as an LLM student, which I was happy to do. He proved to be a solid contributor and, at the end of his year with us, I tried to persuade him to stay on in the United States rather than return to the deteriorating political situation of the Saigon regime. Bich was determined to go home and enter law practice, however, a fateful decision that led to thirteen years of imprisonment for him.

After the South Vietnamese regime collapsed two years later, Saigon scholars, including a legal specialist and a historian in search of employment, turned up in Cambridge because they had heard about EALS. Here was an opportunity to learn more about Vietnamese law, especially the country's precommunist developments. EALS had no funds available, so I persuaded the Ford Foundation to make a grant to support their research. By then, the Ford Foundation had come under the leadership of McGeorge Bundy, who had previously been one of the architects of the tragically misguided U.S. military involvement in Vietnam, and I rightly anticipated that "Mac," as he was known, might welcome an opportunity for an enlightened gesture toward Vietnam.

After several years, and under the leadership of Ta Van Tai, an active and optimistic young scholar, the Vietnamese specialists produced a useful book about the development of law in Vietnam's late traditional Le dynasty, a study that made clear the importance of China's influence. After I left Cambridge, Massachusetts, to take up residence in China, however, Ta Van Tai decided to become a Boston area lawyer and focused on qualifying for admission to the Massachusetts bar and setting up a local law practice. Only a decade later, when my own career in law practice repeatedly led me to Vietnam and then to teaching at NYU School of Law, was I able to resurrect my interest in Vietnamese law.

Indonesia also became a subject of considerable interest, and, with suggestions from our former students Bob Hornick and Gregory Churchill, rare U.S. specialists on that country, we were able to attract a handful of graduate students and visiting scholars from Jakarta over the years. I especially liked Charles Himawan, an experienced lawyer with academic aspirations, and Nono Makarim, a brilliant, articulate public intellectual who had been dabbling in politics as well as law teaching and later became a successful international business practitioner.

I was very lucky near the start of the EALS effort to have the cooperation of an earlier HLS graduate who had gone to Washington, DC, to work as a lawyer and yet yearned to return to academic life and resume his research on China. One day early in 1966, I received a letter from Robert Randle Edwards, HLS Class of 1962, who was working in the legal division of the U.S. Department of Housing and Urban Development (HUD). Edwards, whom I did not know, told me that he had studied both Chinese and Japanese and had been able to use his Chinese while doing military service in Taiwan. Yet he expressed disappointment that his work at HUD offered no outlet for his East Asian accomplishments and interests and asked my advice.

I invited him to come back to Harvard for a chat, which he did. Randy turned out to be a tall, attractive southern gentleman with a dulcet

Alabama accent in English and a superb Beijing accent in Mandarin, which he spoke fluently. He also had a strong interest in China's legal history and was eager to pursue graduate training in the subject as part of Professor John Fairbank's famous East Asian history program. Randy had the good fortune to be married to an able Taiwanese woman whose cooperation was an additional asset to his ambitions.

Randy and I agreed that he would come to Cambridge after giving HUD the requisite departure notice. It was a decision that neither of us has had cause to regret. Randy spent the next seven years with us, honed his skills as an historian, produced some groundbreaking essays on the legal aspects of Sino-Western relations in the late eighteenth and nineteenth centuries, and played an increasingly important role in helping me administer the growing EALS program. He ran the program on his own during the academic year 1971–1972 when I spent a sabbatical year in Japan.

Although reluctant to lose the cooperation of someone who had proved such a good colleague and friend, I began to feel guilty by 1973 about keeping Randy at Harvard when he was plainly qualified to set forth on his own teaching career at another major law school. Randy was offered an assistant professorship at Columbia, where he launched the Center for Chinese Legal Studies that began to play a prominent role not only in fostering teaching, research, and publications but also in promoting training and academic exchanges for the new generation of Chinese law professors who had just been freed by Deng Xiaoping from the repression of the Cultural Revolution.

More than a word should also be said about another person who proved essential to the progress of EALS, the beloved Bertha Ezell. She served as my secretary for the flourishing 1970s from the moment we established our center in the new Pound Hall and stayed on for much of the next decade after my departure for law practice in China. In addition to Bertha's professional competence, I highly appreciated her diplomatic skills in dealing with our students, who liked her very much, and my colleagues in the arts and sciences, whom she had befriended in the several years she worked at Harvard's East Asian Research Center before joining the law school.

INDEX

ABA. *See* American Bar Association
ABC Television, 207
abortion, 286, 292
Academia Sinica, Taiwan, 123, 281, 332
Academia Sinica Law Journal, 281
Academy of Social Sciences, PRC, 228
Acheson, Alice (wife), 52, 53
Acheson, David (son), 57
Acheson, Dean, 3, 20–22, 39–40, 47, 51–53, 56–57
Acheson, Mary (daughter). *See* Bundy, Mary Acheson
ADB. *See* Asian Development Bank
Adjunct Senior Fellow for Asia, CFR, 281, 308–9
administrative law, 4, 47, 57, 64, 68, 76, 104, 200, 284
adultery, 70, 94
Africa, 2–3, 15–16, 334
African Americans, 23, 42, 49–51, 202, 317; law students, 17, 71; lawyers, 58–59, 78, 234
AIDS epidemic, 70
Air Force, U.S., 24, 36–37
Ai Weiwei, 253–54
Alaska, 63–64
Albright, Madeleine, 182

Alexandria, Virginia, 23, 26, 33, 42, 48, 54
Alford, William, 266, 329
Allen, Woody, 237
Alsop, Stuart, 48
Alston, Philip, 280
Amanpour, Christiane, 291
America Center, Kyoto, 150
American Bar Association (ABA), 116
American Communist Party, 77–78
American Historical Association, 115
Americans in China (Lautz), 311
American Society of International Law (ASIL), 138, 140, 321
Ames, Walter, 323
Amherst College, 115
Amoco, 235, 236, 257
Anti-Rightist Campaign (1957–1958), PRC, 80, 91, 92, 96, 142, 225
anti-Semitism, 9, 10, 67, 234, 309, 317
Aquino, Benigno "Ninoy," 259, 312
Army, U.S., 13, 37, 82, 164
Army Language School, Monterey, 82
Arnold, Fortas & Porter, 55
Arnold, Thurman, 55
art patrons, 253
Art Waves/Ethan Cohen gallery, SoHo, 253

Asahi shimbun (newspaper), Japan, 169, 172, 174, 175
Asia Foundation, 168, 194, 201
Asian Development Bank (ADB), 323, 324
Asian flu, 52
Asian Infrastructure Investment Bank, Beijing, 330
Asians, 277, 317
ASIL. *See* American Society of International Law
assassinations. *See* murder
Atomic Energy Commission, 48
Australia, 12, 179, 245, 280, 316
Austria, 68, 86, 104

back pain, 24, 191
Bailyn, Bernard, 114
Baker, Ed, 190
Baker McKenzie, 245, 323
Ball, George, 47
Bancroft Prize, 115
bar associations, 116, 336
bar exams, 8, 20, 276, 321
Barnett, Bob, 296
Barnett, Doak, 124
Barth, Alan, 48
Bates, Larry, 245
Bath, Vivienne, 245
Baxter, Richard, 104
Beard, Charles, 114
BEDC. *See* Beijing Economic Development Corporation
Beijing, 84, 95, 222, 274, 322, 328; hotels in, 101–2, 155, 191, 224–25, 228, 232, 250–51, 273; international business law courses in, 223–24; U.S. embassy in, 279, 288–90, 330. *See also* Tiananmen Square
Beijing College of Political Science and Law. *See* China University of Political Science and Law
Beijing Economic Development Corporation (BEDC), 223, 224–25, 274
Beijing Foreign Economic Law Office, 228
Beijing Municipality, 222

Belkin, Ira, 278–79
Bemis, Samuel Flagg, 13
bench memos, 24, 38
Berman, Harold J. "Hal," 86, 103–5, 116
Bernstein, Robert, 280
Bersani, Matthew, 246
Biden, Joseph, 314
Birch, Cyril, 81
Birch, Dorothy (wife), 81
birth control, PRC, 286, 287
Black, Hugo, 24, 32–34, 42, 51
Blanton, Bob, 235–36
Blick, Roy Early, 61
Boalt Hall, University of California at Berkeley, 25, 104–7; Chinese law at, 3–6, 78, 85–87, 103; faculty, 1, 2, 64, 67–76, 78–81, 83, 85, 103, 108, 140; pre-Christmas show, 71–72
Bodde, Derk, 136
Bok, Derek, 118, 144, 232–33, 310
Book of the Month Club, 178
Boorstin, Daniel, 113
Boston College Law School, 326
Boston Globe (newspaper), 152, 211
Bowie, Robert R., 120
Boxer Rebellion, 162
Brandeis, Louis, 21, 28, 40, 41, 55, 310
Brandon, Henry, 48
Brennan, William J., 43–44
bribes, 99
Brickner, Balfour (Rabbi), 66
Bronx Zoo, pandas, 252
Brown, Bill, 165
Brown, Pat, 72, 108
Brownell, Herbert, 29, 46–47
Browning, Robert, 307
Brown v. Board of Education, 30, 42
Brzeziński, Zbigniew, 130, 131, 189
Buddhism, 111
Bundy, Mary Acheson, 52, 64
Bundy, McGeorge, 116, 336
Bundy, William, 64, 145
Burdick, Carol, 73, 74
Burdick, Eugene "Bud," 73–74

Bureau of Democracy, Human Rights, and Labor (DRL), 278
Burgess, Sarah, 267
burglaries, 111
Burton, Harold, 34, 41
Burton, Selma Smith, 41–42
Bush, George H. W., 327–28
Bush, George W., 182, 201–2, 327, 328
Bush, Prescott, 328
business law, international, 114, 167, 192, 194–95, 223–24, 322

CAFA. *See* Central Academy of Fine Arts
California, 23, 25, 27–31, 66, 122; Army Language School, 82; Hastings Law School, 67–68. *See also* University of California at Berkeley
California Democratic Council, Fresno, 73
California Law Review, 135–36, 139
Cambridge, Massachusetts, 109–12, 120. *See also* Harvard Law School; Harvard University
Campbell, Kurt, 288–89, 293
Canada, 164, 209, 218, 246, 253, 269, 322
Canton. *See* Guangzhou
Cantonese, 90, 91, 95, 243
Canton Under Communism, 93
Carey Law School, University of Pennsylvania, 42, 72, 136
Carnegie Corporation, 97
Carruthers, Tom, 19
Carter, Jimmy, 128–32, 189, 210, 238, 257, 309, 329
CAS. *See* Chinese Academy of Sciences
Casner, Dean James, 112, 114
Castro, Fidel, 82
caviar, 102, 174
CBS Television, 172, 178–79, 207
CCP. *See* Chinese Communist Party, KMT; Chinese Communist Party, PRC
CCPIT. *See* China Council for the Promotion of International Trade
Center for Chinese Legal Studies, Columbia University, 337

Center for Chinese Studies, U.C. Berkeley, 80, 81, 82
Center for Human Rights at the Catholic University of America, 294
Center for International Affairs (CFIA), 119, 120, 259
Center for Japanese Legal Studies, Columbia Law School, 323
Center for the Advanced Study of the Behavioral Sciences, Stanford University, 86
Central Academy of Fine Arts (CAFA), 291
Central Intelligence Agency (CIA), 2, 13–14, 64, 97–98, 119, 140, 163–66, 311
Century Association, 237
certiorari, petitions for, 23–24, 38, 51
CFIA. *See* Center for International Affairs
CFR. *See* Council on Foreign Relations
Chace, James, 52
Challenge to China (Cohen, J. A.), 311
Chan, Jeanette, 246, 269–70, 275
Chan, Kenneth, 243, 244
Chan, Yvonne, 246, 275
Chang, Irene, 84
Chang, T. K., 245, 251, 252
Chang Fu-mei, 262, 332
Chang Wejen, 123, 332
Chappaquiddick incident (1969), 130, 208, 215
Chayes, Abram, 114
Chen, Albert, 333–34
Chen, C. V. (Chang-wen), 331
Chen, Eddie (Chen Zhongwen), 93, 95
Chen, Grace, 81
Chen, Hsutu, 82–83
Chen, S. H., 81, 83, 84
Chen, Yu-Jie, 280–81
Chen Chih-li, 263
Cheng, Teresa, 203–4
Chen Guangcheng, 286, 296–97; detainment and escape, 282, 287–90; legal education, 283–85, 287, 289–95
Chen Kerui, 293–94, 295
Chen Kesi, 293–94, 295
Chen Tiqiang, 142–43

Chen Yifei, 253
Chen Zhongwen. *See* Chen, Eddie
Cherington, Charles, 13, 14
Chi, Wenshun, 82, 83
Chiang (Madame), 123
Chiang Ching-kuo, 257, 258, 261
Chiang Kai-shek, 99, 123, 135, 145, 217, 224, 257; KMT and, 206, 246, 256, 295, 301, 311, 316, 331; regime, 93, 129–30, 138, 161, 206, 232, 255, 301, 325, 328
Chiang Wei-kuo, 263
"Chief, The." *See* Warren, Earl
China. *See* People's Republic of China; Taiwan
China Business Review (magazine), 247
China Club, Hong Kong, 203
China Council for the Promotion of International Trade (CCPIT), 197, 222
China International Economic and Trade Arbitration Commission (CIETAC), 197, 251
China Light & Power (CLP), 99, 241–44
China National Offshore Oil Corporation (CNOOC), 227
China-Pol (listserv), 281
"China Policy for the Next Administration, A" (Cohen, J. A.), 189
China's Practice of International Law (Cohen, J. A.), 139
China Times (newspaper), 280
China Today and Her Ancient Treasures (Cohen, J. F. L.), 253
China University of Political Science and Law (Beijing College of Political Science and Law), 95
Chinese Academy of Sciences (CAS), 154
"Chinese Attitudes Toward International Law," 137
Chinese Communist Party (CCP), KMT, 316
Chinese Communist Party (CCP), PRC, 91–93, 139, 160, 299, 301, 304, 326, 335; Central Committee, 249; *Readings in Chinese Communist Documents*, 82; *Renmin ribao*, 81, 249

"Chinese Communist Party and 'Judicial Independence,' The" (Cohen, J. A.), 139
Chinese language, 11, 81, 134, 279, 325, 327, 329; joint venture contracts, 242–43; learning, 82–85, 133
Chinese law, 80, 245, 320, 325, 330, 334, 337; at Boalt Hall, 3–6, 78, 85–87, 103; *Contemporary Chinese Law*, 139; crime, 79, 89, 91–96, 134–37, 231, 299, 311; firms, 199–200; further studies, 138–40; *Harvard Studies in Chinese Law*, 136; at HLS, 103–4, 164, 266, 312, 322, 324, 329; lawyers, 225–26, 274, 294; at NYU, 278, 312; specialists, 2, 3, 171, 217
"Chinese Mediation on the Eve of Modernization" (Cohen, J. A.), 135–36, 139
Chinese nationals, internment in India, 139
Chinese Society of International Law, 142
Chinese Wildlife Foundation, 252
Chiu, Hungdah, 131, 137–39, 142, 146, 218, 231, 255, 311
Christian Science Monitor (newspaper), 181
Ch'ü, T. T., 135
Chuan Ruxiang, 223
Chun Doo Hwan, 143, 189
Churchill, Gregory, 336
Churchill, Winston, 12, 51
CIA. *See* Central Intelligence Agency
CIETAC. *See* China International Economic and Trade Arbitration Commission
Clark, Charles, 20
Clark, Robert, 266
Clark, Tom, 34, 46, 54
Clarke, Donald, 322
Claytor, W. Graham, 48–49
Cleary, Gottlieb, Friendly and Hamilton, 47, 235, 236
clerkships, 113, 245, 326; U.S. Supreme Court, 6, 20–33, 36–46, 48, 54, 56, 64, 114–15; women and, 24
Cleveland Park, Washington, D.C., 48, 61
Clinton, Bill, 182, 202, 204
Clinton, Hillary, 288, 292
CLP. *See* China Light & Power

CNOOC. *See* China National Offshore Oil Corporation
Coblentz, William J. "Bill," 72, 108
Cohen, Beatrice Flora Kaufman (mother), 7, 8, 9, 12, 16, 150, 309
Cohen, Burton (brother), 8, 10, 11–12
Cohen, Ethan (son), 83, 122, 191, 253, 293, 308; education, 103, 109–11, 148–49, 232, 252; travels, 90, 102, 148–49, 152, 169, 171, 173–81, 241, 291, 331
Cohen, Jerome A. *See specific topics*
Cohen, Jerome B., 88
Cohen, Joan Florence Lebold (wife), 5, 191, 192, 217, 309, 311; with art history scholarship, 6, 19, 26, 38, 107, 111, 128, 146, 154, 252–53, 291, 308, 320; courtship and relationship with, 12, 14, 19–20, 307–8; family, 23, 36, 39, 41, 44–47, 49, 66, 67–69, 75, 98, 102, 109–11, 216, 252, 269, 293, 307–8; friendships, 26, 53–55, 66, 69, 72–73, 78, 98–100, 103, 106–7, 117, 123, 241, 253, 283–84, 333; with HLS chair in Chinese Law, 312, 322, 329; Smith College and, 6, 12, 41, 69, 117; at State of the Union speech, 41–42; with students, 70, 320–21; travels, 23, 26, 48, 84, 88–90, 109–11, 141, 147–50, 152–55, 157–60, 162, 169, 171, 173–81, 183, 219, 230, 232, 237, 241, 244, 252, 283, 291, 331
Cohen, Peter (son), 41, 44, 49, 53, 66, 122, 129, 191, 308; as CBS photographer, 172, 178–79; education, 102, 109–11, 148–49, 232, 252; travels, 90, 102, 148–49, 152, 169, 171–81, 241
Cohen, Philip (father), 7–9, 11–13, 64, 233, 309–10
Cohen, Seth (son), 41, 65, 122, 191, 271, 308; education, 103, 109–11, 148–49, 232, 252; travels, 90, 102, 148–49, 152, 169, 171, 173–81, 241
Cold War, 12, 106, 317
Cole, Robert, 26
Columbia Law School, 47, 86, 103, 136, 219, 310, 323; faculty, 246, 272, 276; visiting scholars, 278

Columbia University, 40, 81, 103, 124, 130, 221, 252, 337
commercial law, 195, 224, 247
Committee on Combined Work in Law and Related Disciplines, HLS, 114
Committee on Rights and Responsibilities (CRR), Harvard University, 120, 121
Committee to Support Chinese Lawyers, 294
communism, 32, 77–78, 80, 93, 301, 331, 335. *See also* Chinese Communist Party
comparative law, 4, 85, 103, 104, 168, 186, 305, 334
conflict-of-interest rules, 46
Confucian China and Its Modern Fate (Levenson, J. R.), 79
Confucianism, 167, 313
Confucius, 1, 6, 135, 156, 211–12, 305, 313
Congress, U.S., 5, 65, 232, 316. *See also* House of Representatives, U.S.; Senate, U.S.
Conner, Alison, 324–25
Constitution, U.S., 61, 73
constitutional law, 4, 27, 43–44, 69, 76, 127, 287, 331
constitutions: PRC, 96, 300; Soviet Union, 96
Contemporary Chinese Law (Cohen, J. A.), 139
Corcoran Gallery of Art, 26, 38
Cornell University, 324–25
corporate law, 191–98
Cortez, Manuel, 19
Coudert, Alexis, 229, 233–34
Coudert Brothers, 229, 233–35, 237, 276, 324; consultant to, 218, 224; PRC and, 217–20, 274, 322
Coughlin, Charles, 9
Council on Foreign Relations (CFR), Adjunct Senior Fellow for Asia, 281, 308–9
Counter, the, 57–60
counterrevolutionaries, in PRC, 2, 94, 273
COVID-19 pandemic, 281, 308
Covington & Burling, 48, 55, 57, 63–64, 321; Dean Acheson, and, 39–40, 47, 51–53, 56; pro bono work at, 49–51
Cowan, Dennis, 2
Cox, Archibald, 118, 126

Cravath, Swaine & Moore, 234
Crespi-Reghizzi, Gabriele, 334
criminal justice system: Hong Kong, 281; PRC, 79, 89, 91–96, 134–37, 229, 231, 299, 311; Taiwan, 260–64
criminal law: at Boalt Hall, 69; pro bono work, 49–51; U.S. Attorney's Office for the District of Columbia, 56–63, 75
Criminal Process in the People's Republic of China, 1949–63, The (Cohen, J. A.), 79–80, 96, 134, 231, 311
CRR. *See* Committee on Rights and Responsibilities
Cruiseville (race horse), 25
Cui Tiankai, 295–96
cultural exchange, with PRC, 154–58
Cultural Revolution (1966–1976), PRC, 140, 160, 177, 228, 298, 337; end of, 142, 324, 325; influence of, 122, 134, 137, 206, 299, 301, 320–22, 334; S. Karnow and, 100; operas forbidden during, 214–15; University of Chicago conference on, 113; violence, 164, 208, 300
Czechoslovakia, 13

Daewoo, 191
Daily Paper. See *Tiantian ribao*
Daly, Ed, 61
Davis, Bette, 307
Davis Polk & Wardwell, 234
Dawson, John P. "Jack," 104, 113, 114
D-Day (June 1944), 10
Death of Stalin, The (film), 313
Debevoise & Plimpton, 70
Defense Intelligence Bureau, Taiwan, 258, 263
defense lawyers, 49–51, 56, 58–59
de Gaulle, Charles, 51
Delhi University law school, 147
Democratic National Committee, 52
Democratic Party: South Korea, 188; U.S., 47, 51, 64, 73–74, 123, 128–29, 131, 171, 208, 292
Democratic Progressive Party (DPP), Taiwan, 259, 295, 315

Deng Xiaoping, 265, 272, 302, 304, 312–13, 317, 330, 337; Open Door Policy and, 192, 196, 223, 250, 298–301; E. "Ted" Kennedy and, 156, 211, 213, 215–16
Denmark, 16
Denny, George, 65
Department of Housing and Urban Development (HUD), U.S., 336, 337
Department of Justice (DOJ), U.S., 46–47, 55, 309
Department of State, U.S., 54, 114, 120, 150, 173–74, 275, 278; Foreign Service, 100, 327; Office of the Legal Adviser, 47, 130, 235, 288–89, 309, 329; PRC and, 165–66, 206, 232, 282–83, 291–92, 327, 329
Department of the Treasury, U.S., 221, 324
desegregation, 22, 30–31, 42
Detroit Edison Company, 48–49, 242
Deutsche Bank, 191
"Development of Legal Institutions" (DLI), 113, 115
DeWind, Adrian "Bill," 238
disabled people, in PRC, 283, 284
Disneyland, Shanghai, 203
dispute resolution, 136–37, 192, 195, 197, 223, 250–51, 330
DLI. *See* "Development of Legal Institutions"
Dodson (Mr.), 23
DOJ. *See* Department of Justice, U.S.
Dong-a Ilbo (newspaper), 185
Dongshigu village, PRC, 284–85, 287
Doshisha University Law School, Kyoto, 147, 149–51, 333
Douglas, Kathy, 34
Douglas, William O., 32–34, 51
Downey, John T. "Jack," 2, 14, 140, 163–66, 311
DPP. *See* Democratic Progressive Party
DPRK (People's Republic of Korea). *See* North Korea
Dreyfus, John, 12
Driver, Cecil, 12
DRL. *See* Bureau of Democracy, Human Rights, and Labor
Dudman, Richard, 160

Dulles, Allen, 164
Dulles, John Foster, 52, 164
Duncan, Andrew, 293, 294
Dutton, Peter, 281

Eagleton, Tom, 181
East Asian Legal Studies (EALS), HLS, 128, 169, 190, 231, 259; development of, 140–44, 167; V. H. Li and, 319–20; students, 143, 167–68, 321–30, 331–37
East Asian Research Center, Harvard University, 101, 231, 337
East India Company, 136–37
Ebner, Hella, 9
Ebola epidemic, 204
education, 22, 30–31, 42, 212–14, 221–22, 279, 302, 311. *See also* legal education
Edwards, Robert Randle "Randy," 246, 272, 336–37
Ehrenzweig, Albert, 68, 86, 104
Eisenberg, Shoul, 251–52
Eisenhower, Dwight D. "Ike," 5–6, 29, 41–43, 56, 60; presidential elections, 22, 30, 37, 64; White House dinner and, 54
Eizenstat, Stuart, 128, 129, 131, 309
"Elegy Written in a Country Churchyard" (Gray), 307
Eliasoph, Ellen, 240, 244–46
Elizabeth (Queen of England), 54
Elizabeth, New Jersey, 8, 25
Elman, Philip, 28
Emerson, Thomas, 4
England, 17, 85, 102, 104, 136, 250
Equity Joint Venture Law (1979), 227, 242–43, 300
Erotic Aspects of Chinese Culture (Gichner), 61, 62
Erotic Aspects of Hindu Sculpture (Gichner), 61, 62
Erotic Aspects of Japanese Culture (Gichner), 61, 62
espionage. *See* spies
Evans, Barbara, 52–53
Ezell, Bertha, 111, 337

Face the Nation (TV show), 231
Fainsod, Merle, 105, 141
Fairbank, John King, 78, 103, 105–6, 111, 124, 305, 337; EALS and, 231; Zhou Enlai and, 159–61, 180
Fairbank, Wilma, 159–60
Fairman, Charles, 32
Far Eastern Economic Review (magazine), 173
farmers, with legal representation, 282
Farrell, Barry, 13
FAS. *See* Federation of American Scientists
Fashion Institute of Technology (FIT), 252
fatingneiwai. *See In and Out of Court*
FBI. *See* Federal Bureau of Investigation
FCC. *See* Federal Communications Commission
FCCC. *See* Foreign Correspondents' Club of China
FDR. *See* Roosevelt, Franklin Delano
Fecteau, Richard, 163–66
Federal Bureau of Investigation (FBI), 46
Federal Communications Commission (FCC), 37
Federation of American Scientists (FAS), 154
Feinerman, James, 322, 330
Felix Frankfurter Reminisces (Phillips), 40
Field, John, 75
Fifteen Strings of Cash (*Shiwu guan*) (opera), 214–15
Finder, Susan, 330
Finkelstein, Buck, 18
Finkelstein, David, 320
First, Harry, 272
First Amendment, 61
First Circuit Court of Appeals, Boston, 24
Fischer, Dorothy, 77–78
fishing, 63–64, 174
FIT. *See* Fashion Institute of Technology
Flaherty, Martin, 294
Flake, Gordon, 191–92
Fleming, John, 68
Fletcher School of Law and Diplomacy, Tufts University, 153, 309, 333
Flom, Joseph, 234

Florsheim, Lee, 12
Flower Girl, The (film), 176–77
Ford, Gerald, 189, 210, 211
Ford Foundation, 5, 103, 147, 273–74, 278–79, 286, 336
Fordham University School of Law, 294
Foreign Affairs (journal), 145, 156, 170, 189, 207, 211, 231, 311
Foreign Affairs Association, PRC, 156
Foreign Correspondents' Club of China (FCCC), speech at, 273
foreign direct investment law, PRC, 222
Foreign Investment Commission, Sichuan province, 248
Foreign Languages Press, PRC, 228
foreign policy, U.S., 129–30, 281, 308
Foreign Policy magazine, 131, 190
Foreign Service, U.S. Department of State, 100, 327
FORMOSA Magazine, 257
48 Group Club, 250
Foster (Mrs.), 90
Framatome, 242
France, 2, 10, 85, 104; Fulbright Scholarship and, 1, 13–17, 36, 65, 105, 115; with nuclear power, 242–43
Franco, Francisco, 16
Frankfurter, Felix, 48; Dean Acheson, and, 39–40, 51, 52; Black and, 24; Brandeis and, 310; Brennan and, 44; career advice, 309–10; clerkship with, 6, 22, 33, 37–44, 114; friendship with, 53–54, 66; Harlan and, 34; with law clerks, 24–25, 27–28, 39–44, 47; W. L. Prosser and, 6, 67; as speaker at Yale Law School, 20, 42; Earl "The Chief" Warren and, 27, 30–31, 37, 39; White House dinner and, 54–55; Whittaker and, 43; work ethic, 38–39
Frankfurter, Marion Denman, 41, 53–54
Freeman, Charles W., Jr., 327
French language, 11, 15, 19
Freshman Prom Committee, Yale University, 11
Freund, Paul, 43–44, 310
Fu, Bob, 292, 293

Fujikura Koichiro, 147, 333
Fulbright, J. William, 65, 165, 206–7
Fulbright Scholarship, 1, 13–17, 36, 65, 105, 115
Fuller, Lon, 104
Fuzhou, PRC, 93, 94

Galbraith, John Kenneth, 117–18
Gang, Kopp and Tyre, 46
"Gang of Four" trial, 229
Garrison, Ellen, 237
Garrison, Lloyd, 237
Gasch, Oliver, 56, 60–62
Gayn, Mark, 181
Gelatt, Tim, 244–45, 257, 271, 278
General Motors (GM), 192–93, 220
George III (King of England), 136
Georgetown University, 58, 121, 245, 307, 330
George VI (King of England), 54
George Washington University Law School, 323
German American Bund, 9
Germany, 1, 16, 191, 305, 334; law, 85–86, 104; World War II, 9, 10, 15, 68
Gichner, Lawrence, 61–63
GM. *See* General Motors
Goldberg, Arthur, 237
Goldberger, Marvin, 154, 162
Gombrich, Ernst, 15
Gorbachev, Mikhail, 270
Grames, Conan, 323
Gray, Thomas, 307
Great Britain, 2, 250–51
Great Leap Forward (1958–1961), PRC, 78, 80, 90, 92, 300
Green Gang, 99
Greg (intern for Paul, Weiss), 267, 269
Gresser, Julian, 333
Griffiths, Andy, 279
Griswold, Erwin, 103, 112–14, 116–17, 127
Griswold, Harriet, 112
Grose, Peter, 207
Guanghua, Gregory Miao, 203
Guangzhou (Canton), 7, 89, 93, 159, 171, 213, 250, 269

Guangzhou University, 214
Guggenheim Fellowship, 146, 169

Habib, Philip, 185
Hagerty, James, 29
Hahm Pyong-Choon, 143, 189, 332
Haig, Alexander, 184
Hall, Leonard, 29
Halleck, Charles, 57
Halperin, David, 322
Hamilton, Bob, 54, 55
Hamilton, Dag, 54, 55
Hamilton, Walter, 55
Handlin, Oscar, 114
Harlan, John Marshall, 33, 34, 45–46
Harper, Fowler, 55
Harriman, Averell, 117
Harrison, Selig, 174, 181
Hart, Henry, 37
Harvard Club of Japan, 152, 158
Harvard Crimson (newspaper), 43, 121
Harvard Journal of International Law, 334
Harvard Law Record (newspaper), 144
Harvard Law Review, 25, 139
Harvard Law School (HLS), 109–10, 139, 144, 169, 332–33, 337; alumni, 24–26, 37, 39, 40, 52, 78–79, 86, 103, 113, 117, 123, 124, 126, 128, 143, 196, 198, 217–18, 252, 272; Chinese law at, 103–4, 164, 266, 312, 322, 324, 329; faculty, 44, 86, 103–8, 111–15, 125–28, 164, 191, 218, 231, 252, 266, 310; ITP, 220–22, 228; new responsibilities, 125–28; personal motivations at, 133–34; students, 111–12, 115, 126–28, 145, 147, 187, 196, 217, 255–56, 260, 279, 319–27; visiting professor at, 101–6. *See also* East Asian Legal Studies, HLS
Harvard Studies in Chinese Law, 136
Harvard University, 10, 14–16, 43, 74, 105, 113–14, 141; CFIA, 119, 120, 259; China-U.S. policy memorandum of MIT and, 124–25, 156–57, 165, 311; CRR, 120, 121; East Asian Research Center, 101, 231, 337; Vietnam War and student protests, 117–21, 323

Harvard University Press, 80, 134, 136, 139
Harvard-Yenching Institute, 120, 186, 231
Hazard, Bobbie, 69
Hazard, Geoff, 69, 71–72
Hazard, John N., 86–87, 103, 105
Heaton, Leonard, 29
Henkin, Louis, 47
Henry Holt and Company, 297
Heyman, Michael, 21, 64, 69
Hilton, Conrad, 307
Himawan, Charles, 336
Hiss, Alger, 48, 54
Hiss, Catherine, 53, 54
Hiss, Donald, 48, 53, 54, 56
Hitler, Adolf, 9, 15, 68
H. J. Heinz, 246, 250
HKIAC. *See* Hong Kong International Arbitration Centre
HKU. *See* University of Hong Kong
HLS. *See* Harvard Law School
Hoffa, Jimmy, 63
Hofheinz, Roy, 124
Hogan, Michael (Sir), 98
Hogan, Patricia, 98
Holbrooke, Dick, 131
Hollywood, 297
Holmes, Oliver Wendell, 27–28, 40, 41, 48
Holocaust, 16
Hom, Sharon, 280
Honda, 247–48, 249, 250
Hong Kong, 190, 218–19, 252, 281, 310, 312, 322; HKU, 88–89, 202–3, 333; PRC and, 171, 173, 244; PRC refugees in, 79, 87, 90–100, 134, 162, 292, 320
Hong Kong International Arbitration Centre (HKIAC), 203–4
"Hong Kong's Transformed Criminal Justice System" (Cohen, J. A.), 281
Hoover, Herbert, 55
Hoover, J. Edgar, 46–47
Hoover Institution, Stanford University, 332
Hornick, Robert, 324, 336
Horsley, Jamie, 235–36, 244, 245, 255, 268–69, 329–30

Horwitz, Morton J., 113–15
hotels, in Beijing, 101–2, 155, 191, 224–25, 228, 232, 250–51, 273
House of Delegates, ABA, 116
House of Representatives, U.S., 74–75, 107, 315
Housman, A. E., 45
Hovland, Jeremy, 323
Howe, Mark De Wolfe, Jr., 104, 113, 115
Howson, Nicholas "Nico," 246, 274, 275
Hsia, C. T., 81
Hsia, T. A., 81
Hsiao Kung-chuan, 135
Hsieh, Frank Ch'ang-t'ing, 262–63
Huang, C. Y. (Ch'ing-yuan), 331
Huang, Jack J. T., 331
Huang, Kathy, 281
Huang, Philip, 136
Huang Hua, 163, 164, 209, 210
HUD. *See* Department of Housing and Urban Development, U.S.
human rights, 2, 132, 185, 264, 278, 294; PRC and, 89, 232, 274, 280, 286–87, 292–93, 297, 303–4, 313–14; South Korea and, 184, 186, 189–90, 238
Human Rights in China, 280
Humphrey, Hubert, 73, 122
Hunan University, 213–14
Hundred Flowers Campaign, PRC, 92, 96
Hurst, Willard, 113
Hu Yaobang, 265, 301, 304

IAEA. *See* International Atomic Energy Agency
IBM, 246, 247, 250
ICJ, UN. *See* International Court of Justice, UN
Ideology and Organization in Communist China (Schurmann), 80
In and Out of Court (fatingneiwai) (film), 229
India, 62, 111, 117, 136–37, 139, 147, 153, 324
Indiana University, 63
Inkeles, Alex, 141
International Atomic Energy Agency (IAEA), 243

International Court of Justice (ICJ), UN, 161
international law, public, 75–76, 104, 137–40, 321, 334
International Longshoremen's Association, 63
International Tax Program (ITP), HLS, 220–22, 228
International Visitor Leadership Program (IVLP), 282
internment, prisoners, 2, 18, 32, 68, 73, 99, 139
"Interviewing Chinese Refugees" (Cohen, J. A.), 94
Intourist travel agency, 101
Isham, Heyward, 100
Isham, Sheila, 100
Islamic law, 127–28
Israel, 173, 251–52, 261
Italy, 15, 86, 334
ITP. *See* International Tax Program
IVLP. *See* International Visitor Leadership Program

Jacobs, Paul, 73
Jaffe, Louis, 104
Jang Sung Taek, 202
Japan, 80, 85–86, 111, 128, 131–32, 143, 164, 173, 312, 314; America Center in Kyoto, 150; *Asahi shimbun*, 169, 172, 174, 175; Coudert Brothers in, 218, 219, 322; Doshisha University Law School, 148, 149–51, 333; *Erotic Aspects of Japanese Art*, 61, 62; HLS students from, 127; language, 147–49, 152, 322–23, 325–26; North Korea and, 174, 175, 182; PRC and, 151–52, 247–49, 305, 317, 323, 326; Red Army, 149–51; sabbatical in, 126, 146–53, 162; South Korea and, 167, 187; U.S. and, 158, 211, 216, 232, 316, 322; in World War II, 6, 7, 32, 99
Japan as Number One (Vogel, E.), 326
Japanese Americans, internment of, 2, 18, 32, 68, 73
Javits, Jacob K., 207
Jefferson, Thomas, 187
Jennings, Richard, 68, 71
Jewish War Veterans of America, 9

Jews, 11, 15–16, 17, 19, 98; anti-Semitism and, 9, 10, 67, 234, 309, 317; internment in Hong Kong, 99
Jiang Nan. *See* Liu, Henry
Jiang Qing, 214, 229
Jiang Tianyong, 287
Johns Hopkins University, 152, 309
Johnson, Chalmers "Chal," 81
Johnson, John, 36
Johnson, Lyndon B., 116, 122, 124, 184, 205–6
joint ventures, 193, 220, 222–27, 241–44, 246–51, 273, 300, 312
Journey of the Buddha, The (TV show), 111
ju-che concept, 170

Kadoorie, Horace (brother), 98–99
Kadoorie, Lawrence, 98–100, 241–42, 244
Kadoorie, Muriel, 98, 99, 241
Kadoorie, Rita. *See* Macaulay, Rita Kadoorie
Kalicki, Jan, 216
Kandukuri, Soumya, 281
Kaohsiung Eight, 257, 258–59, 331
Kaplan, John, 257
Karnow, Annette, 100
Karnow, Stanley, 100
Katz, Milton, 103, 111, 117
Kaufman, Andrew, 25, 26, 38, 40, 43, 44, 114
Kaufman, Beatrice Flora. *See* Cohen, Beatrice Flora Kaufman
Kaufman, Fanny, 9
Kazin, Alfred, 121
Kazin, Michael (son), 121
KCIA. *See* Korean Central Intelligence Agency
Kennedy, Edward "Ted," 123–24, 130–32, 156, 257, 309; Kim Dae-Jung "DJ" and, 168–69; with PRC, 205–16, 311
Kennedy, John F., 117, 131, 152, 238; administration, 64, 74, 184, 206; Eisenhower and, 5–6
Kennedy, Robert F., 122, 208, 212
Kennedy School Institute of Politics, Harvard University, 125, 141
Kerr, Clark, 72, 107, 108
Kessler, Friedrich, 17

Kevorkian, Jack, 37
Khrushchev, Nikita, 77
Kim, Y. J., 203
Kim Byong-Shik, 170, 173
Kim Dae-Jung "DJ," 143, 168–69, 184–87, 190, 259, 311
Kim Il-Sung, 170, 175, 176, 178, 188
Kim Il Sung University Law School, 195
Kim Jong Un, 202, 204
Kim Joung-Won "Alex," 168, 187
Kim Suk-Jo, 169, 190, 191
Kim Woo-Choong, 191
Kim Young-Moo, 167
Kim Young-Sam "YS," 184, 187–88
King, Martin Luther, 121–22
Kinsella v. Krueger, 32–33
Kinsey Institute for Research in Sex, Gender, and Reproduction, 63
Kioppe, Ted, 265
Kissinger, Henry, 125, 138, 157, 163, 165–66, 185, 230, 322; Nixon and, 173, 184, 208–9; with U.S.-PRC relations, 209, 311, 315, 327
KMT. *See* Kuomintang
Koch, Ed, 252
KoGuan Law School, Shanghai Jiao Tong University, 287
Koh, Harold, 288–90, 293
Koh, Tommy, 332
Kohn, Hans, 14–15, 16
Kolenda, Helena, 246, 275
Kong Boji, 253
Korean Central Intelligence Agency (KCIA), 184, 186, 190
Korean conflict, 20, 22, 93, 174, 177, 198; armistice, 5; U.S. and, 2–3, 13, 78, 163, 171, 206, 316
Kotch, John, 130
Ko-yung Tung, 147, 322–23
Kozai, Noriko (wife), 128, 333
Kozai, Shigeru, 128, 333
Kraiem, Ruben, 240–41, 244
Kriegel, Jay, 123
Ku Klux Klan, 33

Kuomintang (KMT, Nationalist Party of China), 206, 246, 256, 295, 301, 316; dictatorship, 257–58, 260–61, 264, 311, 331; with H. Liu assassination, 258, 260–64
Kyoto University, Japan, 128, 151, 333

labor, 2, 91–93, 215, 278–79, 302, 311
Lady Chatterley's Lover (Lawrence), 60–61
Lai In-jaw, 331
Lam, Alexa, 245
Landes, David, 108
Lange, Jack, 203, 275
languages: Chinese, 11, 81–85, 133–34, 242–43, 279, 325, 327, 329; Foreign Languages Press, 228; French, 11, 15, 19; German, 9, 10; Japanese, 147–49, 152, 322–23, 325–26; Korean, 196; legal, 227, 228; Russian, 91; Spanish, 9, 19; U.S. military with, 80, 82
laodong gaizao. See reform through labor
laodong jiaoyang. See reeducation through labor
Lardy, Jean Levy-Hauser, 15
Laski, Norman, 17, 102
Laski, Viola, 17, 98, 102
Latinos, 317
Lautz, Terry, 311
law, 85–86, 104, 127–28, 222, 226–27, 242–43, 247, 300. *See also* Chinese law; *specific types of law*
Lawrence, D. H., 60–61
lawyers, 78, 195, 228, 234, 238, 331; "barefoot," 282, 285–88; Chinese law, 225–26, 274, 294; PRC refugees in Hong Kong, 95–97; with pro bono work, 49–51, 201, 252, 260; U.S. Attorney's Office for the District of Columbia, 56–64, 75
Lebanon crisis, 60, 75
Lebold, Don (brother-in-law), 12
Lebold, Joan Florence (wife). *See* Cohen, Joan Florence Lebold
Lee (Mr.), 184
Lee (Mrs.), 141
Lee, Ji, 198–99
Lee, Myung-Soo, 196–98, 201

Lee Hee-ho, 187
Lee Hoi-Chang, 169
Lee Kuan-yew, 141–42, 219, 312
Lee & Li, 331
Legal Aid Society, 49
legal education, 113, 226–27; Chen Guangcheng with, 283–85, 287, 289–95; North Korea and, 192–204; PRC and, 220–25, 229, 274, 276, 299–300
Legal Institutions in Manchu China (Van der Sprenkel), 135
legal systems, 99, 196, 217, 224; PRC, 79, 89, 91–96, 103, 134–40, 214, 231, 247–49, 270, 273, 298–306, 309, 311–12, 321; refugees and PRC, 93–97; Soviet Union, 86–87, 96, 103, 199–201, 299, 305, 335; Taiwan, 86, 260–64, 279–80, 301, 303
legal terminology, Taiwan, 139, 224
Leitner Center for International Law and Justice, Fordham University School of Law, 294
Leng, Shao-chuan, 139
Lenin, Vladimir, 79, 115, 135, 299
Leningrad (St. Petersburg), Soviet Union, 101, 270
Le Peng, 244
Levenson, Joseph R., 72, 76, 78–80, 82, 103
Levenson, Rosemary (wife), 72, 76, 78
Levy-Hauser (Madame), 15
Levy-Hauser, Jean. *See* Lardy, Jean
Lewis, Margaret K., 278, 279, 280, 311
Li (Mr.), 175–76, 178–79
Li (North Korean Ambassador), 202
Li, Choh-Ming "C. M.," 80
Li, Florence, 332
Li, Fred, 332
Li, Nigel (Nian-tzu), 331
Li, Victor Hao, 319–20
Lianhe Bao (newspaper), Taiwan, 156
Lichtenstein, Natalie, 330
Li Chun, 332
lifetime achievement awards, 312
Li Heping, 287
Liman, Arthur, 234, 235–36, 238–39, 260

INDEX

Li Mingde, 154–55
Lin, Jennifer, 331
Lin Biao, 155, 156
Lin Daguang, 159
Linden, New Jersey, 7–10, 21, 25, 36
Lindsay, John, 123, 124
Lin Yutang, 7
Li Peng, 265, 273
Lipson, Leon, 105
Liu, Henry (Jiang Nan), 258, 260–64
Liu, Tsui, 260, 262, 264
Liu Gushu, 247, 268
Liu Zhicheng, 220, 221
Li Xiannian, 226
LLB (JD) law degree, 143
Local Government in China under the Ch'ing (Ch'ü), 135
London Export Corporation, 250
Louisell, David, 67, 69
loyalty oath controversy, at U.C. Berkeley, 73, 107
Lu, Annette Hsiu-lien, 255–60, 279, 311, 331
Lubman, Stanley, 136

MacArthur, Douglas (General), 316
Macartney, George (Lord), 136
Macaulay, Rita Kadoorie, 241
Macaulay, Ron, 241
MacLeish, Archibald, 52
Macmillan, 297
Macneil, Rory, 245
Maggie (Ms.), 23
Magruder, Calvert, 24
Makarim, Nono, 336
Manchu dynasty, 135–36, 325, 335
Manhattan District Attorney's Office, 56
Manning, Bayless, 238
"Mao and Mediation" (Lubman), 136
Maoists, 2, 81, 85, 138
Mao Zedong, 2, 22, 79–80, 86, 99, 155, 164, 325; death of, 130, 160, 303; regime, 90, 96, 134, 138–39, 206, 305, 317. *See also* Cultural Revolution
March, Michael, 245

Marcos, Ferdinand, 259
Marcy, Carl, 65
Marine Corps, U.S., 13, 59–60, 75
Marshall, John, 18
Martin, John Bartlow, 38
Marx, Karl, 79
Massachusetts Institute of Technology (MIT), 124–25, 141, 156–57, 165, 311
Masters, The (Snow), 74
Mayer, Jean, 153
Ma Ying-jeou, 255–56, 258–60, 279, 291, 295, 331
McCarthy, Eugene, 122
McCarthy, Joseph, 3, 22, 65
McCarthyism, 4, 20–21
McCloy, John, 119
McCone, John, 119
McDougal, Myres, 18, 55, 106–7
McGovern, George, 125, 157, 180–81, 207, 210
McHugh, Margaret, 23, 24, 26, 29
McNamara, Robert, 116, 119
McReynolds, Clark, 27–28
Medical School, U.C. Berkeley, 83–84
Meet the Press (TV show), 231
Meisenheimer, Maylin, 281
Merrill, Charles, 110
Metropolitan Club, 51
Metropolitan Life Insurance, 23
Metzger, Barry, 324
Middle East, 128, 251, 327
Milbank, Tweed, 203, 245
military: Japan, 149–51; PRC, 85, 137, 265–67, 304
military, U.S., 32–33, 78, 80, 119, 166, 315–16, 336; Air Force, 24, 36–37; Army, 13, 37, 82, 164; draft board, 13–14, 16, 20–21, 36–37, 118; Marine Corps, 13, 59–60, 75; Navy, 281, 322; in South Korea, 129, 177, 189
Miller, Merton H., 250
Ministry of Electric Power, PRC, 243–44
Ministry of Finance (MOF), PRC, 220, 221
Ministry of Foreign Affairs, North Korea, 174
Ministry of Foreign Affairs (MOFA), PRC, 156, 222, 228–29

Ministry of Foreign Trade, PRC, 247, 250
Ministry of Justice, PRC, 274, 299
Ministry of National Defense, Taiwan, 258, 263
Minow, Newt, 37–38
Minton, Sherman, 26, 34
MIT. *See* Massachusetts Institute of Technology
Mitchell, Arthur, 323
Mitsubishi Corporation, 248
Mitsubishi grant, 333
MOF. *See* Ministry of Finance
MOFA. *See* Ministry of Foreign Affairs
Moldaschl, Hans, 9
Montefiore family, 76
Moody, Graham, 25
Moore, Tom, 246
Morgan Stanley, 330
Morgenthau, Hans, 15
Morishima, Akio, 333
"Mormon Mafia," 245, 323, 324
Morris, Clarence, 136
Moscow, Soviet Union, 86, 101–2, 104, 117, 177, 270
Moscow State University, 212
Moser, Michael J., 330
Munk, Russell, 323, 324
Munzel, Frank, 334
murder, 15, 32–33, 40, 94, 151; assassinations, 121–22, 143, 189, 190, 208, 258, 260–64; suspicious, 186
Murphy, Janet, 117
Museum of Fine Arts, Boston, 107, 111, 128, 146, 154, 320
My Country and My People (Lin Yutang), 7
Myerson, Toby, 234–35, 322

NAC. *See* November Action Committee
Namkung, Tony, 191–92
National Committee on U.S.-China Relations (NCUSCR), 124, 207, 208, 295–96
Nationalist Party of China. *See* Kuomintang
National Lawyers Association, North Korea, 195

National People's Congress, PRC, 222, 299
National Taiwan University College of Law, 279, 295
National Tax Bureau, PRC, 220, 221
Navy, U.S., 281, 322
Nazis, 9, 10, 15, 68
NBC, 117, 207
NCUSCR. *See* National Committee on U.S.-China Relations
Nee, Amber (wife), 219
Nee, Owen, 219, 223–24, 234, 276
negotiations: dispute resolution, 136–37, 192, 195, 197, 223, 250–51, 330; joint venture contract, 243–44; legal education through, 225–27
Nelson, Bill, 115
Neustadt, Dick, 124
New China Bookstore, 283–84
New Chinese Painting, The (Cohen, J. F. L.), 253
New Deal, 35, 40
New Haven, Connecticut, 19–20
New Jersey State Teachers College, 8
Newman, Frank, 2–4, 6, 64, 68, 75, 85, 105–7
Newman, Jon, 21
New York City, 8, 237, 252, 253, 309
New York Review of Books, 322
New York Times (newspaper), 115, 130, 160, 187, 222, 239; in North Korea, 172, 174, 181; op-eds, 131, 140, 145, 163, 165, 166, 231; U.S.-PRC relations in, 207, 210
New York Times Magazine, 181
New York University (NYU), 221, 266, 289, 290
New York University (NYU) School of Law, 194–95, 246, 255, 310, 312; Chen Guangcheng and, 289–95; faculty, 115, 196, 198, 201, 276–81, 323, 326, 336; USALI, 278–79, 281, 290, 293, 303
Nguyen Ngoc Bich, 335
Nightline (TV show), 265
Niles, John (son), 70
Niles, Russell, 70
Nimetz, Matthew, 235, 237, 238

Ninth Circuit Court of Appeals, U.S., 261
Nixon, Richard M., 125, 138, 141, 153–54, 157, 328; administration, 173, 180–81, 184, 207, 208–9; with U.S.-PRC relations, 165–66, 209, 210–11, 217, 311, 315, 327
Norris, Bill, 34
North Africa, 15–16
North Korea (DPRK, People's Republic of Korea), 143, 153, 167, 183, 186, 188, 232; legal education and, 192–204; PRC and, 163, 177–78, 180, 182, 192, 194, 197, 199–200; Soviet Union and, 177, 180, 182, 200–201; U.S. and, 168–82, 191–204. *See also* Korean conflict
Norway, 17
November Action Committee (NAC), 119–20
nuclear power, 48–49, 241–43
nuclear weapons, 206, 216, 314, 316
NYU. *See* New York University
NYU School of Law. *See* New York University School of Law

Obama, Barack, 202, 204, 292
obscenity, 60–63
Office of Strategic Services, in World War II, 14
Office of the General Counsel of the Air Force, 36
Office of the Legal Adviser, U.S. Department of State, 47, 130, 235, 288–89, 309, 329
Ohio State University, 326
Ohira Masayoshi, 323
oil companies, 51–52, 220, 227
Oksenberg, Mike, 130, 131
Oldman, Oliver, 220, 221
"Old Shoes, Safe Sex" (exhibition), 253
O'Melveny & Myers, 235
1000 Years of Joys and Sorrows (Ai Weiwei), 253
Open Door Policy, PRC, 192, 196, 223, 250, 298–301
Orlins, Stephen, 130, 223–24, 235–36, 240, 245, 296, 327–29
Otunnu, Olara, 334

Otunnu, Omara, 334
"Over the Hill to Hastings," 68

Pacific Gas & Electric (PG&E) Company of California, 28–29
"Painting the Chinese Dream" (exhibition), 253
Pan, Philip, 286, 287
pandas, Bronx Zoo, 252
Park, Choon-Ho, 190
Park Chung-Hee, 168, 184–90
Parker, Carey, 124, 205
Parkfairfax, Alexandria, 23, 26, 48, 54
Parsons, Talcott, 141
patrons, art, 253
Paul, Weiss, Rifkind, Wharton & Garrison, 276, 322; international offices, 234–52, 260–64, 266–70, 272, 274–75, 329–30; with North Korean delegation, 199, 202, 203
Paulson, Nathan, 64
Paul Tsai China Center, Yale Law School, 330
Pearl Harbor bombing (1941), 7, 32
Pearson, Drew, 54–55, 61
Peking University, 78, 162, 194, 198
Pelosi, Nancy, 293, 315
Pelzman, Frankie, 48
Pelzman, Fred, 48
Pennsylvania v. Nelson, 32
People's China and International Law (Cohen, J. A., and Chiu), 131, 138, 142, 218, 311
People's Daily. See Renmin ribao
People's Republic of China (PRC), 1, 116, 167, 227, 294; with American spies, 2, 140, 163–66, 311; Anti-Rightist Campaign, 80, 91, 92, 96, 142, 225; birth control in, 286, 287; CCPIT, 197, 222; "Chinese Mediation on the Eve of Modernization," 135–36, 139; CIETAC, 197, 251; constitution, 96, 300; Coudert Brothers and, 217–20, 274, 322; counterrevolutionaries in, 2, 93, 273; criminal justice system, 79, 89, 91–96, 134–37, 229, 231, 299, 311; *The Criminal Process in the People's Republic of China, 1949–63*, 79–80, 96, 134, 231, 311; cultural exchange with, 154–58; in disabled people,

People's Republic of China (PRC) (*continued*)
283, 284; education and, 212–14; foreign direct investment law, 222; government ministries, 156, 220–22, 228–29, 243–44, 247, 250, 274, 299; Great Britain and, 250–51; Great Leap Forward, 78, 80, 90, 92, 300; Hong Kong and, 171, 173, 244; human rights, 89, 232, 274, 280, 286–87, 292–93, 297, 303–4, 313–14; Hundred Flowers Campaign, 92, 96; Japan and, 151–52, 247–49, 305, 317, 323, 326; Korean conflict and, 2–3, 22, 93, 163, 171, 198, 206, 316; legal education and, 220–25, 229, 274, 276, 299–300; legal system, 79, 89, 91–96, 103, 134–40, 214, 231, 247–49, 270, 273, 298–306, 309, 311–12, 321; military, 85, 137, 265–67, 304; National People's Congress, 222, 299; North Korea and, 163, 177–78, 180, 182, 192, 194, 197, 199–200; with nuclear power, 241–43; Open Door Policy, 192, 196, 223, 250, 298–301; Peking University, 78, 162, 194, 198; *People's China and International Law*, 131, 138, 142, 218, 311; police, 92, 268, 270, 285–88, 302; as Red China, 1, 5, 14, 97, 104, 206, 326; refugees from, 79, 87, 90–100, 134, 162, 292, 320; "rule *by* law" in, 313–14; Singapore and, 200–201; South Korea and, 189, 190–91; Soviet Union and, 77, 103, 301, 305; starvation in, 90, 92, 300; State Economic Commission, 248–49; Supreme People's Court, 140, 164; Taiwan and, 209–11, 221, 246, 255–56, 301, 305, 311, 314–16; taxes, 220–22, 250, 284–85; UN and, 5, 138, 140, 145, 161, 207, 210–11, 225, 248–49, 327–28; U.S. and, 5–6, 122–25, 128–30, 153, 156–57, 164–65, 170–72, 189–90, 203, 205–17, 232, 247–48, 256–57, 260, 282–83, 288–93, 295–305, 311–12, 314–17, 327–29. *See also* Beijing; Chinese Communist Party, PRC; Cultural Revolution, PRC; Guangzhou
People's Republic of Korea (DPRK). *See* North Korea

Perkins, Dwight, 105, 124
Perry, Jack, 250–51
Pfeffer, Richard, 152
PG&E Company of California. *See* Pacific Gas & Electric Company of California
Philip Morris cigarettes, 12
Phillip (Duke of Edinburgh), 54
Phillips, Harlan, 40
Pierce, David, 245
pillow books, 62
Poland, 7, 9, 102
police, 31, 40, 47, 49, 57–59, 172–73, 188; Harvard University, 119–20; PRC, 92, 268, 270, 285–88, 302; with search warrants, 61–62; Taiwan, 257, 263
policy memorandum, of Harvard and MIT, 124–25, 156–57, 165, 311
Politics Among Nations (Morgenthau), 15
Pollak, Stephen, 21
Pollock, Earl, 23, 24, 26
Pound Roscoe, 332
POW. *See* prisoner of war
PRC. *See* People's Republic of China
Princeton University, 10, 19, 217, 322, 325
prisoner of war (POW), 78, 166
prisoners, 215, 282, 287–90, 302, 312; Downey, 2, 140, 163–66, 311; internment of, 2, 18, 32, 68, 73, 99, 139; Lu, 257–60, 311, 331
pro bono work, 49–51, 201, 252, 260
procedural justice, 31, 32
Proceedings of the ASIL Annual Meeting, 140
Profiles in Courage (Kennedy, J. F.), 238
Prosser, Eleanor (wife), 69
Prosser, Tom (son), 70
Prosser, William L. "Bill," 3, 4–5, 6, 67–69
Prosser on Torts (Prosser, W. L.), 67
protests: against FCCC speech, 273; in South Korea, 188; students, 74–75, 107–8, 117–21, 186, 265, 323; Vietnam War, 117–21, 323; violent, 119, 190, 244, 265–68, 301, 303, 326. *See also* Tiananmen Square
public international law. *See* international law, public
public security officers, 93–95

Pusey, Nathan, 118, 119
Putin, Vladimir, 314
Pye, Lucian, 98, 124
Pye, Mary, 98

Qianlong Emperor, 136
Qiao Guanhua, 159
Qing dynasty, 325
Qing Law Code, 137
Qin Shi Huangdi (Emperor of China), 313
Qiu Deshu, 253
quota, Jewish, 11, 17

"Rabbi ben Ezra" (Browning), 307
Radical Socialist Party, France, 15
Radin, Robin, 191
Railroad Court, Harbin, 96
Rakoff, Jed, 279, 321–22
Randt, Clark, Jr. "Sandy," 327, 328, 330
rape, 94
Readings in Chinese Communist Documents (Chi), 82
Reagan, Ronald, 184, 230
Red Army ("Seki Gun"), Japan, 149–51
Red China, 1, 5, 14, 97, 104, 206, 326. *See also* People's Republic of China
Red Guards, PRC, 137
Reed, Stanley, 34–35, 42
reeducation through labor (RETL, *laodong jiaoyang*), 91, 92, 93
Réflexions sur la question juive (Sartre), 15
reform through labor (*laodong gaizao*), 2, 92
refugees from PRC, in Hon Kong, 79, 87, 90–100, 134, 162, 292, 320
Reid v. Covert, 32–33
Reischauer, Edwin O., 124, 129, 131, 143, 184–85
Ren Jianxin, 268, 273
Renmin ribao (*People's Daily*) (newspaper), 81, 249
Republican Party, 8, 22, 52, 123, 292, 297; McCarthyism and, 4, 20–21; U.S. Supreme Court and, 29–30, 42–43
Republic of China (ROC). *See* Taiwan
Republic of Korea (ROK). *See* South Korea

Reserve Officers' Training Corps (ROTC), 119
RETL. *See* reeducation through labor
Revesz, Richard, 278, 290
"revolutionary successors," 114
Rhodes Scholarship, 73, 74, 124
Riesenfeld, Stefan, 68, 86
Rifkind, Simon H., 236, 237
rightists: Anti-Rightist Campaign and PRC, 80, 91, 92, 96, 142, 225; in Japan, 172–73
Roberts, Denys, 98
ROC (Republic of China). *See* Taiwan
Rockefeller Foundation, 2–3, 6, 76, 78, 87, 107
Rockefeller Institute, 124
Rogers, William P., 327
ROK (Republic of Korea). *See* South Korea
Roosevelt, Franklin Delano "FDR," 8, 12, 33–35, 40, 54–55
Rosovsky, Henry, 108
Rostow, Eugene, 20
ROTC. *See* Reserve Officers' Training Corps
Rothman, Bob, 220
Rural China (Hsiao Kung-chuan), 135
Rusk, Dean, 2–3, 116, 206
Russia, in Ukraine, 314, 316
Russian language, 91

Sacco and Vanzetti murder trial, 40
Sacks, Albert, 118, 126, 127
St. Louis Post-Dispatch (newspaper), 160
St. Petersburg. *See* Leningrad
SAIS. *See* School of Advanced International Studies, Johns Hopkins University
salaries, 5, 8, 26, 45–46, 94–95, 172, 294, 297
Salisbury, Harrison, 145, 159, 160, 165, 174, 181
Sally (U.C. Berkeley student), 84–85
Samsung Corporation, 190
Sandra Day O'Connor College of Law, Arizona State University, 324
Sartre, Jean-Paul, 15
Sato, Eisaku, 216
Sato, Sho, 68
Saudi Arabia, 128, 327
Savio, Mario, 107
Saybrook College, Yale University, 11, 328

Scalapino, Robert, 3, 80–81
Scheer, Matthias, 334
Scheer, Robert, 82
Schlesinger, Arthur, Jr., 38, 74
School of Advanced International Studies (SAIS), Johns Hopkins University, 152, 309
School of the Museum of Fine Arts, Tufts University, 146, 154, 252
Schurmann, Franz, 79–80, 91, 146
Schwartz, Benjamin, 79, 80, 105, 124
Science and Technology Center, Beijing, 274
SCMP. See *South China Morning Post*
Scogin, Hugh, 245
Scully, Vincent, 19
SDS. See Students for a Democratic Society
search warrants, 61–62
Searle, John, 107
Securities and Exchange Commission (SEC), 29, 33
Security Council, UN, 5, 140, 161
S&ED, U.S.-China. See U.S.-China Strategic and Economic Dialogue
SEDC, North Korea. See State Economic Development Commission
"Seki Gun." See Red Army, Japan
Senate, U.S., 33, 123, 131, 168, 205, 207, 211, 328; Committee on Armed Services, 58; Committee on Foreign Relations, 65, 73, 163, 165, 206; Committee on the Judiciary, 214
Seoul National University (SNU) School of Law, 169, 184, 186, 191
Seow, Francis, 312
Sexton, John, 272, 277, 289, 290, 294
SEZs. See special economic zones
Shanghai: NYU campus, 289, 290; prisons in, 215
Shanghai Communiqué (1972), 153, 315
Shanghai Jiao Tong University, 287
Shaw, William, 169, 190
Sherman, Laura, 245
Shiwu guan. See *Fifteen Strings of Cash*
Shulman, Harry, 20, 21
Siegel, Stanley, 198

Simhala (dog), 111
Simpson, Russell, 326–27
Simpson, Thacher, 246
Singapore, 95, 141–42, 200–201, 218–19, 322
Sino-Foreign Equity Joint Venture Law, PRC, 222
Skadden, Arps, 203, 234
Skiing magazine, 152
Smith, Chris, 292
Smith Act (1940), 32
Smith College, 6, 12, 14–15, 41, 69, 117
Smith College Museum of Art, 253
Sneider, Richard, 174
Snow, C. P., 74
SNU School of Law. See Seoul National University School of Law
Social Sciences Academy, North Korea, 195
softball games, 25
Sohn, Louis, 104
Solicitor General, Hong Kong, 97, 98, 312
Solicitor General's Office, U.S., 28, 46, 112, 114, 310
Sorensen, Ted, 238
Soros, George, 293
South Africa, 2
South China Morning Post (SCMP), 270, 280
South Korea (ROK, Republic of Korea), 111, 143, 164, 174, 183, 195, 232, 314; human rights and, 184, 186, 189–90, 238; Japan and, 167, 187; legal system, 301, 303; PRC and, 189, 190–91; Supreme Court, 169; U.S. and, 129, 177, 184–85, 188–89, 301, 316. *See also* Korean conflict
Soviet Union (USSR), 13, 21, 48, 75, 115–16, 174, 317; dissidents, 296–97; legal system, 86–87, 96, 103, 199–201, 299, 305, 335; Moscow, 86, 101–2, 104, 117, 177, 270; North Korea and, 177, 180, 182, 200–201; PRC and, 77, 103, 301, 305
Spain, 15–16
Spanish language, 9, 19
special economic zones (SEZs), 202–3, 243, 246
Special Issue (*Academia Sinica Law Journal*), 281

speechwriting, 124
Spence, Jonathan, 329
spies, 127, 155, 186; American, 2, 14, 140, 163–66, 311; Soviet, 48
Stalin, Joseph, 12, 79, 86, 96, 115, 305, 313
Stanford University, 26, 86, 103, 238, 320, 332
Star Is Born, A (film), 177
starvation, in PRC, 90, 92, 300
State Department. *See* Department of State, U.S.
State Economic Commission, PRC, 248–49
State Economic Development Commission (SEDC), North Korea, 202
State of the Union speech, 41–42
State Taxation Administration, 228
Staunton, George (Sir), 136–37
Stella (U.C. Berkeley student), 84, 85
sterilization, 286, 292
Stern, Elizabeth "Bibsy," 25
Stern, Samuel, 24–25, 27–29
Stevens, Charles, 217–18, 233–35, 322
Stevenson, Adlai, 37–38, 47
Stone, Jeremy, 154, 160, 162
Stratford, Tim, 245
Strong, Edward, 72
Students for a Democratic Society (SDS), 118–19
subarachnoid hemorrhage, 271, 278
Sullivan & Cromwell, 234
Sunday Times of London (newspaper), 48
Supreme Court, South Korea, 169
Supreme Court, U.S., 18, 34, 76, 237; with bias, 28–30; clerkships, 6, 20–33, 36–46, 48, 54, 56, 64, 114–15; with desegregation, 22, 30–31, 42; *Kinsella v. Krueger*, 32–33; with obscenity, 60–61; *Pennsylvania v. Nelson*, 32; with petitions for certiorari, 23–24, 38, 51; *Reid v. Covert*, 32–33; Republican Party and, 29–30, 42–43. *See also specific justices*
Supreme People's Assembly, North Korea, 195
Supreme People's Court, PRC, 140, 164
Supreme People's Court Monitor (blog), 330
Surrey, Stanley, 221

Taft, Robert, 30
Taipei, 140, 207, 212, 236, 257–58, 260, 262, 264, 279–80, 332
Taiwan (Republic of China, ROC), 127, 130, 139, 195, 224, 312, 331; Academia Sinica, 123, 281, 332; legal system, 86, 260–64, 279–80, 301, 303; Ministry of National Defense, 258, 263; National Taiwan University College of Law, 279, 295; PRC and, 209–11, 221, 246, 255–56, 301, 305, 311, 314–16; UN and, 5, 140, 145, 207, 279–80, 328; U.S. and, 156–57, 207, 209–12, 217, 219–22, 256–64, 301, 314–16, 329
Taiwan Relations Act (1979), 212, 258, 316, 329
Tan Boon Teik, 142, 219
Tang Muli, 253
Tang Wensheng "Nancy," 159
Taniguchi, Yasuhei, 333
Tate, Jack, 47
Ta Van Tai, 336
taxes, 220–22, 228, 238, 250, 252, 284–85
Taylor, Elizabeth, 58
Taylor, John "Bud," 238–39
"tea money," 94, 95
Temko, Stanley, 48, 49, 56–57
Temple University, 283
Teng Biao, 286, 290–91
terrorism, 173
Theil, Paul, 330
Thomas, Allen, 240–41, 244
Thompson, Kenneth, 3
Thomson, James C., Jr., 124, 131, 328
Thorne, Samuel, 104
Tiananmen Square (June 3–4, 1989), 89, 191, 254, 270, 304; fallout from, 273, 274; violence at, 190, 244, 265–68, 301, 303, 326
Tiantian ribao (*Daily Paper*), 95–96
Tibetans, 302, 304
Timbers, William, 29–30
Time magazine, 100
Times-Dispatch (newspaper), 210
Tiruchelvam, Neelan, 334
"To an Athlete Dying Young" (Housman), 45
Today Show (TV show), 117, 231

"Tomorrow Will Be Even Better," 312
Tong Zhiwei, 287
To Peking and Beyond (Salisbury), 159
torture, 186, 188, 286–87, 302, 314
Toupin, Elizabeth, 253
Towster, Julian, 105
trade, 136, 192–96, 252, 274, 299, 328, 334; CCPIT, 197, 222; CIETAC, 197, 251; PRC and Ministry of Foreign Trade, 247, 250
trademarks, 246–48
Transformation of American Law, The (Horwitz), 115
Trilateral Commission, 129
Trooboff, Peter, 321
Truman, Harry S., 3, 30, 34, 52, 256, 259, 316
Trump, Donald, 204, 297
Tsai Ing-wen, 315
Tsche Chong Kil, 186
Tse, Ada, 267
Tsinghua University School of Law, 283, 286
Tucker, Milton, 67
Tufts University, 111, 141, 253; Fletcher School of Law and Diplomacy, 153, 309, 333; School of the Museum of Fine Arts, 146, 154, 252
Twain, Mark, 13
"Twenty Questions About China's New Joint Venture Law" (Cohen, J. A.), 247

Udall, Morris "Mo," 189
Uganda, 334
Ugly American, The (Burdick, E., and Jacobs), 73
Uighur people, 302
UK. *See* United Kingdom
Ukraine, 314, 316
Ulam, Adam, 105
UN. *See* United Nations
Un-American Activities Committee, 74–75, 107
Unger, Roberto, 334
Uniform Code of Military Justice, 32–33
Union Research Institute (URI), 97
United Auto Workers, 131

United Bamboo Gang, KMT and, 258, 261–63
United Kingdom (UK), 244, 250, 317
United Nations (UN), 3, 76, 159, 164, 191, 237, 279–80, 333–34; North Korea and, 202; PRC and, 5, 138, 140, 145, 161, 207, 210–11, 225, 248–49, 327–28; Security Council, 5, 140, 161; student model conference, 10
United States (U.S.), 61, 104, 112, 115, 154, 318, 336–37; Democratic Party, 47, 51, 64, 73–74, 123, 128–29, 131, 171, 208, 292; Department of the Treasury, 221, 324; DOJ, 46–47, 55, 309; with EALS student numbers increasing, 321–30; embassies, 16, 100, 279, 288–90, 330; foreign policy, 129–30, 281, 308; Japan and, 158, 211, 216, 232, 316, 322; Korean conflict and, 2–3, 13, 78, 163, 171, 206, 316; North Korea and, 168–82, 191–204; oil companies, 51–52, 220; post-World War II, 117, 304; PRC and, 5–6, 122–25, 128–30, 153, 156–57, 164–66, 170–72, 189–90, 203, 205–17, 232, 247–48, 256–57, 260, 282–83, 288–93, 295–305, 311–12, 314–17, 327–29; Solicitor General's Office, 28, 46, 112, 114, 310; South Korea and, 129, 177, 184–85, 188–89, 301, 316; Soviet Union and, 317; spies, 2, 14, 140, 163–66, 311; Taiwan and, 156–57, 207, 209–12, 217, 219–22, 256–64, 301, 314–16, 329. *See also* Congress, U.S.; Department of State, U.S.; military, U.S.; Supreme Court, U.S.
Universities Service Centre, Hong Kong, 97–98
University of California, Hastings Law School, 67–68
University of California at Berkeley, 2–3, 76, 83–85; Center for Chinese Studies, 80, 81, 82; Chinese history at, 78–79, 82; loyalty oath controversy at, 73, 107; protests at, 74–75, 107–8. *See also* Boalt Hall, University of California at Berkeley
University of Chicago, 113, 162, 245, 250, 310
University of Connecticut, 221
University of Hawai'i, 321, 325

INDEX

University of Hong Kong (HKU), 88–89, 202–3, 333
University of Maryland Francis King Carey School of Law, 138
University of Michigan, 1, 76, 103–4, 220, 323, 327, 329
University of Pennsylvania, 42, 72, 136, 245
University of Virginia, 47, 139
University of Washington School of Law, 270, 271, 291
Upham, Frank, 278, 293, 325–26
URI. *See* Union Research Institute
U.S. *See* United States
U.S.-Asia Law Institute (USALI), NYU School of Law, 278–79, 281, 290, 293, 303
U.S. Attorney for the District of Columbia, 56
U.S. Attorney's Office, New York, 56
U.S. Attorney's Office for the District of Columbia: Civil Division, 56, 63–64; Criminal Division, 56–63, 75
U.S.-China Strategic and Economic Dialogue (S&ED), 288, 289, 291
U.S. Naval War College, 281
USSR. *See* Soviet Union

Vagts, Detlev, 114
Valentine, Stuart, 245, 249
Vance, Cyrus, 129–30, 131, 189, 210
Van der Sprenkel, Sybille, 135
Van Dyke, Jon, 321
Vienna, 16
Vietnam, 116, 129, 267–68, 270, 296, 335–36
Vietnam War, 73, 100, 162, 166, 206, 325, 336; protests, 117–21, 323; reacting to, 115–22
Vinson, Fred M., 30, 34, 37
violence, 151, 184–85, 317, 334; Cultural Revolution and, 164, 208, 300; protests, 119, 190, 244, 265–68, 301, 303, 326; torture and, 186, 188, 286–87, 302, 314. *See also* murder
violin lessons, 9
Viorst, Milton, 16
Vivian (secretary at Paul, Weiss), 202
VOA. *See* Voice of America

Vogel, Ezra, 89, 93, 95, 98, 105, 124, 146, 326
Vogel, Sue (wife), 98
Voice of America (VOA), 77, 273
Volkswagen, 224
Von Mehren, Arthur, 103, 332
Vorenberg, James, 232–33, 266

Wakeman, Fred, 82
Walker, Ken, 98
Wall Street Journal Asia (newspaper), 257–58
Wang, Jerry, 192–93
Wang, J. P., 279
Wang, Peter (Wang Youjin), 95–97
Wang, Shirley, 83–84
Wang Chenguang, 286
Wang Hsi-ling (Admiral), 262–63
Wang "Old Wang" (MOF official), 221
Wang Shengchang, 197
Wang Youjin. *See* Wang, Peter
Warner, Jack, 58
Warren, Charles, 113, 114
Warren, Earl, Jr. (son), 70
Warren, Earl "The Chief," 51; with bias, 28–30; as California governor, 23, 25, 27–28, 30; clerkship with, 6, 21–33, 36–38, 42, 64; as district attorney of Alameda County, 31–32; F. Frankfurter, and, 27, 30–31, 37, 39; with internment of Japanese Americans, 32; with law clerks, 26–29, 31–32, 46; with procedural justice, 31, 32
Washington Post (newspaper), 16, 48, 54, 62; Chen Guangcheng interviews, 286, 287; in North Korea, 172, 174, 181; op-eds, 160, 186, 231
Washington Star (newspaper), 62
Watergate scandal, 138, 210
Wellington, Harry, 25–26, 37
Wellington, Sheila (wife), 26
Weston, Julian, 69
Westwood, Howard, 63–64
WGBH-TV, 111, 122
White, Byron, 115
White, Kevin, 253
White, Robert, 78

"White Australia" (Cohen, J. A.), 12
White House dinner, 54–55
"white shoe" law firms, 19, 45–46, 234
Whittaker, Charles Evan, 42–43, 44
Why the Innocent Plead Guilty and the Guilty Go Free (Rakoff), 321–22
Wiley, Alexander, 65
Williams, Bill, 26
William S. Richardson School of Law, University of Hawai'i, 321
Wilson, James Q., 120
Wilson, Pete, 70
Winston Lord Roundtable Series on Asia, the Rule of Law, and U.S. Foreign Policy, 281, 308
Witherspoon Foundation, 294
women, 41, 57; with birth control in PRC, 286, 287; at Boalt Hall, 71; clerkships and, 24; equal rights for, 255; at Yale Law School, 17
Wong, Mary, 245, 247
Woodcock, Leonard, 131, 132
World Affairs Council, 210
World Bank, 323, 330
World Trade Organization, 250
World War I, 13
World War II, 54, 78, 80, 103, 238; communism after, 331, 335; D-Day, 10; Holocaust, 16; internment of Japanese Americans in, 2, 18, 32, 68, 73; internment of Jews in Shanghai, 99; Japan in, 6, 7, 32, 99; Nazis in, 9, 10, 15, 68; Office of Strategic Services in, 14; Poland in, 9, 102; ROK after, 167; U.S. in post-, 117, 304
Wu, Eric (Dong-sheng), 332
Wu Zhipan, 198
WYBC (Yale radio), 11

Xiao Yang, 223, 224, 274
Xi Jinping, 302–4, 309, 313, 317
Xinjiang Muslims, 304, 309

Yale Art Gallery, 19, 26
Yale Corporation, 21
Yale Law Journal, 17–21, 42, 46, 133
Yale Law School: Dean Acheson speaking at, 21–22; alumni, 29, 55, 64, 72, 103, 108, 131, 234, 237, 240; faculty, 55, 104, 105, 238, 288–89, 323; F. Frankfurter speaking at, 20, 42; HLS and, 169; Paul Tsai China Center, 330; scholarship offer, 14, 16; studies at, 36, 70; women at, 17; *Yale Law Journal*, 17–21, 42, 46, 133
Yale University, 6, 19, 26, 37, 67, 105, 221; alumni, 70, 100, 140, 163–64; CIA recruiters at, 13–14, 163; faculty, 163; financial aid at, 10, 11, 328; Freshman Prom Committee, 11; honorary degree, 312; Saybrook College, 11, 328; senior thesis on Yalta Conference, 12, 13; students, 327–28; WYBC radio, 11
Yalta Conference, Yale senior thesis on, 12, 13
Yamani (Sheikh), 128
Young, Alice, 322
Young, Michael, 323
Yu, Daniel Ping, 278
Yuan Weijing, 282, 283, 289, 295
Yuan Yunsheng, 253

Zaloom, Anthony, 322
Zelig (film), 237
Zhang (Mr.), 180–81
Zhao Jia, 229
Zhao Ziyang, 265, 301, 304
Zhou (PRC refugee), 93–95
Zhou Enlai, 125, 157–63, 166, 180
Zhou Peiyuan, 162
Zhu Rongji, 249–50
Zinberg, Dorothy, 110
Zoom meetings, 281, 308, 310